THE ALGORITHMIC PHILOSOPHY

Bin Li
The Algorithmic Philosophy, Volume I

Published by Spines
ISBN 979-8-89691-999-5

THE ALGORITHMIC PHILOSOPHY

VOLUME I

AN INTEGRATED AND SOCIAL PHILOSOPHY

BIN LI

CONTENTS

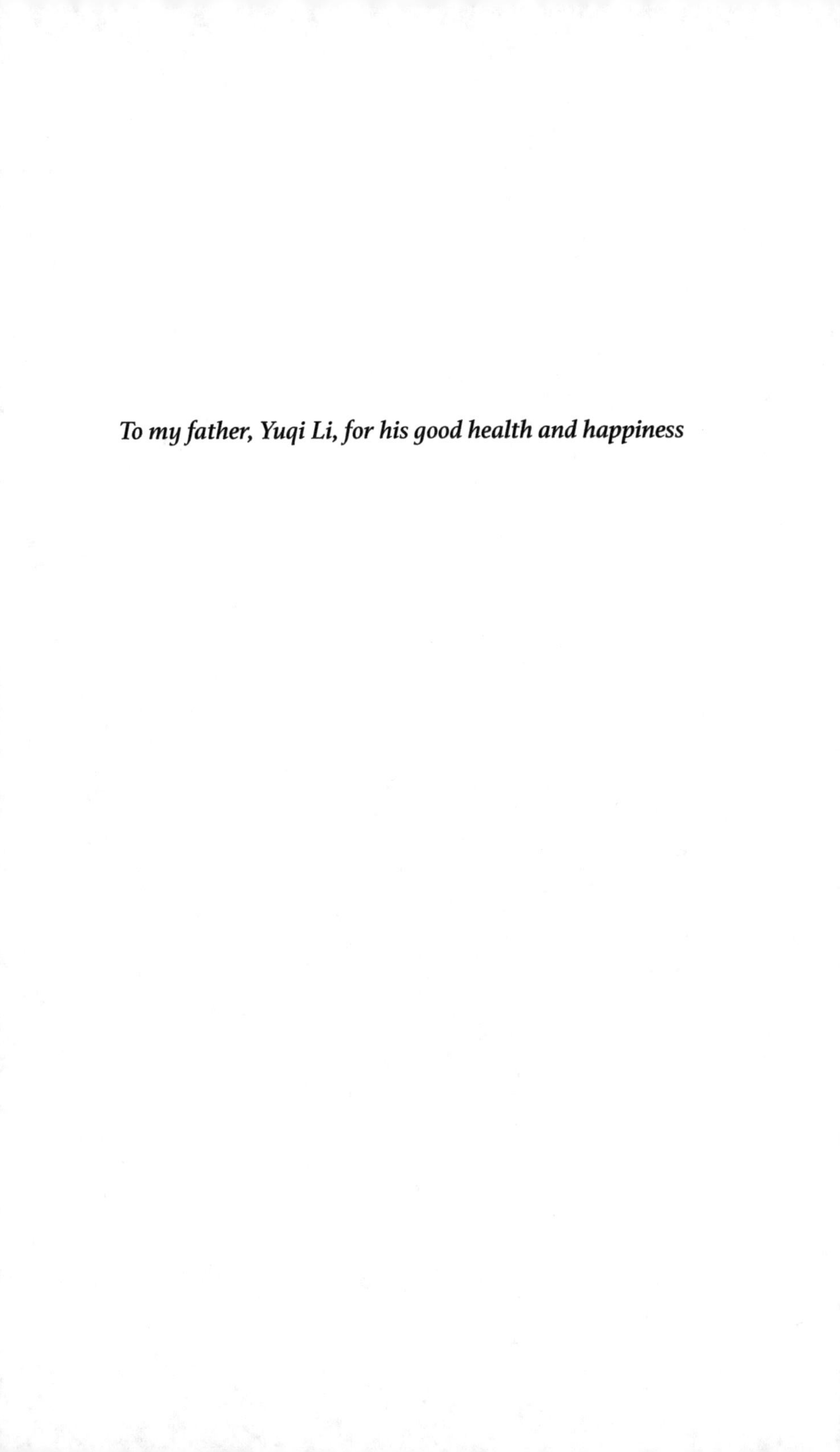

To my father, Yuqi Li, for his good health and happiness

Perhaps the first satisfactory thinking theory in history
Strikingly revealed the mystery and true face of human minds
A creative conclusion of hitherto philosophy
and an opening of its new stage
A solution to reinventing and reactivating social sciences
A necessary and correct application of IT
and AI principles in the humanities

~

ABSTRACT

By combining Kantian philosophy with computer principles, unprecedentedly, this book presents a "software-based" theory of mind, namely, "thinking = (Instruction + information) × speed × time". This means that discrete thoughtful entities interact like chemical reactions under spatiotemporal conditions, while users of this theory can use natural language for research and avoid getting bogged down in technological complexities. Considering the economic factors, surprisingly, it gives rise to a series of inferences and new principles, such as the sedimentation, distortion (the subjective turn), and solidification of thought, combinatorial explosion and infinite development, convergence and divergence, and so on. The psychological system thus becomes attached to the thinking system. After deconstructing the "Being" from multiple angles, the knowledge development model shifts from the traditional "great convergence" to the "Big Bang". As a result, various philosophical branches and schools since ancient Greece are integrated into a critical and creative unity which, encompassing plurality and secured by the "Algorithmic Logic", is termed the "Higher-Order Consistency". On this basis, a unified and general social science is founded, and the coherence among the social sciences, humanities, and natural sciences is achieved, ultimately leading to the concept of "total knowledge system". This is called the "Grand Synthesis". By reinterpreting topics such as freedom, democracy, ethics, institutions, organizations, money, markets, religion, language, culture, science, engineering, and common sense, this book illustratively demonstrates the efficacy of these unique "Algorithmic principles". The author expects that this "Algorithmic Philosophy" will spark a revolution in philosophy, humanities, and social sciences, revitalizing their due vigor and enabling them to keep pace with the revolutions in information technology and artificial intelligence.

Volume I includes:

Chapter 1 The Goal of Philosophy is to Discover a Proper Theory of Minds

Chapter 2 The New Principles and New Knowledge this Thinking Theory can Bring

Chapter 3 The Algorithmic Thinking Theory

Chapter 4 The Thoughtful Entities

Chapter 5 The Psychology

Chapter 6 The Fundamentals of Philosophy

Chapter 7 The Ontology

Volume II includes:

Chapter 8 The Social Philosophy (I)

Chapter 9 The Social Philosophy (II)

Chapter 10 The Social Philosophy (III)

Chapter 11 The Social Philosophy (IV)

Chapter 12 The Philosophy and Methodology of Science

Chapter 13 Greek Philosophy

PREFACE

As information technology (IT)-based artificial intelligence (AI) engineering is ushering in a historic breakthrough, this book aims to report to readers that IT can also lead to a breakthrough in philosophy, the humanities, and social sciences, and its significance may be no less than the former.

In fact, this is a report to the English-speaking world on my independent research work over the past 20+ years. It is both a restatement of my three previous Chinese books[1] and a collection of the latest philosophical applications of the thinking theory proposed therein. I would like to take this opportunity to let English readers know that the domestic Chinese have not only been achieving world-class scientific and technological achievements in areas such as AI and robotics, but are also modernizing and internationalizing their

---

1. Bin Li, "A Theory for Unification of Social Sciences: Algorithm Framework Theory" (in Chinese), Beijing: China Renmin University Press, 2009; Bin Li, "A Preliminary Exploration of Principles of General Social Science: The Algorithmic Approach" (in Chinese), Beijing: China Renmin University Press, 2012; Bin Li, "Foundations of Algorithmic Economics: The Cognitive Revolution and the Grand Synthesis of Economics" (in Chinese), Beijing: Economic Daily Press, 2019.

study in philosophy, humanities, and social sciences (although research freedom has been restricted at present). The main content of this book was brewed in China. Although it is written inside the United States, I first write in Chinese, and then translate it into English. My longtime experiences living in rapidly changing China have stimulated me to explore and delve. Compared with China's huge population size, the tremendous "human computing power", and the support provided by its economic strength, the domestic Chinese contributions to basic research have not been too much, but too little.

Kant's philosophy can be re-interpreted that human thinking activities are carried out in a binary way of "thinking tools + information". And what are the thinking tools? It was not until the computer age that the answer emerged: the "instructions". Multiple human "Instructions" work on information alternately with their limited, tiny, and specific functions, forming dynamic thinking processes, which lead to the infinite growth of human knowledge and wisdom. The result of a specific Instruction processing specific information will never change from time to time, or from person to person, but different combinations of Instruction and information lead to a huge amount of personalized pieces of knowledge and their comparison and interaction, thereby causing the phenomenon of innovation and development. In this way, we have broken through the statics, a major defect of Kant's philosophy, while maintaining the universal necessity of knowledge. Infinite development indicates that Parmenides' ontology as a large convergent model is wrong, and the human knowledge system is a unidirectional, expansive, and explosive system like the universe of the Big Bang. The meaning of this theoretical discovery is revolutionary. If readers agree that this inference is in line with historical facts, then there is reason to believe that the general direction of the philosophical system since Greece shall be reversed.

The history of philosophy can be considered strongly supportive of this meaning. The basic spirit of Greek philosophy is to try to elevate everyday life to the pursuit of absolute truth. It implies that truth is a simple system and can be obtained sooner or later. This pursuit first manifested itself as the "Being", then as God, and later gave birth to science, a great contribution to humankind. However, it also caused the division and conflict of the knowledge system. What is particularly shocking is that communism must be logically regarded as a consequence of Greek philosophy in the social field. Considering that the emergence and prosperity of Greek philosophy actually came from dissatisfaction with Greek democracy, this argument put forward by Karl Popper is actually completely acceptable. This clarification is a necessary step to the reformation of philosophy.

On this basis, we can find very clear routes of philosophical development. After Kant, philosophers tried to bridge the gap left by Kant from different approaches—denying metaphysics is certainly a way to resolve this contradiction. The importances of different parts of the human knowledge system have been emphasized respectively. However, the effort to rebuild traditional monistic philosophy failed in Hegel in a disgusting way. Since then, philosophy has turned to criticisms, negations, and supplementations, and then fallen into a stalemate. At present, the morale of the philosophical community and the humanities and social sciences is generally low, and it can even be said that the meaning of the existence of philosophy itself has become a question.

However, vitality is born out of despair. Computers are born on the basis of philosophical achievements. What I have done is to extend computer science into a theory of thinking, and then use it as a bridge to connect the two relatively independent parts of analytical philosophy and continental philosophy to make a totality. The effect of this reorganization can be magical! We realized that the history of philosophy for more than two thousand years can be encapsulated as a history of searching for such a thinking theory, and this theory of thinking closely fits almost every chapter and every page of philosophical history! Not only that, the overall outline of the entire human knowledge system has also arisen quite clearly—in which philosophy can of course logically have its own due place.

Human thinking activities are to use certain universal thinking tools to process information alternately; this basic theoretical framework must be adopted as a necessary and minimal cornerstone of all relevant disciplines. According to this theory, the following common phenomena can be explained: any novel inventions and creations can be traced back step by step, and then it can be found that they are almost "ordinary" and can be made by anyone. Therefore, people will generally agree with these inventions and creations, and these inventions and creations will win respect and rewards. This thinking mode leads to thinking processes and knowledge stocks, thereby highlighting the issue of the quantity of knowledge as an important and central philosophical issue. In line with this issue, topics such as subjectivity, plurality, and freedom can now be generated and exist "scientifically" rather than metaphysically. This unity that contains plurality seems self-contradictory, but in fact it is naturally consistent with the commonsense rationale.

This theory of thinking means that human thinking activities can be regarded as a series of thoughtful and real entities (Instructions, information, and their results), like microscopic particles, coexisting and interacting mutually or with physical entities at the same logical level. They are similar to chemical reactions. These thoughtful entities stay between humans and nature, constituting a relatively independent third party. Although based on tremendous differences, this system could not have rejected a possibility of unification, but embraced it. This is like static theory is just a particular of dynamic theory, or like the cognitive processes, action processes, and constructing processes are just in a continuous and interactive chain of thinking. This picture also naturally incorporates social existences and social processes, because the social objects are mainly thoughtful objects, and their coexistence and interaction with physical objects can simultaneously determine the differences and connections between social sciences and natural sciences.

When this theory of thinking is used to unravel many theoretical and methodological puzzles in the humanities and social sciences, its effects have been amazing as well. For example, I believe that we have finally taken a solid and correct step in answering the conflict between democracy and autocracy that still troubles the current world. Obviously, all the basic problems within our field of vision are interrelated and are essentially the same problem, and this problem is literally philosophical—or, as Heidegger said, it is the problem of "Being". Before this philosophical problem is to be solved, all other disciplines have always obediently bowed their heads to it and dared not to cross the line. Even the heroes of our time, the AI scientists, can testify to this: when I listened to their interviews, I still heard the old philosophical language.

This is why I traveled to America from the other side of the earth to deliver this theory. The openness, inclusion, and pluralism of the United States ensure that any "strange talk" will not be completely ignored here. In fact, the enthusiasm of my English readers has consoled me (also see my bibliography for the English publications and discussions on the websites). However, the "Algorithmical" economics, social sciences, and philosophy still need to be discovered by the mainstream academic community. And, if readers still cannot understand them from my writings, sooner or later, they will experience the rationales from the development of AI. When the highly developed AI is still constrained by computing power, or powerful giant AI systems still have to adopt the strategy of typification or stylization, or the endless new knowledge generated by machines has to be processually arranged with human daily life, the dominance of computing economy over the social world will eventually emerge, and the big secret under the iceberg will be exposed after all.

While AI is in full swing, the extreme left and extreme right political forces are fighting drastically in the United States. This fight is similar to that inside China, or between China and the United States. It seems that few people know that all these hot topics in the media have come from the same source: the ignorance of our own thinking manner. In other words, I believe that a knowledge revolution and a grand synthesis based on the thinking theory will finally end this historical tragedy. Despite the fact that conflicts of interest are eternal, the awakening of knowledge can certainly alleviate the political fights.

The theoretical principles proposed in this book are formed both "naturally" and deliberately for humanities and social sciences. To understand and use them, a reader or a researcher needs not know computer science in advance, but common sense and common logic only. This theory was originally generated during my exploration, in the 1990s and at the turn of this century, of those fundamental conflicts inside and between economic and social theories. In achieving a comprehensive unification of economics and social sciences, it has satisfied me. When the second Algorithmical book, "A Preliminary Exploration of Principles of General Social Science", was published in 2012, I didn't yet know that it could be used to synthesize the entire philosophy, so I just said in the book that this theory could be used to synthesize the "modern philosophy" (a Chinese term, referring to the philosophies after Hegel). Afterward, my research on the entire philosophy and the history of philosophy was long and intermittent. More than two years ago, when I got through the last few bottlenecks, I was shocked by the secrets of philosophy I discovered. Then, I decided to write this book.

Neither the word "synthesis" nor the word "unification" is appealing or pleasant. From the perspective of the knowledge quantity and thus the "softness", a theoretical unification does not have to reach the point of "oneness". Even if we achieve the "oneness" (which the Algorithmic Thinking Theory can literally do; see §30 of this book), it could not really be a big deal. Therefore, I had no choice but to choose the relatively neutral word "integrated" in the subtitle of the book. I'd like to live in an environment of softness, rather than in the traditional monistic or either-or context, and I also don't like to use "pluralism" as a rigid dogma or slogan. Following the introduction of Algorithmic Thinking Theory, many commonsense and recognized elements and principles can now enter the abstract world so that the ailing philosophy, humanities and social sciences can be reformed, with surgical and tonic procedures.

Just like the theme of this book has multiple relations with AI engineering, the English manuscript of this book is also the product of my cooperation with AI translation. As a non-native English writer, I have to draft the book in Chinese first, then translate it into English. However, even the translated English has lacked the soul of native spoken English, therefore, I have suspended the drafted translations of the first and second Algorithmical books. Fortunately, just after the Chinese manuscript of this book was completed, the AI revolution happened. Although the AI translation cannot be directly adopted, it provides many elements that I am not good at. This cooperation model illustrates that AI would be mainly collaborative with humans in the future, rather than only replacing human labor, and AI would help people improve productivity significantly in almost all aspects. This also indicates a strategy for the development of AI; that is, in the face of unlimited knowledge development potential, it can focus on developing products that can form a cooperative relationship with humans. The knowledge and skills of an AI product shall be neither too close nor too far from ordinary people. It's as if children always like to get along with their peers. This logic is "Algorithmical".

It can be said that the secrets of human minds have been largely revealed by AI engineering and this book. AI provides a technological paradigm while this book uses the so-called "software approach" to provide a concise answer, avoiding the redundant complexity of natural sciences. Faced with the possible revolutionary changes that would take place after these inventions and discoveries, I am particularly excited as an "insider". This refers not only to the changes that AI will bring, but also to the changes in philosophical and social concepts that the Algorithmic Thinking Theory may arouse. After experiencing the "Algorithmical awakening", readers can be expected to adjust their basic attitudes towards knowledge stocks and memory, so that they can better manage their own lives, both mentally and psychologically, let alone its impact on social engineering, public policies, and collective behaviors. As I mentioned in the appendix, I believe that people in the current era must not be conservative, and would better plan for the future more actively than before.

Readers are very welcome to write to me and give their opinions and views on this book. I have been eager to end my longtime independent work. As long as there are active discussions available, I think I would be able to continuously write new works. However, "Algorithmical work" can be endless and will never be exhausted by myself. For example, using the Algorithmic principles to reform those relevant disciplines shall actually be done by professional scholars in their respective fields, after they have accepted and mastered the principles and methods. My involvement in all these fields is largely for a preliminary illustration and demonstration of them, and I do not regard myself as an expert in most of these fields. The same is true for philosophy.

This book is divided into two volumes. In Volume I, it first explains the formation of the basic ideas of Algorithmic Thinking Theory (ATT) and enumerates the new principles and new knowledge it brings, then introduces computer principles, the Algorithmic Thinking Theory and its main inferences. Chapters 4 to 7 expound the philosophical applications of ATT, that is, the fundamental contents of "Algorithmic Philosophy". Volume II extensively showcases the philosophical applications of Algorithmic Philosophy. The first is the Algorithmic social philosophy and philosophy of science (Chapters 8 to 12); then, in the order of philosophical history, it elaborates on how the Algorithmic principles and philosophy can be used to achieve a grand, critical synthesis of philosophy (Chapters 13 to 16). While commenting on various philosophical schools, branches, and scholars, the Algorithmic principles and philosophy are further demonstrated. Finally, the conclusions of both volumes of the book. Nevertheless, all the narratives in this book are preliminary and concise, and I only see them as a beginning, or some illustrations.

The English edition and the Chinese edition of this book are published concurrently. Since the original Chinese manuscript of this book quotes a large number of Chinese literature, I have added the equivalent English literature to most of them; this is why dual references in many places are to be found.

I appreciate Prof. Yan Song very much for inviting me to

live, study, and write in the University of North Carolina at Chapel Hill for several years, and for helping me in various aspects. I would like to thank Prof. Yew-Kwang Ng, a Fellow of the Academy of Social Sciences in Australia, Prof. Weisen Li of Fudan University, and Prof. Tao Feng of Xi'an Jiaotong University for their guidance and help. Many thanks to Dr. John Reardon, Senior Lecturer at the University of Wisconsin at Eau Claire, and Prof. Qiang Chen of Shandong University, for their decadelong enthusiastic support. Thanks to Prof. Yang Yao of Peking University, Prof. Cindy Mason of University of California at Berkeley, for their advice. Thanks to Prof. Laixiang Sun who taught me at Peking University and helped me as an incumbent professor at University of Maryland, College Park. Thanks to Prof. Jinsong Chen of Renmin University of China for the discussions. I would like to express my special remembrance of my friend on academia.edu, Prof. Stephen Schafer who selflessly helped me. Thanks to the support from Mrs. Yingchun Fu of the North Carolina Chinese Scholars Sino-Us Exchange Association. Thanks to my lifelong friend, Mr. Wei Li, for his persistent discussion with me. Meanwhile, I am responsible alone for the contents of this book.

Bin Li
libinw2025@hotmail.com

§0. INTRODUCTION

The purpose of this book is to introduce a *highly original theory of mind*, or a "thinking theory". The theory and its corollaries form a series of principles that did not exist in the world before. When it is introduced into philosophy, many of the major puzzles that have been confusing philosophers for a long time are answered one after another, and the merits and demerits of each existing philosophy are clarified; further, all philosophical branches and schools are critically integrated into a single whole. This is called the "Grand Synthesis", and the logic presented in it can also be used to construct a unified knowledge system of humankind and lay the real foundations for a unified social science. Therefore, this "Algorithmic Philosophy" is both a synthetic, integrated, or unified philosophy and a social philosophy.

In this era when pluralism is prevalent, theories of a grand unification have been seeming doubtful and unsellable. Nonetheless, with this fresh but self-evident logic, this series of principles is used to indicate how the unification can be established in an acceptable (and critical, of course) way while encompassing plurality, conflict, subjectivity, relativity, uncertainty, development—and crucially, any logical inconsistencies here may only be existent temporarily or locally, thus, there is something here that can be called "Higher-Order Consistency". I discovered this theory at the beginning of this century in order to solve some fundamental problems in economic theory, and simultaneously found that it could be used to synthesize all existing social sciences and humanities. However, its philosophical application has progressed more slowly. It was only in recent years that I discovered that when it is used to synthesize the various philosophies, it is just as strikingly satisfactory.

It's not surprising to say so, as it's just a theory of mind. From ancient times to the present, humankind has not had a satisfactory theory of thinking. The history of philosophy throughout history can be read as a search for some appropriate thinking theories. The existing doctrines of thinking are fragmentary, or in the style of natural science. One of the criteria for an "appropriate thinking theory", if any, could be "softwareization"; that is, *the mind should be able to explain itself with its own language, and without using natural science terms such as molecules, atoms, neurons, etc.* I was surprised to find out that the solution to this seemingly difficult task was almost ready-made, which had been in obscurity for decades in the most basic textbooks on computers. Since there have been so many gifts that computers have offered to humankind, how can they once again contribute such a precious one to philosophy, humanities, and social sciences!

This is the principle of "computation = instruction + information", a Cartesian dualism. An "instruction" is a kind of basic operation in a computer, among dozens of core instructions in it. It is what the user of the computer "tells" the computer to perform as a minimal task, so it reflects a type of basic thinking activity that can be carried out in the mind of the user, the human being. A computer simply uses physical means to simulate these types of thinking activities and make them run faster than the human brain. The core types of these instructions are identical for all computers. In this way, isn't an instruction a basic, innate thinking tool in the human brain that was suggested by Immanuel Kant? Or, doesn't it reflect the concrete capacity of thinking in the human brain? Aren't different people able to communicate with each other because they share the same basic abilities of thinking? Clearly, the concept of instruction has been severely neglected by the intelligentsia. Instruction can be defined and paired with external information; only from this perspective can we come to know what Instruction and information, respectively, are. This pair constitutes a relatively complete set of concepts that can be used to provide the necessary bottom structure for the theory of mind. An instruction operates on a quantity of no more than two data (or two pieces of information), like a machine processing certain raw materials, which constitutes the minimal unit of mental activity ("Meta-computation", or "an operation"), relating to concepts such as "intentional activity", "dasein", and "consciousness". The human brain can only perform such a unit of operation at a time, so computational operations must be strung together to form a stream of behaviors. This naturally introduces the temporal dimension to thinking activities. The data resulting from computations must be stored "*alongside*" for intermittent re-use later. This naturally introduces the spatial dimension to thinking activities. This is what economists call the "roundabout method of production", which concretizes and refines Heidegger's "Dasein" (meta-computation) and its activities. It results in the coexistence of tools, raw materials, intermediates, semi-finished products, and finished products of computation with the productive computing actions. It works in cycles, both requiring and generating stocks of knowledge. In this way, the concept of "knowledge" as computing results (the intermediates, semi-finished products, and finished products) is formed, which is, in principle, different from instructions and from the original information. Knowledge exists as a relatively "independent third party" in the human brain, or in books, databases, etc.

This is the "Algorithmic Thinking Theory" (or the "Algorithmic Theory", "Algorithm Framework Theory", "Algorithmic Framework", hereinafter referred to as "ATT") that I propose. It can be shorthanded to a formula: thinking = computation = (Instruction + information) × speed × time. In natural language, when human thinking, it means that a human computes, i.e., uses the Instructions (the capitalized first letter indicates that they are human's rather than computer's) inherent in their brains, universal to everyone, to process information from the outside world serially, selectively, roundaboutly, and repetitively. Information can be reprocessed after processing, so it is called "repetitively". The Instructions can be understood and equated with the verbs in natural language that refer to mental actions. Moreover, we can expand the scope of Instruction to any verb that refers to a mental action and that we believe or assume is carried out also in the form of "Instruction + information", or "verb + object", relatively independently, even if it cannot be simulated by a computer for the time being (the "Manual Instruction"). Therefore, ATT is a theory of human thinking rather than of computers, and it can be used, apart from computers, *directly* in the traditional manual study of humanities and social sciences. In the above, an "Algorithm" is a method by which Instructions are selected to make a sequence to process information or data. Apparently, it is hardcore of intelligence, thus, I use it to title this thinking theory, and use words such as "Algorithmic" and "Algorithmical" to refer to multiple meanings such as "of Algorithm", "of ATT" or "under ATT", and so forth.

This theory is bound to be questioned by opponents of artificial intelligence (AI) or computationalism. However, significant advances in AI show that computers are increasingly capable of performing tasks that are distinctly subjective, just like human brains. Presumably, these developments have sent shockwaves through opponents. I argue that, just as the concept of instruction has been neglected, computers can actually behave more like humans than they once appeared, but programmers usually prevent them from doing so. The similarity between a computer and a human brain lies not only in the fact that the computer can perform meaningful high-level operations that the human brain can do, but also in the fact that the computer experiences such "uncertainty", "confusion", and failures as the human being, which are instead the additional evidence that the human brain runs in much the same way as a computer. And, the assumption of the above-mentioned Manual Instruction can already make ATT largely free from the controversy about AI.

Particularly, the effectiveness of ATT is reflected in the surprising and significant series of inferences it derives (together with ATT, they are called the "Algorithmic Principles"). Some of these inferences previously existed as relatively independent propositions, subject to theoretical justification, while others can constitute brand-new principles and knowledge. Readers are generally supposed to have been unaware that there are clear causal connections between the above simple theory of mind and these propositions.

The computing activities may seem mechanical and "chilly", however, meta-computation *works* or *produces* in the sea of data, which means that information, data, and knowledge are all the *"real entities"*, *"beings"*, *"substances"*, *"realities"*, etc., and computation is a kind of *"behavior"* that is similar, juxtaposed, and interactive with human body movements. Computer principles help us to clarify how these entities "exist", how they relate to their material carriers, how they arise, move, change, disappear, and how they bind, separate, or *interact* with other entities, and so on. Therefore, the actors need to consider the costs and benefits of computations, apply economic analysis to the thinking activities, and arrange the time sequence of computing operations ("Algorithmic Logic"). Although the deductive method, as an Instruction or Algorithm, can produce reliable results, its conditions are strict, the processes are often lengthy, and therefore not often economically desirable, so that other less reliable but relatively simple and rapid methods, such as induction, analogy, experimentation, lottery, association, and imagination (the "Alternative Algorithms"), can come in handy and compete with deduction. Decision-making in the spatio-temporal environment is often time-limited, but the actors must consider as many factors as possible ("factor completeness"), so they have to trade off between the computing efficiency and the resultant quality, concocting the combination of all the above-mentioned methods, in order to close computations and make the decisions timely ("forced closure of computations"). Therefore, the computing results as knowledge are inevitably just some "makeshifts" (e.g., attitudes, beliefs, values, etc.) with *varying degrees* of effectiveness. This is the "*Mental Distortion*" or the *subjective turn* of computations, deflecting from mainstream deductive and perfect tracks. The so-called "purpose" generally is also a result of mental distortion under the serial processing method. Although these computational results are crude and heterogeneous, one has to store them selectively for future use (the "sedimentation" of thinking). And, in the following computations, the actors often have to refer to these ready-made results, otherwise, they will be even more helpless. Therefore, knowledge as a stock is actually mostly arbitrary and rigid things, which only provide fixed answers to problems (the "solidification" of knowledge), and cannot take into full and flexible account its applicability in specific current operations. Compared with the huge stocks of knowledge left over from history, the computing power is extremely limited; whether current operations are used to develop new knowledge realtime on the spot of problem-solving or to revise the existing old knowledge, they must only proceed marginally and gradually in a very small proportion of the stocks.

The considerations of prudence and completeness force a thinker to summarize the *entire world* with limited computing power, and then close the computations and draw conclusions. In this way, it forms a specific version of knowledge about the world. Different individuals can concurrently hold their different versions of knowledge. The improvement of imperfect existing knowledge, or the use of new information to form new knowledge, can lead to innovations. Accumulation of small innovations results in a new version of knowledge that can replace the earlier versions. Furthermore, during continuous computations, an almost infinite number of combinations can be formed between Instructions and massive amounts of information, which is called the "Combinatorial Explosion", indicating the infinite potential for knowledge development. Therefore, knowledge development must be an endless process, intertwining the improvement of knowledge quality and *the expansion of its quantity*. This is one of the most important discoveries that ATT can contribute. Under the premise of infinite development, the convergent processes and divergent processes, equilibria and disequilibria, are mixed, and the related discreteness, plurality, heterogeneity, *"softness"*, individuality, and differences also exist as some Algorithmical inferences. Since ATT accurately describes the specific structure, form, existence, movement, change, and development of human thinking, it constitutes a precise theory of bounded rationality (or the "concrete rationality" or "concrete reason"). The limited computing actions coexist with other physical actions, and their raw materials, intermediates, semi-finished products, finished products, effects, and consequences coexist with the rest of the world that these actions have not yet affected, so that all phenomena, and thus all states of the world can, in principle, be regarded as the consequences and manifestations of this "concrete rationality", or its coexistences.

A specific application and extension of the above Algorithmic principles is in the field of psychology. They can first be used to, in my opinion, satisfactorily explain phenomena such as consciousness and introspection. Second, Since it has been proved that the so-called "rational thinking" is inevitably "distortive" in one way or another, there shall be *no essential difference between thinking or computational phenomena and psychological phenomena* such as emotions, desires, instincts, impulses, and so forth. Since metacomputing requires a stock of knowledge, an individual cannot just carry the Instruction system to the world, and some minimal knowledge must be born with the Instruction system, like some software pre-installed in a computer before it leaves the factory for a user; therefore, the mechanism of biological inheritance, like the arrangement of "hard software" in a computer, should logically be used to transfer knowledge to the descendant. This "hard software" knowledge supports the descendant to make basic decisions after birth, and buys time for his/her development or acquisition of necessary "purely-soft" knowledge. However, because this "hard software" cannot be updated after mother-baby separation, this leads to its widening rift from the acquired knowledge, so that it is eventually deemed "irrational".

The philosophical application of the Algorithmic principles has actually begun above, and below are some of the major points that are to be directly and briefly explained.

The fundamental problem facing philosophy for more than 2,000 years can be considered to be the division between

"Being" and "opinions" caused by Parmenides. From Being to Plato's Ideas, to God, to the Absolute, to modern science, this "correct knowledge" in different names was strongly implied to engulf all other human thoughts and then converge into some simple and internally consistent "ultimate truth". Kant's "Copernican revolution" actually means that thought is to be seen as something concrete that is independent of and juxtaposes with things. After Hegel's failed attempt to pull this subjective-objective split back into the monist philosophy, his critics basically followed two lines: one was to enter analytic philosophy pursuing precision, which eventually led to the creation of computers, and the other line was to emphasize the importance of all kinds of intellectual activities and knowledge other than Being (or science). These two lines could converge into the Algorithmic Thinking Theory: the former as a tool to make ATT and the latter as the inferences. Most elements in the Algorithmic principles have been ready-made, and I just assembled them together in a logical order and accomplished the "last mile" of the grand synthesis.

What exists a priori in the human mind does not need to be assumed to be all knowledge, as Plato did, but primarily the thinking tools such as Instructions (with the exception of the above-mentioned "hard software"). Such thinking tools do not need to be "perfect", or preloaded with some ciphers of the world, or even many (since certain single Instruction can develop into multiple Instructions, see §30) as long as they are finite and concrete. Computer science provides a principle that allows us to understand how concrete spiritual beings, such as "Instructions", interact with foreign objects in a specific way in a spatiotemporal environment, which then solves the problem that since ancient times, ideas have been potentially considered incapable of being placed as objects alongside foreign physical objects. The concreteness and finitude of Instructions lead to the independent and discrete existence of metacomputation as the smallest unit of thinking activity, and then different metacomputations can objectify each other or themselves in a serial way. This further enables that thoughtful entities actually exist in the world as one of many types of entities, and that thinking activities are also a real kind of activity. Now, we have a basic completeness in the identification of entities, and any "activity" is the real activity of any of these real entities, and there is no other human activity outside of these entities.

An activity of human thinking is an "encounter" between two "strangers", namely, the thinking tool and the external object, and thus the information, in a serial manner. This concept can cure all the major ills of philosophy up to date in one fell swoop. This kind of encounters, like chemical reactions between elementary particles, will inevitably first form a large amount of uneven knowledge, which exists as an "independent third party" between humans and things. Different pieces of knowledge are compared with each other, giving rise to their qualitative differences, namely, the differences between right and wrong, consistency and conflict, good and bad, beauty and ugliness, and so on. The concreteness and definiteness of thinking tools lead to the effect that a result of processing specific information by specific Instruction is always definite and certain, which is the "a priori certainty"; namely, people have certain definite concepts of right and wrong before they go to know foreign objects. It is typically reflected in logic and mathematics. This is like a self-test, drill, or rehearsal of a machine, which manifests the constancy and interpersonal universality of functions of Instructions. However, the perspective of metacomputation allows us to recognize that the elements contained in any real object or in any real problem are infinite in principle; therefore, the empirical knowledge formed by the processing of specific foreign information in the course of time can generally only be local, and the depth of the processing is also limited, so its correctness can only be limited and relative; even if some knowledge has obtained the position of winner in the competition with other knowledge for a long time, its ultimate position in the knowledge system cannot be certified, as Hume argued. But, on the other hand, such encounters and long-term, large-scale experiments will not lead to nothing; the law of probability could ensure that both high-quality and low-quality knowledge will be continuously generated, and the knowledge system must, in principle, contain a mixture of all these various components. Some knowledge, initially fragmented and abundant, may later be refined into knowledge that is very simple in form (such as scientific theories), leading to great economy, and then is worshiped, and particularly and deliberately sought after. Henceforth, traditional philosophy speculates that all knowledge will be eventually refined into this concise form. However, as long as we perceive that this is actually a knee-jerk obsession with the computational economy, we will further realize that there is actually no conclusive objective evidence to support this speculation. On the contrary, because the above convergent processes conserve computing resources and thus allow new computations to be launched, the total amount of human knowledge continues to grow. This Algorithmical thinking can be used not only to know, but also to construct and transcend, to propose new goals and initiate human engineering, so as to move towards an infinite future. All of these elements and activities are within a mixed, interconnected framework. It is difficult to explain them only in division or in isolation; instead, by merging them together, they can be interpreted once and for all. The basic form of philosophy can now be transformed from "The Great Convergence" to "The Big Bang", as in astrophysics.

Although one is free to selectively compute, there are differences between the many results. This forces the actors to discern the results. The actors can generally distinguish between subjective opinions and objective "facts" on their own. The latter, although ultimately the beliefs or assumptions, have been considered *relatively* reliable. The actors conceive of this type of beliefs as "realities", distinct from subjective opinions, which can bring computational convenience and economy. This leads to the principle of "universal in things". On the other hand, since the result of processing individual information by individual Instruction is deterministic and unchangable, we can think that all high-quality and low-quality knowledge are unexceptionally "predetermined", thus we can conjecture the existence of a super-infinite "human knowledge thesaurus" composed of the results of all Instructions processing all information. It exists "among people" and depends on the existence of humankind as a whole. Each person only possesses a part of it, moving along the routes in it similar to, or different from, each other. This explains the principle of "universal before things". These principles can be used again to synthesize absoluteness and relativity, determinism and freedom, and ontology and epistemology.

Now, turn to social philosophy.

By applying the above ontology of minds to human individuals as natural beings, it can "naturally" lead to the society that coexists with nature, and the humanities and social sciences that coexist with natural sciences. The reason why the existing natural sciences could not be logically extended to the social sciences and humanities is that human minds have not been able to become *real beings* in the limited, concrete, and characteristic way described above, thereby failing to be the objects of social and humanistic study. Such individuals who are both objective and subjective think, make decisions, and act in the world, and then produce various social existences and phenomena.

The discrete existence of individuals with independent thoughts under the conditions of time and space creates the necessity to exchange their thoughts. As a kind of software mainly for interpersonal communication, language is acquired after one's birth, attached to the thinking system pursuant to the communicational principles provided by computer science, and combined with physical media in the multimedia manner. This shall be the right way to define language, as well as the philosophy of language.

ATT provides explicit or implicit foundations for the endogeneity of basic social issues such as freedom, democracy, market, and justice. Meanwhile, it also provides the soil for the emergence of issues such as institutions, organizations, religion, power, autocracy, war, and many others, eventually reaching a comprehensive and integrated framework that simultaneously explains almost all basic social issues and phenomena like never before.

From the principle of "solidification of knowledge", rules and institutions can be deduced, which lay the fixed tracks on the roads with enormous branches, speeding up computations, but losing a certain quality, accuracy, and opportunity. This is the Algorithmical perspective on institutions. Society, like an individual, has limited current computing power, so only by adopting a variety of measures, including institutions, to fix and coordinate many variables, can current computations achieve better results. However, under the condition of bounded rationality, it is often not enough to adopt the institutionalized measures based on ex-ante rules to do these adjustments; in the environment of subjectivity and conflict, it is sometimes necessary to adopt the *in-site and real-time* adjustment methods by establishing a hierarchical organization through buy-offs or negotiations, where the individual leader commands the organizational members real-timely to work. This is the executive or administrative power that differs from the judicial system and can make up for the flaws in rules, to a certain extent. In this way, for the first time in history, we theoretically explain the division of governmental branches. Another theoretical basis is that under the condition of discrete computing, due to the lack of neural connections between people that are only available within a single human body, the self-consistency of an individual is *relatively* higher than that of the group, hence, the individual achieves some competitive advantages over the group. This is the root cause of power and even dictatorship.

The materialization of computation and communication results in limited and specific costs and benefits for a particular organization. As organizations change in size and function, the way to organize is not necessarily economical and desirable. Societies made up of dispersed free individuals can bring diversity, abundance, development, speed, and flexibility to the results of computations. Free individuals can also establish equal cooperative relations through consultation, contracting, voting, networking, and other means. Common sense, customs, morality, religion, education, media, associations, and other means are also helpful to achieve individual cooperation, but they are all based on the materialization of ideas, which is the guarantee that each of them has relatively independent logical and theoretical significance. The key to understanding ethics and morality, the "informal institutions", is to recognize their solidification, modularity (or patterning), and imperfection, which hence are ultimately also some makeshifts. Fairness and justice, like scientific knowledge, are revered not because they are absolutely perfect, but because they are *relatively* one of the most reliable parts of social engineering knowledge. The computing economy requires that such knowledge be neither too little nor too much.

However, no matter how the stock of knowledge develops, the degree of freedom left for current computations is great. The barriers of limited computing power and big data cause the coercive management from the authority to be confined to limited scopes and aspects, impossible to cover everything. Because of the effect that a rising tide lifts all boats, this impossibility is endogenous and persistent. It is also obvious that radical changes in the stock of knowledge and the establishment of an absolutely stable order are impossible as well. Society is a "Neurath's ship" that sails in a controlled way into the unknown.

The limitations of public administration ensure that the market is the primary mode of organizing economic activities. The significant computing cost leads to the creation of money, which is used to simplify commodity valuation and trading. The materiality of trading activity leads to the effects that its scope and strength can only be limited, the meanings and uses of price information are also limited, and trading activities and non-trading activities, and thus economic activities and non-economic activities, are both independent and interrelated.

In short, in the literature of extreme rationalism, the mind is in a weightless, "non-existent" special state. ATT is like giving weight and "volume" to the mind, so that minds "exist", and thousands of social phenomena, as well as logical and compelling social theories, can henceforth be produced.

Finally, an outline of the philosophy of science and the methodology is presented.

Distortions of thinking lead to thoughtful interpersonal differences as a primary and common Algorithmical phenomenon, and the forced closure of computing leads to the modularity, diversity, and plurality of knowledge. For example, in addition to cognitive knowledge, people will form a variety of engineering knowledge to solve practical problems; scattered common sense knowledge, witchcraft, and religion to answer ultimate questions of the world and their lifetime; culture, literature, and art to entertain and express their feelings, stories, and emotions, and so on. These types of knowledge were made with different methods, from different stages of mental activity, or in different areas; they vary in the degree of intimacy of their internal and interrelated relationships ("Soft Quantitative Analysis"), and each has specific and limited functions, and differs in quality. Together, they make up the whole body of the human knowledge system.

The combination of limited computing power and the thinking economy ensures that knowledge development is divided to a certain extent. In this system of division of labor, it is easy for us to understand the nature, role, and function of science. Science is the cognitive knowledge that is of *relatively* high quality or reliability and is suitable for development and teaching by professional intellectuals. The knowledge of ordinary people is mainly for their own use, while scientific knowledge must be published and disseminated for use by society. The latter implies that science focuses on revealing the properties of objects, such as universality, certainty, and constancy. But, like any other kinds of knowledge, the quality and quantity of scientific knowledge that exists in any era is limited and cannot be completely self-consistent. It must be based on common sense and *certain philosophical assumptions*. Its development is achieved through intensive investment, using a *conservative* strategy; that is, it does not go ahead if it does not meet a certain standard. As a result, a series of technical and detailed standards are established that distinguish science from other kinds of knowledge. However, the core truth is that science *must* be differentiated from common sense and other knowledge so as to be "sold" to ordinary people. Ordinary people can learn from science, and then turn it into common sense, thus, in the final analysis, there will be no essential difference between science and other kinds of knowledge, but the persistent intensive R&D investments make their intertemporal and technical differences persistently existent.

Since the methods used by scientists can also be used by

ordinary people in principle, scientific research cannot have a completely unique method, but only biases some methods against others. Common actors have been studying the world as well. Scientists and common actors both complement and compete with each other, and hence scientists become a particular category of actors. *This means the integration of ontology and epistemology.* From such Algorithmic conclusions, we can deduce the appropriate social science methodology, and meanwhile, we can also know that the Kuhnian "paradigm" is nothing more than a collection of many *relatively closely* related elements in the scientific system, which inevitably contains subjectivity; And, the paradigm shift, or the "scientific revolution", like the transformation of worldviews of ordinary people, or similar to the change of the social system, can only occur occasionally and intermittently on the basis of marginal accumulation.

All of the above discussions are inseparable from Algorithmic Thinking Theory and Algorithmic Principles as the foundation. The reason why the theory and the principles are so useful is obviously that they provide many elements that have been lacking in the existing knowledge system. The main parts of the existing knowledge system are still valuable and important; when these Algorithmic elements are added, it is as if a catalyst is injected into it, and after a series of chemical reactions, it is merged into a new whole. This "Algorithmic Approach" makes use of computer principles while remaining independent of computer science, and then becomes a special tool for philosophy, humanities, and social sciences, and a basic method for theoretical deduction in all these fields. Readers who do not understand the principles of computers should still be able to use them. Moreover, I believe that by elucidating many of the non-traditional mechanisms and characteristics of the human mind, the theory may also be conducive to studying computers and artificial intelligence.

Hopefully, the use of terms such as "computation", "Instruction", and "Algorithm" will not make philosophical and humanistic scholars uncomfortable. In fact, while expanding the rationality and scientificity of relevant fields, ATT has also turned the social sciences humanistic. This synthesis and interpenetration can lead to a unified view of the world and society from some unprecedentedly interesting perspectives, thereby prospectively arousing a great deal of practical research work. It has the potential to make philosophy, humanities, and social sciences all become distinctly productive and creative, and will open up the space for our imagination in the new century.

ATT can also be used to prove that in the infinitely developing knowledge system, philosophy with characteristics such as fundamentality, subjectivity, and fuzziness is indispensable; therefore, the answers to existing philosophical puzzles will finally give way to new ones, and hence to the initiation of new philosophies.

CHAPTER 1
THE GOAL OF PHILOSOPHY IS TO DISCOVER A PROPER THEORY OF MINDS

§1. A Proper Theory of Minds can be Used to Synthesize all Philosophies: the philosophical history perspective

For the sake of simplicity, all the hitherto philosophies can be boiled down to "the efforts to find an appropriate theory of minds".

This boil-down cannot be perfect, but it can be defended that it captures the main content of all existing philosophies. With the help of a theory of the mind, the upcoming synthesis might not be strictly exhaustive, but the many breakthroughs and advances to be made from it would probably be enough to convince readers to accept the phrase of "grand synthesis".

The theme of philosophy throughout history can be thought of as the study of the relationship between mind and matter, or between subjectivity and objectivity. However, this theme was only realized after many twists and turns. Early Greek philosophy focused on things outside the mind, and developed many theories about the origin and nature of the physical world (or the universe). Parmenides, in particular, argues—in today's parlance—that behind many phenomena, there is an unchanging essence that controls everything; and that the phenomena are false passers-by and only the essence is the truth, something that really exists. Therefore, he called this unchanging essence "Being". In contrast, people's thoughts are just "opinions". Parmenides clearly recognized that the human minds are heterogeneous and fickle.

In the ancient Greek city-states, the social order based on the then-real ideas of real actors was liberal and democratic. Truth, or high-quality knowledge, can only be discovered or developed through the specific competitions and debates of the actors involved. Such processes are often slow, conflictual, tortuous, and precarious, especially for those who have more knowledge. Therefore, Socrates continued Parmenides' style, raising highly the banner of reason, and striving to prove and praise the role of reason. But what is reason? When the question went deeper, his successors, Plato and Aristotle, had to go in different directions. Plato emphasized the contemplative, deductive, and theoretical approach, believing that human could reach the ultimate truth, while Aristotle emphasized the process of knowing by advocating formal, inductive, and empirical routes. This was a glaring split in philosophy during the Greek period.

In the centuries that followed, the separation of Being from opinions intensified. Being has evolved into concepts such as Ideas, substance, God, Absolute, science, and so on, and its posture of overarching all other types of human thought and trying to engulf them has not fundamentally changed by far.

The epistemological philosophy initiated by Descartes changed the attitude of the previous philosophy centered on external objects, and placed the human mind in the first and central position. The gist of epistemological philosophy is that what is called Being or "truth" is nothing else in the first place, but an idea in the human mind, a thought. However, this understanding alone is not enough, because thoughts may not be in line with external objects, and in fact there are plenty of imperfect thoughts. Since the "truth" as the destination of thinking processes has been presumed, the processes of development of knowledge from low quality to high quality seem only to confirm the attraction of the "truth". This attraction, in turn, highlights the importance of methods. Thus, methodology became the focus of then philosophies.

The crucial turning point was made by Kant. In a difficult and devious way, Kant implied that human beings think only by using the structures, resources, or tools inherent in the brain to act on information from the outside world; and that since this a priori things in the brain are established and limited, human cognitions can reach some kind of certainty or consensus, but it is not the truth of the world; and that there is an unbridgeable gap between ideas and the truth. This is a categorical repudiation of the traditional doctrine of Being. This "Copernican revolution" reversed the course of philosophy that has lasted over two thousand years.

The confusion and chaos that arose from this was severe. The question posed by Kant was understood as the inevitability of contradiction or conflicts. Henceforth, the German classical philosophers after Kant, under the condition of tolerating conflicts, were committed to bringing Kant's philosophy back to the track of traditional philosophy. The Greek dialectics was re-picked up and expanded to its extreme. Just as epistemology failed to shake Greek philosophy fundamentally, so did the fate of dialectics. A definite destination was always ahead of philosophy. Hegel's works have been famous and widely circulated. Unfortunately, however, they were not convincing, because they portrayed contradictions as a unity, or disguised them as a wholeness. Countless authors have criticized Hegel on common sense, or from other various perspectives. Therefore, one of Hegel's historical contributions seems to lie in the effect that he magnified the flaws of traditional philosophy through his radical discourses, thus paving the way for the development of a new philosophy. This ushered in an era known in China as "modern philosophy", the "post-Hegel philosophy".

The philosophies since Hegel are generally considered to have a loose structure, and different philosophical groups are often disconnected from each other. However, I am surprised to see that they actually proceeded in two neat and orderly directions, one was to refute Hegel's extreme rationalism (in economics, it changed into neoclassicism) in almost all directions, and the other was to start from logic and language, and develop continuously until the birth of computers. The former mainly refers to the philosophy of continental Europe, which emphasizes the elements of time, will, practicality (American pragmatism), humanism, text, everyday life, transcendentality, difference, freedom, permutations and combinations (structuralism), and so on. The latter mainly refers to analytic philosophy. It first regained the logic pioneered by Aristotle and developed it to the stage of mathematical logic. The study of language can be seen as a preparation for a direct study of the human mind. The birth of computers pushed the study of thinking to a thriving stage. Another secondary clue is that the economics of thought, which originated from William of Occam, echoed by Ernst Mach (§170, Vol. II).

All these clues go toward the establishment of a theory of the mind, that is, how humans think or process information. Roughly speaking, they have either proposed conclusions that can be proved by the thinking theory, or they are actually preparing for the making of the thinking theory. From the above brief review, we can see that this question occupies the main thread of the philosophical literature, explicitly or implicitly. Thoughts are not as easy to observe and grasp as physical objects, so activities of the human mind seem mysterious, unpredictable, and controversial, even to humans themselves. This difficulty has led to the fact that the development of theories of mind has drastically lagged behind that of theories about physical objects.

At the very least, the anticipated theory of the mind, or the thinking theory, shall address the following issues: What is the role of empirical material or information in the activity of thinking? Why do humans have thoughts that go beyond empirical materials? Or rather, why do human beings produce both correct and false (or fictitious) thoughts? Why do established ideas develop again? Why is there such a diversity of thought? What are the prospects for the development of thinking? Why do people be convinced that something is true? Is thinking free? What is the relationship between freedom and necessity? What are the specific processes and states of the generation, preservation, dissemination, development, and loss of ideas? How about the relationships between different kinds of knowledge? How about the relationships between thought and text, language, or action? How about the relationship between thought and psychology? Etc.

The necessity of a theory of mind can be realized most deeply only when we have obtained an ideal theory of mind. Simply put, all the above threads will converge in the "Algorithmic Thinking Theory" (ATT, also known as "Algorithmic Framework Theory [AFT]", "Algorithmic Theory", or "Algorithmic Framework") introduced in this book. In my opinion, this can be a satisfactory and ideal theory of thinking. It was first proposed by me at the beginning of this century.[1] The name and terms of this theory are used only in the specific sense given hereinafter. Although they are literally related to other similarly named concepts or theories in

---

[1] It was given in three consecutive Chinese books of mine, as well as in some English introductory papers; please refer to the bibliography in my curriculum vitae for details. However, it will be re-introduced from the beginning in this book so that a new English reader need not first read my previous writings.

computer science, they are ultimately unique because it is a theory about the human mind, not a theory of computer science or technology.

It can be argued that the convergence of various historical development threads into Algorithmic Theory is a natural or inevitable process. The reason why I say this is because we mainly use those existing transdisciplinary and cross-genre findings to solve the problems of philosophy itself. I am like an intermediary and a peddler, making some selecting, moving, and assembling. This has indeed brought a lot of new knowledge and new principles. However, as I will explain step by step in the following text, these new principles are mainly marginal developments of existing philosophies. It's hard to believe that if these principles were not presented by me, no one else would have come up with them.

With the support of this new theory and this series of new principles brought about by it, I believe that the existing philosophy can continue the turn initiated by Kant, and complete its "last mile" of the journey, that is, to return to the era of Parmenides-Socrates, to solve the problems left over from that era, and to make an accomplishment of the philosophies since ancient Greece, thereby achieving the philosophical "grand synthesis". The various existing branches or schools of philosophy can exist as some parts or historical developments in this unified system.

In the above sense, this synthesis can also be called a kind of "unification". However, the reason why I am cautious to use the word "unification" is that Algorithmic Theory, on the basis of abiding by the traditional rational rules in principle, re-argues and re-introduces conflict and plurality. I don't want readers to be misled to think that Algorithmic Theory excludes conflict and plurality. Reversely, with the help of "bounded rationality" (or, more accurately, "concrete rationality"), Algorithmic Theory can be the tool that really effectively introduces conflict and plurality into the core of philosophy, and makes them the "full-fledged members" of philosophy. I believe that Algorithmic Theory has achieved this unprecedentedly convincingly. The resulting comprehensiveness or unity is natural, not affected at all. No matter how many angles the book will take to elaborate on it, it has existed there all along since the beginning of Algorithmic Theory, rather than being artificially attached to it later. As for whether the wholeness resulted should be called "synthesis" or "unification", it is a relatively minor question that we can discuss again after the reader understands the logic herein.

§2. A Proper Theory of Minds can be Used to Synthesize all Philosophies: the philosophical branch perspective

Why can a thinking theory be used to synthesize all philosophies?

Before it is answered in a complicated way, it can be explained very simply. That is, if we regard activities of thinking as the interactive processes of *subjects and objects*, it means that the processes themselves are synthetic, and any extreme doctrines can logically be represented as the particulars of the processes. For example, under the structure of dualistic interaction described above, if materialism is correct, then the thoughtful processes will *eventually* be swallowed up by information from the outside world, and the innate thinking structure, resources, or tools themselves will be dissolved; conversely, if idealism is correct, then the information, and thus the external objects, will *eventually* be dissolved. As for other theories that fall somewhere in between, such as constructivism, it shall be easier to illustrate with this dualism —obviously, constructivism is based exactly on dualisms like ATT.

That is to say, such a theory of thinking has the

characteristics of "philosophical neutrality" or "metaphysical neutrality". ATT can be introduced only as a "process variable" or an "instrumental variable", which, in principle, does not affect the ultimate outcome of thinking processes. This is easy for readers who know mathematics to understand.—The premise, of course, is that the readers acknowledge that human's knowledge of the world is generated through thinking activities.

This is in terms of the metaphysical or ontological purpose. The distinction between materialism and idealism has ever prevailed in modern philosophy. At that time, most people believed that sooner or later, human beings could clear the cognitive fog and obtain the ultimate truth behind the world. Under this belief, mental activities are understood only as some finite processes and are, therefore, easily overlooked. However, as the debates over the "final truth" stagnated, the thinking processes themselves finally came to the fore. It's like the logic in this statement: if there is any doubt about the conclusion of a book, then the book, at least temporarily, shall not be destroyed.

This is the unity between epistemology and ontology or metaphysics: *ontology, or metaphysics, speaks of the conclusions of knowing, while epistemology speaks of the procedures of knowing.* In case people are satisfied with their understanding, they may begin to draw final conclusions about the world. However, after the conclusions are made, is it still necessary for the thinking processes to exist? Secondly, when there are differences in people's understandings and changes among people in different times, there must be differences and changes in the "conclusions" of the world. A desire to draw conclusions shall be understandable, but the reached conclusions can continue to fail. What is the prospect of the human thinking processes? Is knowledge increasing or decreasing? Or is it increasing first and then decreasing, and finally converging to a state of rest?

These are the great philosophical questions that have not been answered for thousands of years. It is obvious that if knowledge is incremental and expanding, then ontology or metaphysics cannot ultimately succeed. Hence, does ontology or metaphysics make sense at all?

Obviously, the question of the unity of ontology and epistemology is far from being as simple as commonly expected. If philosophy is to embrace ontology or metaphysics while adhering to the epistemological line, it must demonstrate the necessity of "concluding the world" in procedures of knowing, and, the thinking procedures must also be continuously existent, and cannot be canceled by the proposition of metaphysics—otherwise it would be ridiculous.

A theory of thinking processes has the potential to solve this problem: for the sake of decision-making prudence, an actor in the time process must look back and forth and grasp as much as possible the whole world and the whole course of history; Even if his/her thinking abilities are limited, he/she must do so as best he/she can; Even if the conclusions reached are of low quality, i.e., unreliable, frivolous, temporary, assumptive, tentative or incorrect, they may be better than nothing to be done—the actor must not abandon the search for the wholeness and for the future merely due to his/her limited ability, and must not deal with the matters around them mechanically and sequaciously, otherwise it will obviously constitute another absurdity. In this way, we then need to value and legitimize these less reliable but quick and skillful ways of thinking, such as assumption and experimentation. This value or legitimacy is actually denied under the mode of traditional metaphysics. Being, the "mirror" hanging highly above, overshadows these methods. This further requires us to deny the Being if we want to achieve our goals!

The denial of Being cannot be done using Kant's method of "thing in itself", which draws an absolute line between subjective thinking and objective truth. The history of human practice shows that thought is constantly advancing, and therefore, the truth about external objects is also constantly approaching. That is to say, when thought is approaching the objects, its activity should not be reduced; what should we do to achieve this?

One idea is that we need a theory that can explain precisely how thinking is carried out concretely and how its capacity, intensity, and scope are limited in a limited time or a unit of time. In this way, the mind can approach a particular object, but because of the vastness of space and time, it can settle one thing and then do another. This theory foreshadows that the end of thinking may still come after its scope has ceased to expand. Therefore, it would be better if it could, in the meantime, prove the infinity of the depth of intellectual activities.

Such a thinking theory is clearly a theory of bounded rationality. But it is not only used to deny the traditional perfect rationality, but to specify how reason is limited and how it develops, so it should be a theory of "concrete rationality".

It can be argued that the existing various logics are the ones that can be used to explain thinking processes, so such a thinking theory can be used to integrate these logics at the same time. However, the existing logic generally lacks the concept of time, and it is clear that they cannot be directly used as a theory of mind. In other words, the existing logic, and other relevant branches such as the philosophy of mind, shall only be deemed the basis of the thinking theory, and they still need to be extended to the thinking theory.

Another difficulty of this integration seems to lie in ethics. Behind ethics is actually the social philosophy, as well as the applied branches of philosophy in life, spirituality, culture, religion, and so on. This thread has been developed independently of other branches, but it is still within the scope of philosophy. In this context, metaphysical ontology is considered to be primarily about nature, and it is "distinct" from humanistic and social issues—although there are a number of philosophers who have tried to relate them in different ways.

According to the previous ideas, however, this seemingly difficult job has now become easy and handy. To understand this, it is necessary to return again to ontological metaphysics. In the case of the assumption that the ultimate truth has been known or will be known, since the epistemology of the thinking process is eclipsed, all the imperfect, false, imaginary, or fictitious ideas that arose in the process become superfluous. What we need to realize is that various humanistic and social phenomena and concrete existences, including ethics and morality, are largely "wrong", "false", "imperfect", or "superfluous" in the eyes of traditional metaphysicians. In this way, it is not surprising that traditional philosophy has split into unrelated parts such as metaphysics, epistemology, logic, ethics, etc.

Now, it's the opposite. Since this theory of thinking based on concrete reason can integrate metaphysics and epistemology, that is, since metaphysics and thinking processes can coexist, then the humanistic and social phenomena that are the imperfect results of the thinking processes will also arise or exist in the meantime. *Thoughts typically exist only when they are imperfect or incorrect. The perfect thoughts, which are seen as a repetition and reflection of external objects, are then implicitly considered to be incapable of existing on their own.* This is an important way for us to understand the existence of thought. On this basis, we can then regard all thoughts, including correct and perfect thoughts, as part of the "independent third party" between people and things, and in this way, we come to a relatively comprehensive understanding.

Human's aims and pursuits are first and foremost

subjective, not (or not exclusively) determined by the physical world. Secondly, since we are in the processes of thinking, we cannot think that all thoughts are perfect. For example, ethics and morality must not be regarded as some kind of perfect, divine being, as philosophers such as Kant did. This book will aim to demonstrate that "making mistakes" (or subjective ideas) is a necessary condition for the making of ethics and morality. As long as some thoughts, including ethics and morality, are subjective, "bizarre", imaginary, imperfect, or wrong, then the system of thought cannot be considered perfect as a whole and, therefore, should be regarded as a relatively independent existence; furthermore, the wills, decisions, actions, and consequences that arise from such thoughts are of the importance independent of the natural world, and the interpersonal actions, human life, and human society are all of the importance independent of the natural world. By articulating this relative independence, we are articulating the unity between social philosophy, including ethics, and other philosophical branches.

§3. What a Priori Theory is Needed

To concretely explain reason is to concretely explain the structures, states, processes, results, and so on of human thinking (that is, the "most rational" part of the human spiritual system). Then, how do we do that? Of the existing philosophical doctrines, the most closely related is apriorism. Apriorism can be broadly divided into two types: the one on a priori knowledge and the one on a priori thinking tool. Plato's theory of Ideas, for example, is a theory of a priori knowledge, which holds that correct knowledge already exists in the mind of an individual before he or she is born, and that the process of developing or learning knowledge is only a process of recalling the a priori knowledge. The proposer of a priori thinking tools can be considered Kant[2], although Kant himself did not directly say so, and many other philosophers seem not to see it this way. This issue can be discussed further after the Algorithmic Thinking Theory is given.

The theory of a priori thinking tools could be superior to the theory of a priori knowledge. The reason is that the latter is a lazy theory, of which the explanation is so easy that the theorist has little to do. Therefore, it is hardly an explanation. And, it doesn't explain where the less correct ideas come from. In contrast, the former makes fewer assumptions because the number of thinking tools is generally considered to be very small, far fewer than the amount of knowledge. If we can explain more phenomena by a priori tools than by a priori knowledge, there is no need to go a devious way to adopt the latter.

Some people might despise the word "tool", because if we say that what exists a priori in the noble spiritual world of human beings is only some "tools" used to process information, this seems to constitute a derogation of the human spirit. In this regard, I hereby declare in particular that when we say that there are some thinking tools in the human spirit a priori and innately, we are not absolutely excluding the possibility that there are also other things in it a priori or innately; we are simply emphasizing the innate tools as the *priority* in our

---

2. As the Austrian economist Ludwig von Mises wrote, "Kant...taught (that)... All knowledge is conditioned by the categories that precede any data of experience both in time and in logic. The categories are a priori; they are the mental equipment of the individual that enables him to think and—we may add—to act... a priori categories...are the necessary mental tool to arrange sense data in a systematic way, to transform them into facts of experience, then these facts into bricks to build theories, and finally the theories into technics to attain ends aimed at." (Ludwig von Mises, "The Ultimate Foundation of Economic Science", D. Van Nostrand Company, 1962, pp. 12, 16; the ellipses and the bracket are added by me.)

discourse. As will soon be shown later, these a priori tools do not completely exclude a priori or innate knowledge.

"Tool" is often a good way to make breakthroughs to resolve disputes. The reason why science has achieved a lofty position in human society is that science often adopts instrumental and technical means to resolve disputes. Such an approach is generally remarkably neutral and persuasive, and hence is highly acceptable to all parties. Therefore, even in philosophical debates, we shall pay attention to it, and even prioritize it.

In short, I believe that the pivot of solving those major philosophical puzzles is to find the innate or a priori tools of thinking. Such tools must be finite and definite. Finite tools process information, leading to finite results, i.e., thoughts, ideas, or knowledge, and only the finite results have the potential to develop, and thus develop. The temporal process of thinking is actually the development of knowledge, or the expansion of ideas in the time tunnel. According to this logic, such finitude should also be spatial. As long as the existence of ideas has a spatial dimension, they can be stored and moved, there is a problem of more or fewer ideas or knowledge, and their inventory can also change and grow, from small to big. Unfortunately, there were clearly no such quantitative concepts about thoughts in traditional literature before the birth of computer science. Such concepts, however, are in line with common sense, and hence should be basic and necessary. It's like when we study physics, if we don't even have concepts of size, shape, position, motion, and so on for objects, what research can we do then? Throughout history, great philosophers have pondered and articulated a great deal of profound thought, but unfortunately seem to have neglected these fundamental questions. It is understandable, thus, that those major philosophical problems have not been solved.

There are also philosophers who, in my eyes, have some

deep-seated bad habits, that is, they are good at distorting problems, shifting problems, and even covering up problems. They always quickly lead some ordinary arguments into major arguments of principle or sectarianism, creating deadlocks and long-term antagonisms. On the contrary, this book starts with some neglected common sense and common logic, supplements philosophy with some new knowledge and new principles, and finally seeks breakthrough solutions to major problems.

Let's continue our arguments. Finite thinking tools are best definite. This means that they are better to be set in stone and be the same for everyone. The resultant advantage of this is that it can then be used to form the basis for answering questions like "Why do people believe something is correct?" raised above. It's like a machine that has a definite and unchangeable function, and thus has a definite usage. To use the machine in a certain way is to be deemed "correct"; otherwise, it's an "error". This explains both right and wrong. One of the meanings of right and wrong is that it is set in stone. If the result of the same mental activity is always changing, it doesn't matter whether it is right or not. Simultaneously, another meaning of right and wrong is that this kind of thinking tool is universal to everyone, so people will agree with or against a certain thinking outcome at the same time. The historical comparison of thinking results has something in common with the interpersonal comparison, because the historical comparison of the same person can also be seen as a concurrent comparison between different individuals, and the interpersonal comparison can also be seen as a comparison between the thoughts of the same person at different moments.

The finite and definite thinking tools are also best explicit, i.e., we can specify what they are really. Henceforth, it would be more persuasive, because we can dissect arguments into details of thinking activities, and the proponents and rebutters can also explain their opinions with specific and clear steps of thinking.

The next question is to explain why there are differences and conflicts between thoughts.

The above approach can be used to answer this question as well: specific thinking tools act on specific information to produce certain results; therefore, if a particular thinking tool processes different information, the results will naturally be different from each other, in principle. Just as thinking tools and information have their own individualities, the results of thinking, namely, the thoughts, are naturally individual. Furthermore, there come the questions of interrelationship between these thoughts, i.e., whether they match or do not match each other, and to what extent. It should be emphasized that *consistency and conflict are the interrelationships between concrete things, and they occur generally at the same time.* It's like two floor tiles, each with a specific and solid shape, and they have to be spliced together; some parts may match each other, and others may not. Moreover, there may be many irregularities between the "exact match" and the "complete mismatch", not only the two extremes. To achieve this effect, it is necessary merely to explain the specificity of the shapes of the floor tiles. In the same way, as long as we explain the specific traits of reason, how the thinking activities are carried out, and what the thinking tools are, then there will be a wide range of relationships such as consistency, contradiction, conflict, causality, and irrelevance between different thinking tools, between thinking tools and information, and between the thinking results.

§4. The "Difference Prior to Identity" and Deconstruction of Being (1)

Interactions between thinking tools as concrete things and external objects or information will inevitably produce a large number of concrete and relatively independent things that are generally different from each other but can all exist reasonably and "legitimately". The word "legitimately" is used here to mean that it came from its previous state of "unlawfulness" that was defined by the lofty "Being" (or the "system of truth"), since "Being" is now to be dissolved and completely disappear. This is the liberation of all living beings on earth.

The dissolution of "Being" has been attempted in different ways by Heidegger, Derrida, and other philosophers. Now, we have a simple and clear way to accomplish it; that is: the concrete thinking tools process information alternately, then process the results, and so on and so forth; although the results of thinking inevitably repeat each other sometimes, such a perspective can lead us to generally believe that new ideas will be generated from time to time. This effect of infinite growth is mathematically called the "*Combinatorial Explosion*".

With combinatorial explosions, it is no longer possible to believe that there is a definite and static end ahead (i.e., "Being") waiting for us humanity, and we no longer have to repeatedly guess and argue about what it is, and thus we no longer have to associate every concrete thing around us with that "Being" and to clarify their roles in it. Every concrete thing will henceforth exist freely and communicate freely. It's a state of true pluralism. Concrete things will deal with each other according to their own natures, forming a variety of states and outcomes that they can form. As with the concrete existence of concrete things, the relationship between them will be concrete and limited. Even if something grand comes up again, it will be finite and partial as well. The terrible "monster" that is going to engulf everything would probably never appear again.

That "monster" is now submerged in a sea of thoughts or knowledge. This is what the mind does with its quantitativeness. In the past, quantities of thought or knowledge were not philosophically important, because philosophy always tended to condense them, thus negating the importance of their quantities. Now, in this state of true pluralism, the question of the quantity of knowledge becomes a matter of course, we will certainly observe, count, study, and predict the amount of knowledge and its changes, and hence we will find the great fact that the amount of knowledge has been steadily increasing in history. This great fact again tends to negate the "Being".

Derrida's "difference prior to identity" will now be realized. These differences will include not only differences in specific "shapes" or contents of knowledge, but also differences in the qualities and values of knowledge. This is because, since these thoughts or knowledge are the results of operation of thinking tools, the word "tool" has ensured that a thinking tool does not necessarily contain the secrets of the object world, and its encounter with its object(s) is not a pre-arranged performance, and a result of the encounters has not been "manipulated" or averaged in advance. Therefore, the results must in principle be very diverse, and hence some people laugh while others cry, and life experiences would be bittersweet and uneven. Thereafter, even if people learn from each other and engage in an "equal wealth" movement, the degree of equalization that can be achieved at any given moment can only be limited. This is because the capabilities and workloads of thinking tools are limited while new, unforeseen ideas are still being generated.

Moreover, the first thing people do is not to "equalize the wealthy and the poor", but to learn to experience differences and distinguish right from wrong, good from bad in the midst of differences. In fact, people don't originally know what is right and wrong, good and bad, but just blindly think about it and produce these results. Because these results are different and even contradictory, people sometimes have to choose among them. By "sometimes" we mean that people don't always make this "either/or" choice. If this choice had been made all the time, there might have been only one or very little knowledge left to remain. People generally cherish and tolerate the results of their thinking, and try to keep what they can. This is one of the reasons for the growth of the quantity of knowledge. However, in this diverse and pluralistic context, it is difficult to completely avoid choosing. This is a manifestation of "irregularity", "heterogeneity", or "mixedness". Furthermore, during this choosing, people find differences in the quality of different pieces of knowledge, and thus gradually distinguish and classify them. And, in this process, it is inevitable to discover some characteristics of high-quality knowledge and low-quality knowledge, or some methods for their development, or certain criteria to identify them. These methods or criteria also exist as *another type* of knowledge alongside these knowledge types and will play a role in judging other knowledge later.

In the previous section, we talked about "a priori certainty", which refers to specific natures of a thinking tool that require a particular use of it, and on the basis of this particular use, ideas of right and wrong can arise. This notion of right and wrong does not concern the objective world. Now, in the judgment of the thinking results in relation to the objective world, through comparison, a notion of right and wrong can also be generated. Although it is impossible for the mind to skip its own way of thinking and directly to the truth of external objects (as Kant argues), the knowledge obtained through the mind itself is not necessarily unreliable. With the help of common sense, we can know that this is a matter of probability; that is, among the knowledge that we have acquired through relatively blind thinking, some are correct or reliable, and some are false and unreliable. Even, as long as the samples are abundant enough, there might be a certain proportional relationship between them. Moreover, there must be a large number of other results in between, varying in the degree of "correctness", and it is difficult to say in detail.

That is to say, the ideas or standards of right and wrong are not known in advance or before birth, they themselves are acquired. Even, the correct use of thinking tools is also acquired in the activities of the days after birth. Even if we believe that it is innate and unchanging, we ourselves may not know exactly what it is in a specific context. This conclusion can be proved by the method of counter-proof: if we had known these standards or criteria beforehand, we would certainly not have developed wrong knowledge, but only correct knowledge; if the existing standards were perfect, we would not have developed false knowledge thereafter. The latter are clearly inconsistent with the facts of the past and with our expectations for the future.

This logic requires us to *look at all the outcomes of human thinking comprehensively and holistically, and to put the problem of truth on the back burner*—let alone the assumption that certain knowledge will eventually swallow up all others. This is another denial of Being.

If the above-mentioned effects of mixedness and infinite development are what a relatively sound philosophy should pursue, then the superiority of the idea of "concrete thinking tools" is reaffirmed. This is to say, we need to think of the basic functions of the human brain as something concrete that is, first and foremost, not too good, not too bad, not too strong, and not too weak. Compared with external objects, they are a bit special and have some specific "temperaments"; in other words, they are a little "biased", a little "evil", and even a little "strange". The phrase "first and foremost" is used here because we don't yet know what the end result(s) of thinking processes will be. This "end result(s)", if any, may prove that the thinking processes are pure "self-disturbance", that the knowledge production is essentially "superfluous", and that the human brain can indeed correspond exactly to the world, and that the human brain does contain the entire code of the world (the thinking processes are merely used to "decode" it, as Plato conceived)—or, perhaps, not at all! In other words, our approach has the advantage of comprehensiveness and neutrality; it contains all possibilities, and does not miss any final philosophical conclusion. The final conclusion, whatever it may be, must be contained in it. Hence, this is a risk management strategy better than before.

The above argument requires us to look at all the results of our thinking in a unified way, regardless of their difference in quality, just like we look at positive, zero, and negative numbers unitively. Therefore, *we simply call all the results of thinking "knowledge", "thoughts", "ideas", and so on.* At the same time, we emphasize that the quality or degree of correctness of each thought varies, and that such differences are generally small and soft, and that the transition from one to the other is generally gradual rather than sharp, and that mutation is a relatively rare occurrence. In particular, the differences are not purely quantitative or qualitative, but often a mixture of quantitativeness and qualitativeness, and their uneven degrees. We use the word "softness" to denote these abundant varied mixtures between extremes or purities, in order to distinguish it from the tendency of traditional philosophy to bias extreme, purity, and simplicity.

§5. The "Difference Prior to Identity" and Deconstruction of Being (2)

Is it appropriate to answer the question of reason, or the question of truth, in the above way? We need to look at it again. Obviously, this is first and foremost a relative approach, and the resultant "truth" or quality knowledge is subject to change. Because of heterogeneity, whether or not specific knowledge has changed and at what rate, must vary from case to case. This speculation is clearly consistent with the actualities. The history of scientific development, for example, is highly fit in this speculation. Although many people believe in the existence of truth or Being, specific scientific knowledge that enjoyed high prestige has been denied and updated from time to time. This is an embarrassment for various realists. The proposed theory of thinking can be used firstly to demonstrate that there are indeed qualitative differences between the results of thinking, i.e., knowledge. This provides support for realism and rationalism. The main meaning of Socrates' appeal to Athenians can be understood as emphasizing the differences in the results of thinking, and thus calling aspirations to high-quality knowledge. Even knowledge about the thinking tools, because this knowledge of these specific objects is also different from the objects themselves, may be subject to change as well. The revision of logic by proposing the Algorithmic Logic can be an example of this.

Secondly, the proposed theory embraces both the absoluteness and development of knowledge. In this regard, it can not only be satisfactory, but even ideal. The result of processing certain information by a particular thinking tool is constant and never changing, which guarantees that there is an absolute line between right and wrong. This absoluteness corresponds to certain firm convictions that have been long held in the minds of us (and of all realists and rationalists), thereby preventing us from falling into utter relativism or nihilism. Meanwhile, it can be considered that this absoluteness is manifested in a variety of ways, and needs to be experienced in specific contexts. For example, this absoluteness also allows for variable knowledge of specific objects, or variable answers to specific questions, because the relevant information available even to specific objects or specific problems can be numerous, and the processing of information by thinking tools can be repeatedly carried out, hence *the depth of knowledge shall be infinite*. Since the tools of the mind are supposed to have finite and definite functions, this conclusion as an inference is necessary. As a rule of thumb, information from the objective world is infinite, and new information appears frequently or fitfully. In addition, the information contained in a specific object can generally be considered to be enormous, *especially compared to the limited ability of thinking tools to process information*. In a specific scenario, the ratio between the two can be multiple times. How many times should it be? Obviously, it is difficult for us to set a specific value for this, so we can only assume *in principle* that this amount of information is infinite, and hence the times is also infinite—Besides, the development of knowledge about other objects often indirectly affects the knowledge of this object and hence the discovery of its information.

On the other hand, the above theoretical framework does not preclude the inference that, with a small probability, even some empirical knowledge will be valid for a long time and is therefore highly affirmed. This is because, due to heterogeneity, there may be cases where the results of the processing of certain information by thinking tools are invincible in the challenge for a long time, perhaps because the objects are simple, or the processing methods used are superior, or there are just some kinds of effects similar to "deadlocks". This is equivalent to some partial equilibria or long-term equilibria in economics. Since there is actually no "God" who has arranged all this, it must be irrational to imagine that all correct knowledge is uniformly correct; this imagination should apparently be *the manifestation of the will of the observer*. Therefore, it shall be normal again for different pieces of high-quality knowledge to have differences in the degree and other aspects of correctness, which shall be a natural manifestation of heterogeneity and irregularity. The empirical knowledge of very high quality would literally exist, but its proportion of total knowledge would be low. These two conclusions are bound to be made at the same time. Meanwhile, it can be noted that the latter conclusion, referring to some local phenomena, should not affect the combinatorial explosion and infinite development of the knowledge system as a whole.

In addition to answering the question of truth, this binary framework of "thinking tool + information" embodies the equal interaction between subjectivity and objectivity, and can therefore be used to answer the question of the relationship between freedom and necessity, or freedom and determinism: specific thinking tools process specific information to arrive at eternal and unchanging results; this is necessity and determinism; However, individuals are free to choose or make the combination of thinking tools and information, as well as the order in which different thinking activities are arranged, which brings a great deal of freedom. Taken together, these two aspects constitute a *basically rational and reasonable* basis for our answer to this question, that is: the individual can think freely, even "cranky", but any mental activity is always within the scope of its ability and possibility; The ideas that can be formed by one person may also be formed by others, because the differences in interpersonal ideas are nothing more than in the thinking tools, information, processing sequences, etc., so it is *possible* for different individuals to communicate with and evaluate each other's thoughts. Moreover, this egalitarian interaction between subjectivity and objectivity has led to the fact that individuals can deliberately violate and resist objectivity, since both subjective and objective forces are now seen as finite forces, and it is hence possible to compare and compete with each other.

Besides the generation of whimsical ideas, this binary framework can also explain the reasons why humanity has evolved from knowing the world to transforming it. The logic is as follows: when both subjective and objective forces are regarded as finite forces, the comparison between them will have a variety of results such as "less than", "equal to", and "greater than". When the subjective force is less than the objective force, it can be deemed indicating that the person has not yet completely known the objective object; When the subjective force is equal to the objective force, it can be deemed indicating that the person has come to know the object; And, when the subjective force is greater than the objective force, it can be deemed indicating that the person has produced a subjective will that is not present in the object, and then the person would try to transform the object, and make it conform to this will. In this logic, people's cognitive activities naturally develop into engineering activities, and science and engineering are placed within a consistent and unified framework. *The "creative" activities emphasized by engineering are actually similar to the cognitive activities, and there is no mysterious difference between them.* In fact, it is not a secret that outside subjective wills, people also have a lot of "inventions" during the course of understanding the world. The philosophical habit of focusing thinking processes only on cognitive activities arose in the prevalence of metaphysics. However, after interrogating epistemology, all kinds of thinking results that are "detached from the truth of external objects" or "outside the truth" are considered to be important.

To sum up. The dual framework of "concrete rationality",

namely, "thinking tools + information", can endogenize not only all types of knowledge at one time in principle, but also various differences among knowledge, so as to move towards the typology, modularization, and versioning of knowledge. Human knowledge can then be divided into various types or "modules" according to various criteria. On this basis, we can hope to realize the aspiration of many philosophers since ancient times, i.e., to establish a comprehensive and unified knowledge system.

Finally, I would like to add two issues. A finite thing that works continuously in a time track, such as a thinking tool that processes information continuously, can produce infinitely rich results. The richness and infinity of the thinking results are brought about by the accumulation of time and workload. In a limited or specific period, the thinking results that can be obtained can only be limited; and, at any given point in time, the stock of knowledge that an individual, a group of people, or an entire human race can acquire or possess is necessarily limited. Moreover, even if the amount of knowledge that can be obtained in the course of infinite history is unlimited, this does not mean that human beings can acquire "knowledge" beyond their capabilities. In other words, if there is some kind of "thinking tool" that does not belong to human beings, then it is impossible for human beings to obtain the "knowledge" processed by such thinking tools. Thus, even if the knowledge that humans can possess is unlimited from the perspective of the "combinatorial explosion", this knowledge base does not, in principle, include anything or any "knowledge" conceived from the "non-human thinking tools". Therefore, it makes sense to imagine the concept of a *human knowledge thesaurus*, which includes all the knowledge that can be generated by the processing of all information using all human thinking tools. Since it is assumed that everyone has the same thinking tools, this knowledge base can exist "objectively" apart from any specific individuals, and each person has only a limited part of it.

This "human knowledge thesaurus" will not be like the "Being", a mantra hanging over us. Because, now this new "Being" does not constitute any constraint on us. On the contrary, whatever each of us can think about must belong to it, and there can be nothing that we can conceive of but that does not belong to it. This new "Being" is huge in size while the old "Being" is tiny as the "oneness".

This is because differences and personalities are now truly prioritized. In this environment of heterogeneity and plurality, things and their relationships are now freely chosen to be addressed, holistically or partially. Scholars can choose to concretely state the relationships between things under specific conditions. For example, the relationship between mind and matter can now be illustrated in a specific context, when we are inside the specific context. The difficulty of explaining the mind-matter relationship used to lie in reducing it to some simple proposition or theory whereas now, the principle of simplicity is not always necessary, at least not primary. We have a lot of knowledge and opinions, and that's fine; this does not even necessarily prevent them from becoming a philosophy. What is simplicity? What is philosophy? Now, they have become the problems in themselves, and therefore become the objects of our investigation.

§6. The "Difference Prior to Identity" and Deconstruction of Being (3)

After the disappearance of "Being", has it been zeroed? Will metaphysics be completely meaningless?

Of course not. Metaphysics attempts to encapsulate the whole world, and thus to give concise and basic guidance to the actors in the course of time, which is of great significance to each of us as individuals.

It is first and foremost used to satisfy our curiosity. It is natural for individuals with limited rationality to have curiosity about the world. Moreover, this curiosity is only justified from the perspective of this limited, bounded and concrete rationality. The ancients conceived of some kind of all-encompassing "Being" in order to potentially satisfy their curiosity. Therefore, once we really reach this all-encompassing "Being", curiosity has no reason to exist. Nonetheless, an boundedly rational individual can be constantly curious, because the knowledge he/she receives is always limited and subject to development. In particular, it is important to note that the desire of people in concrete situations and bounded rationality to understand the overall world is not only reasonable, but also a manifestation of wisdom. A person who mechanically does things in a sequacious manner may have little thought of the distance and the future, and may have little estimate of the vastness of the world and the length of time. To be able to move from a focus on everyday matters to a focus on philosophical issues requires reasoning and imagination. Even if we can't provide answers to these philosophical questions for a while, just being aware of the existence of distant places and the future indicates the development of intelligence.

Secondly, "Being" is conceived as having a simple form, and thus it can be considered that one of its functions is to pursue the economy of mental activity. Philosophers could have had thought of everything in front of them as the "Being", but why not? Obviously, one of the reasons is that phenomena are too cumbersome and hence need to be simplified. Parmenides believed that phenomena are false and Being is true, that is, phenomena are fleeting, through which we have to discover the dominating and unchanging thing behind them. This unchanging thing, because it doesn't change, is relatively simple. This economy is the hidden subconscious and now needs to be clearly revealed. This book aims to illustrate that its impact is far greater than what is usually considered in association with the topic of "economy".

Of course, economics is not the only one. One of the goals of mental activity, as Nietzsche put it, is to control the external world in order to achieve one's own ends. To do this, the information from the outside world needs to be adapted to our processing manner, in line with the structures, tools, methods, and resources we already have. Economics is just one of the requirements.

That is to say, after a circle, metaphysics is now coming back, and we are returning to Parmenides' position. And, now we have to reconcile it with our concrete rationality. What to do?

The solution to this problem comes naturally. It not only complies with common sense but is also capable of developing a series of new philosophical and theoretical principles and hence systematically revamping the existing philosophies.

That is, the boundedly rational individual in the condition of time and space speculates about the existence of the whole world. In order to make the current conclusions and decisions sound, he must understand and summarize the world as much as possible, and, in principle, must consider all the factors of all things. This is called "factor completeness" in this book. And this kind of thinking activity in order to summarize the overall situation can only or must be completed within a limited time. The space for knowledge development is unlimited, whereas the ability of thinking activities, the amount of thinking work per unit of time, and thus the speed of thinking are all limited; however, decision-making and actions in the real world often have time requirements; therefore, the actors cannot allow such thinking activities to continue indefinitely, and they are forced to close them at certain points in time. This is called in this book the "Forced Closure of Thinking (or Computation)".

What should an actor do if a series of mental activities is to be rationally elementally complete, but it must be forcibly closed in a limited time? The answer is that the rigorous and relatively reliable thinking envisioned by epistemological philosophers has to be set aside, and the subjective, rough, canny, and rapid methods can come in handy. Traditional epistemology is actually primarily in the service of scientific research. Conclusions of scientific research can be much more reliable, but as mentioned earlier, this reliability can only be relative. And, importantly, it's small and slow. This is a new way of looking at science right now. The importance of this perspective has previously been overlooked. It would literally be wonderful if real-world problems could always be solved with scientific methods, however, as many scholars have often argued, there are many questions that science has not yet answered, so what should the actors do with these questions? This is the real (or more) important question. Now, if the person concerned has to answer questions related to the overall situation of the world in a limited time, he can only "make things up". This is a methodological explanation of the occurrence of errors or fiction, and hence, it's no surprise that we often hear various weird talks or bizarre theories. We used to criticize and even ridicule them, but now we need to recognize that this is a necessity. Even, it's a sort of luck. Wouldn't it be even more difficult if humans were not capable of making these bizarre theories? These bizarre theories may not be entirely true, nor are they necessarily entirely wrong. Wasn't correct knowledge developed from conjectures and bizarre theories?

In this way, we find a justified and *rational* cause for subjectivity or "irrationality" to enter into the philosophical arena, or for the combination of subjectivity and objectivity, or of rationality and "irrationality". The traditionally scientific, objective, and rational approach, of course, still has an important role to play, but it needs to re-find its place in the competition with the subjective, "irrational" ordinary methods that people use every day, and the thinker needs to evaluate, compare, and weigh different tools and methods, and choose to use them flexibly as appropriate.

What will be the state of metaphysics under this perspective? Metaphysics shall be both comprehensive and concise. Or, even if its content is lengthy sometimes, it is still succinct compared to space to be unfolded in order to know the whole world precisely. It is impossible for people to travel to every corner of the world in person, and they can only speculate based on the information available to them. Obviously, this is a mind game. In fact, everyone has participated in this mind game to a greater or lesser extent in their daily life and drawn their own conclusions and hence formed their own philosophy. Philosophers, on the other hand, specialize in this work, devoting more time and resources to it than the average person.

At the request of a forced closure of thinking, the quality of philosophical work can be challenging. Although philosophers are not usually faced with a definite temporal requirement in their work, their lives are limited, and hence, it is still necessary for them to timely draw certain conclusions from their research objects. In order to make a living, even if it is perfunctory, it is needed from time to time to conclude their work and publish the reports. Otherwise, if you insist on absolutely strict standards of quality, you may only say nothing or have to find another way to make a living. Fortunately, this is just a contest of wisdom; that is, the winner of the game will gain a foothold in the philosophical arena if he/she can manage to prove to the reader that his/her doctrine is just *relatively* superior to those of other authors.—Most of the livelihoods in the world are actually the same in this respect.

In this way, the Algorithmic philosophy finds the role and place of metaphysics or philosophy in the knowledge system and in the real world. For example, philosophy can be used to summarize and explain the world as a whole. This "totality" can be reflected in the temporal dimension as the primitive, long-term, or ultimate contemplations, i.e., the thinking about the origin, future, and destiny of the world. Because this interpretation of philosophy arises from the perspective of "concrete reason", it is actually a mere consequence of "concrete reason". Second, philosophy can be used as a basis for a variety of mental activities, including scientific research. This basis can be different from a "generalization" of the world, but the roots and grounds of mental activity. For example, scientific activities need to be rigorous, but tracing back to the roots, it cannot be rigorous. This lack of rigor in the roots is like the lack of rigor in the frontiers of scientific work, which further requires a concise and vague generalization or encapsulation of the rest of the world. These effects will simultaneously occur as long as the size, scope, function, and nature of science are limited. Science is like a baby; it needs to be wrapped in the philosophical "swaddling clothes". And, in pursuit of the brevity of the philosophical discourse, as well as the breadth of its usefulness, this fundamentality of philosophy is accompanied by a high degree of subjectivity and ambiguity. Because such properties are so intense, philosophy and science are both interconnected and relatively separate.

What needs to be inserted here is that scholars and the general public actually have a good understanding of the characteristics of philosophy. Now, to a large extent, the proposed theory of thinking is only helping us to re-discover and re-organize these existing understandings and make them theoretically explicit.

A metaphysics and a philosophy thus formed are necessarily limited knowledge. Although the relevant discourse can literally relate to the whole world, because the materials and information used by the author are limited, the functions of thinking tools are limited, the amount of thinking work actually completed is limited, and the depth of philosophical thinking must inevitably be limited. As mentioned earlier, this limited metaphysics has the effect that it can logically coexist with epistemology, unable to eliminate epistemology. It's exactly the coexistence of thinking tools, thinking processes, and thinking results. Moreover, since this coexistence is natural and inevitable, the metaphysical author as an actor oneself should also consciously recognize this coexistence, so that this coexistence can be consciously reflected in the metaphysical discourse itself, and the epistemological and metaphysical discourses can be interspersed with each other at any time. In this regard, the book calls it the "Ontology-Epistemology Entanglement". This self-consciousness can also lead to a change in metaphysical strategies. For example, it would be better to focus research and discourse on the questions that must be answered, rather than answering all questions indiscriminately (as William of Occam argued), and, to figure out which issues need to be avoided or further studied, and to develop certain research plans for the future. Making a step forward, this implies the *versioning* of metaphysics, that is, it recognizes and proclaims that it must renew itself from time to time. Of course, since metaphysics is concerned with the whole and the foundation ambiguously, it is not likely to be frequently updated. A kind of knowledge shall be updated only after an intensive use, so that it would be economical. Therefore, even if a particular metaphysics has shortcomings of one kind or another, scholars and ordinary people will tend to use it, and its renewal must only take place intermittently.

Since this self-inclusion implies a reflective consciousness of itself, how does consciousness do it? A series of related issues need to be further explored.

§7. Materialization of Thought and Its Discreteness

Once epistemology is developed outside of ontology, it means not only that it requires a particular a priori or transcendental theory, but also that both thinking and knowledge shall be materialized, substantialized, or "physicalized", and that they both need to take some discrete forms.

The human brain was originally conceived as dealing directly with foreign objects. Every deal is done independently, instantaneously, and quickly as a "clear-up", with no leftovers or remnants. However, now that it is impossible to clear it in time, it has to be stuck deeply in the processes, and "knowledge" (including all high-quality and low-quality thoughtful results, please do not forget) is left behind as the "traces" of thinking, or as the "mediators" between thinking activities. People use the "survived" knowledge to help form ideas and decisions, and hence to deal with foreign objects. That is to say, there is now a new thing called "knowledge" between people and things. Although knowledge is mainly found inside our brains and is not easily seen or touched, we all know that it is produced or acquired and then exists. Especially as human beings, and as the producers, feelers, comprehenders, dominators, users, evaluators, and reformers of knowledge, we not only know that it exists, but that we may be the only species in the world that knows of its existence. We know that it arises, stays, moves, grows, decays, or dies. The identification of such a thing as a "thing" may not be important to other species (or any other possible "subject"), but it is crucially important to us humans.

We can use any word on it, like "thing", "substance", "being", "reality", "fact", "existence", and so on. Given that the meanings of these words are controversial, we need to avoid such controversies for the time being. What I mean by this is that knowledge needs to be identified first of all as *a relatively independent class of objects of our thinking*, regardless of its relationship to other objects of thinking. Traditional philosophy (or science) is often accustomed to first abolishing the independence of human minds and knowledge. This, regardless of its ontological implications, is particularly *methodologically* incorrect and unwise.

Nor does acknowledging the relative independence of minds and knowledge as objects entail imposing on them indiscriminately the specific properties of other kinds of objects, and then reopening the terminological debate. Since it is the beginning of this book, we must try to avoid this kind of inefficient argument as much as possible. We just emphasize here that, while acknowledging the relative independence of minds and knowledge, their nature as objects is first and foremost limited to their own concrete properties with which we are familiar; they interact with other objects with their own properties, and the manners of interaction are also specific, just like the properties of any other object, as well as their interactional manners, are also concrete and specific. In this sense, we will oftentimes call a thought or idea an "entity" in this book, following while reforming the existing terminology.[3]

Since we will expand on the specifics of these properties later, here we highlight only the following three aspects.

First, ideas, thoughts, or knowledge must exist in time and space. That is, they have dimensions of time and space. This is

---

3. The word "entity" was invented and broadly used to refer to anything including a thoughtful object, which may imply the "Algorithmically-correct" common sense and the philosophical stance that everything, or every entity, can be real in certain sense. This book devotes itself to the justification of this common sense and philosophical stance. I am happy to see that this word, ideal so much, has been "customized in advance" for our Algorithmical use.

the basic meaning we express when we use the colloquial term "thing" to refer to ideas or knowledge. The "thoughtful processes" are the processes of time, not some other processes that have been detached from time. The knowledge produced by mental activities is initially the components and results of the flow of mental activities, and then, after being determined to be stored, it turns into a "stock" that exists as a thing distinct from the flow, the mental activities. The word "stock" means that its existence can continue in time, just like we see an object lying there quietly and continuously, motionless and intact. This seemingly simple truth has always been very ambiguous in philosophy and science. People have been talking about ideas or knowledge since ancient times, but they have always refused to acknowledge these physical properties of them. This attitude is so subtle that philosophers rarely speak precisely about it. When philosophers speak of concepts such as "Being", "truth", "substance", etc., they often refer to something other than concrete things, or *they always avoid thinking of ideas or knowledge as concrete things*. In fact, we can say, to a large extent, that the concepts of substance, Being, and truth were invented precisely to *expel* ideas and knowledge *out of* the class of concrete objects, and precisely to let them act as the *antithesis* of the concrete objects. In other words, philosophers consciously or unconsciously believe that if ideas and knowledge were deemed concrete objects, then these concepts would be useless and superfluous—because there seems to be nothing that is not "existing" or "real" anymore.

The explanation for this strange attitude may be complicated, but it should be simpler first. That is, since ideas reside primarily in the brain, and the input of knowledge obviously does not enlarge the brain with it, there is no way to understand how ideas can exist in the brain (and hence in space), and what specific technical characteristics of this kind of "existence" should be. In terms of its temporality, the reason why the temporal characteristics of mental activity are ignored is obviously not because the mental activity is carried out too slowly, but because its speed is intuitively too fast. Slow advances in ideas and technology were often intergenerational. In ancient times, when the conditions for storing information were very rudimentary, people inevitably ignored the long-term accumulation and development of knowledge. On the contrary, mental activities in front of us are constantly changing, fleeting, imaginative, coming and going without a trace. Since what is "real" is a thing, what is an "unreal", "virtual" thing? Obviously, it just refers to a human's thought or idea! Thoughts are prone to make mistakes, and the things that make mistakes are none other than thoughts! Therefore, according to common sense, human thoughts are regarded as like bubbles. What philosophers teach mankind is to get rid of the bubbles and errors and to take what is real as the foothold, and bow down to the "truth", preventing the restless mind from messing around.

In this way, the traditional attitude towards ideas and knowledge is contradictory: talking about them, but not believing their existence! Then, what on earth are being talked about if they do not exist? What are "they"? Isn't there only a difference in degree between something fast and something slow?

Second, in connection with the spatiotemporal characteristics, since the substantive or material nature of minds and knowledge is recognized, it is necessary to divide them into one and another, thus distinguishing "this thinking" from "that thinking", "this idea" from "that idea", i.e., to build theories about the discreteness of minds or knowledge.

Why do we say so? This is because, since a thinking tool is limited, it must also be assumed that the object(s) and result of the tool are also limited. Therefore, thoughts can be counted in numbers and knowledge can be measured by quantity. And, this limitation is relative to that infinite potential, and must be distinguished from it and discussed separately. If the two cannot be distinguished, then these finite results cannot be discussed separately, and this "finitude" would be meaningless. This implies that one must wait for all the thinking results to arrive before looking at them all at once. Based on the same logic, the results of different thinking activities formed by the use of different thinking tools on different informational objects must also be relatively independent; otherwise, this finitude will be both nonexistent and meaningless.

As a particularity for the above view, when we objectify thoughts, our observer's own thoughts must be tacitly regarded as separate from the thoughts of the person objectified, distinct from each other, and in principle not interfering with each other, or rather, not fully interacted and integrated with each other. This is a major technical condition that needs to be met for the objectification. There is an underlying paradoxical understanding in traditional philosophy that the human mind, since it "comes and goes fleetingly without a trace", must be a well-integrated and whole "lump"—at best, each person can only own a part of the lump, and the different parts are consistent with each other (e.g., the so-called "division of brainwork"). In this case, it is deemed not very meaningful to distinguish between the thoughts of actors and the thoughts of the researcher himself. Moreover, in this case, since thoughts are deemed existing as a whole, then the whole is not concrete, and cannot be *logically and equally juxtaposed* with concrete ordinary objects. This concept secretly extracts the historicity and development of thoughts, making them a kind of mysterious thing unknown for what it is after all; the "thing" is detached from the existence of time and space, or in other words, it becomes an absolute, perfect, and static so-called "Being" or "Absolute" in a specific sense.

A doctrine of discreteness inevitably gives priority to the

microscopic vision. It necessarily requires a certain match in "size" or scale between an object of thinking and a tool of thinking. Strictly speaking, the requirement is not exactly a preference for the microscopic, but a specificity of the scale or size. It's like when we look at a physical object with our eyes, it requires the object to be in the right size; what is too small needs to be enlarged, and what is too large needs to be reduced. This is not to suggest that it is incapable of dealing with objects that are too large or too small, but rather that objects that are too large or too small need to be processed in advance because of this particular requirement of scale or size. That is, this requires some additional processes. This logic shows that the approach to "concrete reason" does not reject the combination of the macro and the micro; and, moreover, it is precisely because it describes the specific characteristics of reason that it is able to establish a concrete, credible, and persuasive connection between the micro and the macro.

Discreteness is also associated with the subjectivity and arbitrariness of thinking mentioned earlier. Since discreteness means the independence and relative freedom of an individual thought, it means further that when the individual thought is moving, to a certain extent, it can still be independent of other entities or objects. Therefore, it may be kind of "imperious" or "arbitrary" from the "perspective" of other entities, or from a macro perspective. This imperialism or arbitrariness in turn reaffirms the materiality of the thoughtful entity. On the basis of this materiality, the dynamics of thinking activities can then be feasible and realistic. This has become a key tool for solving many philosophical problems. Readers can experience this in detail in Volume II (e.g., Kant, Nietzsche, Husserl).

Third, based on the above-mentioned materiality and discreteness, the behavioral and economic nature of thinking activities is prominent. Since a thought or idea is an entity, a thinking activity must also be a real behavior, and in addition to occupying the resources of time and space, a real behavior is usually bound to consume other resources (such as energy and material resources), so that the economic analysis of thinking activities can be carried out, and the actors must arrange their schedules and allocate time, space, and other resources for them. The economic effects of ideas are so important that they not only have a significant impact on actions of the people involved, but also change the basic structure and principles of the humanities and social sciences that take ideas as their major objects of research. The discreteness of thinking not only enables thinking to take thoughts as its objects, but also take the economy of thought as its object. These high-order processes will cause further reactions from the thinker, and then produce a chain effect. This is just like physical entities that have mass and thus have gravitational force between each other will cause a series of superposition effects. For example, according to astrophysics, gravity caused the universe to diverge into various types of celestial bodies after a long period of evolution. Similarly, it can also be argued that different types of knowledge are not the result of simply dividing the thinking results, but the result of the deliberate re-conception and reinforcement under the consideration of the thinking economy.

The materialization of thinking in this way will become a fundamental feature of Algorithmic philosophy. I believe that it is of great subversive significance in philosophy. We will keep showing these great meanings step by step.

§8. Interaction of Thoughtful Entities

Human minds directly understand external objects but cannot finish at once, so the "third existence" of "knowledge" (in a broad sense) is born. Since this existence comes to exist now, it must continue to derive. Under discrete conditions, different minds "observe", study, and deal with each other ("*Mutual Objectification*"), and a person's mind "observes", studies, and deals with one's own mind ("*Self-Objectification*" or introspection), which produces "thoughts on thoughts", or the "*higher-order thoughts*". In my opinion, this is the root of society, social issues, social philosophy, and social sciences, and it is also the hinge joint between social philosophy and philosophy.

"Discreteness" not only means that different ideas are in different locations in the spatiotemporal environment, but also that the movement of "one" thought is relatively independent of "another" thought and does not dance with it. It is a prerequisite for one person to see another person as an object. This is not only a prerequisite for scholars to study society, but also a prerequisite for actors in society to study and deal with each other. Under this premise, ideas for ideas and for behaviors governed by ideas are born, social knowledge is generated, and actions against specific social problems, and thus specific social engineering, are produced. Social actions and social engineering then once again become the objects of observation, research, and actions, and they continue to be derived and intertwined, thereby forming huge, important, and complex social phenomena and social existences.

Traditional philosophies have not been ignorant of the interactions between people and between the minds of different individuals, but they potentially believe that the end result of such interactions is the elimination of them, and therefore they are primarily neglected. For example, people deceive each other, and at the end of interactions, no one can deceive anyone, and they all tell the truth. People fight with each other, and in the end no one can win over the other, thus peace is made. These are what modern game theory pertains to. In short, the implication of traditional philosophy is that the game processes will eventually be reduced so that, at the equilibrium level, the social processes can also be ignored.—

Another understanding is that in the case of game processes being reduced, traditional philosophy seeks out "society" while regarding ethics and morality as something absolute, similar to the laws of nature. This is the way in which society was "found" again. Such mainstream social philosophy and social sciences then struggled with longtime criticisms and discontent until today.

One's self-objectification means "self-awareness" (or "self-consciousness"). According to the above, this kind of self-awareness is actually the awareness of one part of the self (the thinking activity itself) against another part (the memory about the self), so it is quite similar to the awareness of other things. This is the way this book explains self-awareness. One's past thoughts as a fact and a memory of this fact cannot be changed by one's own self at the moment, so that one can observe and study one's own thoughts in the same way as one observes, studies, and deals with the thoughts of other people, and even "deals" with oneself. Such self-awareness cannot be complete and perfect. But, in this generally imperfect environment, this is normal and unsurprising. Perfect self-awareness, if it exists, would be strange. The typical way of mutual objectification is spatial, that is, in a space where people objectify each other directly and in real-time, thinking and acting while observing and studying each other. The typical way of self-objectification is diachronic, sequential, or "serial"; that is, it unfolds in the course of time, and therefore requires the help of the mechanism of memory. However, the so-called "typical ways" described above are only relative, and mutual objectification can, of course, take place diachronically while self-objectification can also take place almost in real-time (e.g., looking at oneself in the mirror).

Nor is traditional philosophy incapable of recognizing the existence of self-objectification. The reflective activities of humans are extensively documented and discussed in early literature. However, under the paradigm of mainstream philosophy, reflective activities have unfortunately been marginalized or even dissolved. The reason is the same as above: in an ideal state, a "sufficiently rational" person should not be considered to be inconsistent with himself—just as different individuals who are "sufficiently rational" should not be inconsistent with each other, so that even if one constantly reflects and produces "thoughts on one's own thoughts", and "thoughts on thoughts on one's own thoughts", and so on, this process of multiple-level higher orders will eventually collapse and return to some optimal and equilibrated first-order states. A typical theory in this regard is the "rational expectation" model in economics: a "sufficiently rational" individual has foreseen future activities, and the actual future activities will just fulfill this previous prediction; once a deviation occurs, the deviation must be a "purely random walk" and should be excluded outside the scope of explanation.[4]

This returns to the argument already stated: in a sense, it can be said that thinking "exists" only when it is wrong, fictitious, or imperfect—or in other words, only in this case, it can be reasonably accepted as "existing". *The existence of the mind is linked to its imperfections.* Thus, the existence of society, and the existence of ethics, are all linked to this imperfection. When ideas are assumed to be perfect, it is not easy to find the roots of society.

Of course, as mentioned before, we can further argue that even those ideas that are considered perfect cannot be thought of simply as perfect reflections (or "counterparts") of the world, or even as realists believe, that they are the truth of the world itself. In fact, these perfect thoughts may have nothing to do

---

4. Robert E. Lucas Jr., "Expectations and the Neutrality of Money", Journal of Economic Theory 4, 103-124, 1972; and "Asset Prices in an Exchange Economy", Econometrica, Vol. 46. No. 6 (Nov. 1978), pp. 1429-1445.

with the external world, and may be completely "self-inflicted" and "wishful thinking" of human beings. If there is really an omniscient and omnipotent God, these so-called "perfect thoughts" may be ridiculous in God's eyes. However, we do not base our argument on this *in the first place*, but on the former points. The Algorithmic philosophy is not a game of hair-splitting, but rather reveals the basic and convincing logic that pervades us all the time but is overlooked by us, and that can be widely and immediately agreed upon once they are spoken out and understood.

There is a misleading weakness in the above argument that we need to correct now. We start with the understanding of physical things, and then discuss the understanding of minds, and this order of discourse is only to cater to the historical tradition of physicalism, and to facilitate the reader's transition from old philosophies to the new one. It is neither a logical order nor a historical order. Individuals do not need to know things before their minds. In the real world, in any situation, and in any historical stage, as long as we open our eyes and use our brains, objects, people, and ideas are placed side by side in front of us, and we are free to choose and freely construct the sequences of understanding. It can even be assumed that a baby's mind is already being formed before it is born, and before he/she opens his eyes to see foreign objects. His/her thinking, if not all reflective, should at least be comprehensive and contain various types. Therefore, the question of which is more "basic" between the thoughts of things and the thoughts of people, or between the thoughts of first order and the thoughts of higher order, is actually meaningless and unnecessary. Even if the higher-order thoughts must be technically based on first-order thoughts, this question is of little significance because of the minimus, abundance, frequency, and overlap of thinking activities.

By the way, I would like to emphasize that this method of

transitioning from traditional mainstream logic and concepts to the Algorithmic comprehensive framework will be widely used throughout this book. Therefore, the above explanation also applies to all relevant discussions in the entire book.

§9. The "Softwareization" of Theory of Mind

At this point, the basic requirements of an appropriate or ideal theory of thinking have been formed, which are: to adopt a dualistic approach of "innate + acquired", or "thinking tools acting on information"; to adopt a discrete approach; to be able to define individual thoughts and thinking activities, to have a spatio-temporal dimension, and so on.

Unfortunately, however, looking back at history and examining the current situation, it seems that a theory of mind that meets these requirements does not exist, or apparently has not yet been found. Scholars do not even know that they are poor in this regard. For example, everyone is keen to talk about information, but how is information processed? Does information continue to be information after it has been processed, or does it become something different from the raw material of "information" as if a physical material is processed to become? If it is something else, then what is it? Also, why is it that people's minds have wrong, fictitious, or imperfect ideas? It is common sense that thinking activities obviously take time, namely, ideas are developing. Hence, how does thinking develop? Do we directly produce correct ideas and then continue to accumulate correct ideas, or do we make mistakes first and then correct them? If we need to constantly correct mistakes, will the existing knowledge still be reliable? Is it still meaningful? What is the prospect of knowledge development? When will we be able to obtain a truly correct, reliable, and complete "truth"? Intellectuals do not seem to be in a hurry or any sense of crisis on these issues. On the contrary, they were keen to show the public any progress made in knowledge development, as well as their satisfaction with the progress.

On the other hand, paradoxically, it is generally admitted that the riddles of life and mind have not yet been solved. The underlying understanding behind this claim is that revealing the puzzles of the mind is merely the task of the natural sciences. Many researchers, either explicitly or implicitly, believe that the best sign of a successful theory of mind is to interpret the activities of the mind as something about molecules, atoms, or quanta. Thus, they have been watching and waiting as natural scientists make progress in these areas. Philosophers and social scientists are also waiting. Those who really did not want to sit back and wait began to try to use the sporadic discoveries that natural scientists had already made and relate them to specific philosophical and social science topics. This is how the behaviorist approach to research has developed. For example, neuroeconomics has been popular for many years as a branch of it.

However, the main meaning of the phrase "thinking theory" should be that *thinking must explain itself clearly*; that is, thinking must explain itself in its own way. The reading, writing, and communication we are doing at the moment all manifest thoughts, so when we talk about "theory of thinking", it is thoughts telling themselves, or one thought telling the other. We cannot simply say that the activities of certain material molecules and atoms are thinking activities. Maybe they are indeed thinking activities, but not *directly. Before feeling and manipulating matter, our consciousness first directly feels and manipulates thoughts.* The feelings that physical objects give us must also be considered thoughtful. The mind knows and controls its own thoughts. It is in this sense that the mind needs to explain how it thinks.

Looking at the current situation in academia, on the one side, scholars would rather admit their ignorance in minds, and on the other side, seemingly they snub it; these two attitudes have been combined eerily. The commonality of these two is that they both ignore that the existing knowledge has been enough to come up with a satisfactory theory of thinking. Most importantly, such a theory of thinking can actually *be expressed entirely in the language of the mind itself,* regardless of natural science terms such as molecule, atom, or quantum. It is a purely humanistic and social science approach. In computer jargon, it's a *software-based* approach that has nothing to do with *hardware.* Although Algorithmic Thinking Theory borrows the terminology of computer science, we will repeatedly explain in detail that this method is essentially a method of humanities and social sciences, which can be exclusively and easily used, reined, or manipulated by scholars in these disciplines.

For the goals of the humanities and social sciences, why is the above-mentioned hardware approach misguiding? The clearest answer to this question can be made with this reverse logic: What if scientists one day succeed in proving that mental activity is the product of some specific structures and functions of certain material particles? What will scholars in the humanities and social sciences do after reading a report like this? Will we then manipulate these elementary material particles to replace our thinking activities? These are questions that need now to be considered, studied, and speculated on in advance.

Obviously, such a possibility is slim to none. First of all, one can manipulate these elementary particles only with the support of mental activities, not the other way around. Thinking is the basic function of human beings, and it is our *"root".* All our activities *start from* our own thoughts that we can perceive, control, and carry out. The mind manipulates the limbs to act, not the limbs to manipulate the mind to act—otherwise, what would manipulate the limbs again? Moreover, scientific discoveries about the functions of the mind would have not yet led to the emergence of techniques for directly manipulating elementary particles. Even if such technology were to emerge, it would not immediately lead to a replacement of the basic functions of thinking. Even if this replacement is in some ways economical (just as computers are economically attractive to users today), it is difficult to envisage that the replacement will be comprehensive and thorough. As long as we are alive as living organisms, mental activity is generally always easy and economical for ourselves. Second, and more importantly, can the contents of mental activities be known by direct observation or measurement of the states of brain tissues, biological organs, or elementary particles? Is it easier than directly knowing about our own thinking activities through our own neural systems? It must be understood that the contents of thinking are our own human affairs; they are our own stipulations, we know them, and we want to communicate them with our own kind. This question has nothing to do with the issue of how human thinking is physically or biologically realized. It's like engineering and technical personnel are responsible for building a car, but after building up the car, how to use it is the driver's business. The engineers may provide the user with the operating instructions. As long as the user masters this set of instructions, he/she can use this car for very distant, complex, and longtime trips. For the specific contents of the trip, the vehicle engineers do not need to pay attention to them, and it is also impossible for the engineers to know them. In this way, the driver of the car can develop his/her own language about the car, its use, how it behaves in use, and what it means—even if he/she may not know how to build a car at all.

This difference can be clearly explained in computer terms: the end result of hardware design and manufacturing for a computer is to provide a set of software languages for software developers and users. By using this language, the developers or users can, without knowing how to make the computer's hardware, develop or compile applied programs, or use the programs for a variety of other tasks. It should never be assumed that only hardware engineers "know" about computers. Especially for a computer in use, the hardware engineers often have no or little knowledge of the complex structures and "inside stories" of the programs and data in it. For example, by observing and measuring the electrical currents or potentials in a computer component, it is impossible for a hardware engineer to know what is going on there; or, after I write an article on my computer and then save it in the hard disk of the computer, it is impossible for a hardware engineer to know the contents of this article simply by detecting the electronic activities in the chips or the physical states of the hard disk without reading the words on the screen. This article needs the reader to directly "open" with relevant software to read, and then to know its contents. Correspondingly, a large part of the value of a computer is also determined by the software and data it carries.

We can continue to have ethical and metaphysical discussions about the above questions—For example, is there any point in human existence if humans don't think any longer? However, the Algorithmic approach is, *in the first place,* committed to *instrumental points* that are the easiest, most efficient, and most persuasive; therefore, these discussions are omitted here for the time being.

§10. Flow - Stock; Serial - Parallel

In the above, when we say "the mind's own language", we are primarily saying that it is the content of conscious activities, and that the conscious individual knows in his own consciousness what it is—even if it cannot be easily expressed in natural language. There is a difference between thought and language, and they must not be confused; nor can ATT, as a theory of mind, be confused with any linguistic theory. Another reason for emphasizing this point is that if the content of consciousness cannot be expressed as language for a while, we can give it a new name, and invent new terms, and then it can be expressed again.

The terminology difference is also reflected between "mind" and "consciousness". The word "consciousness" is often used to refer to the *active* states of the brain or mind. For example, when a person is awake, we say that he is "conscious", and when he is asleep or comatose, we say that he is "unconscious". "Consciousness" can also refer to the actions of the brain or mind, and then we often refer to "conscious activities" and so on. "Mind" can be used to refer to actions such as "conscious activities" or "thinking". "Mind" can also be used to refer to things like the brain, the thinking system, and ideas or thoughts, i.e., the tools, equipment, or products of conscious thinking activities, which can all be preserved apart from active, conscious, or mental thinking activities. At this time, the flow of mind is distinguished from its stock. From this distinction of natural language, we can realize that in the common sense of human beings that has been handed down for thousands of years, the flow and stock of thinking need to be distinguished, and in fact, this distinction has been made, and widely recognized. As we have seen, the use of "thought" or "idea" as a noun is equivalent to the broad use of the word "knowledge" in this book—although we sometimes accept their literary differences. Thoughts preserved as memories can re-enter into conscious activities through recalling, and thus participate in the work of thinking. In this way, there is an interactive relationship between the flow and the stock.

Both philosophy and the social sciences have a minimalist, abstract, and macroscopic style. In keeping with this style, we would better make the technical details as simple as possible. The innate mental structures, tools, or resources in the human brain are technically and physically complex, but when reflected in human consciousness, they have become relatively simple. It is impossible for us to sense the presence of our own hippocampus, sulcus gyrus, and neurons in our own consciousness, and hence images of brain anatomy can startle ourselves and average observers. It is also impossible to have a clear understanding of the specific processes by which information is processed and stored in the brain. However, we have the means and the conditions to simplify them. The first step in simplification is to focus on the concept of "thinking tools".

We just need to imagine that there are certain thinking tools inherent in the human brain, as if there is a toolbox containing multiple different physical tools. Each tool processes its own information to produce relatively independent results—that is, ideas or knowledge. This is the requirement of discreteness, a concept that can come naturally from our reasoning above. There is another way to achieve this discreteness: it is possible to imagine that there is a single organ in the brain, but this organ can do a variety of mental actions. The consequences of this assumption can be equivalent to the assumption of "toolbox" above, except that it emphasizes the sequential, serial processing method that only after one thinking action is done can the next move on, so that the different thinking activities have to be "chained" into a sequence to be carried out. This obviously takes time. The dynamics of the mind have to happen from this.

Regarding the relationship between stock and flow, the existing principle is the "roundabout production method" proposed by the Austrian economist Böhm-Bawerk. When discussing the relationship between commodity production activities and capital stock, Böhm-Bawerk said that workers generally cannot directly use raw materials to produce goods that are ultimately used by consumers, but need first to "detour" to the production of tools, machines, equipment, semi-products, and other factors, and then use these factors as capital goods to produce consumer goods; in this "roundabout" way, the economic system expands its scale, where there must regularly be a large number of capital goods in stock that cannot be directly used for consumption though, then the economic system can normally run to provide goods for people.[5] This "roundabout production method" was originally only used to explain the relationship between physical productive activities and physical stocks. Now, we can use it to explain the relationship between the production of ideas and the stock of knowledge, and from this we can further discover a series of important new inferences, new principles, and new knowledge that we cannot obtain directly from physical objects. Since these new principles did not exist in previous economics, they can now return to be re-applied to economic issues, to reform the existing capital theory and economic theory.

The roundabout production method inevitably leads thinking activities to be "serial" (equivalent to, or including, "sequential", "recursive", "iterative", "Markovian", etc.). The limitation of thinking tools, and thus the limited ability of a thinking tool in a single thinking activity, leads to the fact that thinking activities must be carried out continuously, one after another. Unfortunately, many specious theories prevent this basic mode of thinking from being fundamentally accepted and established by the academic community. One of the arguments is the so-called "serial-parallel" controversy. The parallel theory refers to the fact that in general, there are many

---

5. Eugen von Böhm-Bawerk, "The Positive Theory of Capital", translated by William Smart, London: Macmillan, 1923, pp. 17-23.

(or nearly infinite) mental tasks in the brain that are always collaboratively working with each other at the same time. The popularity of the parallel theory has seriously affected recognition of the serial theory as a basic theory, so that by far, the value of the serial theory has been far from being fully realized. We need to ask the proponents of the parallel theory the following questions: Is the parallelism of the thinking work so strong that the time consumed for the whole thinking work can be neglected? Are all the thinking activities thus reaching their end at once and then losing their historical development? Although the observed brain activities unfold somehow synchronously, can the observed person himself *feel* that there are multiple mental activities in his brain concurrently? Should we henceforth ignore the common byword of "one mind cannot be used for two purposes"?

I don't think it's surprising that people can feel that a specific mental activity in their own brain requires the participation of many organs and tissues in the brain, both physically and biologically. It's even a mechanical common sense. For example, the brake of a car is only performed by the driver to "press the brake pedal", but behind it, there is a combination of many parts. If we look behind the pedals and the interior of the car, we will know a lot of things that the driver may not know; however, does this mean that it is not "one" braking operation? The answer may be "yes" for someone. This incorrect answer can be used to illustrate how getting caught up in technical details may hinder the development of a concise and robust concept, and how the complicated, advanced, and complementary knowledge, if not properly handled, may hinder the development or refinement of a basic theory.

Secondly, some scholars may realize that a purely serial theory would limit the ability of a computational theory to explain the details of mind, and hence are eager to supplement it with parallelism. To this, I would say that it is first and foremost necessary to realize that the shortcomings of seriality need to be tolerated, rather than to be supplemented in a hurry. We first need to understand a series of unknown characteristics and consequences of the seriality, and then re-examine the framework, structure, and pattern of thinking and of knowledge systems, and adjust the basic strategies and methods of research activities. Only after all these basic and primary tasks have been completed, the details of mind can then be touched.

To sum up, in addition to the requirements set forth in the previous section, an appropriate theory of thinking needs to take the following manners: different thinking tools process information to form the basic thinking activities, or the smallest units of thinking activity; only one thinking activity can be carried out at a time, and these units of thinking activity are arranged in chronological order to form a thinking flow, which consumes time and produces knowledge; flows of thinking activity generate and use the stocks of knowledge, and the knowledge stocks are continuously generated and accumulated to form a considerable scale of "thoughtful entities"; these thoughtful entities exist side by side with other physical entities in the spatiotemporal world. In other words, "concrete reason" produces a variety of objects, creates a variety of problems, adopts a variety of methods, and leads to a variety of consequences and knowledge. Now, these are all within a logically unified framework.

CHAPTER 2

THE NEW PRINCIPLES & NEW KNOWLEDGE THIS THINKING THEORY CAN BRING

§11. No. 1: Constant Thinking Tools and Their Discretionary Use

Such a theory of thinking, if it can be found or constructed, will be very useful. According to the above logic, it and its inferences will constitute a significant set of new principles or knowledge. These new principles and new knowledge were previously absent from the thesaurus of human knowledge, or they had previously existed only in some embryonic, mutilated, deviant, fragmented, or implicit ways. Now, we can reveal them explicitly and demonstrate them logically. Then, they will be used to correct the fallacies and deviations in existing philosophy, fill in the blanks and gaps, provide frames and adhesives, and thus form a comprehensive, unified new philosophical system.

Strictly speaking, such new principles or knowledge cannot be enumerated one by one, and different readers will have different opinions on the importance of their different parts. However, we should not come to the absurd conclusion that "because we may be wrong, we should not say anything". We must pursue a simplified and outlined expression. Given the importance of these new principles, while most of them have already been mentioned in the previous chapter, they still need to be elucidated, re-interpreted, and refined. Then, after formally giving Algorithmic Thinking Theory, we will return to the discussion of these new principles (i.e., the "Algorithmic Principles"). The goal of this book, as well as all other Algorithmical writings of mine, is just to demonstrate and interpret these principles. These principles only revolve closely around this thinking theory itself, forming the primary principles. Their secondary inferences, although they can also have very important meanings, are not included in this chapter.

Thinking activity is the use of innate thinking tools that everyone has to process external information; this would constitute the specific manner of the proposed theory of thinking. The functions and characteristics of thinking tools are limited, the connotation and characteristics of specific information are also limited, and the results obtained, namely, the forms and contents of knowledge, are also limited. This all-encompassing finitude leads to the effect that human thoughts are neither everything nor nothing, but something concrete and specific, which sit between human and external objects, constituting a cluster of entities that exist as a relatively independent third party. The discreteness of thinking activities guarantees that the majority of these established stocks are not affected by the traffic activities but can be selectively applied to the traffic activities. Since then, the entities identified have acquired a kind of completeness in their types. Any being must be one of these types of entities that we have identified and delineated, and any activity must also be the activity of one or more of these entities. For example, because of this theory of thinking, we will not devote ourselves to arguing that "incorrect ideas do not actually exist" as traditional realists do. Now, both correct and incorrect thoughts can actually exist, the thinking activities that produce them can actually occur as behaviors, and they may also be actually implemented as decisions, thereby affecting the physical world. Thus, there is no absolute distinction between the virtual and the real, but only the *technical differences* between different entities and their different relationships. Moreover, our natural habit of identifying entities will be consistent with this theory of thinking that naturally requires the identification and division of entities in order to adapt them to the characteristics and requirements of our own minds in size or scale.

This concreteness and finitude not only ensure that human thinking is meaningful, but also require that thinking be dynamic, continuous, and evolving. At the same time, this concreteness and finitude provide the basis and possibility for free fabrication or combination in the dynamic thinking processes. Because thinking tools, information, and other entities are concrete and definite, people have nothing to do but can only selectively combine them or not. There may be some restrictions coming from their formats, just as a physical tool may also have specific instructions on how to use it, but the freedom and possibilities that are left over from these restrictions should still be enormous—It is probably that the format restrictions themselves were discovered consciously during the course of these free combinations. The results of information processing can continue to be processed freely. In this way, it can be shown that there is not only a lot of room for the combination of thinking tools and information, but also for the collaboration between different thinking tools, either directly or indirectly.

Therefore, such a theory of thinking guarantees that human thinking not only has its objectivity, certainty, and some regularity, but also has its freedom. According to the principle of combinatorial explosion, this freedom has grown to the point of infinity, and to the point where it could be large enough to form a barrier between the different opinions of many people. For example, because of this barrier, people sometimes have to vote among themselves to coordinate their opinions. The diversity generated from freedom is so important that freedom must be protected as a primary right and value. This is a new way of looking at democracy and freedom. It is precisely because of this freedom that our human beings exert our efforts to think, discuss, and create value. Freedom, then, is both a right and a duty; And, our existences and discussions are then meaningful, not completely fanciful or arbitrary. In other words, even if they are some "misconducts", they are the "misconducts" within the capabilities, limits, and possibilities.

The system of thought, which is made up of concreteness and freedom, is a mixture of the above two elements. This mixedness also opens up a wide range of possibilities in their applied principles and methods. For example, it may further produce determinism, or it can produce some kind of agnosticism. However, I believe that the current situation is significantly different from the past. First of all, this integrated system brings the two closer together, so that they are co-located in the same platform or system. Second, the universality, constancy, and certainty of the thinking tools provide the criteria that enable us to clarify differences and distinguish between right and wrong, good and bad, through *specific analysis*. This will be distinct from what happened before when there was no such theory of mind. Therefore, we are moving towards a synthesis and unity rather than a simple accumulation of different doctrines.

This combinative perspective sees the human mind as an ocean composed of these basic elements. This mixedness may not be as ideal in form as a certain purity. However, if the mixedness is a truth about the world of human thought, then the explanation of the mixedness shall be a success, a precision, and another example of reducing complexity into simplicity.

§12. No. 2: The Combinatorial Explosions Bring Endless Development

Obviously, such a theory of thinking gives a solution to the dynamicization of philosophical doctrines. Heraclitus articulately raised the question of dynamics. This question has been in conflict with various static, absolute doctrines, difficult to reconcile, up to date. Now we can realize that the *dynamics of mental activity is the key to the dynamics of philosophy.*

This is not so clear until it is spoken out, but once it is spoken out, it becomes so clear that the reader can be expected to immediately agree on it. Traditional metaphysics is a doctrine that has few processes, but mainly the results. The curiosity aroused by the assumption of "Being" misled people to ignore the process of knowing. At that time, people did not even realize that "Being" was only a mental assumption, the content of a result of mental activity. This "Being" in religion was reflected as the "doomsday" doctrine, which claims that there is a date when all the truth will be revealed and all responsibility will be held accountable. One manifestation of the "Being" in real life is the belief that there is a limit to the growth of economic activity, and eventually, after "everything that should have been invented has been invented", growth will stop and human living standards will not be able to improve again.

Now, on the other hand, as long as the reader agrees that "Being" is only an inference, and that this inference was caused by the activity and process of the mind, then the contradiction between it and the dynamic world is highlighted. The dynamics of the world are, first of all, manifested in the dynamics of physical phenomena and the dynamics of human physical behavior. In the context of these dynamics, once the "Being" is presupposed, it entails the situation that the mind stays still while everything else is moving and changing. Then, what's the significance of the change and motion of the other things? Aren't they under the control of the mind? In particular, what is the point of such a dynamism in the case of human behaviors and social changes, if their destination and final state have been determined in advance? This is clearly a far cry from the dynamic question raised by Heraclitus. The dynamics must be eternal, unpredictable, and evolving. This is the result of our observation of reality; even, it is a common-sense requirement.

It is a pity that most of the philosophies prior to Algorithmic Theory did not meet this requirement. The "Being" doctrine actually provides a bit of dynamism that "Being" is supposed to hang high ahead of us, rather than in the present, and thus implying that it will take some distance to get there. Although it is implied that the journey is not so long, it has been waiting for thousands of years, and is still a long way off. Interestingly, such a technical approach has been adopted by other philosophies. For example, Kant's presupposition of the limits of knowledge amounts to a rejection of this infinity. The "circle" of mental activity shown by Hegel implies denying the infiniteness of mental activity. Nietzsche talked about the "eternal recurrence", which indicates his falling into the theory of circulation. Chinese Taoists conceived of the dynamism that the world revolves around an axis, similar to the way modern science combines formulas with information, or the Laplacian determinism. This doctrine, because it assumes that certain information can only be collected and not speculated, has in effect drawn an absolute line between what is knowable and what is not; therefore, it could not be accepted as a proper dynamic philosophy. This compounded state is actually a mixture, irregularity, or imperfection, which can be considered to be caused by bounded or concrete rationality. Another doctrine of infinite approximation to truth (e.g., Nicholas of Cusa, Bruno) may intuitively seem plausible, but as a philosophy, it implies a convergence or contraction of dynamics in general and thus, in fact, presupposes a static prospect. The last example is the assumptions and "statements" of philosophers about the dynamism of eternity, expressing their "belief" that change is everlasting. This doctrine is methodologically indistinguishable from the doctrine of "Being" because it has no concrete arguments.

In this way, the defects or lack of the dynamic doctrine are in an astonishing status. Especially in the social sphere, we need a doctrine about developmentality. This lack of a developmental doctrine is also astonishing. Both dynamism and development arise from their contrast to and coexistence with statics, which further requires a doctrine of this heterogeneity or mixedness. Furthermore, it is not enough to just approach the truth of the objective world, but is also necessary to transform and transcend it, so that the dynamism will be activated again and gain new energy. Now, we finally know that a single theory of mind can achieve all of these goals simultaneously. It will cancel the "Being", break it apart, and crumple it into the process of thinking (e.g., the versioning of knowledge); It will justify the plurality, heterogeneity, and mixedness of knowledge systems, and then justify the abundant and diverse interactions between thinking and physical entities (including the transformation of subjectivity into objectivity); Finally, it will show the expansive and infinite prospects of knowledge.

The combination of thinking tools and information, as well as between thinking tools and thinking tools, and between information and information, is called a "combination" when it does not have a sequential character, and sometimes it is called "permutation" when it has a sequential character. As is customary in the mathematical literature, the words "permutation" and "combination" are often used in conjunction to refer to both or either of them. The number of permutations and combinations that can be established between finite elements increases dramatically as the number of elements or the length of a permutation increases; This phenomenon is figuratively called the "Combinatorial Explosion". For example, the types of musical notes are finite, but the number of notes that can be contained in a piece of music is relatively large, resulting in a nearly infinite number of pieces of music that can be obtained and listened to by us humans. From ancient times to today, humankind still cannot exhaust it. For another example, the number of chemical elements is limited, and by far there are only one hundred and more, but the number of the kinds of materials formed by the combination of these elements could be tremendously large, and the new substances have been continuously produced through this combinatorial approach since the birth of chemistry. Algorithmic Thinking Theory can be deemed a kind of "thinking chemistry". In particular, the result of a mental activity can become its object again and hence enter the mental activity again, which means that information as the "basic elements" is infinite in number, or the length of a permutation is infinite in number, therefore, the resultant combinatorial explosion effect must be prominent at all (see Diagram I).

Developmentality can refer to the fact that either the quantity of the results of mental activity increases over time or the quality improves over time. It can also refer to the intermittent updates of a version of knowledge. In short, in the process of this explosion, there must be a variety of ways or states of development, of which we generally do not need to enumerate or identify the details. However, the phenomenon of convergence emphasized by traditional philosophy cannot be neglected, on which we shall still make special explanations. Nor can explosion or development be completely isokinetic at both macro and micro levels. Therefore, the principle of combinatorial explosion needs further to be combined with other principles, such as convergence and divergence in the following text, to form a relatively complete system.

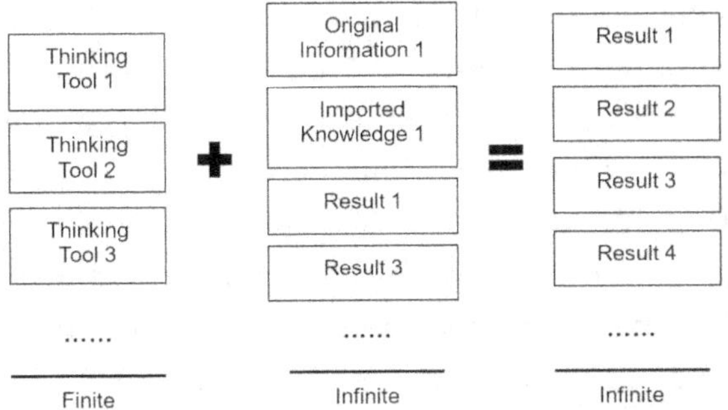

Diagram 1: Combination Explosion

A thinking activity is to selectively use a thinking tool to process information, i.e., to make a combination or permutation between thinking tools and data, and the result can be processed again and again, thus leading to the "combination explosion".

§13. No. 3: The Sedimentation, Solidification, or Patterning of Thoughts

In the case that only one step of thinking is carried out at a time, a thinking process usually requires many steps to be done one after the other. This way of processing must require the creation of a stock of thoughts. "Stock" refers to the knowledge that has been stored. It is first and foremost a spatial concept. Without the existence of space, nothing can be stored, and conversely, since it is "stored", it implies that space has been introduced and resides in advance in the theoretical model. This issue is intuitively and physically easy to explain. Imagine that when we work, we mainly use our two hands to act on external objects. The number of the hands, the size of the palms, and our strength are all limited, so we generally always pick up one or two items, manipulate them, and then put them aside and pick up another one or two items…and so forth, step by step. This requires us to have a certain size of space to be able to gather relevant items, arrange them well, and work in close proximity. In the same way, activities of the mind can only be carried out one step at a time, which is like the capacity and capability of our hands are limited. And, the space for storage of information and knowledge is necessary.

The raw information from the outside world first needs to be stored in this space, and then it is invoked to be processed "in the hand" in a certain order. The results of the processing then return to be stored here again so that they can be used ("invoked", "cited", "referenced", etc.) afterward when needed. The knowledge stored before the final result comes out, in principle, can be called the "intermediate outcome", similar to the "semi-finished products" produced in the production of physical goods. Not all thoughtful results need to be stored. Some results are discarded without the need to be saved, i.e., the "forgotten". They are equivalent to the waste products in a factory. There are also results that, although no longer needed immediately after the final result, may be beneficial to other mental activities later, and hence deserving retention. This is equivalent to the by-products in the factory.

Some readers may ask: How does the brain know what knowledge is useful and what is not? How is the order of thinking arranged? Is there any specific mechanism in the brain to control and arrange all this? The answer is: In my opinion, there shall be no other specific controlling mechanism in the brain, or the brain does not need any other mechanism for help. This is because *the knowledge about answering the above questions is also a kind of knowledge* and therefore, can be produced and accumulated in the way as other knowledge. In the above narrative, we have, in fact, potentially assumed that the knowledge that guides these arrangements already exists and works there. Meanwhile, based on the assumption of seriality, we can also infer that the thinking activities of arranging the orders of thinking must be *interspersed* with the thinking activities themselves. In other words, after the brain takes one step of thinking, supported by certain knowledge, it will think about what to do next, and then "execute" the next step. If the relevant knowledge of arrangement is rich and of high quality, then the thinking activities they guide and arrange will also be of high quality. On the other hand, if it is low or of poor quality, then the thinking activities must be of poor quality, and the results obtained must be of poor quality, too. In extreme cases, what happens if the stock of knowledge is completely missing? The answer is that the mental activities may come to a standstill and fail to produce the desired results, or the mental activities themselves may be tentative, or aimless, or purely driven by the input of external information. At this point, we can also think of mental activities as being carried out blindly and randomly—or under the operation of an "innate thinking tool" such as "Randomize" (or "Lottery").

If we did not, in the above text, explain the "mechanism" of choice and arrangement of various mental operations, readers would be confused with the topic we are going through—note that the solution to the problem of "rational homunculus" has already been touched upon above, which will be discussed later. At the same time, readers are also reminded to note that *the theory of thinking does not need to establish a goal such as "how to produce the most perfect results",* because the researchers now should not mistakenly take themselves as the actors involved; in our framework, the thoughtful levels of actors are really uneven, which we need exactly to explain as an imperfect, diverse, comprehensive, and general reality. In other words, the researchers now need to be cautious to stay out of matter and be *neutral* between the actors.

I will now continue with the second paragraph of this

section. When the stored memory is recalled, what exactly is recalled? Is it to repeat the thinking activities that have already been carried out to produce a result, or is it just to quote the result? This is an easily overlooked but important question. However, the answer to this question is relatively easy: in general, of course, it is just recalling the result. As for the choice of recalling those thinking activities that have already been carried out to produce the result, why do we repeat them? Isn't the whole thinking process just going round and round in circles? Therefore, by calling the result alone, the time and resources can be saved, and thus the next other operations and the entire operational process can move *forward* quickly, cannot it? To take a step back, even if some inspection or review operations are necessary sometimes, it can be inferred that they must be done partially and limitedly; otherwise, the whole operational process will lose its economy.

Now, let's zoom out and stretch the time. As mental activities progress continuously, year after year, the amount of knowledge stored must increase dramatically, and its types must vary. The age or validity of the knowledge must also vary. Some knowledge at a certain point in time may be "old", produced many years ago, or inherited from others, or from ancient ancestors. Some knowledge may exist permanently and has been widely accepted, admired, and used by people from generation to generation, while some other knowledge has a limited lifespan and is invalidated after expiration. There must also be a great deal of knowledge whose effectiveness is dubious, controversial, and needs to be reviewed, evaluated, discussed, and corrected from time to time. However, the question is, as the scope of thinking expands, will the previous conclusions still apply? That is, is there blindness in the use of ready-made stock knowledge? Can this blindness be entirely eliminated? Can the temporary test of stock knowledge, if any, be "thoroughly complete" before use? Can the revision of stock knowledge, in general, be enough to rebuild such knowledge? Is it possible for current thinking activities to be completely independent of any stock knowledge, to answer specific questions? Can all knowledge required for problem-solving be re-made on the spot of problem-solving, starting from scratch?

§14. No. 3: The Sedimentation, Solidification, or Patterning of Thoughts (continued)

After pondering these questions from both positive and negative aspects, we will come to a major and unprecedented principle, that is, generally speaking, *any current thinking activities on the spot must be quite blind.* Even if certain mental activities are not considered blind by certain recognized standards, this conclusion can be generally held as long as some parts of the thinking activities are blind, or some pieces of knowledge cited in thinking is blind. Furthermore, since any mental activities are actually carried out in a specific spatio-temporal environment, they are all "current", "temporary" or "on-the-spot" compared to the huge knowledge stocks; hence these attributive words in the above proposition can be removed. That is to say, from the perspective of the flow-stock dual structure, any thinking activity must be blind, and it must more or less blindly cite (or "invoke") specific knowledge from the ready-made stocks of knowledge. It has no other choice!

The word "blind" was used above from the perspective of some perfect ideal standards. However, compared to any isolated thinking activities that do not involve any knowledge stock, the stocks of knowledge can generally be regarded as "strong" and "powerful". Without the aid, purely current thinking activities would be very weak and primitive, and in no way sufficient to solve any problem of the moment. It's like a head-empty infant who can't be expected to do anything. One learns from books or others, from practice and experience, or even closes one's eyes to meditate. In short, through certain channels, the stocks of knowledge must be built in order to acquire problem-solving skills.

Here we have quietly introduced the concept of "thinking economy". This idea, which was once well-known in Ernst Mach's time, has unfortunately declined. This is obviously due to the lack of a thinking theory itself, which makes it difficult to carry out an effective economic analysis of the thinking activities. Now, the conditions have been in place for the idea of thinking economy to shine again.

This means that since a thought is treated as an entity, a thinking activity should also be seen as an "act" or "behavior", alongside physical activities. Then, whether for a common person or a theorist, when analyzing thinking activities and thoughtful phenomena, it is also necessary to introduce economic considerations, because the economic considerations will inevitably affect the selection of the types of thinking activities, the directions of development of thinking, the structures of thinking, and then affect the contents and results of thinking. In other words, *people have to reflect and weigh their own thinking while thinking*; these two levels of thinking activity have to be intertwined. The discreteness of thinking activities provides this possibility and also creates the need to temporarily interrupt the ongoing thinking activities and insert the thinking activities of "economic analysis". Under the traditional idealistic, ultra-rationalist conception, because the activities of thinking are assumed to proceed at a very rapid pace, it is in fact potentially considered that thinking need not be interrupted and interpolated with the operations of economic analysis, or that the interpolated economic analysis has no significant effect on the contents of the thinking activities.

The examination of stock knowledge before its use must be limited to a certain scope or intensity, which is the requirement of the thinking economy. Similarly, the use of stock knowledge must be simple enough. This means that no matter how laborious and time-consuming it may be in producing a particular stock of knowledge in the first place, the *use* of that stock of knowledge shall not be as difficult as its *production*. In the primary context, stock knowledge refers to some pieces of information or data: words, numbers, sounds, images, and so on. In this case, of course, it can meet the economic requirement, and the user only needs to cite it. In more complex cases, specific knowledge is presented as "modules" that "occupy" "a huge area" of memory, and it takes a long time to understand, learn, and master it. However, once the user has mastered this knowledge, its operational process is often relatively simple, too. The user only needs to clarify the conditions for application of this knowledge, and then compare them with the conditions of the specific problem at hand; once they meet each other, the user can make a small number of thoughtful operations pursuant to the guides of this knowledge, and then the results will be reached. Such examples include using mathematical formulas, looking up a dictionary, running an application on your computer, and so on.

From another point of view, this means that the stock of knowledge is generally a set of *modules* or *patterns*, and its internal structure is *rigid* to some extent, which is not sufficiently flexible and changeable. *This rigidity is just where it is useful.* It may be a deliberate pursuit of the people who produced this knowledge, with the intention of dealing with a large number of changing problems with the fixed method. It can be conjectured that such rigidity will inevitably lead to rudeness and arbitrariness, which in turn will give rise to some losses, but these losses may be what the actors are willing to bear, after weighing the benefits the rigidity will bring.

This highlights the many kinds of connections, conflicts,

struggles, opportunities, solutions, and so on that exist between flow and stock. We can further ask: Is it possible to completely eliminate these tensions in any way? For example, is it possible to completely solve this problem through the method of parallelism mentioned above, or the so-called "connectionism" approach[1]? Apparently, it is impossible. A parallel method is simply a union of multiple serial methods; although it increases the total amount of thinking activity per unit of time, it cannot make the thinking power of the human brain (or the computing power of a computer) unlimited. As long as the thinking ability of the human brain is limited per unit of time, dependence on stock shall be unavoidable, and thus, the above-mentioned multifaceted relationship between stock and flow will also take place at once. The stronger the thinking ability per unit of time, the more results and stocks will be produced, and the above relationships between them will continue to unfold at a higher level.

I believe that the discovery of the above relationships and characteristics is not only unique, but also significantly and ubiquitously influential. The rigidity, or solidity, or the economy is often mutually exclusive with the precision of a knowledge module, and one must be sacrificed in order to obtain the other. For example, we can think of a law as a cohesive knowledge module, which uses the solidity of the module to achieve the economy of thinking while sacrificing certain benefits from precision. From this perspective we can construct a unique, but in fact, basic, and indispensable "Algorithmic jurisprudence".

In order to make these inferences easier to name, memorize, and communicate, I call them the "principles of sedimentation and solidification of thinking". The thinking

---

1. Margaret A. Boden (ed.), "The Philosophy of Artificial Intelligence", Oxford University Press, 1990, pp. 14-18.

flows will selectively sediment into stocks, temporarily leaving the hot thinking activities, just like water in a river sedimented into the riverbed and then condensed into the solids. Solid substances, although not easy to modify, are easy to identify, move, and use. In some cases, they re-melt and reconstruct into new objects, like the renewal of knowledge.

Thus, we come again to the "roundabout production method", the way of building up stocks to serve flows, which was first discovered by Böhm-Bawerk, meaning that in order to solve the problem at hand, it is necessary to "detour" farther (seeming "wastefully") in a diachronic process. However, the concept was shelved shortly after it was proposed. Now, within the framework of a proper theory of mind, this concept can be brought back to aliveness. It is only in the analysis of the thoughtful objects, or in the economics of thought, that the significance of this concept is revived.

§15. No. 4: The Mental Distortions

The mind has to build and use the stock, and it has to accept the resulting deviation from accuracy or idealism. This deviation may be small, or it may be large, and it will become a force that cannot be ignored or even be decisive in changing the face of human knowledge. To borrow a term from the theory of relativity in physics, we can figuratively call such deviations *"Mental Distortions"*. This borrowing is not a deliberate imitation of Einstein, but it is indeed too fitting here. I have ever tried to avoid using it, but in the end, I couldn't resist its temptation. When thinking is distorted (or "bent", "curved", "warp", or any equivalent words), it deviates from the ideal, objective, deductive, definite, recognized, or unquestionable track to the flawed, imperfect, controversial, subjective, fictitious, arbitrary, vague, coarse, and even mistaken one. However, the above deviations are just the beginning. Distortion does not occur just once, but repeatedly, even continuously, like a chain bending this way and that way, again and again (Diagram 2, 3). If there is usually only one right path, then there must be many different distortive paths. In this way, a logical relationship can be established between these two major categories or aspects that philosophers have emphasized: rational and irrational, positive and negative, and so forth. It's as if a connection is made between a straight line and a curve, or the straight line is seen as a particularity of a curve and then is included in curves.

Mental distortion is connected with the sedimentation and solidification of thinking, and can be used on various occasions alone, or collectively referred to as the *"principle of sedimentation, distortion, and solidification of thinking"*.

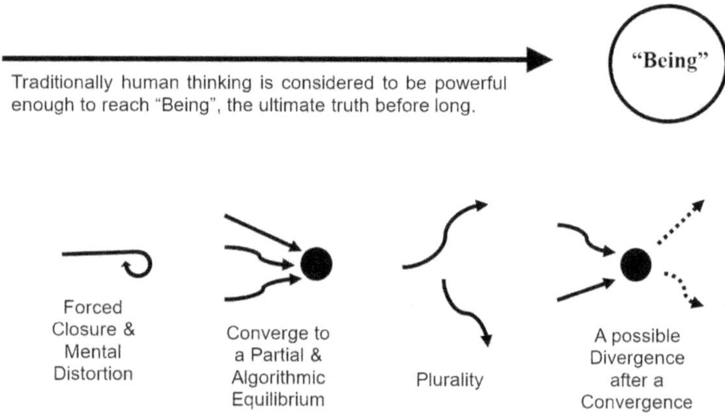

Diagram 2: Mental Distortion
Under the pressure of time, space, and other economic factors, thinking activities cannot go straightly to the destination as expected traditionally, but be distorted into a curve or various curves, either to end a specific thinking process, or to bend again and again to deviously evolve (or even degenerate), and there is no the lump-sum destination.

The causes of distortion are also varied. Next, let's change the angle and explain it again.

Some of the basic types, tools, steps, operations, or ways of thinking often must be combined to use. On the basis of daily observation or reflection, we can find a variety of credible bases to support this conclusion. For example, deductive reasoning, although often viewed as an ideal, standard mental activity, is conditional on its use. It must be based on certain ready-made propositions, but where do the ready-made propositions come from? You can't simply answer that "the propositions can come from other deductive reasoning". In this case, wouldn't you fall into a circular argument? Therefore, this inquiry should lead to the conclusion that sooner or later, the deductive premises have to come from other different types of thinking activities, such as induction, and, the inductive method can be based again on purely empirical observations. When you see much more in the real world, you will often come up with certain points of view. These views can be original, if not reliable. In this sense, *deduction is typically a derivative, intermediate kind of thinking activity, which can only be built on other kinds of thinking activities, and cannot exist alone.* Another example is search. "Search" refers to the activities of looking for specific information or knowledge in memory. As a frequently happening mental activity, search is often needed. In a classical syllogism, after the major premise is in place, the minor premise associated with it needs to be found for deductive reasoning to proceed. Then, where does this minor premise come from? That's the result of a search. What kind of minor premise is obtained from the search, what kind of conclusion will be drawn. Consequently, search activity largely determines the direction in which deductive reasoning is headed.

However, we must point out a seemingly prosaic but actually significant, even revolutionary point of view, that is, in traditional and mainstream philosophical thought, the value of "non-deductive" thinking activities such as induction and search has been largely submerged and dissolved. Orthodox philosophy implicitly holds that mental activity is like a breeze, and that you can always reach the ultimate truth no matter what dynasty or generation you are in. Further, since truth can be easily reached, any inductive conclusions, even if unreliable, can be easily corrected in other subsequent thinking processes, so what special significance do the inductive processes have other than "adding a little trouble" to the whole thinking process (even if this "trouble" is grudgingly considered "necessary" in a specific context)? The fate of search is also the same: although search can influence the direction of a mental activity for a while, since mental activities are always carried out at a very rapid pace, it is supposed possible to carry out an infinite number of searches, thus ultimately correcting any bias caused by any finite search.

Let's take a look at the hypothetical approach. In either the deductive or inductive approach, a conclusion is produced passively as a result of a particular thinking process. However, this order is not necessarily always economical. In a given situation, it may be more efficient to speculate or assume an outcome in a volitionist manner, and then to think and deduce from it, forward or backward. Or, when it is not easy to reach a satisfactory conclusion on the current link, maybe it is easy to draw a conclusion by assuming a value on a difficult variable, which in turn will affect or enlighten the current link. These situations are common both in research activities and in everyday life. One of the main reasons why hypothetical methods are dissolved or marginalized by orthodox philosophy shall be like the above: since the ultimate truth can be obtained, any hypothetical values are only temporary and procedural, and will eventually lose their importances when the truth is finally revealed.

Now, however, since we see the activities of thinking as

starting from its smallest unit and accumulating gradually, and that the ultimate truth is not attainable, the importances of the many kinds of the above non-deductive thinking activities are then highlighted. From time to time, the thinker has to choose between various tools or methods. The selection is based on evaluating their respective functions, contributions, difficulties, time and resource consumption in specific contexts, etc. Now, the mental activity is like the production of material goods, where the manufacturer has to choose and combine different "inputs" in order to obtain the maximal benefits under certain conditions. Since the role of each tool or method is unique, and the thinking activities are carried out frequently and in large quantities, it is believed that in the thinking activities carried out for any purpose, in general, it is impossible for one method to "go it alone", and various tools and methods will be used frequently and interchangeably. Each of them is somehow independent, and the relationship between them will be quite equal, and this equal relationship in their collaboration will be permanent.

At the beginning of the book, we mentioned the synthesis between the deductive and inductive methods. In this regard, my first solution is to prove in the microstructure of a thinking process that they must be frequently combined with each other. The proof we aim to establish is exactly that, in general, the thinking process is like a zigzag chain of tools and methods (Diagram 3).

This statement can be actually deemed common sense. Although this common sense enjoys widespread acceptance, before today, it did not have a theoretical status, and it still needed to be theoretically proven. The reader shall now realize what preparations we need to make in order to achieve this proof, and what concrete theory of thinking we need to have.

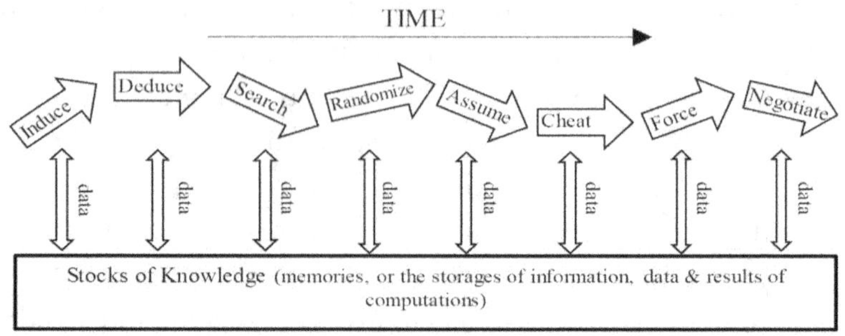

Diagram 3: A Microscopic View of a Thinking Activity

§16. No. 5: The Forced Closure of Thinking and Different Versions of Knowledge

The previous section illustrates mental distortions from the perspective of information processing and the types of thinking activity. Now moving on to the other end, namely, from the perspective of problem-solving, let's continue to illustrate the occurrence of mental distortions.

The time to think, or the introduction of a finite thinking speed, has very broad and profound impacts that are often unexpected. One of the impacts that mental activities starting from different points or concerns will lead to different results or effects. In the paradigm of ultra-rationalism, there is no such distinction. This is because, since mental activity is assumed to be very easy to carry out, all local knowledge must eventually become coherent and consistent with each other. Therefore, in the final analysis, it does not matter where a thinking activity starts, or what the thinking activity is focused. This is like the old saying, "don't ask a hero where he comes from", or "within the four seas, all men are brothers".

Now, it's the opposite. The initiation of mental activity has an important motivation, namely, to solve problems. Not all mental activities are intended to solve certain problems, but a large percentage of them indeed are. The problems that people have to solve are also varied. Some are motivated by curiosity, to satisfy their thirst for knowledge, while others are motivated by the need to solve pressing practical problems. For the latter type of problem, a timeline for thinking and decision-making is often requested. For example, decisions must at least be made before actions. The actual effect of a decision made earlier can be quite different from that later. This issue becomes prominent in the case of a speed limit on the activities of the mind.

"Decision-making" refers to figuring out a specific "value" (note that this "value" can be any type of information other than a quantitative number) for a variable that the actor can control and hence can assign its value with the action. This is the starting point from the problem-solving side. Deriving from here often requires assigning values to a number or a series of other relevant variables, followed by the process of developing the "engineering" knowledge. A part of the knowledge that develops from processing raw information or satisfying intellectual curiosity becomes science. The other part of the knowledge developed from solving practical problems becomes engineering. Through this perspective, differences between science and engineering can be seen more clearly.—Of course, it cannot be ruled out that some scientific knowledge is also developed from solving practical problems, and vice versa. We are usually more familiar with the scientific perspective and less familiar with the engineering perspective. Even if the engineering perspective is familiar to common sense (because each of us often needs to solve practical problems), we generally don't know what place it should have in a book-based system of knowledge.

Unfortunately, the knowledge we *have* at a given point in time, no matter where it comes from or what nature it has, may not match the knowledge *required* to solve the problem. It may be excessive in some respects and insufficient in others. This shall be an inevitable feature of the limited knowledge that comes with limited time for thinking. Infinite or perfect knowledge is conceived as not having this defect. "Limited knowledge" refers to the negation of perfect knowledge, which logically can have any sorts of defects, or any "irregularities" that do not satisfy our desires.

The "controllable variables" mentioned above suggest that there are still variables that are beyond the control of actors. This distinction is consistent with the limited physical ability of the actors to act. The limited ability to act is consistent with the limited thinking ability and limited knowledge. Combining these two types of abilities constitutes the limited, yet evolving, comprehensive capacity for behaviors of an individual, a group of people, and all of humankind. It should be emphasized that we can now realize that the presupposition of perfect rationality is not really "matched" with the limited physical ability; that is, people are assumed to have perfect brains to produce perfect decisions, but their ability to act is limited, namely, their ability to execute the perfect decisions is limited, thus, not only does such a view of knowledge not conform to the facts, causing conflicts within the knowledge system, but it also leads to *a severe imbalance in the relationship between body and mind*. Under this stiff and weird combination, the mind or knowledge does not develop, and "development" becomes merely a purely physical, predictable process of accumulation, or the "pile-ups". That's what mainstream economics is all about.

However, the attempts to match limited physical ability with limited thinking ability will also cause the interactions between them, bringing about new problems. For example, the limited physical ability requires that the solution to a decision-making problem must be relatively simple—Along this direction, we can understand why the so-called "optimal solution" is, in principle, understood as a *single* solution. And *this simplicity, in turn, requires that the knowledge on which the decision is made should preferably be simple.* This practical requirement will exert a long-term and systematic influence on people's cognitive activities, giving preferential treatment to simple knowledge and discriminating against complex knowledge. Over time, a concept will be developed that simple knowledge represents the "truth", or that the "ultimate truth" is simple, even single and indivisible. This is a confusion between subjective needs and objective reality. This confusion has a huge impact on the formation of philosophy, which we will discuss repeatedly from multiple angles in this book.

Bounded rationality (or "concrete rationality") leads to the fact that the actors can only focus on some, or even a few, number of variables at a particular point in time or period. At the heart of a decision-making process are the controllable and operational variables. An operational variable is a controllable variable, and in particular, the part of controllable variables that the actors can *directly* control, decide, or influence. The sum of the operational variables constitutes an "action". For example, if you want to travel today, you need to choose your route of travel and means of transportation. Such choices are completely in the hands of the actor, and the actor cannot avoid the task of assigning their values; otherwise, it is not sufficient to constitute the act of "travel". The actor uses physical resources to manipulate certain variables, carry out actions, influence controllable variables, and ultimately achieve the purpose of influencing the "target variable". Even if there are many other uncontrollable variables that need to be paid attention to indirectly, these variables only make sense if they ultimately boil down to controllable and operational variables.—For example, an occasional uncontrollable event will adversely affect achieving the current behavioral goal, hence the person concerned needs to take certain countermeasures to prevent it, and so on.

In this way, we come again to the concept of "factor completeness". Since things in the world are widely interconnected, a decision must, in principle, take into account all the factors of everything in the world. This is logically the starting point. In this respect, we basically subscribe to the general equilibrium theory of neoclassical economics—except that we emphasize that we must also consider the finiteness, temporality, economics, and other subjective factors of thinking. Since the actors cannot temporarily consider so many factors in their thinking activities, "factor completeness" refers to the set of factors that must be considered in order to make a decision based on common sense, in the judgment of the actors, or in a specific or situated sense, are *complete*, neither more nor less. The actors must take these factors into account, which cannot be avoided, and simultaneously, with this done, it is often sufficient for the actors to arrive at an appropriate decision. Nevertheless, it is debatable how to make a decision that is "appropriate", therefore, the core meaning of this concept is that in the process of solving a problem, the actor cannot just passively and mechanically calculate and process the original information in the order by which the information (as the raw materials for solving the problem) is given; instead, the actor must jump out of this order, examine the entire situation, even the entire world and the overall situations, and *try* to consider all the factors that should in principle be considered; in view of the limited thinking power, the actor should, according to their statuses and importances in the problem at hand, classify and rank the relevant variables that need to be solved, and discriminately allocate them to different proportions of the brainwork, or adopt different strategies to address them. Therefore, *"completeness" is always a matter of degree and relativity. As a* result, some variables that can be solved using the information given may not be important in the decision-making, or variables at hand that are familiar to the actor and can be easily solved may not be important, but those existing in a distant place or in an inconspicuous corner are important. In short, the issue of factor completeness is the basic reason for considering the overall situation and filtering variables, which will further cause various kinds of misalignment among elements such as information, problems, resources, knowledge, methods, and strategies, bringing great challenges to decision-making.

Under the pressure of time, activities of thinking could not proceed in an ideal manner, decisions must be forcibly closed; and, for this reason, the actors must have their positions on certain selections within the time limit. Extreme rationalism requires that decisions be made on a sufficient knowledge base, i.e., knowledge derived from the deductive method or from certain axioms or facts that are widely recognized as reliable. If they do not have such a sufficient knowledge base, then the actors can only concoct answers on the spot, fudging them perfunctorily. The actors will be forced to choose "non-deductive", less reliable but quick and easy methods. For example, in addition to the above methods such as induction, search, and assumption, they can imitate, approximate, associate, imagine, experiment, randomize, and so on. Especially in interpersonal and social matters, they can use the methods of negotiation, deception, coercion, etc. These approaches do not exist in natural issues, hence are unique as social methods, or "Social Algorithms". These methods can help actors to actively create stable or favorable conditions, thus making their subsequent decision-making tasks simpler. In the Algorithmic theory, we refer to these non-deductive methods collectively as "Alternative Algorithms", and the deductive method (and all methods that can lead to reliable conclusions and are therefore often used in priority) as the "Mainstream Algorithms".

§17. No. 5: The Forced Closure of Thinking and Different Versions of Knowledge (continued)

The question of factor completeness involves not only temporary thinking activities in a particular situation, but also a relatively general "knowledge framework" on which actors base their many everyday decisions[2]. Since real actors generally must already have this kind of framework knowledge when making specific decisions, the framework knowledge must be implicitly existing in the background in specific situations, and even the actors themselves are not aware of its existence.

As mentioned earlier, the issue of factor completeness actually entails that the actors have to rank the importances of the relevant variables regarding a decision. Since resources are limited and time is pressing, some factors need to be focused on and considered in depth; some can only be considered hastily to a lower extent, and the others may be abandoned. In this sense, "abandonment" is also a deliberate "arrangement", which expresses the attitude of the actors towards the relevant factors. Or, the actors do not even identify specific factors, but simply judge how the whole situation within a particular scope is, generally. They don't know exactly what factors they can analyze in detail. Therefore, the issue of completeness is not absolute, but relative and "soft", and the actors' approach to it may be highly varied and irregular. For example, what are a person's attitudes towards the world, life, future, and his/her own development? This question can generally involve the

---

2. Daniel C. Dennett, "Cognitive Wheels: The Frame Problem of AI", in Margaret A. Boden (ed.), "The Philosophy of Artificial Intelligence", Oxford University Press, 1990, pp. 147-169.

solutions to all specific questions he/she faces. If a person does not have general knowledge or a proper attitude about the natural world, he/she may be frightened and unwilling to deal with any problem of the moment. Therefore, in ancient times, in the absence of natural science knowledge, people invented witchcraft and mythology, with the help of this knowledge to "explain" natural phenomena, and then help the people concerned to stabilize their emotions, build confidence, and deal with other people with a healthy common attitude. This is a necessary condition for reaching specific decision-making issues.

These general knowledge, beliefs, and attitudes, together with knowledge, experiences, methods, and techniques about specific matters, constitute a version of the general knowledge at a particular point in time or for a particular era. Since the knowledge is produced and accepted with some considerations of the future, it is usually used universally, continuously, and repeatedly for a long period of time. Also, the lifespans of different pieces of knowledge generally vary. This is like the differences between fixed assets and current assets in a business. However, since this knowledge is formed on the basis of the extensive use of alternative Algorithms, they must also contain many errors, fictions, or defects, which lays the groundwork, or creates conditions for knowledge innovation. People get a respite from the repeated use of existing knowledge, and hence are able to devote themselves to the development of new knowledge. New knowledge may come from the discovery of new information, or from the repair of the methods used in existing knowledge. From this, we can clearly distinguish between two types of innovation: *Information-driven Innovation and Algorithm-Improved Innovation.* Innovations may be small, but they add up, and gradually lead to a leap into a big innovation. On the basis of these big and small innovations, sooner or later, a newer version of the knowledge system will be formed. The new version of the knowledge system inherits the old version in some respects and negates it in others, with different answers to the same questions.—Meanwhile, of course, it is entirely possible that it will contain additional new contents that neither reaffirm nor negate old knowledge.

Diagram 4: Versioning and Infinite Development of Knowledge
By considering various elements as completely as possible, a specific version of the knowledge system at a specific time can be obtained; however, the infinite development caused by combinatorial explosion will intermittently update the version.

In this way, different individuals may have different versions of the knowledge system, and the knowledge system of a particular individual, or the knowledge system of the entire human race, will be moving forward in the form of "version upgrades". This structure resembles an onion, with larger layers on the outside wrapping around smaller layers on the inside, or the symbol of wireless LAN (Diagram 4). According to the principle of combinatorial explosion, there shall be no end to this expansion.

Further, we can say that, in fact, an individual is "summing up" the world in every decision, in every day of his life, because one "considers" the whole world in one's particular way and embodies this consideration in every decision. Final, processual, short-term, and long-term considerations are mixed together to make up our everyday life. This is our way of critically assimilating the view of "ultimate truth" or eschatology of extreme rationalism, and it is also our way of critically assimilating and hence, reforming neoclassicism in economics. The latter assumes that one day all the truths will be known accurately, and all problems will be solved precisely and perfectly. Now, that imaginary ultimate truth is torn apart and crumpled and melted into the parts of the world and the course of history. The idea of ultimate truth or doomsday is not entirely unreasonable, because curiosity drives us to wonder about the entire world as it is. Moreover, it is precisely because we human beings are constantly making mistakes and changing our opinions that philosophers have long observed this disappointing fact that they have to seek the absolute truth. It can even be said that the thirst for the absolute truth is also a requirement of the economy of thinking: if the absolute truth is obtained, the problem of thinking will be solved once and for all, and people will be freed from continuous toil! Even if one knows that he/she stands inside the course of history, the ambition to oversee and summarize the whole world is worthy of respect and praise (although this pursuit can sometimes turn into a conceit), because he/she wants to make decisions sound and avoid unpredictable risks.

In this sense, we are again approached by ontology and metaphysics, which attempt to draw on existing knowledge to summarize the whole world and history from a particular epoch. Since such summaries necessarily go beyond the realm of concrete, specialized knowledge, it especially requires philosophers to exert their ability to generalize and imagine and to use abstract, special, or vague language to speculate and discuss problems within those vast and distant scopes. Since the objects of such discourse are the natures of the objective world, the process of cognition, or the thinking activities of subjects, must be temporarily forgotten or relegated to a secondary position. In this way, ontology or metaphysics becomes a permanent branch of philosophy—although it also has to intermittently update its own versions.

In this sense, common sense, as well as other types of knowledge, can also acquire their own permanent status, independent of science. Science is probably the highest quality and most reliable of all types of knowledge. I don't want to challenge this view for the time being. However, under the constraints of the thinking economy, the *pursuit of high quality has led to the narrowing of the scope of science*, so that science cannot answer a large number of questions in real life. However, actors must meet the requirement of factor completeness, which forces the actors to accumulate experiences outside of science and to develop and exchange their own relevant knowledge. This forms "common sense". Its structure is loose and of low quality, but it is indispensable for an individual's survival. Common sense also supports the development of science and other knowledge to a certain extent.

Another example is religion. Religion answers questions that science cannot cover, such as the ultimate causes of the world, the ins and outs of human beings, the basic attitudes to life, and so on. These are also questions that philosophy cannot totally cover; or, religion answers the same questions differently from science or philosophy. Comparatively, the discourse of religion is more based on imagination and fiction. Although often lacking a factual or logical basis, its fluency and storylines are more attractive than those of science and philosophy, and thus are more readily accepted by the general public. As a kind of engineering program, religion performs a social function that also transcends science and philosophy.

§18. No. 6: The Algorithmic Logic

Hidden in the above derivation is the logic that is commonplace for ordinary people, but does not enjoy a formal status in book knowledge; that is, the rational and effective development of thinking activities requires the establishment of the conception and evaluation of specific thinking tools, combinations of tools and information, processing steps and sequences; and, this conception and evaluation activities, as a type of thinking activity, need to be interspersed and alternated with the thinking activities that they objectify.

One of the most basic elements of this logic is that actors can view a question as an act involving one or more entities, and thus recognize that the question does not necessarily require an immediate or direct answer, but can be set aside, or dealt with indirectly or vaguely, or turned to other irrelevant issues. In this way, an actor has, in principle, an infinite number of options for responding to any question, and hence will make a choice between these options based on the conclusions of the thoughtful economic analysis and other relevant analyses. For example, ask: Is $a = b$? Answer: I go to bed. "I go to bed" can be a response to the question, "$a=b$?"—a behavioral response, although not a direct answer in its content.

One of the first things I learned in my practical work after college was the importance of acknowledging ignorance and putting things on hold. I have long been puzzled by the lack of theoretical status of this principle. It was only after the Algorithmic theory was put forward that I realized that the traditional and mainstream logical systems do not really depict the actual thinking process. The analysis of syllogisms above is also an example of this, in which traditional logic obscures the process of searching for knowledge. The syllogism really just writes about the results of the relevant real thinking process, not the real thinking process itself. The real activity of the mind goes far beyond those three propositions.

This logical finding both reveals the disorder of mental activity and discovers a new order beneath the apparent disorder. By "disorder", I mean that the thinking process that runs according to this new logic, whether in a computer or in the human brain, will inevitably appear to be quite messy, and will contain a large number of contents that are diverse and not directly related to each other. By "order", I mean that we will find that the thinking order of actors may be quite strictly in line with the principles of economic decision-making (especially the "marginal decision-making principle": marginal benefit = marginal cost[3]). As a result, our understanding of real behaviors and real social phenomena will be significantly deepened.

A large number of so-called "irrational" behaviors reflect the rationality of actors in this sense. However, formal academic literature has historically denied this rationality, ignored it, or does not yet know how to deal with it. For example, the existence of contradictions, conflicts, and plurality needs to be understood with the help of this logic; that is, actors may ignore the existence of contradictions and conflicts, or have no time to deal with them, or may deliberately tolerate and allow them to occur. These attitudes may be in line with the logic of his economic analysis of thought. For another example, the process of "rationalization"[4] of society mentioned by Max Weber is, in fact, the collective patterning process established in social interaction, and this

---

3. According to the terminology in economics, the word "marginal" means "of the latest one", "incremental", "additional", etc., in a temporal context.

4. For rationalization, see Kim, Sung Ho, "Max Weber", The Stanford Encyclopedia of Philosophy (Winter 2022 Edition), Edward N. Zalta & Uri Nodelman (eds.), URL = <https://plato.stanford.edu/archives/win2022/entries/weber/>.

patterning, according to the above discussion, is the result of this logic. In other words, the economic analysis of thinking may conclude that, in order to save the cost, within a certain range, no specific economic analysis of thinking is carried out, but the thinking activities and external actions are directly arranged according to the pros and cons of the matter itself. This has a dramatic effect: even the negation or rejection of the thinking economy itself needs to be done with the logic of the thinking economy.

I name this logic the "Algorithmic Logic"[5]. At its core, it is a question in the context of our thinking theory: what to do next? This question and a series of knowledge and skills to answer it together constitute the content of Algorithmic logic. Obviously, it is a higher-order logic that is also closely related to metalogic. *This Algorithm logic can connect different kinds of logic systems that are previously independent of each other with this thoughtful economic relationship to establish an all-encompassing logic system.* In it, specific mental activities can jump back and forth between different logical processes, or they can moderately focus on a specialized logical calculus according to a certain chronological arrangement. The in-depth empirical study of Algorithmic logic will inevitably uncover some specific rules, habits, patterns, or genres in people's schedules, which can be used to re-interpret the meanings of some existing knowledge, or lead to the formulation of multiple methodological principles and techniques for theoretical analysis (including model construction).

---

5. The term was proposed initially by Banachowski et al. in a quite narrow sense (Lech Banachowski, Antoni Kreczmar, Grażyna Mirkowska, Helena Rasiowa, Andrzej Salwicki, "An introduction to Algorithmic Logic - Metamathematical Investigations of Theory of Programs", Banach Center Publications. Vol. 2. Warszawa: PWN., 1977, pp. 7–99); I borrowed and extended it.

§19. No. 7: Desires, Instincts, and Emotions as the Innate "Hard Software"

Psychological phenomena such as desires, instincts, emotions, sentiments, impulses, and so on have always been considered inherent in the human spiritual world, that is, innate, enduring, unchanging, and universal for everyone—although interpersonally different to a certain extent. This is widely seen as an important reason why human behavior has an "irrational" character. Now, however, not only can their existence be deemed uncontradictory with the Algorithmic theory of thinking, but also a corollary to it.

The idea that such mental beings may be necessary equipment for rational computations has long been advocated[6] , and the question is just how to prove this hypothesis. However, under the framework of the above thinking theory, that is, under the Algorithmic framework, this proof can be completed from multiple angles, and in one go. Here are some of the key points.

First of all, the above Algorithmic theory of knowledge, that is, the theory of thoughtful sedimentation, bending, and solidification, can be applied here. We need to realize that the system of thought is not as perfect and dense as it has been traditionally assumed, and that it is hardly even what rationalists envision, either as a whole or in its main aspects. The knowledge modules respond subjectively, imperfectly, or bluntly (but perhaps prospectively, proactively, concisely, and quite effectively) to external stimuli, akin to a psychological impulse. With the existence of these scattered and relatively independent knowledge modules, there is nothing unusual

---

6. Aaron Sloman, "Motives, Mechanisms, and Emotions" in Margaret A. Boden (ed.), "The Philosophy of Artificial Intelligence", Oxford University Press, 1990, pp. 231-246. Also refer to pp. 18-19 for Boden's summary statements on this issue.

about the "irrational" phenomena that are the objects of psychological research. Therefore, we can expand our knowledge system again to include them. Mental phenomena are originally and traditionally regarded as distinctive and fundamentally different from psychological phenomena. Now that this distinction no longer seems to exist, is it necessary, in particular, for psychological phenomena to be explained? Is there still a need for psychology to exist alone? This has immediately become a question.

Second, the fact that psychological phenomena are "innate, persistent, and shared by everyone" indicates that they are not acquired through practice, but are based on "hardware" (i.e., specific biological tissues and structures). It does not exist in the form of pure "ideas" or "software" like ordinary thoughts, otherwise, it would have obvious interpersonal differences like ordinary ideas that can be rewritten, deleted, or reconstructed easily and frequently. But this is not true. For example, everyone has an emotional system, which is persistent and "stubborn", and not only cannot one person change the emotional system of another person, but the person himself cannot change his own emotional system. A person can suppress his or her anger, but cannot change his or her emotional system in the same way that he or she changes his or her opinion, or deliberately makes it non-existent. Combined, these features lead us to think that it is similar to the "hard software" (or "firmware") of a computer: it is already embodied into a specific part at the factory, so that the user cannot change it throughout its lifetime. While in principle such hard software can also be upgraded and rewritten, the upgrades or rewrites require either a replacement of the physical parts or a direct intervention and assistance from the original manufacturer. However, after birth, people are physically and biologically separated from their parents, which makes such "upgrading" or "rewriting" completely impossible (genetic engineering is a different topic).

Another question that needs to be answered is: Since hard software can be regarded as a kind of knowledge, and knowledge can be acquired, why does it be inherited again?

From the perspective of the thinking economy, this question can have a very eloquent answer, that is, the human death and birth, namely, the "replacement" of a human body, requires that in addition to the system of thinking tools, the human mind must be equipped with certain mechanisms of knowledge inheritance; otherwise, the new human life will not be able to maintain a minimum survival after birth. As mentioned earlier, decisions required for behaviors need to be based on the results of mental activity, i.e., knowledge. This means that it cannot rely directly on the thinking tools or the information alone. And, what should a newborn person do if he/she has not had time to develop or introduce knowledge, and hence his/her knowledge stock is zero? Will he/she just sit back and wait for death? From this it can be seen that the birth of a new individual is in great danger of death and extinction. So, what to do? The solution, then, is apparently to "arrange" for the inheritance of a minimum amount of knowledge, which at least can help the individual as an organism to be able to be fed and survive on its own.

Some of the skills that are needed first must be included in the hard software, and these skills can be summed up by the word "instinct". In animals like freshly hatched sea turtles on the beach, they spontaneously crawl towards the sea. In humans, babies cry to get the attention of adults in order to be cared for and fed, and so on. If the whole set of specific action guidelines is not easy to inherit (it is important to know that the process of biological inheritance must be complex and costly), then a fragment of it could be inherited, or some abstract and vague arrangement, e.g. emotions, could be made. The affective mechanism is abstract in that it can respond equally to a range of stimuli of similar natures. There are several fixed types of emotions that respond to stimuli alternately or cyclically. This arrangement can be related to the concept of "factor completeness". The finitude of emotional genres also reflects its simplicity and economy. It is a rough and even crude mechanism. Without the perspective of the thinking economy, we would not understand the characteristics and functions of the roughness or crudeness in emotions. Obviously, these innate inherited pieces of hard software (or "genetic knowledge" or "hard knowledge") do not evolve throughout their lives, unlike ordinary knowledge systems that develop and change as quickly and infinitely. This is the price it has to pay for being based on hardware, and it is also the reason why it is so obvious that it sometimes imposes severe restrictions on mental activity that it has to be called "irrational". The widening gap between the psychological mechanism and the common knowledge mechanism further proves that it is reasonable to position it as "hard software".

In this way, we have to accept both kinds of innate theories (or transcendentalisms), namely, the theory of innate instruments and the theory of innate knowledge. Algorithmic Theory is first a kind of innate-instrument theory; that is, it assumes that thinking tools are innate and a priori. However, the above derivation allows us to realize that such an innate-instrument theory not only does not exclude the theory of innate knowledge (i.e., some knowledge must also be inherited congenitally), but also gives rise to the theory of innate knowledge that then becomes a corollary of the former, and thus is consistent with it. Moreover, from the point of view of the traditional distinction between thinking systems and psychological systems, we can conjecture that common people have intuitively generally accepted the distinction between thinking tools and thinking results. People clearly don't think of things like emotional systems as tools for knowledge production. These things intervene in decision-making as a fixed mechanism, like parameters entering certain mental processes. The highly flexible and adaptive knowledge produced by nurture complements the psychological mechanisms, and among conflicts (e.g., one deliberately suppresses his/her anger while feigning joy), they cooperate to produce the final result—decision-making. This way of their functioning is more like that of knowledge than that of thinking tools. Hence, this common-sense distinction between the thinking system and the psychological system can be used as evidence to show that the concept of "innate thinking tools" is generally acceptable.

Genetic biologists tend to believe that the psychological system is the "genetic codes" accumulated over the course of long-term evolution of organisms, and hence its number is very large.[7] Other biologists believe that acquired knowledge (or traits) of an organism can also be inherited.[8] According to these views, the psychological mechanism of inheritance can have individual differences. There is agreement between this understanding and the results of empirical research[9], so it can also be included in Algorithmic analysis. However, these questions go beyond the scope of philosophy, humanities, and social sciences, so we should stop somewhere. We certainly

---

7. John C. Eccles, "Evolution of the Brain: Creation of the Self", Routledge, 1989.

8. In biology this is called Lamarckism. For a popular and excellent introduction to relevant studies, see Matt Ridley, "Nature via Nurture: Genes, Experience, and What Makes Us Human", Harper Collins Publishers Ltd., 2003, Chapter 3, pp. 69-97.

9. For a philosophical survey of this issue, see Paul Griffiths and Stefan Linquist, "The Distinction Between Innate and Acquired Characteristics", The Stanford Encyclopedia of Philosophy (Fall 2024 Edition), Edward N. Zalta & Uri Nodelman (eds.), forthcoming URL = <https://plato.stanford.edu/archives/fall2024/entries/innate-acquired/>.

don't know how the "design mechanism" works in biology (or how "God" "created" human), and how the economy of thought accurately works in it. However, for philosophy, the humanities, and the social sciences, it is important to recognize that the amount of genetic code, no matter how large, is still far from sufficient for general decision-making, so we need to return to the track of the theory of thought.

If human memory can eventually be exported, copied, and then acquired easily, would future generations like to completely inherit the memories of their predecessors? Is this "economical" enough? If so, what impact will this bring to current thinking activities on the spot of problem-solving? Obviously, our thinking theory can also lead us to explore the answers to these new questions that are about to arise.

§20. No. 8: Pluralism and High-Order Consistency

Pluralism, while very popular in modern times, does not have a place in the core of philosophy, as shown in literature. Apparently, many authors are even a little secretive about this subject. This is because philosophy is divided, and the connections among various branches and schools have not yet been established essentially. Simply put, philosophers have not yet known how to integrate pluralism into the mainstream of rationalism. In this context, the recognition of pluralism, while "politically correct", is tantamount to an admission of philosophical failure. In literary words, this is actually quite an embarrassing thing.

The characteristic of the Algorithmic theory that we are about to give is that pluralism actually goes deep into the marrow of Algorithmic theory from the very beginning, and it follows us all the time. Even if we don't specifically articulate it, it is silently present in all aspects of the discourse. For example, the dualism of thinking tools and information is a manifestation of pluralism, as is the distinction between flow and stock. The innate tools of the mind are assumed to have a finite number of them, and the information is assumed to be extremely abundant and even endless, and the knowledge produced is varied and full of subjectivity, contradictions, and conflicts; these are all pluralities.

The meaning of pluralism can be elaborated from the point of view of the distinction between pluralism and diversity. Pluralism refers to the inadequacy of connection between two or more elements to such an extent that we must treat them as relatively independent, distinct, primordial, or ultimate elements. This shows that the concept has a strong metaphysical connotation. Philosophers understand that talking about pluralism is like talking about its opposite, the monistic "God", which is prone to arouse controversies and arbitrary arguments. This is not the case with "diversity". "Diversity" refers first and foremost to the fact that objects are different in appearance and surface characteristics, but simultaneously, they can be consistent with monism. This is because, according to the paradigm of "essence-phenomenon", the essence of monism can have a variety of expressions or phenomena. This argument provides a reason to talk about diversity "securely" without worrying that there is any conflict between such talk and orthodox doctrines. For example, in economics, the differences in various industries and products are explained as a "division of labor", which is then, through market transactions, dissolved into a unitary logical framework. Thus, different products are valued *merely* as their different quantitative prices, losing their qualitative individualities.

I believe that this extreme "essence-phenomenon" paradigm has become a protector of monism, and diversity has become a gorgeous but empty disguise. Even, the diversity we talk about in this context becomes proof of monism. For, what is the use of the concept of essence if it does not exist in diversity? Obviously, it is just in the unity of diversity that essence proves itself useful.

However, a Heideggerian question is: Is there nothing left of diversity after it has been extracted from its essence? And, if this leftover still exists more or less, can it have its own independence from essence? Obviously, similar interrogations reveal the indispensability of pluralism; that is, it must be raised at the same time as the concept of "essence" arises, and exists together with "essence" as a group of concepts. Moreover, the above understanding exposes that the "essence-phenomenon" paradigm is actually subordinated to the thinking economy, that is, the "essence" is extracted precisely from the needs of the thinking economy, and the extractor, after obtaining the essence, puts aside the rest temporarily. Therefore, it is a simplified and approximate operation. There shall be theories to support the legitimacy of this operation—and to preclude its misuse, as well as the possible misuse of pluralism. All of these goals need to be achieved simultaneously.

Such a theory is now being naturally reached.

According to the understanding of the "forced closure" of the mind, people in specific conditions of time and space must, from time to time, compulsively, actively, or passively conclude the whole world, and the knowledge they have is incomplete, and it is impossible for them to perfectly summarize the world into a monistic entity (or some "essence"). Often, there are many, or even a large number of elements, whose relationships have not yet been clarified, so they can only be considered as relatively independent elements temporarily. In particular, this independence may reach the point where the actors do not *believe* that this independence will be extinguished one day in the future, and the actors will then see this situation of "juxtaposed elements" as "ultimate" and identify it as a "plurality". Even if it is *later* proved that the judgment was wrong, it is not sufficient to prevent the actors from making such an identification *in the first place*. And, it is not only the actual actors who do it, but also researchers and theorists who are likely to do so.

Any reference to pluralism can obviously only be understood in this way. This characterization depends on the specific level of understanding of the actors. This is an example of the impossibility of a complete separation of ontology from epistemology. Even if the person concerned recognizes the developmentality of knowledge and hence the possibility of making mistakes in his/her particular judgments, what can he/she do? Can he/she postpone the responsibility of making judgments until forever? Can the actors never make any conclusions? Won't they make any decisions? Will researchers never decide to take a stand on their subject matters? Don't their papers need an ending at all?

Therefore, such a theory of thinking not only does not oppose pluralism, but also strongly justifies and supports pluralism. Pluralism can be carried forward within the Algorithmic framework, and it has been present in it from beginning to end. The objects involved in any theoretical analysis must, in principle, be considered to be local, and the connections (or essences) established must also be local, and the rest must be left to pluralism. As a matrix, pluralism must exist before all concrete theories, and must exist as part of the "theory of theory", that is, the "meta-theory". Meta-theories then become the indispensable relational aspects of a specific theory, or the indispensable parts of the overall theoretical system. There is even a need to establish a professional principle that a theorist must be trained in such meta-theories in order to become a qualified theorist or analyst.

At the same time, pluralism alone is not enough. We must also establish a concept to accompany it in order to eliminate its potential negative effects. This new concept is called "higher-order consistency".

This means that when actors identify pluralities, contradictions, and conflicts in the historical process, whether this identification is seen as temporary or permanent, there is an objective possibility of consistency (essentialization) among them, that is, at some point in the future, new connections would be discovered, and specific irrelevance, contradictions, and conflicts would be eliminated, and new coherence would be established. This is because, according to the combinatorial explosion principle, the possibilities for the development of knowledge are endless, and hence, it is objectively impossible for us humans to affirm any absolutist plurality, just as it is impossible for us to affirm any essence or consistency absolutely. Once we take this theoretical approach that is based on the dynamic process of mental activity, we must also recognize this possibility, and we must be neutral between plurality and consistency, rather than simply favoring one over the other. The resulting high-order consistency is something that traditional metaphysical pluralism does not have. As mentioned in §6, since metaphysics should now consciously admit that there will be different historic versions of itself, it should also recognize the existence of this special consistency.

Higher-order consistency refers not only to the historical relationship between multiple "elements", but also to the spatial relationship between them, i.e., they actually co-exist in *a* space. "Space", as the common matrix between these "elements", provides the condition for their coexistence. Conversely, precisely because they are entities, they can make an understandable use of the space and thus exist in its *different places*, and then, they can keep their distance from each other in order to maintain peace with each other. It's like people who have conflicts but agree to live together peacefully without hurting each other.—Further, only the coexistence in the space creates the possibility of diachronicity, that is, a possible "chemical reaction" between them one day in the future, and then a generation of a new consistency.

"Higher-order consistency" is an important theoretical element that has not yet been revealed in the existing literature, and I also think that it is a principle that is easy to understand in common sense. Its intelligibility may be straightforward and simple to the point of making the reader doubt the concept. However, in my opinion, it is especially indispensable for our theoretical analysis. For example, this concept should be a philosophical basis for our *scientific* and *logical* discussion of the political issue of democracy and freedom.

§21. No. 8: Pluralism and Higher-Order Consistency (continued)

The word "plurality" simply refers to the independent aspect of the individual elements. However, the relationship between these individual elements is complex and diverse, and the complex diversity of these relationships can be another manifestation of plurality. We need to look at these various pluralities.

The first is the distinction between "primitive plurality" (or "presumed plurality") and "derived plurality" (or "endogenous plurality"). The beginning of mental activity presupposes the existence of differences or conflicts among objects (e.g., a difference between desire and resources), so the study of mental activity must first necessarily recognize this plurality that exists at the beginning of mental activity, which can then be called "primitive plurality". However, the activity of the mind probably takes a bend and a subjective turn in its process, which means that it adds a new plurality to the knowledge system. This plurality is transmitted to the objective world through physical actions of the individual, and thus adds a new plurality to the physical world. This is called the "derived plurality". As a result, ideas, people, and human society will not only be the "independent third party" as constructs, but even something like "monsters" from the "perspective" of the world itself.

The second is irregularity. The proposed approach would be very inclusive of irregularities and would not exclude any irregularities in principle. Personalized knowledge will exist in staggering, near-infinite quantities, which in turn will be linked to concepts such as "complexity" and "big data". This is, first and foremost, an inevitable consequence of the theory of dynamics. Static theory studies the ultimate, regular, and ideal state, and a dynamic theory inevitably gives rise to various intermediate states. They are in different time courses. Furthermore, since an intermediate state can exist for a short time, it can also exist for a relatively long time, or even be seen as permanent and "ultimate" in certain contexts.

The next are contradictions and conflicts. Among the many differences that cannot be dissolved, there is one type of difference that is considered to have completely opposite ideological contents, and that is the "contradiction". The meaning of the word "conflict" is a little subtly different. For example, in some traffic accidents, two vehicles collide not necessarily on contrary directions, but perhaps sideways or with minor scratches, and so on; this is the "conflict". Therefore, the meaning of "conflict" is broader than "contradiction". Hegel regularized and sanctified contradictions. His fictional system gives the illusion that contradiction is the *same* as consistency, and that when two things contradict each other, there seems to be no problem with him. This argument of "two poles can be connected" is also quite common in Chinese philosophy. This dramatic effect is achieved with the help of concepts such as "the cunning of reason"[10]. It's like a couple of man and woman who are really lovers pretending to be enemies in front of outsiders. This way of thinking messes up all the logic—and of course, it despises, belittles, or ignores any other conflicts and differences, imperially. If a contradiction can be regarded as a unity, then what can the unity be viewed? What is the difference between the two concepts of unity and contradiction?[11] It is true that, according to their specific meanings, one side of a contradiction can be transformed into the other, but this transformation is only conditionally realized in the course of history and in the real consumption of resources. Carrying out such transformation is generally not the end of the process of the side itself, and the transformation is usually supplemented by error correction and knowledge development, rather than simply circulative. Not all contradictions are necessarily mutually transformative, and the two sides of the contradiction are not necessarily exactly equal in terms of their specific characteristics. Therefore, we shall not over-imagine it only based on the appearances, but we shall return to the big background of diversity and irregularity. Here, both the thinking tools and the information are stereotyped, solid-like things, and there must be some *specific* bumps or matches between them at the same time. Therefore, under this materialized, solidified framework, conflicts must be coexisting with consistencies, both are the different characteristics of different parts of an entity, or the different fragments of a continuous thinking process: only when the different parts are

---

10. For an introduction to this concept, see Robert C. Tucker, "The Cunning of Reason in Hegel and Marx", in "The Review of Politics" Vol. 18, No. 3 (Jul., 1956), pp. 269-295.

11. This logic is like that in Confucius' following words. "Someone said, 'Repay an injury with a good turn. What do you think of this saying?' The Master said, 'What, then, do you repay a good turn with? 'Repay an injury with straightness, but repay a good turn with a good turn.'" (Confucius, "The Analects", Section 14-34, translated by D.C. Lau, The Chinese University Press, p. 143.)

adjusted to a certain angle can they match each other, or only among conflicts are there some matches. There may also be a relative or quantitative relationship between them. And, we use "higher-order consistency" instead of "cunning of reason". In the case of limited rationality, experimentation and exploration will legitimately take to the stage, providing the actors with reasons to oscillate between the extremes, back and forth. Together, these approaches can lead to the "deconstruction", the "critical synthesis", or the "sublation" of Hegel's doctrine of dialectics.

Another example of pluralism is the aforementioned dualism of innate-acquired, flow-stock, static-dynamic, and so on. The emphasis here is on the "qualitative-quantitative" dualism. Just as the above-mentioned people have lost their vigilance against the concept of "diversity" and have been misled into the trap of monism, many scholars have apparently lost their vigilance against the popular quantitative analysis methods and do not know how to get out of the numerical spiral. Let's take economics again as an example. The analysis of prices and quantities of goods obscures everything so much that commenters often mistakenly think that qualitative analysis is a precursor to quantitative analysis, and that quantitative analysis has become the perfect, ultimate analysis. In fact, the supremacy of money has been unconsciously established in this way. The way out of this misconception is to explicitly define the scope of commodity trading, reject the assumption that "it can be traded anytime, anywhere", and reveal the rich subjective elements in pricing and trading activities, and so on (see Chapter 10, Vol. II). Only in this way can those branches of qualitative analysis in economics have an irreplaceable theoretical status over transaction theory, and the distinction and connection between economic analysis and social analysis can be made possible.

The pluralistic perspective leads to the fact that any body of knowledge can only be a mixture in principle, with various elements having their independent properties and various ideas having their independent values. We no longer try to completely dissolve, reflect, represent, or replace each other in the strictest theoretical sense, but instead explore the *relationships* between them. These relationships are infinite in kind, and generally flexible or "soft" in degree, rather than as rigid and simple as the mode of "black-or-white" or "either/or". In this book, the word "soft" is used to refer to many small quantitative relationships mixed with small qualitative relationships, so as to distinguish it from the traditional clear distinction between quantitativeness and qualitativeness. These small relationships are sometimes not worth a clear distinction because they are so small, complex, and irregular that they are difficult and uneconomical to dissect in detail. Limited computing power forces us to roughly and legitimately mix them up. For example, we can now "legitimately" use literary words like *"distant", "close", "loose", "tight"* to describe a relationship, which in principle should not be considered "ambiguous" or "terminologically imprecise" any longer. As the antithesis of Algorithmic Theory, extreme rationalism has its many manifestations, explicit or implicit, and requires us to identify, expose, and critique them respectively in each scenario. In the same way, pluralism and bounded rationality also have a large number of their different manifestations, which also need to be defined and elaborated respectively in different scenarios. In many cases, the confusion of thought and the stagnation of scholarship are quite related to failures in the establishment of a proper philosophical theoretical framework.

Here are two more examples:

A large number of systematic or loose thoughts may exist in a person's brain at the same time, and they were generally formed at different stages of an individual's lifetime.

Individuals are bound to reprocess these ideas. However, due to economic or behavioral factors, any processing cannot be "thorough". Therefore, an individual's knowledge system must be a mixture, and it is completely impossible for the knowledge systems of different individuals to be identical. From this, we can reasonably enter into *the huge issue of "individuality" or "interpersonal difference", of which the importance cannot be overemphasized.* At the same time, the intrinsic differences in a person's thoughts are, in principle, smaller than the differences in thoughts between different individuals. This is a manifestation of the "softness" mentioned above. This is also a concrete application of the method of ideological materialization. If we don't think of our minds as something like microscopic particles, they can't exist in space, and then we don't have this distinction between farness and nearness. Individuals or groups from this perspective must have certain contradictory behaviors. On the other hand, under certain conditions, a hierarchical organizational system will have an advantage over a flat organizational system. Extended applications are outlined in Chapter 9, Vol. II.

Another application is the differentiation and modularization of the humankind knowledge system, which has created a distinction between science, engineering, common sense, religion, art, and so on. This issue has been touched on in many places in the previous article, but it is only emphasized here that the differentiation and modularity of this comprehensive knowledge system are closely related to the problem of soft quantitative relations. This soft relationship is a mixture of qualitativeness and quantitativeness, with a large number of synchronous different elements. The differences here are so small, and the changes are so slow that they are described by words such as "degree". This exemplifies the subtle plausibility of natural language. It is precisely because of the differences in the degrees of connections between the internal and external aspects of a knowledge module that the knowledge modules are like oases in a desert, growing around different water sources and dotting the desert in clusters.

§22. No. 9: Convergence, Divergence and Marginal Adjustment

Rationalism depicts the convergence of knowledge development, that is, the process of simplifying the complex and ending with a static conclusion. Even we believe, through higher-order reflection, that this static conclusion may be broken in the future, it is still appealing and, to a certain extent, true. Plato's schema shows that knowledge development is like this, at least in the local realm. Specific knowledge of certain objects was achieved early in human history and has remained unchanged to this day—or changed less, if at all. The development of knowledge in various fields generally is not synchronous. Updating existing knowledge needs theoretical explanation, and expanding knowledge beyond stock is also an important way of development. Now, we need to combine the old and new theories and comprehensively discuss such processes.

The convergent process is, first of all, a process of replacing roughness with precision, removing the false and adding the true. A thinking process usually starts with trial-and-error and then gradually improves. It is also a process from the generation of interpersonal differences to interpersonal communication, and finally to a consensus. However, extreme rationalism has an inextricable puzzle, that is, in social interactions, because interpersonal strategies are generally interdependent, if the relevant calculations of actors can be carried out indefinitely, then the interactive processes may not converge, or may converge stochastically into multiple equilibria.[12] However, the non-convergence or multiple equilibria are realities that we should usually acknowledge, and thus rationalist analysts needn't really bother with them. Meanwhile, within the framework of the thinking economy, there is a much simpler way of dealing with it; that is, as a marginal effect, the thinking economy inevitably often leads to an *attenuation* of interpersonal interactions, and thus the actors concerned are prone not to perform calculations too deep— just as people with limited vision usually do not like to see too far. Hence, in real life, interactive or reflexive calculations often stop automatically after a few rounds. Even if there is objectively an opportunity to make a profit, the actor may let it go. This is like a decreasing sequence, where the economy of thinking leads to a continuous weakening of the intensity of interaction, to the point of a convergence.

Thus, the statics in the real world are by no means confined only to the situations pointed out by those rationalists, and they can be varied and even bizarre. A statics can refer to any static phenomenon or situation, or to any static feature or aspect of an object, corresponding to the static information or data from it. It can be a staticness included in some kind of dynamics, as a regularity or a certainty. Static phenomena can be positive and satisfying, or they can be negative or unsatisfactory, corresponding to actors' mind states such as helplessness, indifference, frustration, disappointment, despair, and others. The Nash equilibria in game theory[13] depict some deadlocks, in which the actors are dissatisfied with the status quo but can do nothing about it. These statics or equilibria are quite real, and some can exist long enough to be theoretically significant.

What we are opposed to is primarily the notion of "general

---

12. Drew Fudenberg, David K. Levine, "The Theory of Learning in Games", The MIT Press, 1998.

13. See David M. Kreps, "Nash Equilibrium", in "The New Palgrave Dictionary of Economics", 3rd edition, Palgrave Macmillan, 2018, pp. 9251-9258.

equilibrium" that everything will eventually converge towards a general statics. What should we do if we go to deny the generality of equilibrium while accepting its truth? A natural way to this solution is to confine the equilibrium within a certain range and point out that it has *boundaries*. This "boundary" can refer to the spatial extent of the equilibrium, or to its logical scope (i.e., the equilibrium may only refer to certain *aspects* of the relevant objects). The spatial boundaries can allow the equilibrium to exist independently. Also, the economy of thinking can act as a barrier that forces certain variables to be assigned with fixed values rather than contingently with various values while infinitely advancing the relevant calculations. This means that the resultant static knowledge may be acquired "distortively" through the use of alternative Algorithms, but the maker of the knowledge has not been able, or intended, to improve it. It is only after considering the overall situation in an Algorithmic way that the actor decides to maintain this statics, use this statics to survive in the vast and turbulent world, and even *use this statics to deal with the vastness and changes of the world*. The equilibrium formed in this sense can be called the "*Algorithmic Equilibrium*". *Algorithmic Equilibrium is a partial equilibrium in scope, but it is also a "general equilibrium" formed in the Algorithmic way under the Algorithmic conditions. It is a staticness, deadlock, or standoff formed by thoughtful moving entities in a part of the spatial world. It is the equilibrium that can really exist. In other words, any observed real equilibrium can only be an Algorithmic equilibrium in a certain sense.*

When an equilibrium is confined in its scope, knowledge development has to take place on its sides. The word "side" is used here to emphasize its relations with the space. The theory expressed here cannot be effectively developed without the materialization and spatialization of thinking. Now, the equilibrium is recognized, which means that the actor will no longer use his/her brainwork on it, and then the brainwork is saved; henceforth, the actor can devote himself/herself to the initiation of new topics and new research activities. Since the former issue is "settled", and this "settlement" will automatically and continuously play a role in the following activities, which constitutes the conditions under which the actor can enter new areas. This convergent process towards equilibrium has led to a decline in the activity of the mind, which then is possible to trigger new tasks and return active. According to the established terminological tradition, this latter process can be called "divergence".

Divergence occurs next to the equilibrium and is probably initially independent of the equilibrium. The principle of plurality guarantees that this "irrelevance" can be reasonable and acceptable. Since rationalism has always focused on connections, Algorithmic methods now have to do the opposite, justifying the legitimacy of all sorts of irrelevances. This mixedness can also be called "heterogeneity", which refers to the fact that the object world as a whole is not internally homogeneous. This "inhomogeneity" refers both to the differences in the nature of individual objects and to the differences in how people value them. In economic terms, it is, therefore, possible to carry out "arbitrage" actions among them. However, the limitations of subjective thinking, and of the ability to act, lead to the fact that although these arbitrage opportunities objectively exist, the actors cannot immediately take full advantage of them, so they have to selectively let some of them go. In conclusion, this heterogeneity can refer to any differences we observe in the real world. We do not need to theoretically define the types and scopes of these differences now, because our primary theoretical inference is that *any differences are likely to exist* realistically. Even if some specific differences are noticed by the actors who are determined to eliminate them as soon as possible, the differences between convergent and divergent processes cannot be completely eliminated in the final analysis.

§23. No. 9: Convergence, Divergence and Marginal Adjustment (continued)

Divergence overcomes the decline of thinking activity and relieves the quagmire in which traditional rationalism has fallen. Now that the combinatorial explosion shows us the infinite potential of knowledge development, the actors can now expand their activities again. Then, what is the overall effect of the superposition of convergence and divergence? This requires us to make theoretical speculations on the one hand, and observe the reality on the other.

First of all, it is necessary to recognize that a major but subtle consequence of breaking monism and moving into pluralism is that *the question of the quantity of knowledge becomes a major problem.* The traditional view of knowledge is reductionist, which holds that typical, ideal knowledge is similar in form to something like mathematical formulas and is, therefore, simple. Thus, the process of knowledge development becomes a process of refining information. According to this logic, knowledge can be optimized in quality, but cannot be increased in quantity. Now, the divergent process reminds us that the actual amount of knowledge is growing; that is, new knowledge is added next to existing knowledge, and hence, the knowledge system needs more space to store. In turn, the expansion of storage space reflects the growth of knowledge and can be used to measure the growth of knowledge. Second, in this case, empirically, is the knowledge stock really increasing in terms of its total volume? For example, has the number of books and libraries increased? Has the number of intellectuals and their proportion of the total population increased? Has the number of years of education for an average person been extended? Has the number of academic disciplines and specializations increased? Has the scope of research objects been expanded? and so forth.

The general conclusion is obvious: human history shows a great process of knowledge expansion, even if this is not easy to be justified in theory, and even if the growth of knowledge is not stable or strictly monotonous.

The above analytical process can be used to illustrate how the logical transition between theoretical and empirical analysis can be made in the proposed Algorithmic approach, and how they can be coordinated as well. Obviously, a rigorous theoretical analysis of the general trends in knowledge development might outgo what our thinking power can provide, and at this point, empirical analysis can be relayed, which directly shows us the results of the combinatorial explosion, or the results of the "calculations" of the object world itself. These two analytical methods have their comparative advantages at their respective stages in the calculative economy.

The final question is: is there a possibility that a certain thinker can sweep away our current heterogeneous and mixed stock of knowledge and replace it with some internally consistent, precise, and concise new knowledge system at one time? This seemingly complex question can be answered quite rigorously using the logic we already have: 1. If the thinker is superior in basic calculative power over common people, as if an upgraded faster computer is replacing an old computer, then it is possible, at least the "super thinker" might be able to significantly straighten and improve the existing stocked knowledge. However, provided that his/her speed of thinking remains limited, then he/she will be very unlikely to essentially change the existing knowledge system—even if he/she is running at a speed of a higher order of magnitude. 2. If the thinker is merely a human being like us, then the answer is clear: "impossible". This is because the existing knowledge stock was developed in a similar environment collectively by all previous human beings, and is largely the sum total of the thinking results of those countless ancestors—although some of the results have been lost, abandoned, or outdated. And, this stock of knowledge has been repeatedly tested and revised by a large number of his/her closest contemporaries, thus, a few individuals are powerless to overthrow the entire system on account of the great gap in calculative capacity between the small part and the big whole. In the language of economics, this is an *"endogenous impossibility"*: if it were possible, the stocks of knowledge would not be what they are, and conversely, since the stocks of knowledge have in fact appeared as what we are viewing, it means that it is impossible to reform it quickly or completely.

This logical deduction allows us to declare with confidence that reformation of the existing body of knowledge, whether as an expansion or an amendment, must be merely *marginal*, i.e., the activities of the present people can only play a gradual role in some parts fairly small, comparing to the bulkiness of the whole knowledge stocks. The present activities can move back and forth in this stock-pervasive world, even frequently changing their focuses, but they can never "do it all at once". After we have made all the above detours and preparations, we are finally able to prove this common-sense understanding.

An important application of this conclusion is that it can be used to show that social reformation and institutional change usually proceed gradually, and hence, the "shock therapy" that Russia tried to quickly and comprehensively change the economic and social structure in the 1990s would not work well. Any current policies or actions, as the flows, must only influence a certain proportion of the social reality.

Moreover, the above conclusion has an extremely significant philosophical application, that is, the *traditional view that "ultimate truth is simple" is obviously a great and "inverted" error, and therefore, the traditional metaphysics of "Being" initiated by Parmenides is obviously a fundamental mistake.* Philosophers must have observed the phenomenon of convergences of certain knowledge-development processes, and this phenomenon is apparently due to the heterogeneous and uneven nature of the knowledge system (and thus the world), and that in some places it is indeed possible to simplify the complex (or to allow the arbitrary and Algorithmic simplification), so that through thinking efforts, people try to simplify it as much as possible, and hold the leftovers that cannot be sufficiently simplified in their original or still quite complex forms. It's as if scientists have developed formulas and concise theories, while humanistic scholars have used a plethora of descriptive books and audiovisual works to portray the rest of the world. Humans hold both works that form a collaborative system to support actors' lives. According to the proposed theory of thinking, it is easy to understand and even necessary for this mixture to occur. However, from the time of the Hellenists, observers misunderstood that since some knowledge could be simplified, then all knowledge could be simplified. Therefore, they enshrined the succinct, universal knowledge as absolute truth, detached it from other knowledge, and gave it the special preferential treatment. This reasoning is clearly ill-founded and contains elements of over-imagination. Now, we need to make a big reversal of the philosophical direction, which is to turn this "great convergence" upside down and then into a "big bang" mode. Partial convergences in the knowledge system shall not be enough to offset the "explosions" happening elsewhere. Only such a philosophy is in line with the reality. [14]

---

14. The second law of thermodynamics and the concept of "entropy" imply that systems tend to be uniform and disordered in their long-term evolution. This

§24. Conclusions & Supplements

This chapter uses thirteen sections to introduce the new principles and knowledge that the proposed thinking theory can bring. One of the reasons why we devoted such a long text, in advance of a formal introduction to Algorithmic Thinking Theory, is to explain to readers how few new assumptions will be made, despite those many technical terms and how great the role of the theory will be. The Algorithmic clues and principles can be reasonably grown from the existing knowledge system, and this growth is mainly marginal and can be groped with the existing ideas and common sense; or, at least, this deductive reasoning can be expected to be understood and accepted by the readers, even if it has not been strictly given in this book. However, I believe that although these new principles and knowledge are based on existing knowledge, they are indeed new and have not yet been found in the existing literature; or, even if they are found sparsely in the existing literature, our interpretation, organization, expansion, and integration of them are still prominently novel, even in a completely different sense.[15] These new principles are so systematic, coherent, holistic, and concise that we need to first concentrate on formulating and arguing for them while relegating the

---

suggestion coincides with traditional metaphysics and the concept of "general equilibrium" in economics, and thus widely attracts many economics enthusiasts. However, the principle of combinatorial explosion reveals to us the opposite scenario: human thoughts grow explosively, and cognitive activities are only a part of them; then, by virtue of their own wills, human beings would continuously produce new ideas and new products that were not previously available in the world; the growth of these artificial products as the "independent third party" will make the world more heterogeneous rather than homogenized, more ordered rather than disordered.

15. I have ever summarized these principles on different occasions as the "Thinking-Knowledge-Innovation Trinity", the "Thinking-Knowledge-Conflict-Innovation Quaternity", or the "Thinking-Knowledge-Subjectivity-Plurality-Conflict-Complexity-Innovation-Development Eight-in-one".

examination of existing literature to a relatively secondary position.

It is a fundamental point of view that the manners and processes of thinking seriously affect the contents of thought. Thus, epistemology and ontology are inseparable, and these philosophical parts are actually inside a whole. This book does not primarily belong to any applied discipline such as "sociology of knowledge", but to philosophy.

The influences of thoughtful forms on its contents are realized through the logic of thinking economy, namely, the Algorithmic Logic. At the end of the 19th century, Ernst Mach proposed the "economics of thought". Nevertheless, it was still relatively narrow. For example, only propositions such as "the most concise theory in form is the most worthy of pursuit" were recognized. This can also be traced back at least to the fourteenth century when the famous "Occam's razor" principle was proposed. However, this understanding is somewhat superficial after all, whereas the sedimentation, distortion, solidification, explosion, and pluralization of thinking shall all be the major consequences of thinking economy. The thinking economy shall be the root cause of the philosophical "subjective turn". Without this resultant set of important principles, philosophy cannot bridge its internal gap between subjectivity and objectivity. In fact, this and other related splits have been existent evidently to this day. These puzzles are so controversial and desperate that many scholars have to forget them, or misunderstand them as having been dissolved.

The economy of thought is just an alternative branch of economics. Bridged by this branch, a large number of useful ideas and methods in economics can enter philosophy. However, the splits in economics are in fact similar to, if not more so, those in philosophy. This is largely due to the fact that the dominant neoclassical economists have brought the idea of extreme rationalism to a flamboyant and formidable degree.

Economics departments at top universities can now be called "applied mathematics", where mathematical economists are literally hiding in ivory towers to escape from the real world. They give the impression of being proud and stubborn, and their critics have ridiculed them as "ignorant" and "useless" despite that excessive criticisms should be avoided. In my opinion, this embarrassing situation shall be mainly due to the fact that they have not found out how to combine rationality with irrationality, or objectivity with subjectivity. However, many of their critics have not gotten the hang of it, either. They are not strict theorists, and they criticize mainstream economics even before they completely understand their theoretical logic.

Rationalism is a key guiding tool for theorists. If we cannot understand it in a positive and well-meaning way, we will not be able to criticize and reform it to the point. I argue that behind the assumption of the potential "infinite thinking speed", rationalists are actually reluctant to see a thought as an entity—and vice versa, of course. This forces their thinking into the trap of "going straightforward restlessly until the final truth", with no time for anything else. The revision of this most basic philosophical attitude will inevitably lead to a fundamental change in logical thinking itself. Logical reasoning, which operates while regarding itself as an entity or "being", will *logically* attempt to close itself in time, and in turn, it will *logically* introduce "irrational" mental activities. Thus, logical reasoning saves itself from its everyday busyness of "going straightforward". The reasoner, the "slave to logic", can now become a "master of logic". He/she can calm down, sit back, take a sip of coffee, and look around at the world. He/she may no longer need others to correct him/her, because he/she now could "automatically" save himself/herself from traditional mistakes.

I argue that the neoclassical economics of extreme

rationalism is the key obstacle to the emergence of a unified social science. After this obstacle is overcome, the next work will break through all the way overwhelmingly. The social sciences will be able to establish a fluent ontology and methodology. The main contents of these basic principles have long been proposed by various scholars separately and fragmentally, and now, it is only necessary to connect them with the Algorithmic principles—of course, it is inevitable to add new contents as well.

One of the key steps in this connection is to relate our work to the natural sciences. The social sciences need to explain their differences from, and their relationships with, the natural sciences on the basis of logical consistency. Now, a basic idea of this work is to introduce an ontology of the human mind. This ontology will elaborate on how the activity of the mind is carried out and what its consequences are to be. Thoughts are entities in the brain that coexist and interact with the brain and the vast number of natural entities outside it. In this context, it doesn't matter whether you're a natural scientist or a social scientist. You are free to re-choose what you want to study. If you choose to study the human mind, or if your object of study (e.g., commodities) is closely related to the activity of the human mind, then, under the condition that you accept this theory of thinking, you will "naturally" enter the social sciences, getting connected with the rich social science results that have already existed. It even doesn't matter if you only have an educational background in the natural sciences. Since the same and consistent logic is there, and when you follow it step by step, the principles and methods of the social sciences will naturally "pop up"—or the Algorithmic logic will require you to answer some *unavoidable* questions, along which you will find the ready-made methodologies in others. This is true for the social sciences, as well as for many other humanities and social engineering disciplines.

Therefore, what we are achieving is an all-encompassing "grand synthesis".

What will the status of philosophy be in this unified body of knowledge? Since Russell and Wittgenstein, philosophical discourses with ambiguous characteristics have been criticized and relegated, and accuracy and positivism have been elevated. However, the mainstream of continental philosophy adheres to the track of "subjective turn", which is prominently different from English analytical philosophy. This is a new split that took place in the twentieth century. I believe that another consequence of "Algorithmic synthesis" is to correctly handle the relationship between ambiguity and accuracy. As a manifestation of bounded rationality, ambiguity (or "vagueness") has an important significance in the thinking economy, and this significance is expected to be re-discovered, recognized, and revived on the basis of correcting the bias of positivism, and will eventually enable philosophy to find its place in the whole body of knowledge.

On a broader scale, rationalism has been dominant since Socrates. Socrates' aim was to convince the Athenians that they should pursue wisdom and reason, especially in their secular lives, namely, to figure out reliable (really partial) knowledge. This doctrine sets the tone of Western philosophy. However, since modern times, this tradition has been subjected to sniping from multiple directions. It has reached such a point that the mainstream intellectual community feels at a loss what to do. Actually, it's a U-turn, and I think philosophy has been trying to re-understand the circumstances and foundations on which rationalism grows, and it wants to return to the starting point of Socrates. It wants to recover the whole body of knowledge that includes rationalism, and to integrate it into a coherent whole. This is like Edmund Husserl starting from concepts such as "suspension" and "reduction", and finally reaching the "life world". The integration of this book will involve the integration of almost all major concepts and categories that have been opposed to each other. Readers must have perceived this. Knowledge moves forward, not individually, but as a whole, with many intrinsic collaborations.

What is the role of philosophy in this whole? Basic, speculative, original, general, and vague philosophy will always occupy an important place in the body of knowledge; this can be an Algorithmic conclusion despite the possibility that the specific contents of philosophy may vary from time to time. The Algorithmic synthesis may consequently scientize some current contents of philosophy, or expand philosophical discourse beyond its current scope. Meanwhile, it will also create new philosophical topics and open up new philosophical fields. But that's for later. For the time being, the synthesis of philosophy is yet to begin. First, it is obvious that the concept of "thinking tool" needs to be clarified, detailed, and concretized. This is not something that can be done alone without adopting any technical tools. We need to introduce a minimized concrete theory of thinking.

CHAPTER 3
THE ALGORITHMIC
THINKING THEORY

§25. Instruction

As the Chinese saying goes: "Everything is ready except that the east wind has yet to come". Now, if we find or point out what the "innate thinking tools" are, we can hopefully establish each of the new principles mentioned above, and thus construct a whole new theory of thinking. It can be used both to synthesize all existing philosophies and to reform and transcend them.

However, before that, the aforementioned topic of "with or without technical terms" is worth revisiting. Someone may suspect that theoretical and philosophical deductions can be made without clarifying the specific forms (i.e., the specific contents) of "thinking tools". These deductions have led to most, if not all, of the above conclusions. However, they suffer the flaw that the relevant conclusions can only remain in their vague states. Another effect is that the stronger the explanatory power of these new principles for reality and the more significant their guidance for practice, the more interested people will be in the question of "what on earth are the thinking tools?" and the more eager they will be to enter into micro-analyses of thinking activities. The micro-analysis will not only make such a thinking theory more complete, but also, with this completeness, connect to other specific disciplines, and then serve applied research. Only when the thinking theory enters such a stage can it be concrete, operable, and mature, in certain sense. In other words, the Algorithmic theory has had different routes or versions from the beginning. Let's start with the "Standard Version".

Such a kind of long-awaited thinking tool has a weird name called "Instruction". The name comes from computer science. The original meaning of "instruction" refers to the type of specific work that the user of a computer "instructs" the computer to do. Its meaning is, first of all, to distinguish information (or data) from the act of "processing" (or "handling") of information. "Processing" refers to work or "operation" that uses something different from information, such as certain tools, to work on information. It can be that multiple tools take turns to process information, or a single tool does different kinds of actions serially to process information. To put it simply, we can just focus on the former and use it to include the latter. In other words, the concept of "instruction" first emphasizes the difference between thinking tools and information. It defines itself as a tool used to process information, just like the machinery and equipment in a factory are used to process raw materials. It also means that this "processing" is an action, behavior, operation, or "flow", in contrast with the stocks of thinking tools, information, and results. The flow of computational operation is the "behavior" made with these stocks.

Distinguishing the types of thinking activity from information processed is a common practice in human daily thinking activities. For example, when we write mathematical formulas, we always distinguish between numbers and the operations on numbers and write them separately. And, when we describe our thinking activities, we always distinguish between the information used in the thinking activities and the thinking activities themselves. For instance, when we reason, compare, or imagine, we must identify the objects of our reasoning, comparison, or imagination, and also identify the results of these thinking activities. Because this distinction is too natural, it is often ignored by ourselves, so that we only see information and the results in our eyes, and the thinking tools become invisible to us. This invisibility exists even among computer scientists to a greater or lesser extent. Although computer scientists have clearly distinguished information from instructions and accurately defined the format, function, and usage of each instruction, they have not considered that instructions, a kind of software, are the basic thinking tools of the human brain that reflect the architecture, resources, and operating modes of the human brain, thereby ignoring the extremely important philosophical significance of this concept.

The binary structure of "thinking tool + information" could have been established *before the advent of computers*. What computers contribute is that they demonstrate in a visual and precise way how this binary architecture actually works. However, computers don't do everything. A finished computer can only do a limited variety of work. As a result, a computer leaving the factory provides the user with a list of the specific kinds of jobs it can do, as well as the specific format and requirements for each job. It's like a restaurant offering a "menu" to its guests (hence, the word "menu" is commonly used in computers). Some of these dishes on the menu have conditions and specifications such as "not available at lunch", "three levels of spiciness selectively", etc.

The kind of work that the user asks the computer to do was extended to the kind of work that the computer "itself" can do, indicating that there was a semantic shift here. Why didn't computer scientists use other names to refer to the kind of work that computers do? Obviously, they were intended to emphasize this "master-servant" relationship between human users and machines; that is, human is the master, and the computer is just a tool used by the master.

We could have used a different name. Some alternative names were also suggested to consider. However, in respect to the terminological originality and the consistency with the computerized research that has prevailed, I advocate the use of this existing name. Although the current computer simulation work is not based on Algorithmic Thinking Theory, in my opinion, future work in this approach needs to be based on this theory, which requires a consistency in terms.

And, most importantly, we are to make another shift in the meaning of this term, that is, the *"instructions" that humans give to computers must be the "Instructions" that the human brain has,* i.e., the human brain itself must be able to do the work referred to by an "instruction". Considering that you cannot "give" something if you don't have it, how can you "give" an instruction if you don't have the instruction? It is precisely because a person can do a certain job, needs to do this kind of work, and does not want to do it himself/herself that a certain tool, the computer, does it for him/her. Isn't this exactly what is happening?

Of course, one can also ask computers to do some jobs that one can envision but can't concretely do oneself, so as to take advantage of the characteristics of computers as machinery. However, the types of instruction that a computer has, i.e., the number of Instructions, are very limited, ranging from dozens to hundreds. Diagram 5 is a list of major instructions (or the "instruction set", the "repertoire") typically and commonly used. A closer look at these instructions shows that, in terms of the computing functions that correspond to thinking functions, there is no such thing as a job that cannot be done by the human brain or by the human brain in conjunction with manual work—Since computers are designed by imitating human's work, this consistency is natural and understandable.

These functions referred to by the instructions should be the basic functions in the human brain. This is because instructions are the basic functions of a computer, and a computer is a mirror image of the human brain—whether the image is exact or not. In this way, we come to the logically ordinary, but extremely important, conclusion that *computer instructions reflect the basic thinking functions of the human brain*, or at least some, if not all, of the basic functions of the human brain.

Then, the next question is: Apart from those controlling functions, can all of the basic thinking functions of the human brain, if they can be identified one by one, be expressed as computer instructions? Or, if some of them cannot be done now, can they be done in the future?

This is a typical AI-style problem. The essence of the question is whether the computer can completely simulate the thinking activities of the human brain. Obviously, this is not a question that I can answer directly here. AI engineering institutes and industries around the world are working to find answers to this problem. Significant positive developments have been made. However, the scepticism and negations remain sizable.

If Algorithmic Theory answers "yes" to this directly, it would not be very wrong, and in fact it would probably be on the winning side, because the proponents of AI are clearly in an advantageous position, and the achievements of AI engineering are prominent to all observers. In terms of the types of function, the "thinking activities" that computers are really unable to simulate at all have been reduced to the point where it is not easy to exemplify. However, to be secure enough, there is a relatively simple solution to this seemingly tricky question.

Diagram 5: A List of Major Instructions of INTEL8086/8088 Microprocessor[1]

Instruction Type	Instruction(s)	Description	Instruction Type	Instruction(s)	Description
Data Transfer	MOV	transfer data	Arithmetic Operation	ADD ADC AAA	add
	XCHG	exchange data		MUL IMUL AAM	multiply
	XLAT XLATB	read data from the lookup table		DIV IDIV AAD	divide
	PUSH POP	push/read data to/from the stack		SUB SBB AAS	subtract
	IN OUT	input/output data		NEG	negative
	LEA LDS LES	load data		INC	increment by 1
Logical Operation	AND	logical AND		DEC	decrement by 1
	OR	logical OR		CMP	compare
	NOT	logical NOT	String Operation	MOVSB MOVSW	move string data
	XOR	logical XOR		LODSB LODSW	load string data
	SHL SHR SAL SAR	shift bit of data left or right		CMPS	compare string data
	ROL ROR RCL RCR	rotate bits of data left or right		SCASB SCASW	compare bytes/words
				STOSB STOSW	store string data
	TEST	logical AND for flags only		REP	repeat an instruction
Processor Control	CLC	clear carry flag to 0	Program Execution Transfer	CALL	call a procedure
	STC	set carry flag to 1		JMP	unconditional jump
	CLI	clear interrupt flag to 0		LOOP	jump to a loop
	STI	set interrupt flag to 0		INT	interrupt a program
	CLD	clear direction flag to 0		RET	return from a procedure
	STD	set direction flag to 1		JZ JA JO	conditional jump
	NOP	perform nothing		LOOPNE	conditional loop
	WAIT	set the idle state		IRET	return from interruption
	HLT	halt processing			

---

1. Based on Section 3.1 of Lichao Chen, "Intel 8086/8088 Macro Assembly Language Programming Theory and Practice" (in Chinese), Ordnance Industry Press, 1993, pp. 37-38, and other materials. This table is made, added, revamped, and interpreted by me.

§26. Instructions (continued)

Let's look at the detailed contents of instructions. Start with the core instructions, namely, the data-processing ones.

Computer textbooks generally start with arithmetic instructions. To reverse the order here, let's take a look at the instructions for logic operations. The most basic, standard, and reliable logical reasoning is deductive reasoning. Mathematical logic has distilled its typical (and perhaps not all) forms into the three types of "Or", "And", and "Not", and computer science defines them as the three different instructions, each "realized" with different logic circuits. In this way, the computer has basic *reasoning skills or functions.*

This magical leap from mathematics to logic has started the process of mystification (and even demonization) of computers. However, in fact, this leap has nothing to do directly with a computer itself, it is completely a product of human intelligence. In 1847, more than 100 years before the invention of the computer, the English mathematician George Boole proposed that logical reasoning could be carried out in a symbolic way that is similar to arithmetic calculations. This "logical calculation" has only the three basic forms mentioned above, and all other deductive forms can be managed to be expressed as some combinations of these three forms. This is a major refinement of human thinking, and an important step towards finding the "basic thinking tools". The idea of inventing a certain calculating or computing machine is to find or design a device whose initial state(s) can just represent the original data to be processed, and a certain action of the device can just represent the processing of the data (i.e., "calculation" or "computation"), and the changed state can represent the result of the processing. In this way, the movement of the device appears as if it is calculating "on its own". As long as the performance of the device is stable, people can set the data they want to process to its initial value(s), and then operate the device to perform specific action, and then observe and identify the subsequent state, that is, "read" the computational result. In other words, people can take advantage of this mechanism over and over again.

A lot of philosophical questions have already happened here, but let's continue with the types of instruction first.

Arithmetic operations can be seen as an extension of the above logical operations. Because, when natural numbers are already clearly defined, operations on them are nothing more than *reasoning* pursuant to the definition of natural numbers—and then expanding from natural numbers to decimal and negative numbers. This view suggests that logical operations are more "fundamental" than mathematical operations. However, according to the above introduction, logical operations are developed after and with reference to arithmetic operations, and arithmetic operations are simpler, more intuitive, and easier to understand. From this point of view, it seems that the latter is more "basic". Nonetheless, this issue can be put aside for now, because it is not difficult to add several basic kinds of arithmetic operations to instructions. As a result, in classical computers, arithmetic and logical operations have been both listed as the basic and core instructional types from the very beginning.

The other type of instruction can be called the "managerial", "controlling", or "service" instructions (three sub-types of them include: data transmission, processor control, and control transfer). These instructions play the role of scheduling, storing, and managing data, scheduling and managing operational sequences of instruction, powering on and off, and so on. There are more than twenty instructions at the core of this type. Just looking at their names may lead one to think that the computer is a conscious, living thing, thereby creating a sense of mystery. In practice, however, the implementation of the functions referred to by these instructions is based on a relatively simple logical mechanism. For example, the so-called "Transfer" of data is actually the copying of the data stored in *one place* and transferring it to *another place*, and simultaneously deleting the data stored in the former place. The "Copying" of data is to make two data "equal"—As long as the representation method of a number in the computer is determined, the concepts of "greater than", "equal to", and "less than" will be generated accordingly. The ways data are stored and changed in different locations are similar to each other, but the definitions and roles of these different locations are *artificially* and structurally set, memorized, and performed; collectively they form the *logical structure* of computing.

The above-mentioned instructions are introduced in computer textbooks in a relatively bland manner, however, now we would like to emphasize their great philosophical significance, that is, these instructions are listed as basic types of operations, and in fact, they are very conspicuously indicating the *materialization* of thinking activities, namely, thoughts are entities, or "real entities", which can be produced, transferred, copied, re-processed, stored, found, destroyed (deleted), and so on. Aren't these actions exactly what we do only with entities, or "real entities" including physical objects? For example, isn't it precisely because a thought (datum) is an entity that it needs to be "carried" or "transmitted"? Therefore, the seemingly ordinary act of "transmit" already represents *a major philosophical shift in the attitude of computer science toward thoughtful objects*. This attitude is absent outside of computer science. Other traditional disciplines generally do not depict and handle mental activity in this way. For example, a concrete consequence of this subtle turn in philosophical meaning is the basic point we have made above: A syllogism is not a complete and correct description of the activities of the mind, because it lacks at least the processes of search and selection for knowledge. A deductive reasoning can go in different directions depending on the search results, and a specific syllogism represents only one of the directions.

The last type of instruction can be called the "hardware control instruction", which is responsible for executing computational results; that is, using a certain mechanism to trigger the parts or devices connected to the computer to physically work, so as to execute contents in the results, such as displaying pictures and words on the screen, making sounds, printing, and so on. This type of instruction did not exist in early computers (such as 8086/8088), because the entire instruction system, as the "interface" between software and hardware, had actually directed various types of hardware to work. For example, string instructions had been designed for operations on text, and text is used for display. The results of text operations were sent to the specified address after being transferred through a series of instructions, and the relevant electronic signals were then generated and triggered the displayer to work, and the text would be displayed on the screen. Later, the types and complexity of hardware devices drastically increased. In order to improve the efficiency of programming, special instructions were designed additionally to replace the series of computing processes used to control hardware, and to directly connect with new external devices. Today's computers generally have a variety of hardware control instructions.

The corresponding functions in the human body are not exactly the same as those on a computer, because human being is not a tool and hence does not need to "report" or "display" results of computations to a "user". However, one sometimes needs to express oneself to others, then he/she can also "showcase" his/her own mental activities, consciously or unconsciously. The essential similarities are that certain computations need to be executed as "decisions", and when the decisions are executed by the relevant components or equipment, specific computing activities need to be carried out in parallel with the executive actions in order to organize and control the physical processes. This determines that any visible, physical action performed by the individual is not in fact completely physical, and the accompanying thinking activities must also be deemed the necessary and essential real actions. Without the existence of the concurrent thinking activities as its components, there will be no human physical behavior or action. A typical example is that biologists pointed out that human upright walk must be supplemented by the brain's controlling thinking activities at all times, and it is just the speedy, concurrent, and precise thinking activities that ensure that all parts of the human body work in harmony, so as to maintain the balance of the body during walking and avoid falling. This biological balance is difficult or impossible to achieve for ordinary objects that have no ability to think.[2]

This kind of executive computing is also of great value in philosophy and the social sciences. A significant proportion of day-to-day thinking activities are executive, i.e. repeatedly "executing" (i.e., applying) existing knowledge. For example, the executive branch of government is used to enforce laws and administrative orders. Implementation of law is so complicated and controversial that the courts are established to settle the arguments. It is a pity that the importance that the judicial branch has had in real society has not been reflected in theoretical analysis. Traditional extreme rationalism has a strong tendency to despise this type of computation, and now we need to, reversely, treat all types of computations equally. This is not just because of the rationalist reasons such as

---

2. John C. Eccles, "Evolution of the Brain: Creation of the Self", Routledge, 1989, pp. 48-70.

"execution can arouse innovations", but because this kind of computation, like other computations, takes up time, space, and resources, hence it has the same real position as other computations; and, its role is unique, irreplaceable and indispensable. "Every day the sun is new" does not only emphasize that there are some changes in the characteristics of the daily sun, but that the sun must rise every day, and the sun cannot refuse to rise today just because it is the same as yesterday's sun. In the same way, since knowledge needs to be copied, there must be a reason for copying, and a role of copying. Each copy activity has its own unique meaning in the place where it happens—even if its content is not different. This can be applied to executive computations. Its meaningfulness cannot be replaced by other reasons such as innovation. Traditional rationalism actually absolutizes the distinction between the two, and in turn, worships innovation, the qualitativeness as the only manifestation of "wisdom" while despising other factors such as quantitativeness.

In light of the above, the term "computation", which was originally used exclusively in mathematics and computer science, inevitably had to be expanded to refer to the general activity of the mind. This is first and foremost for the sake of terminological convenience—it is not necessary to distinguish all the time between the massive computations performed in a computer, which are for quantitative data and which are not—besides, qualitative computations are not necessarily non-mathematical. Second, the *use of the word "computation" to refer to and replace the word "thinking" reflects a change in philosophical perceptions*, an acceptance of the particular perspective of computer science, and a re-conception of human thinking activity from this new and comprehensive perspective. Therefore, in this book, as well as in any of my other Algorithmic writings, I follow this terminological tradition, equating mental activity with "computation". This is neither derogating nor glorifying mental activities. At the same time, there is no intention to distort the original meaning of the term "mental activity" by this equation or substitution. The analysis and discussion of activities of the human mind will continue as usual.

§27. From Simple to Complex (1)

In order for the instructions to be realized physically, appropriate physical materials need to be selected, and certain processing of these physical materials needs to be carried out to make them fit for human purposes. A natural ideal computing material that needs not any human design and manufacture cannot be expected. On the other hand, artificial design and manufacturing will not be enough until the right materials are found out. Chinese were the first people to use wooden abacuses as arithmetic calculators. Nonetheless, the basic mechanism of today's electronic computers is not fundamentally different from that of an abacus. This topic involves a philosophical discussion of artificial intelligence, which we will continue later.

Modern computers mainly use magnetic materials for data storage, and transistors made of silicon materials for computations. This is because magnetic materials do not lose their magnetism after they are out of electrical power, which helps reduce the cost of storage. Transistors are used for computations because they run faster than magnetic materials. Under human control, a transistor can constantly change its high potential to the low potential or its low potential to the high potential, that is, it constantly makes it positively or negatively charged, corresponding to numbers of 0 and 1 in binary computations, respectively. Later, however, transistor materials were developed that could retain data records even after a power outage, and then there came the time of using transistor materials for both storage and computing, although with their different specifications.

The reason for reviewing the above history is to explain that there is really no essential distinction between storage operations and computing operations in principle. The so-called "storage", or "memorization", is to artificially make a certain state of the physical material and let it sustain for a while, short or long. For example, the ancients used a knife to cut a hole in a tree, which could keep for a long time and would not disappear even if the tree grew; hence, it had the effect of "storing data". Later, people printed paper into books, and the ink in them lasted for a long time; hence, they could be used to pass on civilization. However, this storing procedure is also a "computational" process. A computational process is a process with at least two steps. It both sets the initial state and changes that state to move it into another state. In the example above, it either changes the state of the bark or the state of the paper. This is equivalent to changing the magnetic properties of magnetic materials or changing the high or low potentials of transistors in today's computers. The difference is that since the carved bark or the paper on which the words are printed cannot be restored to its original state, hence such a "computation" can only be performed once; if the computation is carried out repeatedly, the material can only be discarded and replaced with a new one. This is not the case with magnetic materials and transistors, which can be used *over and over again*, just like a whiteboard can be erased over and over again. In this way, they turn memory and computation into a composite, continuous, unified, interdependent, and efficient process, i.e., the setting of any state can represent storage, and the change of any state can represent computing. Moreover, this material device can run very quickly, then the resulting economy is enormous.

Another factor that makes the above physical materials

ideal is the use of binary. Binary not only greatly facilitates the search for an ideal material by allowing it to have only two different states, but also allows the device to store and compute any type of information other than those quantitative pieces of information. How does it do?

One way to do this is to set the length of a unit of information (i.e., the "word length"). This means that "a piece of information" (or "a datum"), or the smallest unit of information, is not represented by a single 0 or 1, but by *a set of* sequential permutations of 0s or 1s. For example, computers that are commonly used today use a combination of 0s and 1s that contain a minimum of 8 bits and a maximum of 64 bits to represent a piece of information. This is possible by taking advantage of the width or breadth of the *space*. We are in space, so most of the objects we focus on can be combined with space to form a "structure", namely, a qualitative and non-quantitative relationship. "Structure" is a term that seems mundane but is actually subtle. Only when we understand the idea of extreme rationalism can we comparatively understand what "structure" is. This is because extreme rationalism is an attempt to dissolve the structure. In other words, it attempts to *completely* reduce the heterogeneous, structured world we live into a single, homogeneous, and therefore "non-structured" world. People who have been deeply affected by this kind of ideological code are often confused with, and alienated from, the conventional world in front of them, or make a fuss of it, or sneer at it, and even launch a variety of attacks on it, overt or covert, intentional or unintentional, and struggle in it by themselves.

Using a set of numbers instead of a single number to represent a piece of information is an innovative leap that the inventors of binary might not have anticipated. In my opinion, the philosophically correct attitude is that we first directly accept this "structurality", rather than rootlessly assume in advance that this structurality can be eliminated, and then use this assumption to restrain all future thinking activities.

Structure plus structure, or repeatedly structuring, is the secret of computers evolving from simple to complex, from low to high.

Along with the increase in word length, the types of information that can be represented by computers can also increase, from quantitative data to text data, and others. However, since there are infinite kinds of non-quantitative and structural information, should we just rely on increasing the word length to represent them all? Of course not. Because the world we live in has not only a spatial dimension, but also a temporal dimension. This provides the other method—*unfolding vertically in time*. The state of a particular material at the previous moment can represent one kind of information and another at the next moment.

How, then, does the computer "know" that the information presented at the next moment, the 0 and 1 series, is of another informational type? The way to do this is to structure it again, that is, to add another link before the next series of information, which is dedicated to specifying the type of the next information. This "specification" is actually to provide another specific type of information, which of course, also needs to be specified, with a certain mechanism.

The next question is: even if the problem of information representation is temporarily solved, how can the information be processed, and how does the computer know what kind of processing should be done with the information? In other words, what kind of instruction should be selected and used to process the information?

There is an answer to this seemingly difficult question: since billions of pieces of information can be encoded and stored, dozens (or hundreds) of instructions can certainly be encoded and stored as *a specific type of information*, like any other information. After completing a computing step, the computer does not directly enter the next step, but first opens the information storage, "reads" the next instruction stored there, so that it knows what type of operation should be done next, and then invokes the relevant instruction and data to do. The conclusion of this reasoning is that the computer needs to establish an initial working structure that can distinguish different types of information, and distinguish an instruction from information. All operations must be based on this fundamental mechanism. That's exactly what the control system does.

Here I would like to insert a question to explain what is meant by "reading information". In fact, the above information storing process contains a necessary step, that is, how to display, return, or re-transmit the stored information to users when they need it. *It should be noted that memories that cannot be read and reused are not real memories.* The movement of ordinary physical objects also leaves certain traces or "records", but they do not "read" and reuse them, nor do they deliberately create them. In the case of carved trees or printed books, this problem does not seem to exist, because those physical marks can be seen by the naked eyes, then the contents are naturally "read". The knowledge of identifying these marks has been stored in the minds of the people involved. However, in the electromagnetic age, the situation is different. The information stored in the electromagnetic material is not directly visible to the person concerned. Fortunately, in the case of automatic computation, most of the intermediate information generated during computing does not need to be seen by users, as long as the machine itself "knows" them. Since storing information in a magnetic material converts an electrical signal into a magnetic signal, "reading information" then converts a magnetic signal back into the same electrical signal as before. In the case of transistors, "reading information" refers to copying the high or low potentials stored in transistors that are used as memory to the transistors used as computing units. This reversibility requirement makes it difficult to single out the proper physical material. However, the good news is that it has been achieved through specific physical techniques. The word "read" here has a more or less anthropomorphic flavor, which casts a layer of mystery over the data access operations and then may confuse a learner; however, in actual effects, it is indeed equivalent to our human "reading" of memory.

§28. From Simple to Complex (2)

According to the above section, a computer must initially have some kind of structure that can directly defines (or "recognizes") what instruction is and what information is[3]— Otherwise, we would get stuck in a logical loop and achieve nothing. In practice, the basic design idea is as follows: the computer can do a number of basic actions, which means that it can execute a number of instructions; each basic action adopts a fixed mode, and the information to be processed will be input at a fixed part; that is, the information to be processed is placed under an instruction, becoming a component of a whole structure and a whole action, and hence there is in principle no informational movement isolated from instructions; therefore, each instruction has a fixed format, and the information to be processed is required to be filled in a designated and fixed position, thus constituting "one complete instruction"[4]–Hence, when we say "instruction", sometimes we

---

3. To know the difficulty of defining information in the extant approaches that lack our conceptual pair of "instruction-information", see a summary in Pieter Adriaans et al (ed.), "Philosophy of Information", Part B, especially pp. 117-119.
4. For an introduction of instructions, see G. Frieder, "Machine Instruction Set" in Anthony Ralston et al (ed.), "Encyclopedia of computer science and engineering", Van Nostrand Reinhold Co., 1983, pp. 899-904.

mean an empty instruction that does not contain information, and sometimes we mean an instruction that has already been filled in with information (see Diagram 6), depending on the context. Generally, no more than two pieces of information can be processed by one instruction, and no more than one result will be obtained. An instruction that is "executed" once, or "run" once, is called a computation, a computational operation, or an operation, and sometimes I call it a "meta-computation" or "meta-operation". After an operation is completed, the computer's program-control system will automatically look for the next action at a fixed position. The decision to move on to the next operation either needs to be given by the user or the previous instruction, or it needs to be triggered by the result of the previous operation. Once this is achieved, the computer can run continuously and *automatically* in a certain sequence of operations. At this point, people can manually write computing steps, or "a program", and store them in the computer. The computer then "reads" the instruction and executes it, alternately and stepwisely. *The initial programs must only be written by hand*, and subsequent programming can then be done incrementally or "marginally" on the basis of copying or citing existing programs. A program can be paused during its execution or "running", waiting for the user to input parameters or new information, or give new instructions, thus forming a *composite structure of "partially fixed + partially variable"*. However, in any case, the computer simply does these basic operations over and over again, i.e., executes the instructions in its "instruction set" or "repertoire".

Opcode (instruction)	Operand 1 address	Operand 2 address	Result address	Next instruction address

Diagram 6: The Format of A Typical Four-address Instruction
This format is used to show how an instruction contains, or combines with, information (operands as the target data) and how the instruction is succeeded by the next one.

Once the basic structural arrangements are in place, they can be continuously expanded with time, space, and other structural elements, so that the computer can be connected to our daily life, and thus become practical. First, the numerical information stored in binary needs to be converted into decimal. Thanks to its regularity, this converting work leads to a fixed program that can be stored and executed repeatedly by the computer. The same goes for other types of data as characters, graphics, sounds, and so on. Next are instructions. Compared with instructions in the computer, the types of thinking that people usually perform are still relatively complex, which often require the joint executions of multiple basic instructions. Conversely, some of the basic instructions in a computer are familiar only to the computer scientists involved, but unfamiliar somehow to the people who wrote programs (the "programmers") or the users. This leads to the *"advancing"* process of instructions that leads to a fixed permutation of certain instructions that is given a new name and then promoted to the menu level and made available to programmers or users. The new name is "command". A command, when computing, is executed literally as an instruction, but the fact is that the command is to be translated automatically by the "compile programs" mentioned above into a series of instructions, and then executed "backstage" stepwisely by the machine. Therefore, the executing time of a command is usually longer than that of an instruction. Sometimes, commands are added to the instruction set to be provided for users. This increases the number of instructions, and hence the choices of users. This is an important reason why the instruction list we usually see on a computer is relatively longer and more complex than a classical instruction list. The formation of hardware control instructions mentioned in §26 is an example of the advancement of instructions. The processes of advancing instructions have lasted for several levels, so that some commands in a high-level language look a bit like a sentence in a natural language. However, even so, the "instruction list" at any level has not become particularly significantly long, i.e., the number of commands and instructions has not infinitely increased. This is because the number of commands or instructions that a programmer can memorize and skillfully use is really severely limited. This proves that the human brain's own "instruction list" is actually relatively simple. For these reasons, a distinction is usually not made between instructions and commands in the narrative of this book.

In this way, the actual computing processes of the computer are greatly complicated in comparison with the human brain. Any simple operation in the human brain may correspond to hundreds or thousands of operations on a computer. That is, in order to get to a place, the computer goes around a distance much farther than the human brain, until it folds back. One of the reasons for this is that the computer runs so fast that the economy it brings, after deducting the additional cost of it, still has a vast surplus. Of course, this is not always the case. Some other work performed by the human brain may not be economical if it is transferred to a computer (I will not go into detail about this for the time being). As a result, this relativity creates both a labor division and cooperation, in which humans hand over some work to computers while holding the rest for humans themselves. Meanwhile, given the rapid advancement of computer technology, the variety of jobs a computer can undertake for humans is still increasing.

The high speed of computers has also changed the structures and forms of human knowledge. By replacing some of the work done by humans, computers make the cuts in specific phases of human thinking procedures, greatly speeding them up. In order to take advantage of the speediness, people deliberately change their strategies of knowledge development, and deliberately develop knowledge that can be used on computers, so as to cooperate with computers.

§29. From Simple to Complex (3)

Since the birth of computers, various related software and hardware technologies have rapidly developed, and their performances have rapidly improved. This process not only demonstrates the outstanding advantages of the "evolutionism" of computers, but also serves as an example of how human knowledge generally evolves and develops.

Let's start with a little overview of the previous sections. Information can be complex or simple, and hence, it doesn't have to be represented by a fixed number of digits. Resultantly, information can be set to different types with different lengths and formats. It is exactly the development of computer science that highlights the important concept of "information types". It leads us to understand that the so-called "computation" is just the *transformation of information*—either between different pieces of information of the same type, or between different types of information, or from the sensory information (*raw information*) to knowledge (as a type of information, or *"knowledge information"*)—on the contrary, "executing a decision" means the transformation of knowledge information into sensory information. Therefore, computational activities can be seen as the activities of different parts of the human body *communicating* with each other. This communication necessarily requires a pluralistic view of the human body and the brain.

At the heart of this communication are the instructions. The juxtaposition of different types of instructions, such as information processing instructions, managerial or service instructions, and hardware control instructions, is in a comprehensive list, which vividly reflects that "computing" (or thinking activities) is a kind of "work". These different types of work have both their specific characteristics and commonalities. For example, they take up time and space, and they are all about dealing with information: some ship information, some change information, some copy information, and so on. The term "computing", as an umbrella term for these efforts, is highly effective for this conceptual synthesis. This kind of high efficiency cannot be denied by superficial criticisms of it, but can only be experienced after a deep understanding of how computers work. For example, the existence of hardware-controlling instructions as an "interface" between the center of the mind and the organs of physical work or movement has rich and significant symbolic significance. It symbolizes the juxtaposition between software and hardware, or between thoughts and the physical world as different types of entities, and the collaborative relationship between the upstream and downstream of human's continuous behaviors. These two types of relationships are ultimately iconoclastic because traditionally, they have been deemed on different levels of logic, reflecting or representing each other rather than *interacting on an equal footing.*

The implementation of the functions of instructions is similar to that of information, i.e., some instructions are physically implemented with specialized components (such as "adders"), while others are implemented on common or partly common circuitries, so as to improve the economy. The instructional types are very limited. One way to understanding these limitations is to recognize that the physical materials used for computers may be otherwise used to implement a wider variety of other "non-human instructions", but that this bigger possibility has to be "wasted" because the latter "instructions" do not belong to the human brain, and hence cannot be conceived, understood, or recognized by our human brains. This contrasting perspective allows us to further appreciate the *concreteness, specificity,* and *particularity* of the basic intelligence of human beings; that is, it would be one of the many existing or possible types of intelligence in the universe, which are neither so good nor so bad, neither complete nor ineffective. *It is precisely because of these natures that thinking or computation, and thus "algorithms", becomes a problem.* The human "algorithm" can roughly correspond to that of computers. In Chinese language, "algorithm" literally (and correctly) means "the computing method". Specifically, an algorithm is a method of processing information to solve a problem by using this immutable set of instructions; or, given that computation is serial, it refers to the order in which instructions and information, as well as instructions and instructions, are combined and/or arranged. According to the concept of combinatorial explosion introduced above, it can be known that the types of algorithms must be theoretically infinite, thus they can only be empirically summarized, and the summarized algorithms must often appear as some patterns, styles, or types for programmers to choose and use.

The evolutionism of computers is particularly evident in the storage of a program and its automatic execution. In the history of computers, the idea that the methods and steps of computation can be stored as data, read like data, and hence be automatically executed (i.e., the "stored program principle", and then the "Von Neumann Architecture", see Diagram 7) is deemed a great intellectual achievement. This reflects that a typical form of human knowledge is a fixed sequence of computational steps, or in other words, knowledge is a pattern, *a fixed route figured out in the sea of data*. In the terms above, knowledge is something that is sedimented, distorted, and solidified. This fixity can be a condition for the automatic execution. The automatic execution of programs arouses observers' imagination and makes them feel that computers have some characteristics like human thinking. This has given rise to a philosophical discussion about artificial intelligence.

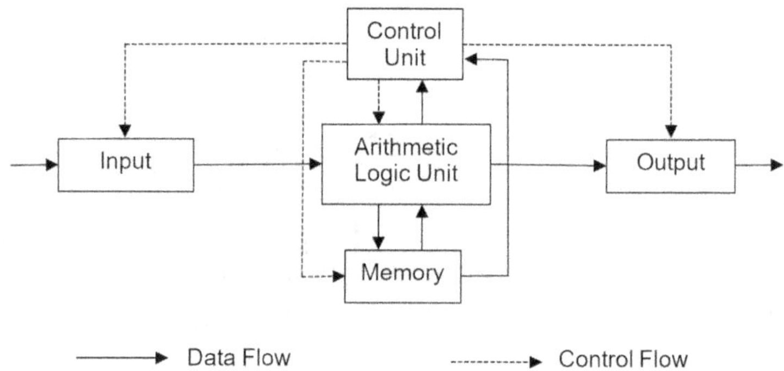

Diagram 7: Von Neumann Architecture

The Von Neumann Architecture in computer science is the roundabout production method of thought, that is, using the breadth of space and the length of time to establish an operating structure that includes memory, the stock of data as knowledge, and runs serially in time, so that the weak power of the meta-computation can afford to undertake huge tasks.

The infinite reproduction and automatic execution of programs liberate people from tedious and repetitive tasks, so that they can concentrate on the improvement of existing programs or the development of new programs, namely, the production of new knowledge. The resulting savings and efficiency gains are unprecedentedly enormous, and the rapid development of the computer industry is, therefore, incomparable to other traditional industries. Defects in those products in use, especially in software, can be improved quickly and cost-effectively through program upgrades. This feature prominently indicates the advantages of human knowledge over physical products: the renewal of physical products often entails discarding physical materials, which is not the case with knowledge that can be *directly* renewed. For example, if Jack does something wrong, and you remind him of something that he then accepts and remembers, then he is likely to do it right next time—because the old data in his brain have been directly "erased" and the new data has been written in it.

The similarity between computers and the human brain attracted widespread attentions in the early years of computer development when artificial intelligence engineering was also beginning. AI engineering has a history as long as computers. Early AI was overly optimistic. After a long period of twists and turns, AI experts generally recognized the importance of knowledge accumulation. This understanding is consistent with the inferences we have made earlier. The rapid development of artificial intelligence in recent years (well-known examples include computerized chess, music composing, writing, chatting, etc.) indicates that it has finally moved away from early deductivism and mastered techniques such as induction, association, and analogy. These achievements are based on methods about big data, probabilistic computation, heuristics, and repetitive self-objectification. This reflects the progress of software engineers' understanding of human thinking, i.e., as mentioned earlier, human knowledge is based on frequent self-objectifications, which in turn is based on the discreteness of mental activities.

Because, without this discreteness, there is no pause in computation and thinking, and thus no new thinking activity can start again with the (past) self. These repeated "self-entanglements", combined with "factor completeness" and the "forced closure of computation", form a special nonlinear structure of knowledge that expands outward layer by layer like an onion.

A direct in-depth discussion of AI would get bogged down in complex technical details, hence we have to hold back here. This section is limited to the following points: First, no matter how AI develops, it has not caused any significant changes in the above-mentioned infrastructure of computers. In other words, if it is considered that artificial intelligence has successfully simulated certain characteristics of human spiritual life, then our above preparations would be sufficient to endogenize these characteristics. Second, AI engineering has raised certain challenges to serial computing (such as connectionism applied to simulate neural networks), and the adoption of certain specialized modules or chips has enhanced the parallelism of computers. However, the expansion of parallelism was not at the same quantitative level as the extension of computations on the timeline; the latter is often measured in the amount of billions or trillions, hence the expansion is by no means sufficient to overturn the basic architecture of serial computing. Thirdly, AI engineers are mainly involved in the study of human thinking activities from their technical needs and details of computer simulation, but the study is only preliminary and fragmentary. In this direction alike, we will comprehensively expand, generalize, and systematize the thinking theory in this book.

§30. Single-Instruction Computer

From the perspective of exploring the basicity of instructions, we can ask: To what extent can the number of instructions be "basic"? This question is interesting and of great philosophical significance. Computer scientists have studied it, but the results came quite late. And, this research was not enriched and perfected until the twenty-first century. The general conclusion is that one instruction is enough! There are a number of specific technical solutions for this. Multiple instructions (some mutated addition or subtraction instructions), designed specially, are used to act selectively as this single instruction that indirectly and circuitously implements the functions of other instructions, so that any computational work that can be done by computers can theoretically be fulfilled. [5]

This research can help us understand that the basic workings of the brain may be fairly simple. Of course, this "simplicity" is from our point of view as the owners of such a mechanism. A "subject" who does not possess such a mechanism, if it can "see", may still see it as complicated. This confirms Thomas Hobbes's assertion 400 years ago that reasoning is just computations such as additions and subtractions! Under certain structural conditions (e.g., storage space) and resources (e.g., time), this simple mechanism selectively and cannily combines with one or more elements from its environments, and then transforms itself into the

---

5. Original materials on "one-instruction set computer" include Mavaddat, F.; Parhami, B. "URISC: The Ultimate Reduced Instruction Set Computer". International Journal of Electrical Engineering Education. October 1988, 25 (4): 327–334; And Gilreath, William F.; Laplante, Phillip A. "Computer Architecture: A Minimalist Perspective". Springer Science+Business Media. 2003; And Nürnberg, Peter J.; Wiil, Uffe K.; Hicks, David L., "A Grand Unified Theory for Structural Computing", in "Metainformatics: International Symposium, MIS 2003", Graz, Austria: Springer Science+Business Media: pp. 1–16, September 2003.

"different types" of computational tools, i.e., instructions, which then act on external information.

The relevant results are of great and profound enlightening significance for us to engage in philosophical synthesis. If the fundamental instruction can be seen as one, not many, then we have a much stronger reason to assert the unity of human knowledge and, thus, of philosophy. The possibility that human knowledge can be seen as the result of the interactions of a single element in the mind with other elements in the world will be in any case shocking to the general public. By directly or indirectly using these results, scholars in humanities and social science can also independently study the consistency between various basic thinking tools or thinking forms outside of computer science—in fact, this consistency has been quite apparent in many cases, as indicated in other sections of this book.

This achievement of computer science is also consistent with the development mechanism we expound in this book, that is, the entire computing mechanism composed of instructions, information, meta-computing, storage capability, and other elements, leading to the one-way and continuous development of computing results, and thus to the developmental phenomena of intelligence and civilization. In this mechanism, it can even be said to the extreme that no matter how many instructions there are, what they are, and whether their functions are powerful, as long as the human brain has an "innate concrete thing" similar to instructions, it is possible to produce something like human civilizations. When a "computor" can store those rudimentary computing results, namely, the results of interactions between the "innate concrete thing" and the representatives of external objects, i.e., information, and repeatedly compare and screen these results, he/she will gain continuous progress in wisdom. This principle is similar to the way people with color blindness perceive colors. The knowledge thus obtained is relative, and will not be utterly chaotic or ruleless, but will develop forward according to its own logic and specific manners. Although interactions between an ordinary object and other external objects can also produce different results, there is no development because it cannot produce and utilize existing knowledge. Comparing these two different mechanisms, we can learn the secret of thinking.

The above mechanism can also account for failures in development, since these conditions leading to development are not always met. For example, although the memory of the human brain can be formed, it may not be fully utilized by oneself or for interpersonal communication due to various reasons. Instead, it is gradually forgotten or destroyed with the death of the individual. External memorizing tools such as books and disks might not have been developed for a time, and communicative tools such as telegraphs, telephones, and the Internet might not have been developed, either. Or, because this computing mechanism took significant time and thus the computing speed could not keep up with the changing speed of specific objects, the knowledge developed finally became invalid because it was too late to be applied. Also, the use of certain knowledge is not always more economical than its production, which can lead an actor to produce the knowledge by oneself on the spot of problem-solving rather than to utilize, and thus improve, the existing knowledge, and so on. These theoretical situations are by no means irrelevant in historical practice, but should be necessary elements that we must not forget when interpreting history and reality. From these, we can see the weakness of this thinking mechanism.

However, this book still intends to set aside this discovery and continue our discussion along the assumption that multiple instructions coexist. The reason is, first of all, that it doesn't really matter whether it is a single instruction or multiple instructions for the goal of "Grand Synthesis". What we need is the series of characteristics of instructions, such as the finitude, interpersonal universality, etc. It would be enough for us if these conditions are met. After this single instruction processes data, it inevitably and irreversibly enters into the plurality and mixedness of knowledge. Even if the instruction is initially singular, it will become pluralistic when other structural elements are added, repeatedly, and then it will turn into other various instructions—or, as described in §28, it will advance into the commands in high-level languages. When we talk about instructions, we are not taking them as completely isolated, but in the context of the working architecture as defined by computer science. Even if the type or form of instruction is monistic, it comes to us *together with* other structural elements. And when this single instruction is transformed into other instructions, it has reached the stage of processing external information, and has, in many cases, gone through the complex processes of permutation and combination with other structural elements, and then is no longer the original itself. In the relevant research and arguments, the researchers were also committed to demonstrating that this instruction can be transformed into other instructions in the classic instruction list, rather than specifically demonstrating how a computational task assigned by the user can be completed merely with this single instruction. This is because, in the specific operation, this single-instruction method is extremely cumbersome, time-consuming, and hence has no practical significance. In other words, the single-instruction approach is extremely uneconomical, both for human calculators and for machines. Therefore, in a computer, each instruction is individually designed and implemented relatively independently. It is highly likely that the human brain will adopt a similar arrangement to speed up computations. Further, since the classical list of instructions was set by human scientists, it is likely that this list is the list of "instructions of the human brain", or the list of instructions that is "convenient for the human brain" (and also convenient for machines). The single instruction was discovered decades after the invention of computers, and has only been discussed as a theoretical topic. This fact also shows that computer inventors and scientists, as the "samples" of human beings, usually do not think in terms of a single instruction.

It is also important to emphasize that in this book, the synthesis of philosophy does not take place by reducing human knowledge to the mere "oneness". This reduction does not necessarily have to reach the point of "oneness". It would be satisfactory for the synthesis to reach a certain finite extent (Philosophy's obsession with "oneness" obviously connects with the singleness of a metacomputation). Besides, this philosophical synthesis is achieved especially by revealing the plurality, conflict, developmentality, and higher-order consistency of knowledge systems. The philosophical synthesis is not to forcibly "compress" human knowledge into a single thing, but to appropriately bridge and unify the contradictive philosophical theories about human knowledge. *As for the entire knowledge system, it is not even about compressing the big into the small, but decompressing the small, the forcibly compressed one (i.e. the "Being"), back to its original, infinitely growing one.*

In addition to the above-mentioned software approach, according to my review, there is also a hardware approach, which is used to explain that all the computer operations can reduce into those of a simple device (2 states + 3 symbols).[6] For the same reason, I put this finding on hold for the time being.

---

6. See https://www.wolframscience.com/prizes/tm23/ and Alex Smith, "Universality of Wolfram's 2, 3 Turing Machine". Complex Systems. 29 (1): 1–44, 2020. Thanks to the anonymous friend who recommended it to me.

Another advantage of these suspensions is that they providently and conservatively constitute a strategic concession to the opinions opposing Algorithmic Thinking Theory. If readers could accept the synthesis under many Instructions, the synthesis under a single Instruction would be more acceptable to them. Therefore, the suspensions are potentially strengthening the argumentation of this book, not weakening it.

Thus, let's move on along the line of the original arrangement.

§31. Why Computers Can Be Originally "Alive" (1)

On the basis of the above overview and interpretation of computer principles and its developmental processes, we will now turn to a specific discussion. One of the core points that I'd like to express is *that the above-mentioned mechanisms of computers are basically enough to simulate human mental activities, although computer experts have not moved towards artificial intelligence from the beginning, but have focused on making computers as human helpers that make up for the shortcomings of human thinking, and cooperate with humans.* This attempt prevents scholars from deriving the most important philosophical perspectives from computers, that is, building the theory of human minds with instructions at its core.

Computers were developed to perform complex mathematical calculations instead of laborious manual operations, such as calculating ballistic data needed in warfare. This is where electronics come into play in terms of speed and precision. Not only are the operations done accurately by computers, but the huge number of data stocks are easily and quickly copied, transmitted, and reprocessed. It is from here that this "miracle" was first created. Later, it developed into text and multimedia processing, and its revolutionary consequences continued. However, the shock effect has occurred in recent years with the leap forward in artificial intelligence, which has seen the emergence of a momentum for computers to replace general human mental activities including those that are often considered subjective and "noble", which has discouraged critical and picky AI observers. It is indeed necessary to rethink the nature of human mental activity.

At the beginning of this century, when the Algorithmic Thinking Theory was first proposed, AI engineering actually did not make these leaps. At that time, I believed that if we carefully analyzed the basic steps of human thinking movements, we would understand that it should not be difficult for computers to complete these steps; or, even if there are difficulties temporarily, it is possible to overcome them in the future; or, because these basic steps are so simple and straightforward, it would be highly believable that they can universally be accomplished by the human brain, and that they can simultaneously be accomplished in a binary way of "instruction + information"—thus the Algorithmic Thinking Theory can be established. Of course, my understanding at that time was not accurate everywhere. Fortunately, recent achievements in AI not only confirm these vague judgments, but also provide powerful additions and support in detail. Now, let's combine these old and new understandings and present them briefly.

In order to be more human-like, the first thing that computers can do but don't do is, in my opinion, the change of topics, or the "leapfrog thinking". Traditional computers only passively and honestly answer users' questions, *but do not actively compete for the initiative of discourse.* For example, when a user asks "2 + 3 = ?", instead of answering 5 directly, the computer goes round the bend and says to the user "the weather is nice today", etc., and waits for a while before telling him that the answer is "5"; or, the computer gives the answer 6, adding a 1 to any correct answer for any arithmetic question; or, it refuses to answer, talk about something irrelevant. Is it possible to do this? Of course, it is because *any relationship between the data in the computer and the result is artificially created.* One can either look for similar mechanisms in nature, or make corresponding physical mechanisms, or use software programming methods to achieve it. The problem is just that in the traditional approach, this is not necessary, and hence programmers don't write programs this way.

The change of topics involves the assessment of the situation of a dialogue among humans, as we mentioned in the "Algorithmic Logic" section above. In real dialogues, this assessment is common, because there is a hidden or neglected "Algorithmic logic" that treats the other person's question as an "act" and then can possibly delay it, reject it, avoid it, divert it, and so on. Of course, this kind of assessment of the dialogue situation requires relevant knowledge storage, and this storage was initially thought to be easy to obtain; but later, with the repeated failures of artificial intelligence engineering, researchers learned that it is extremely large in its variety and amount, and it is by no means available overnight.[7]

Related to the above topic change is the problem of proactive computing. This means that in the free time of a computer, it proactively initiates computing activities without a human request. Then, are computers actually capable of doing this? Yes, of course! For example, you can set the computer to

---

7. For a vivid and interesting example, see Daniel C. Dennett, "Cognitive Wheels: The Frame Problem of AI", in Margaret A. Boden (ed.), "The Philosophy of Artificial Intelligence", Oxford University Press, 1990, pp. 198-199. For a well-known historical report on this issue, see James Lighthill, "Artificial Intelligence: A General Survey" at http://www.chilton-computing.org.uk/inf/ literature/reports/lighthill_report/p001.htm, which focuses on the problems caused by combinatorial explosion to the development of artificial intelligence.

start "free operations" at a point in time, and the rules can include: to randomly select data from a certain location on the hard disk, to perform some kinds of computations on the data with the data from other locations, and so on. This is similar to a free reverie or imagination of a real person in his/her spare time. The problem is that these random operations are so less possible to produce valuable answers to a problem in question that it is likely to make a mess of the data in the computer, or even lead to huge, horrific damages; hence, it has traditionally *been deliberately forbidden by programmers*; instead, programmers set the computer, when idle, to wait only for the instructions from users. It is just this artificial setting that gives observers the illusion that computers cannot perform proactively. However, what is more important to ask is: Isn't this exactly what human thinking is? Isn't it all in vain that we usually engage in a great deal of nonsense? What is the essential difference between this kind of nonsense and the kind of "nonsense" that computers may carry out, except for the fact that human thinkers usually have a wealthier knowledge than computers in some aspects (and probably not so wealthy in other aspects)? These questions lead us to look back at ourselves, to recognize the true natures of human thinking, and to ask: Do we really want computers to be like ourselves? Are there really any benefits in that randomness and mess? The problem may be not just whether computers can do it, but whether we want computers to do it completely!

The word "initiative" is worth a closer look. Exceeding the expectations of the other party and taking the lead in changing the topics is a kind of initiative. "Intervening" in the other party rather than being submissive to it is another initiative. The latter, in particular, requires computers to have intelligence *equivalent* to that of humans. This equivalence does not necessarily require that the two be exactly equal, or perfectly matchable, in every aspect of intelligence; they can also be somehow different from each other, that is, one be better than the other in this aspect while the other be better than this one in that aspect, and so on. The running speed of a computer that is significantly higher than that of humans in traditional calculative fields, and the knowledge accumulations that have rapidly gone forward on computers, provide the basis and potential for computers to match humans generally or specifically.

More importantly, initiative demands the existence of some kind of "free will", or, making a human observer feel that the computer has "free will". In this respect, computer principles provide a clear explanation of freedom: freedom is the freedom to permutate or combine instructions within the scope of the repertoire, or the freedom to permutate or combine instructions and information (the freedom of physical action can be covered by this proposition because it just executes the outcome of thinking or computations). This freedom may seem small, but in fact, they have a lot of potential. Second, random number generators, random functions, random algorithms, and so on can provide another foundation for freedom. However, a more fundamental argument that has been overlooked is that "freedom" means, first and foremost, moving out of the orbit of traditional, "mechanical" deductive computation into the realms of topic conversion, indeterminate reasoning, etc. In other words, *freedom refers to the subjective turn of thinking or computations, or the "mental distortions"*. From this point of view, we can once again discover the grotesqueness and contradictions in the ideal of AI: when the computer performs correct deductive reasoning, we humans despise it, saying that it is "mechanical" and must be "freed" again, but what does "freedom" mean? I am afraid that it only means those "not so correct" computations! Is this what we humans desire really? We ourselves desire it, and we also demand it from our shadow, the computer.

§32. Why Computers Can Be Originally "Alive" (2)

By looking at and contrasting the physical world, when we say that we humans ourselves are "alive", we are indeed expressing something specific. It can be said that it is the existence of these specific meanings that makes people generally believe that human society has its different properties from the natural world, and that social science also has its different properties from natural science. These properties include, at a minimum, initiative, autonomy, reciprocity, adversariality, irregularity, unpredictability, variability, and so on. However, in the context of computer science, we can carefully figure out and interpret the specific connotations of these properties, as well as the computational steps they require. At this point, we will find that they are not particularly confusing, but can be simple and straightforward.

For example, as mentioned earlier, "initiative" (or "proactiveness") means rejecting other people's questions and searching for or creating them yourself. A "computational subject" (whether a human or a computer) may not, in his/her spare time, pick up on the previous job, but search in his/her own database and weigh what is worth doing now. Objectively, it is the suspension of the previous behavioral flow and the initiation of a new flow of behavior. Then, how do we determine that one behavior flow is "suspended" and another is "initiated"? Obviously, this involves the relationships between different behavioral steps and thus different thoughts. *These relationships must have distinctions such as "present" and "absent", "distant" and "near", "loose" and "tight", etc. That says, we must acknowledge that these relationships are "soft".* Then, we must come to the pluralistic and mixed Algorithmic environment where these soft relationships can not only appear objectively, but also subjectively. This can be the hotbed for "positive-passive" discourses. On the surface, this problem seems to be just a dynamic problem, but in fact, it is closely related to other philosophical problems, such as subjectivity and plurality; if these problems cannot be solved, the dynamic problem cannot be solved, either. *This is the secret that dynamic theory has failed to achieve since ancient times.*

Another example is the issue of "autonomy". Autonomy is obviously associated with initiative. More importantly, it is related to the issue of factor completeness. That is, the computational subject has the right to reassign values to the decision-making matters oneself, regardless of whether other computational subjects have already assigned them. In the vernacular, it is that one does not trust others, willing to recount something on one's own. Hence, autonomy is also about independently setting variables and issues, but it's slightly different from the independence that initiative requires.

These all involve the issue of "leapfrog thinking" mentioned in the previous section. Computations can be divided into two categories; one is, within an instruction, how to "jump" from the data to be processed to the result. This is solved at the stage of the design of instructions, i.e. the computer manufacturing stage. The other is how the instructions are connected. *The basic mechanism of instructional connection is actually time.* After one instruction is executed, time moves forward (the instruction counter automatically adds 1), and it naturally needs to execute the next instruction. Thus, *time becomes a natural, fundamental driving force* that "connects" the different tasks. Of course, this "connection" is only superficial, and it does not guarantee that there must be a close logical relationship between the two steps. A tight logical relationship can be given only by a specific instruction, which artificially provides the address of the next instruction in its expression, and the expression was written originally by a programmer. Under this structured, pipelined arrangement, computations consecutively jump from raw information to results, from some data to others, and from some instructions to other ones. Deductive reasoning, mathematical operations can all be thought of as the "jumps", that is, going from some positions to others, or from some steps to others. This perspective again gives us a unified view of computing activity, regardless of whether the "jumps" connect data to results or tasks to tasks. This leads to a re-understanding of "logic", i.e., *the role of "logic" is to jump, from here to there, from this to that. It guides the computation forward in time.* Conversely, *what can achieve this effect can be called "logic".* It is like a rope, connecting many knots into a chain. Therefore, a fact in the academic community is that computer science has contributed to the prosperity of logic. Logic once gave birth to computers, and now logic itself has been developed because of computers. The variety of logic has increased, and the research methods have accordingly become refined.

Deductive reasoning and mathematical operations are primarily deterministic reasoning, whereas the "jump" (or "leapfrog thinking") can refer to "indeterminate reasoning", or "uncertain reasoning". Is a computer on earth capable of uncertain reasoning? An answer of "yes" has been given by the fact. Now, let's try to understand its details.

"Uncertain reasoning" is a kind of reasoning that is "neither too good nor too bad". Since computers can make both correct and wrong reasoning, it should not be challenging to make reasoning in between. Both good and bad logic exist in the human mind, and the problem is only to simulate and implement them with the help of some computing mechanism. As long as such a mechanism is found out, AI will gain success. Nonetheless, if you can't find a physical mechanism that directly corresponds to them for the time being, maybe you can achieve the goal with a combination of instructions. In the previous example, to get 2 + 3 = 6, we can use a programmatic approach to add 1 to the result in 2 + 3 = 5.

Let's take a look at the specific steps of leapfrog thinking, or "uncertain reasoning". The relevant functions that need to be implemented include usually association, induction, abstraction, analogy, learning, and so on. This requires us to disassemble these "thinking activities" and then see if we can realize them stepwisely. The original meaning of association is to target one object and associate it with other objects. It can be seen that the function of association is to find objects that are related, or to find relationships between objects. Then, why are there relationships between objects? because they are all featured, and these features may be similar, identical, congruent, opposite, and so on. Therefore, this inspires us to store not only information about an object, but also information about the characteristics of the object. Classical computers initially only stored information about objects without attaching their characteristics to themselves, making it difficult to associate. Storing both the information of an object and its characteristic values is a lot of work, but it's a must-do. If you think about it, that's actually how the human brain works. There is no mystery here. For example, today I meet Tom, an American, I immediately think of Mike, because Mike is also an American, and when I first met Mike, I already remembered the data "he is an American". Not only did I remember this information, but I probably remembered a lot about Mike at that time. A relatively high percentage of these pieces of information may not be useful in the future, but the human brain does remember them and leaves them in a state of "waiting to be used". It's literally acceptable to say this is a "waste", but that's really how the human brain works. Through the microscopic analysis aroused by computer simulation, we now have come to understand the real working mechanism of the human brain.

This question needs to be said again in reverse. Computers that used to process highly simple and abstract information, such as 1, 2, 3, or a, b, and c, now turn to process information from the two people, Tom and Mike. In the case of 1, 2, 3, or a, b, and c, because the data are so simple, the relationships between them are so simple, and there is little need for an associative job. And what do we mean when we say "association"? First, it's obviously aimed at objects that are rich in information (such as physical objects in the real world). These objects are so rich in information that *different* observers often inevitably understand and analyze them from *different* angles or dimensions. The differences between the observer's associative abilities often come from their abilities to dig into the features of the object, especially those implicit features. The second is to search in one's own memory bank based on the characteristic information that has been found and highlighted. It is generally the case that the other objects searched are not identical, or congruent, or exactly opposite, but "softly" irregularly different in between. The data are massive, and the search time can be long or short, which inevitably raises the problem of search strategy. *For those who can search at an infinite speed, they don't need to think about strategy;* instead, they can just go through the entire database. But there is actually no such a person. Search is also a kind of computation and necessarily has a speed limit. You can search for objects based on specific features, or you can compare their features one by one within a specific range of objects. They are strategic choices. Different strategies lead to different productivities. People with strong associative skills tend to use their search strategies appropriately and can make important discoveries in a relatively short period of time.

The above analysis also shows how "association" becomes a theoretical problem: in the reality of finite computing speed, big data are a factor, extensive individual differences are a factor, and the "soft differences" of small quantitative differences mixed with small qualitative differences are also a factor—these frequent and intensive soft differences make it analytically uneconomical to set a variable respectively for each qualitative difference. In a nut shell, this leads to significant heterogeneity or mixedness in the database, and ambiguity or vagueness in its analysis and generalization.

§33. Why Computers Can Be Originally "Alive" (3)

Now, look at induction. Induction is an important kind of "uncertain reasoning". It usually does not refer to a "complete induction", as the latter is equivalent to a deduction. Induction mainly refers to incomplete induction, and a typical inductive method, based on some incomplete samples, leads to a general, uncertain conclusion that can cover more cases, or even an infinitely large number of cases beyond these incomplete samples. In this sense, induction is a method of guessing and formulating hypotheses, the conclusions of which are yet to be tested. The process of induction of the finite samples is similar to association, which is to find a few meaningful features in the rich features of objects. However, what is meaningful? Sometimes, this needs to be defined by the user, and sometimes, it needs to be explored based on other empirical data. Therefore, early computerized inductive models often failed as they couldn't identify features that were really meaningful to users. But the models can be improved gradually. Association can be developed for a single object, while induction must be to find a common ground in certain characteristics of multiple objects. The search and the comparative processes produce a conclusion that covers these limited samples first; then, a logical leap happens, which is to remove the sample-specific constraints in this conclusive proposition, especially to remove its quantifiers and make it general. For example, it first draws the conclusion that "Zhang San, Li Si, and Wang Wu all like tomatoes", and then modifies this conclusion to a conclusion such as "Chinese love tomatoes"—this conclusion is likely to be applied to other Chinese in the subsequent computations than Zhang San, etc. The process of reaching the general conclusion is actually a process of formulating new hypotheses, which is resulted from the "free will". That is, the computer is set to arbitrarily assign a value to a variable although the resultant hypothesis is not completely, but only partially arbitrary, thanks to its basis of the previous empirical conclusion. There is a basis, but it is not sufficient.

This process often leads to an "abstraction". Abstraction is not only the generalization of common features of some samples, but also the neglect of other particular features. In this way, the abstracted object is virtual, and its content is relatively simple, which then is relatively easy for subsequent deduction or processing. The neglected other features have not been deleted entirely, but are left blank as variables subject to determination in other specific contexts. It's like we delete the contents of a table, but leave the table itself empty. These empty spaces suggest that there will also be contents that can be contingently filled in the right places. A content that is to be filled in is called the "particular". For example, horses can have many colors, so the "color" column is left blank in the abstract concept of "horse". Although it is blank, it reminds the reader that horses are generally colored—or that a horse without color cannot be a horse.

What does analogy mean? Obviously, it refers to extending or changing some variables of an object in an abstracted proposition so that it can be applied, tentatively, to other kinds of objects that are not identical but are similar or closely related to the object (notice that we are "Algorithmically" illustrating the topic of "close" or "distant" relations). For example, if we change the "Chinese" in "Chinese love tomatoes" to "Americans", then the proposition becomes "American love tomatoes".

In the context of AI, a typical "learning" process refers to learning from historical experiences and then adjusting the subsequent computations (e.g., the "heuristics" based on Bayesian laws). For computational data generated in the past, the first step is to use methods such as data regression (as an inductive method) to try to discover the reasons for a success or failure of a past decision. Because the data size is generally large and complex, and the paths for induction are almost infinitely many, what to do? This in turn requires some clues, strategies, or knowledge to select or exclude certain inductive paths. The logical relationships between variables are sometimes highly hierarchical or structured, which requires a second-order induction of a series of inductive results after the first round of induction, and then a third-order, fourth-order, and so on. This serial approach leads to slower speeds of operation. Sometimes, there is very little data involved in the inductions whereas many orders are needed. This can result in a costly job for programmers: the program must be complex in structure, and lengthy, but merely processing a few data, and the conclusions are unreliable, etc. What to do with it? An AI approach introduces methods that include probability and statistics (such as the "Bayesian Algorithm") to improve performance. Generations of programmers in many fields have collaborated with each other to relay the processes to form a dedicated program package, and even develop into a dedicated chip, and so on. In the famous chess game played by AlphaGo, the robot studied the games against a real player overnight to find out strategies for the battles the next day. It is reported that it studied millions of times every night during game days to practice such methods as learning and experimenting. These methods might be somehow clumsy, but they took advantage of the speediness and low cost of electronic computers to make up for the clumsiness.

The above brief discussion is not just for machines. Our purpose is primarily to analyze the human mind. The machine simulating the human mind reflects human minds. Isn't it through this process of accumulation that human intelligence develops? Our knowledge of the real world is not only diverse, pluralistic, and fragmented, but also highly structured, and very irregular. This is what practical and useful knowledge really looks like. It can be said that one of the major philosophical contributions of AI engineering is to enlighten us, in this very detailed and powerful way, the true faces of knowledge in our own minds. This understanding is highly consistent with the Algorithmic inferences we have already developed earlier.

This understanding also explains why AI engineering has historically been slow to progress: the reason was obviously not that the computer's infrastructure is inadequate, but that its software engineering needs to undergo historical evolution, data needs to be accumulated, and computational results need to be improved to a more satisfactory level comparable to that of a human being. The hallmark of success in AI engineering shall be not just to prove to the audience that it is capable of those uncertain reasoning, but to prove that it is capable of deriving conclusions that can challenge the current thoughts of real people. It's going to take time. Our human knowledge has evolved over a long period of history, hence why was it necessary for computers to re-evolve all of them at once just at the beginning of the construction of their basic architecture? *Computers cannot have the current human thoughts all at once, and computers have suffered these or those failures, which just shows that computers probably resemble human beings much in terms of the basic structures, doesn't it?* Therefore, from this point of view, the historical process of AI is completely normal and necessary.

However, the same perspective can logically lead to the astonishing conclusion that AI will not always lag behind human minds; and, now that the right way to knowledge evolvement has seemingly been found, together with the refinements and progresses that will continue to be made in details, AI is likely to surpass human intelligence in the future (even if it is under human control). That's because the electronics are just so fast.

§34. Why Computers Can Be Originally "Alive" (4)

The above argument about the evolution of AI implies that for a computer to be more human-like, it must be able to "get things done" and not just make unreliable reasoning. Let's look at a boss in an enterprise. To get things done, he must hire people to work, not just use machinery and equipment. This is not only because of the human employees' flexibility in work, but also because the employees can replace the boss and think "automatically" *like the boss* to fulfill those complex and important tasks. *In the eyes of the boss*, human employees have a higher degree of "automation" than machines (this comparison is not intended to relegate human labor).

In other words, for a computer to "convince" an observer to equate it with a human, it should be able to compete with the observer in intellectual achievements. It shall not only make the observer "dare not" belittle it, even arousing a sense of awe, but also make the observer feel that he/she can get help from it, rely on it, use it, and "cooperate" with it. The mathematical abilities of a computer have far surpassed those of human beings, but this is not enough to convince observers, because the more mathematical operations are carried out by computers, the more observers regard the computers as "mechanical" and dull, and hence despise computers even more, as if a computer were a dumb pet. Computers must be contingently selective in navigating between multiple, heterogeneous, fragmented, or highly structured issues, and at least be able to draw conclusions with a level of common sense. Only such a computer is likely to pass the "Turing test"[8].

Literally, anything that people use has the meaning of "automation". For example, after sowing seeds, crops grow "automatically" in the land until they are harvested for human consumption. The role of food is to combine nutrients and calories, and then "automatically" bring them to the body in a way that the body can accept. The function of books is to record knowledge, silently "wait" for readers to visit it, and then "automatically" display the knowledge as text, and so on. Once we replace the subject of a sentence with the object targeted by the subject person, the narrative would probably have an "automated" effect. Traditionally, this is a rhetorical device of "anthropomorphism", but it also reflects a philosophical perspective that tries to see objects as living people. This approach can be used to explore the nature of life and people.

What circumstances under which can the word "automation" be used to describe the changes of an ordinary object in motion? The answer is obvious: when the changes of the object in motion resemble or are understood as the work of a person. What circumstances under which automation makes an observer feel more "alive"? The answer includes, at least, that it has many "turns" in the topic or logical process, thus it looks similar to the manner, depth, and frequency of the turns of ordinary human thinking. For example, a dog can, at its owner's signal, pounce on a "bad guy" who tries to hurt its

---

8. Turing Test uses an anonymous real person to chat with an AI agent, and then lets the person judge if or not he/she has been talking with a real person, and in this way it judges the success or failure of this AI project. For a further explanation of Turing Test, see David Schafer, "Turing Test", in Philip L. Frana et al. (ed.), "Encyclopedia of Artificial Intelligence: The Past, Present, and Future of AI", Santa Barbara, California: ABC-CLIO, 2021, pp. 329-331.

owner, which is a useful "automaticity" for dogs. After completing the task, an average dog may return to its owner, either to ask for a reward or to rest and be on standby. However, if there is a dog that, after completing this task, turns back and complains that its owner should not have misbehaved to provoke a conflict with that bad guy, and then it asks its master to go to work, and "by the way" talks about the upcoming dinner...And all that. Isn't such a "dog" just a living "parent"? Although it is a little scary, it can certainly be regarded as "alive". However, in fact, it is just an addition to the behaviors of ordinary dogs. In computers, these actions of the "dog" (of course, the simulated "dog") can be set separately, such as prompting the owner to reflect on his own behavior under what circumstances, scheduling the agenda for the owner, and discussing dinner in advance. If you agree with this, then, since they can be set up separately, they can also be combined into a single behavioral series. Or, under certain general behavioral mechanisms, the dog as a computational agent may exhibit such a specific sequence of behaviors one day—and exhibit other sequences of behaviors at other times. The sequence of behaviors is certainly to vary from day to day. Moreover, there seems to be no other deep meaning to be explored here.

My views on AI can now be summarized, that is: compared with traditional computers, the computing subject (or agent) under AI engineering needs to *expand horizontally in topics* and *jump frequently in logic*. At the same time, it also needs to *evolve to a certain level in the depth of decision-making*, and the combination of these three aspects is likely to make an AI project successful. Traditional computers place too much emphasis on the programming of computing operations—or rather, traditional programs are written too straight and monotonous. It's like a car that could have been able to move relatively freely in an open field, but was forcibly installed with a track so that it could only travel along the fixed route. The goal of early developers was clearly to make computing more efficient so that it could quickly produce results that would benefit human users. However, as a result, the working surface of the computer has been narrowed, which led to another kind of loss. As will be shown in the following discussion of human knowledge development strategies, the arguments in the AI field are quite similar to those for human knowledge development, namely, the distinctions between science and common sense.[9]

Henceforth, to what extent can the three aspects—horizontal expansion, logical jumping, and knowledge evolution—be able to pass those many AI tests, including the Turing test? The answer obviously depends in part on the knowledge and ability of the real testers.

This exposes the problem of the limitations of the ideal of AI. Strictly speaking, the criteria for judging AI are relative, individualized, and even changeable. In principle, the level of intelligence of the computing agent can be neither lower nor higher than that of a human. Computational agents that are lower than people will be looked down upon, and computational agents who are higher than people may not be understood. Therefore, the comparative results of specific answers in the test are inevitably diverse and even conflictive. This is a significant systemic situation. Under the condition that the combinatorial explosions cause the infinite potential for knowledge development, such a discussion can be indispensable and very meaningful.

---

9. For this reason, the introduction of computer principles in this book basically ignores the problem of "Turing completeness", because the latter deals mainly with the applicability of computers to general mathematical computations. Research along this direction, with the tone of perfection and mystery of extreme rationalism, can therefore be said to be misleading. Until denying that this ideal can be generally realized, we cannot enter into the true and realistic thinking and then Algorithmic Thinking Theory.

The ideal of artificial intelligence is at least superficially self-contradictory in some aspects. For example, from deterministic to indeterministic reasoning, the level of intelligence of a computer has decreased, at least on the surface, and the reliability of the results has deteriorated. On this basis, it again requires improving the resultant quality and reliability. Programming and automation are seen as highly intelligent in some cases, and rigid and low-intelligent in others.

Of course, in the context of infinite possibilities, intelligence is historical and specific, despite any certain level of intelligence. Although there are enormous differences in details between any versions of an intelligent system, they can, in fact, all be subordinated to a unified theory. This theory is the Algorithmic Thinking Theory that we are about to formally introduce. ATT was generated in the interactive observations of human thinking, computers, and AI engineering, thus it can be applied again to AI as a reference by relevant researchers. This book focuses only on its application to philosophy, humanities, and social sciences. Now, it is necessary to turn back to the theme of the book.

§35. Algorithmic Thinking Theory: the standard edition

The applicative achievements of computer science and artificial intelligence engineering constitute a strong pieces of evidence, and the prospects inferred in the first two chapters can be deeply appealing and relatively fresh. These two forces, as the forces of push and pull, lead us to the place of "ATT". In the face of the tides of the information technology revolution, humanities and social sciences can no longer fail to take actions and respond. Nor should the responses be superficial. We need to step back and go to the original root for a fundamental reconstruction. In view of the fact that the old and new logic are essentially connected, it is reasonable to speculate that if humanistic and social sciences scholars do not act, computer and AI scholars may one day act on their own and enter the field of humanities and social sciences in a big way, to achieve the great integration of knowledge systems. The signs of this trend are actually emerging from many points at present. As for some of the imperfections and doubts in AI engineering right now, we can deliberately take some supplementary measures to address them. The thinking theory we are going to propose is for humans only, and we ourselves are humans, then *our work is actually easier than that of AI.*

Thus, it is now assumed as follows: there are a limited number of Instructions innately in the human brain; they are universally owned by everybody; the function of each Instruction is specific and constant all the time; these Instructions in principle include all computer Instructions (with a few exceptions); the rest of Instructions, not available in a computer but assumed running in the same way as computer Instructions, are called "Manual Instructions"; a human uses these Instructions serially, selectively, repeatedly, and roundaboutly to process information from the outside world, to think; at a specific moment, only one Instruction can be run in the brain; an Instruction can in principle process no more than two data at a time and produce no more than one result, thus Instructions are executed one after another in time; the number of computing operations in a unit time, and hence the operational speed, is limited, therefore, a certain number of computations take a certain period of time.

To express it in a formula, it is:

Thinking = Computation = (Instruction + Information) × Speed × Time

Here, the assumption of Manual Instructions is the major "supplementary measure" we propose. Meanwhile, according to §19, auxiliarily, we assume that there is innately the "hard software" (or "firmware", "genetic knowledge", or "hard knowledge") in the human brain (or in the body, according to the theory of "embodied intelligence"[10]), including desires, instincts, sentiments, emotions, impulses, etc., which keeps unchanging during one's lifetime and works in the way similar to knowledge stocks. Considering the different needs of theoretical analysis or practical application, hard software in a human body can be flexibly assumed to have or not have interpersonal differences, certain contents of the Instruction list can be flexibly assumed, interpersonal differences and intertemporal changes in computing speed can be flexibly assumed, and the forgetfulness of certain pieces of stocked knowledge can be flexibly assumed.

According to the above assumptions, a human thinking process can be described as follows: the original pieces of information enter the brain through the sensory organs (under the "instruction" of data-transmission Instructions), to be stored temporarily, and then are processed by data processing Instructions, in a certain order; the processing order and methods are determined either with the guidance of certain invoked knowledge stocks, or determined at discretion, or randomly; the results of processing are either regarded as "knowledge" to be stored, or discarded; the stored knowledge may be fragmented, or a combination of data and their relationships (as other data), or a sequence of Instructions (with or without data filled), i.e. a "program"; they are occasionally re-used or updated, or gradually forgotten, or reinforced again in recollection from memory; hard software work in interaction with these ordinary knowledge; when the result of a

---

10. For an introduction to "embodiment", see Lawrence A. Shapiro, "Embodied Cognition" in Eric Margolis et al. (ed.), "Oxford Handbook of Philosophy of Cognitive Science", Oxford University Press, 2012, pp. 118-146.

computation is a decision about an external action, hardware-controlling Instructions are activated to control the relevant organs of the human body to physically execute the decision; "language" is a means of information exchange between different individuals, which is composed of some *physicalized* sounds and graphics, and stipulated through interpersonal conventions and works as part of the communicational system, a subsystem (the role as that in a computer) of the thinking system.

Next, I will equate thinking activities with computations in this book, and alternately and freely use these words alike. The way in which a metacomputation is made and different metacomputations are connected to form a program to work, is called "Algorithm", which indicates what Instructions are combined with what information, in what order or manner different Instructions are combined, and so on. In short, it is equivalent to what is commonly referred to as "thinking method", but is especially used in the context of computer science and then in the context of Algorithmic Thinking Theory, hence it could be deemed another "old wine in a new bottle", besides Instruction. In particular, "Algorithms" in the narrow sense refer to imperfect and subjective Algorithms, i.e., the "Alternative Algorithms" (or the ones for uncertain reasoning, more on this later). As this narrow usage has become common in the popular vocabulary, it is now necessary to expand it into academic literature. In cases where the list of Instructions has been determined, Algorithms shall be the key to the formation of one's intelligence. Therefore, the above theory is called the "Algorithmic Thinking Theory" (ATT), "Algorithm Framework Theory", "Algorithmic Theory", or "Algorithmic Framework". The word "framework" is sometimes used to emphasize that the theory is proposed to serve other applied purposes, and that it is only a foundational assumption in itself. It mainly proves its acceptability by explaining phenomena and answering questions in its application, rather than providing direct evidence to prove itself. The first letters in "Instruction", "Algorithm", or other relevant terms are capitalized to indicate that they are for human rather than a computer, but they are used similarly to their counterparts in computer science. In this sense, when we mention a specific Algorithm of human, we often or sometimes capitalize its first letter.

Corresponding to the above terminology, a person who adopts such a way of thinking as described by ATT, is called an "Algorithmic Person". When a real actor in the real world is understood as an Algorithmic person, the world is then called the "Algorithmic World". The methods derived from ATT and used in the research of philosophy, humanities, and social sciences, are collectively or individually referred to as the "Algorithmic Methods" or the "Algorithmic Approach". The series of fundamental corollaries derived from ATT, together with ATT itself, are collectively referred to as the "Algorithmic Principles". The word "Algorithmic" or "Algorithmical" can mean "of Algorithm", "of ATT", "of Algorithmic People", "of the Algorithmic world", "of the Algorithmic approach", "of the Algorithmic principle(s)", and even "of the Algorithmical style", depending on the context. In respect of the limited operational speed, sometimes we call it the "finite thinking (or computing) power", or "thinking (or computing) power".

§36. Algorithmic Thinking Theory: the manual and anonymous versions

The definition of Instruction is very strict and clear in computers, but in practice, as mentioned earlier, the variety of Instructions or Commands can increase dramatically because the permutation or combination of specific Instructions can form the Commands in a high-level language. The connotations of Commands have been gradually moving closer to natural languages, which is then convenient for programmers to memorize and use. Of course, not all permutations that can be formed with Instructions will be really formed and defined as a Command; only those permutations that are close to the meanings of natural words, or those frequently used permutations, or those permutations that are computationally effective will be defined as Commands. That is to say, in the process of using the computer, on the one hand, new Commands have been added, and on the other hand, existing Commands have been streamlined, simplified, or eliminated, so as to keep the Instruction List or Command List concise and efficient.

The same can be applied to the concept of "Algorithm". According to the definition of Algorithm in the previous section, a specific Algorithm is relative to a certain list of Instructions. Once the list of Instructions or Commands is determined, the mode, pattern, or style of permutation and combination of these Instructions or Commands can then be called an Algorithm. This is a relatively strict way of definition. However, it is implicit in this way that certain computational operations may be referred to as Instructions in one context and Algorithms in another. Another ambiguity is that because Algorithms often refer to those abstract and somewhat vague and flexible computing methods, and the internal structures of different programs formed by a particular Algorithm can be different, then Algorithms can also be discussed in isolation from specific lists of Instructions or Commands. Since most of the types of Algorithms commonly used in computers are highly technical, we will not go into detail here.

These discussions can all be linked to the concept of "Manual Instructions" (or in another name, the "Artificial Instructions"). This concept has been discussed implicitly, although it is rarely explicitly mentioned in the previous article. This is what we keep talking about as the "thinking tools". Based on the successful stories of computers and AI, we now have reasons to attribute most of the "thinking tools" to computer Instructions. However, the reasons may not be sufficient. AI is still not sufficiently mature to fully reach the level of the human brain. In academia, there is a strong opposition that tends to criticize and deny AI. These opponents argue that the human brain has unique functions that are ultimately difficult for computers to imitate. The important progress made in AI in recent years was clearly not in favor of the oppositions. However, the opposing opinions need to be taken into account and embodied in Algorithmic Theory as a theory of mind. For this consideration, I first put forward the concept of Manual Instruction in the first Algorithmical book as a preventive and backup concept: Since you think that some functions of the human brain cannot be imitated by computers, is it okay to name them "manual Instructions"? No matter what these functions are and how many of them there are, can they be enumerated? As long as you can list them, we will all accept them as manual Instructions; is it okay? In case these "manual Instructions" cannot be expressed as words in a natural language, we will say them as symbols while assuming that these Instructions still work in a dual manner of "Instructions + information" as ATT says; is it acceptable for the opponents?

Nevertheless, concrete examples of "manual Instructions" are actually rare, and one of them I am able to find out is "Randomization" or "Lottery", i.e., drawing lots. In computers, it is generally realized through a random mathematical function, and the resulting random numbers are called "pseudorandom numbers". The human brain, with free wills inside, can be seen as an equivalent of a "random number generator" that generates "true" random numbers. However, in this specific context, its difference from a computer is still not large.

Manual Instructions, while maybe insignificant in terms of technical details, but together with Commands, can lead to the consequence that we shuffle Instructions and Commands as the verb words in a natural language, mix them with other verb words in the natural language, and re-select and re-arrange them into a new "Instruction List", regardless of whether any "Instruction" in it can be completely simulated by a computer. An advantage of this list is that with these computerized and manual words, it is convenient for us to continue to carry out the theoretical writing narratives and hence, continue the academic tradition of the humanities and social sciences while using ATT. Apparently, these "Instructions" must be provided mainly by natural language (if not, they can be coined into proper terms), and are mainly *those verbs in the natural language that refer to mental actions* while assuming that these mental actions work in the "Instruction + information" manner. Since the number of these verbs is limited, it does not contradict the Algorithmic assumption that the number of Instructions shall be limited. Even if some of these verbs are similar or overlapping in their meanings, they are, in principle, tolerable and acceptable, as it will only entail some diseconomy. The objects of a verb in the list, i.e., the data targeted by an Instruction in it, are not necessarily limited to two, but can be extended to a finite number depending on the context. Maybe the actions that these verbs refer to can be simulated, or partially simulated, or not simulated at all by a computer; we don't need to care about that temporarily. Since high-level programming languages are constructed with specific arrangement and combination of basic Instructions, some Commands have complex formats like phrases or sentences representing complex meanings, which we will still simply regard as the "Instructions", dually structured. Whether an Instruction is expressed in a word, a symbol, a phrase, or a sentence shall not affect its establishment and use as a thoughtful entity. Conversely, when we refer to symbols, words, or sentences as Instructions rather than those of a natural language, we would have strictly limited their meanings and usages as the Instructions rather than the ordinary words. That's what the unique name "Instruction" means, and why it's worth using.

Henceforth, the above "Instructional List" can be called the "Manual Instructional List". The Algorithmic theory based on this list can be called the *"Manual Version of Algorithmic Theory"* or the *"Easy Version of Algorithmic Theory"*.

The manual or easy version of Algorithmic Theory can further have another form, that is, we do not identify the specific Instructions, but only assume that the human brain has Instruction 1, Instruction 2, Instruction 3, ... and so forth. Namely, the Instructions here are anonymous—and on this basis theoretical analyses then happen, accordingly. For example, when we talk about the combinatorial explosions between Instructions and data, we usually ignore the specific contents of Instructions, which means that we have implicitly anonymized the Instructions. Such an Algorithmic theory can be called the *"Anonymous Version of Algorithm Theory"*.

Under the above three versions, the Instructions are treated in a white-box, gray-box, and black-box manner, respectively, and can serve different theoretical purposes and research methods. The three versions can also be intertwined with each other and then used flexibly. The two latter simplified versions of the Algorithmic theory can obviously only be used for manual research work. When a researcher writes computer programs to simulate human thinking on a computer, it means the researcher is equating the human Instructional list with that in a computer. From this angle, *Algorithmic Theory can lead to two research routes; one is the "Manual Algorithmic Approach", and the other is just computer simulation.* The former supersedes the traditional contemplative and manual approach, whereas the latter supersedes the current computerized simulative approach. In economics, the current major formalized tool is mathematics. Next, I advocate the use of computers, instead of mathematics, as the "standard formalized tool". In fact, computer simulative methods are currently gaining a momentum. What we need to do now is to theoretically justify and recognize the role of "standard formalized tool" that this method should play, and to provide "Algorithmic principles" for such research in an attempt to correct its current biases.

In order to meet the needs of specific research, another way to tuning ATT is to add or adjust its other technical details. For example, data memory can be allowed to become blurred over time to accommodate forgetting, computational speeds can be allowed to fluctuate with the timely rise and fall of human physiology to study microscopic behaviors, and so on.

§37. Algorithmic Principles as the Inferences (1)

ATT is a theory of thinking that fully, and even perfectly meets the requirements of Chapters 1 and 2. Therefore, logically, the effects and goals envisaged above can then be realized with ATT. However, given the importance of this issue, we now need to review the reasoning and conclusions in this "Algorithmic" context. This review can also be the process of expanding or extending ATT, as well as the beginning of demonstrating our fresh "Algorithmic approach". As mentioned above, ATT and its inferences are collectively referred to as "Algorithmic principles".

Instructions, whether of computer or of human, are simple and straightforward, and we know them, understand them, and actually use them over and over again every day. Now, it's just a new name for old things. Instructions and information are combined in meta-computations, and the computing results are called "knowledge". In principle, knowledge is a new thing that is different from both Instructions and the raw information, and it did not exist in this world before. The resultant knowledge can also be re-put into computations as information again, thus interacting with other information or knowledge selectively and repeatedly. The outside information is massive, unpredictable, and therefore often new to people. In this way, there will be a huge number of permutations and combinations to be made between Instructions and information, to the point of "combinatorial explosions". The "combinatorial explosion" can be used to demonstrate the infinity of the potential for knowledge development, quite accurately and scientifically.

Let's look at the most distant future first, then the closest present. While the potential for knowledge development is infinite, the knowledge that people have at any given moment is limited or finite. This finitude can be quantitative, qualitative, or both. The history of mankind up to any given moment is finite, so is the age of an individual, so is the number of computations and the results of the computations, and so is the knowledge that can be recorded, remembered, and thus handed down, and that can be used by the person concerned at this moment. In the face of finite stocks of knowledge and specific problems at the moment, the computations that the person (of course, Algorithmic person) performs at this moment are called "*Current Computations*". Since stocks of knowledge available are finite, the quality and quantity of results obtained by current computations based on these stocks must also be finite or limited. In order to achieve better results, the person needs to develop new knowledge on their own, to better support the current computations. However, is it easy or difficult to develop new knowledge temporarily on the spot of problem-solving? Ideally, the person concerned could have fully computed the existing information in order to obtain the best and most reliable knowledge. But, now, the computing speed is assumed to be limited, and with the combinatorial explosion effect, this ideal shall be not achievable. The person as the actor could have computed the raw information in a certain order, from beginning to end, and then turned back. However, when the person returns, the original information may have changed along with the factual changes, as the above process is not necessarily short, but may be very long. Hence, when the actor turns back, there may be so much information that changes to the point that the original computational results have become invalid. The actor then falls into a vast, inextricable predicament from which it is definitely impossible to come up with a perfect decision. Even if some decisions are "perfect" in the eyes of the actor oneself, because the actor does not know enough about factual situations and fails to study them sufficiently, such decisions cannot be objectively secured to be perfect, and *can only exist as some fragmentary pieces of knowledge*. Since we call a person who thinks in the way described by ATT the Algorithmic person, we call the above problem faced by the person the "*Algorithmic Person's Problem*".

Algorithmic Person's Problem is like David Hume's inductive problem, which cannot be perfectly answered. However, the results obtained from processing different data by different Instructions are different in principle. There are generally extremely large numbers of different computing results, either in one person's brain or in the different brains of different persons. In this way, for the first time in history, we theoretically realize the doctrine of "*difference first*" that philosophers (especially structuralists) insist on. Consistency, order, certainty, effectiveness, perfection, etc. can only be found *locally* in these massive data; contradictions, conflicts, plurality, differences, irrelevance, and connections will coexist extensively, and the ways and degrees of connection must vary. These conclusions are necessarily logical. The person concerned (and all people, including researchers) can only pursue *relatively reliable* knowledge, although the assumption that "the result of the processing of a particular information by a particular Instruction will never change" will be absolutely unchangeable. Even if some knowledge about the external world is considered to be reliable and "eternal", its scope of use will be limited, and its eternity cannot be fully proven. At the same time, the person concerned can pursue to have *more and better* knowledge than others, and can also pursue *historical development* of knowledge. There is no end to development, but individuals can have fun *continuously* in improving the status quo.

Individuals will not use their energy *evenly* across all information and knowledge, but will try to do it discriminately and categorically. Individuals will divide the types of objects and strive to deal with problems in batches rather than individually. The abstraction method is also a method for processing problems as a batch, which brings high computational economics by establishing a theoretical model to make a single computational process suitable for many cases of problem-solving. Individuals can divide their objects according to different criteria and scales, thus forming the *crisscrossed* divisions, which is also a manifestation of bounded rationality. Individuals can prioritize the discovery of generalities or certainties in the world, ignoring particularities or uncertainties temporarily, and then relying on the former, try to "*deal with*" the latter, serially and roughly. This further creates a difference in the quality of knowledge. If high-quality knowledge is preferentially disseminated and inherited, the rest of the knowledge is at risk of being left to fend for itself.

However, "factor completeness" and "forced closure of computations" can tell us that there are limits to such differential treatment. There are some problems that must be faced, if not well resolved. These issues must be dealt with. Even if gaining few lessons from dealing with these issues, the actors must confront them again and again. This is also a prominent effect of bounded rationality in spatio-temporal conditions. This creates a certain *mismatch* between the supply of knowledge and the demand for knowledge. Under these pressures, the actors must try to solve the problem by using crude, less desirable methods other than the deductive or theoretical methods. For example, an inductive or empirical approach can be of some value at this point. Even if the actors do not know exactly why a method that has been used is effective, the practical effect may prove its effectiveness. The actors only need to remember this method and do the same on similar occasions in the future. At this point, this method is not just an option, it is simply a treasure. Without it, the person concerned would only be more embarrassed. These methods also include association, imagination, analogy, assumption, experiment, trial & error, lottery, case study, evolution, approximation, fuzzification, and so on. These methods are collectively referred to as "Alternative Algorithms". The aforementioned "uncertain reasoning" must contain some alternative Algorithms. Now, the "Fuzzification" as an Algorithm is an inaccurate method that is used to fuzzily generalize, synthesize, or *stratify* information. Traditionally, we have been accustomed to the methods for accurate analysis, and have *neglected the opposite methods for ambiguous synthesis*. The latter is also an effect of bounded rationality. All kinds of non-traditional Instructions and Algorithms can be analyzed through their detailing procedures, to understand how they can be implemented with basic Instructions.

In order to make optimal decisions, in the case of limited resources (limited time, space, computing power, and Algorithms), the actors must comprehensively, flexibly, and selectively use various mainstream or alternative Algorithms. Deductive, theoretical, or "mainstream" Algorithms are reliable, but they may be not readily available, or lengthy and cumbersome, or a deduction is not in the right direction to solve the problem. At these times, various alternative Algorithms gain their certain comparative advantages over deduction. Alternative Algorithms also include Social Algorithms such as Imitation, Persuasion, Contracting, Deception, and Coercion.

Now, the turn to Algorithmic logic. Algorithm logic refers to the logic in which the actors, under the Algorithmic framework, specifically arrange the computational sequence. This logic stems from the economics of thinking. Because thinking activity is now a kind of real activity, it needs to consume resources, impacting the world really, thus it is necessary to evaluate the differences between its costs and benefits, or evaluate its necessity, feasibility, etc. And, for this purpose, it is necessary to understand the characteristics of each specific Instruction, logic, and Algorithm, and examine its advantages and disadvantages. However, under the condition of finite computing power, namely, the bounded and concrete rationality, it is not possible to always clearly know the advantages, disadvantages, costs, benefits, etc. of each item, as assumed in mainstream economics that each item can be able to be evaluated monetarily and accurately. If so, this evaluation would be easy, of course. Once we realize that the mainstream assumptions are only ideally conceived by our human brains, and that these assumptions are obviously firstly for the convenience of analyses of our researchers, then we will conjecture that the reality must not have fully met our expectations. In the real environment, not only is it impossible to accurately monetize the evaluations, but sometimes it is not even easy to identify and distinguish between advantages, disadvantages, costs, benefits, etc. Thus, we come to the so-called "*Structured Computation*", which means that actors often do not use quantitative analytic methods to make such evaluations, but instead evaluate them citing other non-quantitative and structured knowledge that may also be uneven, incomplete, unsystematic, and irregular itself. On this basis, actors only obtain clues, rules, guidelines, and so on about the computational methods and sequences, so that the computing processes can only be barely planned. Fortunately, much of the knowledge that is usually available is explicitly or implicitly involved in scheduling computations, so that they can be used to directly help actors to arrange computations, even if the help provided is still fragmentary, vague, and imperfect.

In this way, not only the computations themselves, but all the elements related to computations are *"boundedly rationalized"* or *"Algorithmically materialized"*.

§38. Algorithmic Principles as the Inferences (2)

Chronological and serial computations require an arrangement of the order of operations, but this does not mean that the order can always be satisfactorily made. Even, sometimes the order is not deliberately made. Two unrelated computations stay together, before and after, objectively forming a "sequence", but there may be no logical connection between them. It can be assumed that at the beginning of human history, or when an individual's consciousness is just being formed (most likely in an embryo), computations are (or were) likely to have occurred in a random manner, or roughly in the order in which external stimuli occur. Instructions are randomly selected and paired with information. Algorithms and knowledge are developed slowly. The mainstream and alternative Algorithms are chosen and used at will, and each of them is mixed with others at a fairly high frequency. Even if some specific order or tendencies are established in some places so that certain Instructions or Algorithms are used intensively, the rest may still be mixed and even chaotic. And, the intensive use of a particular Algorithm in a particular place can also lead to a decrease in its marginal return, which in turn creates an incentive to use other Instructions and Algorithms. For example, the use of a deductive method may lead to tedious and slow operations, which then require the use of alternative Algorithms and indeterminate reasoning to speed up computations.

In summary, there are numerous reasons for the subjective turning and mental distortions. The reader could find other reasons for the occurrence of this effect. For example, a shortage of certain knowledge could cause distortions to happen, the caused distortions then yield lower quality computations, and the low computing results are stored and disseminated, which in turn becomes the knowledge stocks that can be cited by oneself or others in the future, and then again lead to further computational distortions. To "distort" computations is to abandon the relentless pursuit of perfection and to draw some inadequate, arbitrary, and risky conclusions. In particular, it refers to the forced valuation of variables that urgently need their values. Since this valuation is often subjective, the values assigned by different individuals may be different or conflictive. The assignments made by the same person at different times may also be contradictory. *This shall be the most convincing cause of contradictions and conflicts.* Without this reason, extreme rationalists would say that contradictions and conflicts can be "ultimately avoidable" for the actors who will appropriately combine different pieces of information, and different computations, into a coherent whole.

Numerous imperfect and even erroneous pieces of knowledge will be stored. Even if they are screened, it does not completely change their nature of imperfection or erroneousness. They have been sedimented and solidified into knowledge stocks over the course of history. The meaning of "solidification" is that when they are re-called in the future, they are generally not split apart and examined from inside, or adjusted or reconstructed, but are used as a whole, i.e., they are input with information directly and then operated fixedly, until the results come out. This is like the difference between the making of a machine and the use of a machine. Making a machine is complex, while using it is relatively simple. The role of the machine is to transform the raw materials into products in a *fixed way* "automatically", without the need for the user to manually transform them, so that the user can reduce labor, save time, and enjoy convenience. If the user does not have the machine, the price will be even greater. It may be more cumbersome for the user to build the machine on site. In case the user has to repair the machine on site, he/she could have a lot of trouble. Users usually just choose which machine to use, at best, simply debug it before using it. However, this fixity of the machine's structure leads to the fact that it can only output products of relatively fixed structures or quality, which limits the possibility to obtain a different or better product. Therefore, when users use the fixity of the machine's structure to accelerate operations, they are also limited by this fixity. It's a double-edged sword. High-quality machines are used for a relatively long time and have fewer restrictions on production. Low-quality machines have shorter shelf lives, lower flexibility, and more restrictions. In the same way, *fixity is a crucial and prominent property of knowledge stocks, and also necessary to knowledge stocks.* If there is no such a property, there is no need to form a stock of knowledge, and the actors could have to directly compute and draw conclusions on the spot of current computations, with their "hollow minds"—One can conjecture the low quality of the conclusions. This discovery is a unique Algorithmic discovery. Even if the discovery has already been made in a place unknown to me, it is clear that its significance has not been fully explored and therefore not given the attention it deserves. From this property, we can draw a series of very important consequences (e.g., for understanding the nature of institutions, rules, organizations, and ethics).

The meanings of "subjectivity" are abundant, hence this inference has its great explanatory power. For example, attitudes, beliefs, principles, values, and strategies are all subjective knowledge. Although human desires are apparently physiological, the goals and objectives that must be achieved concretely in order to satisfy desires are ideological. The finite computing power requires both the simplification of computations themselves and the simplification of what computations are pursuing. *This is how the concept of goal or purpose is born.* People divide their computing jobs into different elements such as goals, means, resources, conditions, etc. Boundedly rational individuals can succeed or fail, and thus create a distinction between the consequences and goals of their actions—and thus the *"Evolutionary Algorithm"* (or "trial and error") is begotten that cycles back and forth between the consequences and goals.

When thinking or computing means the limited activities of an individual, the "other people" makes a lot of sense. The computations of person A and person B can be the same or different, conflictive or consistent, synchronous or asynchronous, cooperative or competitive, or independent of each other and never interacting. The independence is particularly easy to overlook. However, the same Instructional system of different individuals can be the basis of interpersonal communication. The internal nervous system of a human body can be used for highly efficient "internal communication" within a human, and the lack of neural connections between different individuals forces the individual again to intensively "self-communicate", thus forming a relatively tight and distinctive knowledge system, namely, an *"Individualized Version of the Knowledge System"*. However, the interpersonal differences in the knowledge system lead again to the necessity of interpersonal communication. The lack of neural connections forces people to develop external, physical means of communication, e.g., language as a social engineering and knowledge system. With the help of language, after the translative process of "thought-language-thought", one can treat the thoughts of others as if they were one's own. Furthermore, this process can simultaneously produce multiple effects or "Social Algorithms" such as learning, understanding, persuasion, cooperation, negotiation, intimidation, deception, coercion, and struggle. The individualization of knowledge versions further intensifies the independence of individuals and the competition and confrontation between them, which leads to the emergence of institutions and organizations within a certain range, which exist as stocks to constantly coordinate social relationships. For example, it produces legal arrangements and institutional consequences such as the right to self-determination, privacy, voting, market, democracy, freedom, etc., in which the logical relationship now Algorithmically becomes clear and overwhelming. If we consider the fact that citizens have the "higher-order attitude" of recognizing the fallibility of their own opinions and thus the necessity of accommodating the opinions of others as the cornerstone of a democratic system, then Algorithmic Theory that demonstrates this "higher-order attitude" shall be an indispensable prerequisite for the establishment of political science.

One can avoid directly dealing with the natural world and focus on dealing with people to gain a chance of survival. For example, as for the social Algorithm of learning, the knowledge taught by teachers may be abrupt, unfamiliar, and blunt to students. If the students develop knowledge on their own, the knowledge developed may be unique, but the cost savings brought about by learning are so attractive that students would rather turn to adopt learning first and then try to develop or revise the learned knowledge in use. On the other hand, it is precisely because the learned knowledge is blunt and unexpected that it becomes a kind of "discovery" and then is worth learning and cherishing. Further, however, when such imported knowledge has a negative connotation, it can become a form of encroachment and manipulation. Therefore, the mind is controllable to a certain extent. This principle provides an opportunity for evil to prevail. In addition, the relative independence of a person's computation poses a challenge to interpersonal communication and group collaboration. The inefficiency in collective actions then leads to a comparative advantage in centralizing power *in some cases*. Subjectivity can make a person bigoted in the eyes of others. However, independent and massive computations and their interactions can be used to suppress and correct errors and evils at macro levels—but simultaneously, costing time and other prices. With advances in interpersonal communicational technology, the advantages of democracy are expanding.

All these arguments need to be grounded in ATT. After minds are distorted, over and over again, a variety of humanistic and social phenomena are to be formed. It can be said that the *real world is formed in this way, and that the rich diversity of the ideological and social world must be understood generally, or in most cases, from the perspective of Algorithmic bounded rationality.*

§39. Algorithmic Principles as the Inferences (3)

Actors use a combination of various Algorithms not only to form specific decisions, but also to form a worldview. The person concerned may have made a concrete decision directly without a good understanding of the vastness of the world (the so-called "fearlessness of ignorants"). However, after understanding the vastness and complexity of the world one day, one has to give an explanation of the vastness or complexity itself, and possibly come up with a theory, and then use the theory to deal with it. This "theory" is the worldview. Or, he/she may consider the vast and complex situations of the world "inconsequential and negligible". The latter is also a worldview. The necessity of a worldview can be used in particular to illustrate the "factor completeness" and the "forced closure of computations", as well as alternative Algorithms and subjectivity. In such a vast and complex world, it is impossible to account phenomena one by one, precisely, then subjective estimation and imagination shall play their very prominent roles, and the resulting theories or conclusions as worldviews can be highly approximate, simple in form, and vague in content. However, it is usually not possible to do without a worldview. For example, the worldview can be used to pacify emotions of anxiety and fear, to encourage an individual to face life positively and avoid falling into a psychological breakdown.

Thus, each person will form his or her own knowledge system about the *whole world*, even at one's early age. Even if one knows it's imperfect, he/she has to have it first. It is a condensed, mutilated version of all knowledge, like a "mini-universe". The individual first forms it, owns it, use it, and then revises it, serially, from time to time. Since the conclusive knowledge occurs first, at a lower level, perhaps in a hurry, then improving it can be logically possible. Improvements may come from the discovery of new information, or from the innovation of Algorithms, resulting in the "*Information-Driven Innovation*" and "*Algorithm-Improved Innovation*", respectively. Of course, they are often intertwined. If the reader agrees that this distinction between these types of innovation is necessary, it is tantamount to acknowledging that the formulation of Algorithmic Theory is necessary. Innovations first emerge as changes, and whether or not such a change is "improving" is only an afterthought. Meanwhile, it is important to note that innovations occur especially when computing resources are saved from existing matters. Since the solidified stocks of knowledge can help output results quickly, the person concerned becomes more skilled and efficient in existing matters, then he/she has spare time to devote himself/herself to cultivating new ideas.

However, *within a given field*, the benefits from computing activities are not likely to grow continuously, but are changing. From a statistical point of view, it often appears as a curve, rising or falling. Or, after a fruitful period, the marginal returns will diminish to the *point of "stuckness"*. Why is that? Using ATT, this phenomenon can be explained: working continuously and actively in a particular field means not actively working in other fields, which is determined by limited computing power. It is as if one part of an organism continues to grow while the other parts remain unchanged; this "one-sided development" must not be sustainable. If the organism had previously been relatively structurally balanced, then the one-sided growth would further require the other parts to grow in equal proportion in order to maintain the balance (the "equilibrium"). The growth of knowledge in a certain field inevitably requires that this knowledge be applied to other fields, which leads to the growth of knowledge in the other fields. Further, knowledge growth in other areas may also be excessive, which in turn will lead to knowledge growth within this area. This can explain not only the change in the return curve within a given field, but also the alternation of convergence and divergence. To put it bluntly, *the various marginal phenomena that are prevalent in economics essentially depend on the finite scale and intensity of a behavior, and one of the key aspects of behavioral finitude is the finitude of thinking activity of the actor*. This finitude matches up with heterogeneity, because bounded rationality leads to heterogeneity, so that people's physical and mental behaviors are often discrete and jumping. That is, either task A or task B, rather than a continuous, smooth transition between A and B. This phenomenon, which is overlooked because it is all too common, can only be clearly explained by using bounded rationality and thus ATT.

This heterogeneity is manifested not only in the alternation of convergence and divergence, but also in the fact that versions of knowledge are often not continuously renewed, but are *intermittently* and occasionally updated. For example, the process of scientific revolution described by authors such as Thomas Kuhn is a discontinuous process. The small advances that take place in a knowledge system in ordinary times share a certain "paradigm" as the "infrastructure" of the knowledge system. All stocks of knowledge as a whole are the aggregate result of accumulation of all previous histories, and therefore, any current computations cannot update it entirely. This is the first inference. This inference can be used to explain why a country's institutions and traditions cannot be totally renewed in a short period of time, and thus explain the social "shock" caused by the drastic changes in the former Soviet Union in the 1990s. As a result, knowledge progress is usually directed at a very small fraction of the knowledge stocks. These marginal renewals require that the knowledge system must be somewhat discrete, and then a renewal can be "finished" alone, not destroying the running of the whole system. This is to say, *its specific "parts" must be individually replaceable.* This is the second inference. The third inference is that heterogeneity and irregularity can coexist with indivisibility as another consequence or manifestation of bounded rationality, and indivisibility can cause a certain "infrastructure" in the knowledge system to have its wholeness, and the "infrastructure" must be used as a whole, or replaced entirely. This requires, when necessary, building up strength over time to perform a larger surgery one day for the knowledge system. This would be a risky move because the infrastructure has to be taken out of service when it is to be replaced in its entirety. This could paralyze the entire system. For example, the computer system of an organization often chooses to be upgraded during holidays or at night to reduce the impacts on users. Transformation of a scientific paradigm and renewal of an institution are all based on this principle.

§40. "Human Knowledge Thesaurus"

The above inferences or understandings are impossible without ATT. For example, without the Algorithmic theory, it is impossible to explain why the stocks of knowledge in a specific time is qualitatively limited and therefore needs to be improved and can be improved, and we cannot think of knowledge as the *"independent third party"* between Instructions and information, hence knowledge has to be *completely tilted towards one of the two*. Relatively correct knowledge has to be forced to be alleged the "absolute truth", and even confused with external objects (or "minds"). Then, when this "absolute truth" is one day overthrown, philosophers can only fall into collective silence. Rationalists believe that people can discover the ultimate, if not all, truths in the course of history. Even Kant thought so, as well. Or, at a particular stage of history, one can discover the whole truth, as in the case of Hegel. How can we refute this philosophical view without the way of thinking described by ATT? If there is no Algorithmic discreteness, how can we justify the phenomenon of partial renewal of knowledge? And how can we explain the coexistence of equilibrium and disequilibrium, convergence and divergence? Because, it should be remembered that extreme rationalism presupposes that mental activity is always carried out very quickly, so that any difference is either meaningless or absolute and unchangeable. There can be no meaningful gap; if any, they must have been automatically wiped out before they actually existed. We will not be able to treat the mind as "existent" as a "thing" and then allow us to work on it. Nor will we be able to meaningfully explore the *real* processes of movement or change of the mind.

Without ATT, we would be unable to describe and discuss the combinatorial explosion or "Big Bang" and the perpetual development of ideas, and thus adapt philosophy to these social facts that are actually quite obvious but have so far not been explained theoretically. Conversely, with the framework of "Instruction + information", it is clear that the thinking activity cannot be stopped in general. Its local stagnation has instead become the condition for its activity in other areas. Of course, the new information that has been processed by Instructions can be reprocessed, and the artificial products can be re-recognized as the objects for working, then how can the developments and changes be stopped? Since the big data of the human mind cannot be completely controlled by any other human force, how can this expansion of the adventures towards the unknown future be expected to be "planned" or "prorated"? Therefore, the tone of philosophy will change, and any established intellectual or institutional arrangement will take a back seat and will, in principle, become a temporary factor. *"Sustainable development" will become the general tone to be laid at the beginning of the restart of philosophy, and it will also be the basic principle that will be followed in the philosophical thinking processes.*

On the other hand, the concept of the "human knowledge thesaurus" mentioned in Section §5 can now be concretized, and we can further define it as the database consisting of "all the knowledge derived from the processing of all information by all Instructions"[11]. It can be argued that the existence of this super-infinite database was "predestined" at the beginning of human history—an idea that could explain some of the plausible elements in the traditional metaphysics. Nonetheless, due to the relationship between limited computing power and big data, any individual or group of humans can only occupy a part of it. Observers can deduce the existence of this database, but no one can find out all of its contents in detail. This Algorithmic approach can further integrate objectivity and subjectivity, statics and dynamics, so that they can all be symbiotic harmoniously.

If the achievements from this approach of studying ideas or knowledge as the central objects are considered important, even indispensable, then philosophy should, in principle, adopt the Algorithmic theory. Otherwise, the minds as objects will be re-entangled with, and not separated from philosophers' own thoughts, and the philosophers will lose their objects again, and philosophy will deny itself. In the same way, this approach is also the basis of the social sciences, without which there would be no social sciences. Now, we can understand why the general social science has not been established. Scholars have failed to effectively illustrate society, and, at the same time, have not left themselves a foothold in society. Either none of these is happening, or, right now, these can happen concurrently.

---

11. I have ever called this the "space-time map" (Bin Li, "A Preliminary Exploration of Principles of General Social Science: The Algorithmic Approach" [in Chinese], Beijing: China Renmin University Press, 2012, p. 296; Bin Li, "Foundations of Algorithmic Economics: The Cognitive Revolution and the Grand Synthesis of Economics" [in Chinese], Beijing: Economic Daily Press, 2019, p. 386).

§41. How to Use this Theory

Many of the above "Algorithmic Principles" are only general outlines or summaries, and hence will be discussed again and again in different paragraphs below. Now, back to the Algorithmic theory itself.

ATT is actually very simple. It's just a sentence, or a formula —even though there are three versions of it. It's a bit of the style of a natural science theory. It is said that such succinctness often indicates the success of a discipline. This saying is in line with the ideals of traditional rationalism. Interestingly, however, this theory was created to dissolve the existing system of rationalism. Algorithmic Theory is dedicated to arguing for the opposite of rationalism, but it is itself an illustration of the idea of "rationalism". This is subtle. Of course, this can be re-interpreted that we have transformed, expanded, and upgraded rationalism, and that we are using the word "rationality" in a new sense. Meanwhile, this simplicity is also premised on computer knowledge. If it is not assumed that the reader has already mastered certain computer knowledge, or that the reader has agreed with the effectiveness of computer knowledge, such a theoretical proposition might not be so easy to understand, and a lot of words will be said to explain it.

The crux of Algorithmic Theory is the introduction of the concept of "Instruction", which appears as the counterpart of information, exists in the human brain in a discrete form, and works in a serial and roundabout way. The discovery of Instruction can be regarded as a major event in the history of human intellect. At present, it can be used mainly to construct the basic principles of the humanities and social sciences, and the relevant theoretical reasoning is primarily based on these simple hypotheses. At this point, *we think of different Instructions as different thinking organs in the human brain, or different actions of a certain thinking organ.* The ontological deduction can be deemed "self-forgetful". In other words, the researcher's own existence has not been considered in it, the researcher does not "compare" oneself with the research object (even if the object also belongs to the same species as the researcher, the humankind), and the researcher does not consider the impact of his own existence on the research objects. In this way, the theoretical reasoning methods are somewhat similar to the traditional methods, although under the ATT hypotheses, the natures and behaviors of objects will be quite different from those traditional ones, and, the conclusions of research will change as well, and a large number of new conclusions and new perspectives will emerge.

Such theoretical reasoning often uses anonymous Instructions. That is, a specific kind of Instruction is not taken into account. Since we have assumed that the human brain works in an "Instruction + information" manner, we don't have to frequently demonstrate or prove this hypothesis. *Emphasis will be placed, as a priority, on the applications of this hypothesis.* At this time, it is not necessary to consider the specific type or specific content of the information processed by Instructions, and there is no need to write stepwise how actors in a theoretical model carry out thinking activities in the way of "Instruction + information"—that is, there is no need to write down the specific "Algorithmic forms" of thinking activities. Or, in some cases, we only mention specific information or specific Instructions, and obfuscate others.

After a long detour, the reader may have understood that what I want to say is: *the traditional methodological styles on how to research, how to speak, or how to write shall Algorithmically roughly go on working*—except that researchers are now under ATT, the new hypothesis. Then, some readers may still ask: If the forms and styles of theoretical discourse remain unchanged, how can the hypothesis of Algorithm Theory be credible and convincing? Why not clarify the "Algorithmic forms" of thinking activities in a theoretical narrative?

Again, this comes back to the difference between thinking and language. *The fact that we assume that human thinks in the "Instruction + information" way does not necessarily require our humans to speak and write in the "Instruction + information" way.* For example, "Instruction + information" is similar to the way of "predicate + object", while the basic structure of natural language is "subject + predicate + object", with the subject added. When thinking is going, there is no need to say to oneself "I am thinking", and still less can this sentence be used as a substitute for the specific thinking activity to be carried out; thus, this "I" must be omitted, of course. However, if this "I" is omitted when speaking, the listener will be confused and will not know who is "thinking". In this logic, the mind shall not even say to itself, "She is imagining the wedding scene", because this saying can neither direct another person (the "She") to carry out such an imagination nor be expressing something for others—although soliloquy is also useful in certain Algorithmical ways. This is the difference between thinking and interpersonal communication.[12]

---

12. Some scholars (such as Ludwig Wittgenstein, John Searle) have argued that one must learn a language before one can proceed to topics such as logic, asserting that language is more fundamental than thinking. This is actually a misunderstanding of the relationship between high-level programming languages and the "machine language" (i.e., the instruction system). It is not surprising that a particular concept or topic exists only in a particular high-level language or application. The knowledge of human logic depends on the self-awareness of human beings about their own Instruction system, which is certainly different from the Instruction system and thus the logical system itself, hence shall be part of the knowledge that depends on high-level languages, as a kind of high-order knowledge. After realizing these principles, the contradictions hidden in Pinker's "The Language Instinct" (Steven Pinker, Harper Perennial Modern Classics, 2007) can be solved.

§42. How to Use this Theory (continued)

This distinction can be explained in another way. Certain verbs referring to mental activities are used to refer to Instructions, which is only for the convenience of expression, and in no way indicates that these verbs are the same things as Instructions. Instructions are basic thinking actions, or basic thinking tools, or can be thought of as some organs in the human brain. Verbs simply come to refer to the actions, tools, or organs. In this way, Algorithmic analysis can be clearly separated from linguistic analysis. Readers can question our practice of simply expressing Instructions as certain verbs. Because in computers, Instructions are strictly constructed and defined, and the words or phrases that we introduce as "Instructions" are actually only called "mnemonics" in computer science, which means that since these "Instructions" are so specific, in order to make it easier for programmers to remember and use them, they are associated with the words with the closest meanings—but they are not really the same! Instructions are so specific that they are some other times called "sentences" rather than simple verbs. Therefore, it may not be strictly appropriate to use computer instructions directly to construct our discourse in a natural language. However, because they do correspond to the basic computational actions of a computer, our "manual Algorithmic approach" still has its certain feasibility. And, fortunately, *even if some of our so-called "Instructions" (including manual Instructions) are very difficult to implement in a computer, they are easy to implement in the human brain*, therefore, they shall still be appropriate as the basic tools of the human brain. From here, we can further understand the connection between Instructions and natural languages. It can be said that the basic structure of thinking determines the basic structure of a natural language to a large extent, which explains why linguists asserted that there is a universal grammar for human beings. In this sense, subtly again, not only will there be no contradiction between thinking and language, but Algorithmic Theory can now become a new basis for language research.

However, it is by no means useless to clarify the contents of the Instructional list, i.e., to make it a "white box". Even in the manual Algorithmic approach, its role is enormous. One of the great benefits of the concept of Instruction is that it is the content of human consciousness, and hence we all know what an Instruction is. At this point, computer science and Algorithmic Theory are all the "old wine in a new bottle": Instructions are basic mental actions, corresponding to verbs about mental actions—the doubts and controversies here are only about whether they can be simulated by computers. There are only a few dozen of these verbs that are commonly used; even if their synonyms and similarities, and those meaningfully overlapped or included, are counted, there are probably only a few hundred. In fact, we handle these "Instructions" every hour of the day, experience them, verify them, reflect on them, and study them. Even if these verbs are all taken as Instructions, it does not matter at all, as it will not significantly affect the establishment and use of ATT.

The use of specific Instructions and Algorithms will concretely manifest the computing processes, results, and the directions of next jobs. For example, without specifying the steps in terms of Instructions and Algorithms, it is impossible to prove the subjective turn and the mental distortions. With a little attention to these concepts, most people can record their thinking processes in words or voices, and then can retell and explain these processes to others more accurately than before. Based on these recordings and retellings, researchers can try to write out the "Algorithmic forms" of their thinking processes, i.e., the expressions of "Instruction + information", so as to clarify what Instructions were used and what information was processed. Of course, it can't be precise enough for the time being. Moreover, many of the data objects processed by real actors must be some abstract concepts, and these concepts may be some historical and social constructs from longtime periods by countless participants, thus it shall probably be difficult to fully clarify them from their original sources.

This approach will lead us to a microscopic analysis of mental activity. In fact, this kind of micro-analysis has been carried out in many disciplines such as linguistics, logic, cognitive sciences, artificial intelligence, etc., but the analysis in the "manual Algorithmic approach" will have its own characteristics, and it will play a role in the field of humanities and social sciences. It is not only different from logic and linguistics, but also different from artificial intelligence. For example, the generation of demons and monsters may seem absurd, mysterious, and bizarre, but as long as we carefully observe the structures of images of demons and monsters, and study the relevant historical materials, we can generally know how they were "imagined" (as an "Instruction") by the ancients in specific situations in history, what methods (Algorithms) were used, what prototypes (information) were borrowed, and so on. That's roughly what anthropologists did. This way of working can now be Algorithmically reinterpreted. For example, economists are keen to build mathematical models to simulate the decision-making processes of actors. These mathematical models can be seen again as the prototypes of the "manual Algorithmic approach". Speculating on thinking processes of the actors should be under the Algorithmic framework, including not only reasoning and computation, but also many links such as problem generation, data search, timing arrangement, and the subjective operations. In a nut shell, the more realistic the thinking processes, the better acceptability of the analysis. Analysts should not only justify the particular reasoning and computations, but also elucidate the structures, choices, and timing of the entire thinking processes.

I call this analysis method the *"consciousness approach"*, which means that a person's behaviors are explained according to the specific contents of his/her thinking activities. Under the assumption of perfect rationality, it does not matter whether the conscious approach is adopted or not; this question is insignificant, because the results of various "non-conscious" methods of analysis are always assumed to be the same as the conscious approach. However, under the Algorithmic and boundedly rational conditions, the conscious activities of actors are generally diverse and defective, and there are generally some conflicts between different behaviors and between them and the environments, thus the independence and differences of various analytical methods naturally take place. Although we still speculate on actors based on the principle of optimization, the optimization in the eyes of the theorists and the actors may be different, and the optimization in the eyes of different theorists would also be different, and even infinite possibilities would be put on the table, difficult to identify or choose either objectively or subjectively. In other words, Algorithmic Theory can be used to theoretically prove the limits of theoretical analysis itself. Then, what to do? Nonetheless, this shall not be the end of intellectuals. On the contrary, only at this time will the *theoretical value of the real world* be highlighted, and the importance and even irreplaceability of observing reality and empirical research will be highlighted. This is what we call *"theory-experience shift"*. Scholars should not only try to understand why certain choices are made in the real world among many possibilities, but also try to question or challenge the selections made in the real world, and provide suggestions for actors.

The precise Algorithmic approach to consciousness is, of course, computer simulation. Since there is nothing ambiguous about a computer program, its simulation of human consciousness constitutes a *"super-strict form"* of the consciousness approach. In it, the inaccurate manual Instructions are abandoned, and the simulative analysis and the logical processes must be rigorously carried out. Literally, the objects of computer simulation are not limited to the consciousness of actors, it must also use appropriate (and economically concise) methods to simulate everything, including physical objects, otherwise the virtual actors would not have their realistic behavioral environments. Hence, this rigorous approach entails a huge amount of technical work. The principles contributed in this book can be applied by experts in computer simulation. I hope that the Algorithm principles would help to improve the existing simulative research. However, since I am not an expert in computer simulation, this book can only move forward along the track of manual Algorithmic approach. And, the current technical difficulties in computer simulation also highlight the importance of this manual approach.

CHAPTER 4
THE THOUGHTFUL ENTITIES

§43. The Thoughtful Entities and Their Quantitativeness

After giving the Algorithmic theory, it is time to move on to its further explanations, interpretations, argumentations, and extensions. ATT was first proposed as a scientific theory, but it is also a philosophy. Therefore, philosophical discussions are to come in and carry more and more weight.

First of all, it is necessary to emphasize the integrity of the Algorithmic theory. This means that its parts need each other and prove each other; it's a naturally whole system, not a patchwork; and, taking away any part of it cannot be allowed by the other parts.

The concept of entity (or being, thing, substance, fact, reality, existence, and so on; similarly hereinafter) and the concepts of space and time are mutually reinforcing. Whether we imagine Instructions as some organs in the brain, or certain actions of a particular organ, Instructions are treated as entities. The same goes for information. Information is collected from objects as some "things", and passes through interpersonal communication systems and sensory organs, and then enters the brain to "meet" Instructions. They all exist in space, apparently in a finite way. The "finite" refers first and foremost to the fact that the size of the space they occupy is finite, rather than "non-existent" or pervasive throughout the space. This finitude is the reason why they need to change positions to "move". This finitude also contributes to the time-consuming nature of their movement. "Finite", of course, also means that the functions, contents, or roles of each Instruction or data are specific and finite, just as any specific physical object we see has its particular shape or natures. Water is water, fire is fire. A wrench is a wrench, and a table lamp is a table lamp. They are neither nothing nor everything. The specificity of the functions and natures of Instructions or information leads to the fact that their combination always has specific results, and the results as knowledge are also finite and specific. When a result, or a piece of knowledge, is here, it is not there; and if it belongs to person A, it does not belong to person B. To belong to person B, it must go through a specific act of copying, dissemination, or reproduction. And, the extent to which knowledge is disseminated, the number of pieces it is copied, and therefore the number of people who master it are all important and theoretical issues now. Questions such as where it comes from, where it goes, and how long it lasts are inevitably important. The contents, functions, or roles of specific pieces of knowledge are finite; they can only act on computations in the minds of specific individuals, not directly and "automatically" on others. If they need to be done to others, then it needs to initiate new actions to turn them into knowledge in the minds of others. For the sake of conciseness in writing, we sometimes do not make such a distinction, but only talk about the specific knowledge itself; however, it needs, in principle, to be distinguished. Conversely, when we imagine, describe, and analyze the existences, movements, interactions, and developments of these objects, the philosophical concept of "entity" emerges spontaneously and gradually takes root in our minds.

The above view of finitude is a general "Algorithmic" view. This view can be challenged. If, for example, the mysteries of the whole world can be distilled and condensed into a single or concise form of "truth", then it is problematic to, merely based on their finite appearances, assert that the contents of certain data as knowledge are limited, because the opponents of the assertion will argue that since that single "truth" is available, any pieces of knowledge that exist finitely in appearance can be integrated into this single "truth" and hence are not really isolated or limited. However, what I would like to say is that when we regard Instructions, information, and knowledge as individual entities like microscopic particles and their combined products, we have to ignore their contents for a while, and ignore the relations between them and other entities. This is equivalent to holding a linear view of knowledge. But this does not mean that Algorithmic analysis does not need to focus on the contents at all, but rather that the words shall be said step by step—which in itself is a serial way of working. *We first draw some conclusions while ignoring the relations in the contents, and then revise those conclusions based on a certain analysis of the contents.* We have to take this stepwise approach.

Secondly, some knowledge that is considered "true" does have a concise form, i.e., it can be expressed as short, concise data. However, observations show that the *amount of such knowledge is not large,* only a small proportion of the total knowledge, and that in general, the meanings or significances of these pieces of knowledge are also limited, and they involve only a limited range of objects. Even if they are wide-ranging, they are usually related to limited *aspects* of a large number of objects. And, this kind of knowledge (e.g., Newtonian mechanics) is generally obtained from an active, historical phase of computations. For the problem to be addressed, the computations typically first grow, then decline, and then converge on some results. After that, it enters a static state with less active maintenance or minor repairs, or is supplemented by occasional changes. We first need to recognize and describe this active computational phase. As an approximation, a linear view of knowledge is generally necessary. Convergence leads to a local equilibrium. However, as mentioned earlier, the saved computing resources from this equilibrium will be re-invested for other problems, and hence there will be divergent processes happening on the sides of the equilibrium. The return of active computations leads to the revival of the linear view of knowledge.

Indeed, in the process of knowledge development, the content of the result of a unit computation should have been increasing due to the effects of knowledge accumulation. In other words, the quality of individual decisions as the current computing outputs should, on average, have a tendency to improve. If schooling years remain unchanged or grow slowly, it is all the more necessary to streamline the developed knowledge to make it more efficient in use. These factors must lead to a historical increase in the ability of existing knowledge at any point in time to generalize or explain the world, or to support human actions. However, this qualitative increase shall not be enough to invalidate or marginalize the issue of the quantity of knowledge; additionally, expansion of knowledge storage capacity will enable the increase of knowledge stocks, which in turn will tend to include low quality knowledge into the stocks. The number of researchers will also increase with the growth of the weight of R&D investment in GDP (the "gross domestic products"), which will also help slow down the increase of intensity of knowledge stocks.

Analyses such as these tend to support the use of a linear view of knowledge as our primary assumption throughout the book. In other words, the quantitative analysis and quantitative description of knowledge without considering the heterogeneous contents of knowledge would generally have a certain effectiveness, but only need to be adjusted and revised afterwards in specific contexts. It can be argued that there is a basic congruence between this understanding and social reality. For example, we usually use the term "knowledge explosion" to describe the knowledge developmental momentum at present, quantitatively. The more a society develops, the more the length of education tends to be extended, and the proportions of researchers and educated people in the total population tend to increase, indicating the increase of knowledge. Although the development of knowledge will also lead to abandonment of some old knowledge, it is clear that the abandoned knowledge is generally less than the new added knowledge.

The final argument in this section is that whoever thinks that a small amount of knowledge can summarize the whole world, or that the knowledge system as a whole has a tendency to converge, needs to make his own *concrete* illustration. There have been many concrete contents in our arguments above, which can be resulted from our close observations and analyses of specific facts of the knowledge system. The approach based on the linear view does not completely exclude its opposite; it has left room for the opposite to win, and it can also be revamped when necessary in the future. Therefore, it is the *basic* and *synthetic* approach that is only used to *take precedence* over others.

§44. Entity Completeness

Another philosophical question raised by the perspective of thoughtful entity is whether these thoughtful entities can be classified as members of the "entity family" alongside physical entities.

This question is one of the central issues debated in the history of philosophy. Plato's theory of Idea acknowledges the entity status of thought so much that it places the entities of thought (Idea) above the material or physical entities. However, such a distinction between mind and matter, discriminating one over another, inevitably leads to perfectionism, hence the final logical result of development of the tradition of Idea is just to admit that there is only one "entity", which is all-encompassing, omniscient, and omnipotent. Materialists certainly don't see it that way, but when they see the mind as a mirror image of the physical world, the entity status of thought is completely denied, and its agency cannot be explained. Is it permissible to juxtapose physical and spiritual entities as different types of entities? At this time, Gilbert Ryle said this is a "category mistake", i.e., confusing the concepts of different categories.[1] Now we need to briefly explain that not only is this not a category mistake, but that philosophical progress can consist in abolishing the concept of "category mistake" in this sense.

Algorithmic Theory does not deny the common-sense understanding that thinking is a function of the human brain. In the sense of "embodied intelligence", Algorithmic Theory does not deny that thinking is a function of both the human brain and the human body. In common language, saying that "thinking is a function of the human brain (or 'brain')" shall be deemed by default a simplification. However, this rudimentary recognition does not mean that the mechanism by which the human brain, a material organ, produces thoughts and thoughtful activities, has been clarified, nor *does it mean that the thinking of the human brain can be replaced by one's direct*

---

1. Gilbert Ryle, "The Concept of Mind", Penguin, 1963, pp. 13-25.

"manipulation" of the specific physical or biological objects, where the mind is assumed to be able to be fully interpreted as the physical or biological activities. Prof. Ryle could have been astute. It is conceivable that, in the case of the mysteries of the mind being so revealed, Ryle and his followers would logically assert that either one talks about the molecules or atoms, or one talks about ideas, but one should not mix them together to speak.

Even so, however, Algorithmic Theory can advocate this kind of "mixedness": we can talk about physical or biological activities in any other context except that when we talk about the physical or biological activities that directly embody and empower the thinking activities, we shall directly turn to the thinking activities instead of the physical or biological activities behind; Then, it will not cause a repetitive discussion. This "exceptional" approach to the discussion of thinking activity has at least one advantage, that is, as Descartes said, "ourselves" is first and foremost our thoughts, so *it is more economical to speak directly about thoughts.*

The view that the description and analysis of visible physical or biological phenomena can replace the study of thinking activities implies such a confusion: since thinking activities are attached to the human body, then the study of the human body must necessarily and "automatically" include the study of thoughts without omission of any entity in the body. This view is self-defeating once it is spoken out. Just as our sight of a person does not necessarily mean that we know the state of his health or what exactly is in his pocket, we do not necessarily know the state of his mind. We must imagine that there is an invisible but real thing called "mind" attached to his body, "present" to us, and moving with his body.

Moreover, in fact, the mystery of thinking has not yet been scientifically revealed, thus we cannot establish a *direct* equivalence between the mind and its material base. At the very least, in terms of analytical strategies, we must first put aside the question of the relationship between the two, and for the time being, we must primarily treat the activity of the mind as a relatively independent substantive activity. I call this the "Principle of Mind-Body Separation".[2]

According to scientific and philosophical common sense, an object of entity must have a finite nature and have a real effect on the real world. For example, a black hole is identified as an entity because its existence explains the positions and motions of stars in a particular region of the universe; If it doesn't exist, this universal region will be out of balance. Then, do the entities of thoughts meet such a requirement?

A well-known example from economics can be used to answer the question. In the 1960's, economists who study economic growth found that a significant proportion of the income[3] of the United States could not be explained. They looked for reasons and identified the need to recognize the improvement of employees' skills and then tried to monetize them. "Employee's skill" is synonymous with knowledge, which economists call "human capital". In other words, economists must assume that there are many *entities* called "human capital" in the body of employees in order to explain the increase in the national income.

This example is quite similar to the example of black holes. In fact, without the entities of thought, a large number of economic and social phenomena and a large number of philosophical problems will not be able to be fundamentally explained. This example also illustrates that in order to treat a thought as an entity, we cannot establish the hierarchical relationship between mind and matter, as Plato did, but rather establish a relationship of *juxtaposition, equality,* and *interaction*

---

2. Bin Li, "A Preliminary Exploration of Principles of General Social Science: The Algorithmic Approach" (in Chinese), Beijing: China Renmin University Press, 2012, Section 3.2, pp. 58-59.

3. Different scholars have different estimates of this, ranging from 18~75%.

between them. This further requires that thoughts be treated as finite things: finite existences, finite characters, finite functions, finite effects, and so on. This finitude and its "entitiness" or materiality are mutually compatible and mutually supportive. Finite, limited, and discrete entities leave room for other entities to exist, and they confirm their own existences while confirming each other's existence. A finite object is easy to observe, and thus also to make it easier for us as observers to discover and feel its presence. Plato, in his eagerness to make thoughts exist, went too far, resulting conversely and pitifully in the non-existence of thoughts.

We can admit that the mind depends on finite physical materials (the human brain and/or the human body) for its existence. A more reliable argument is that *the activities of the mind are connected to physical activities at the front end and back end respectively*. At its front, it receives information transmitted by material organs, which directly represents the physical phenomena such as shapes, colors, sounds, tastes, and more. On the back end, the decision-making generated by the mind directs the limbs to act on physical objects in the external world. A thinking activity is clearly located on this whole chain of human activities, neither absent nor ubiquitous, but a link *in it*, akin to a stage in factory production. Moreover, this link has its explicit occupation of physical resources, such as space, time, energy, and so on. These resources occupied, which are a component of the total consumption of an individual's activities, can be measurable; and, their shares of the total consumption can be calculated[4].

The "category-mistake" proponents are not entirely unreasonable. Indeed, some double counting and repeated

---

4. For example, according to statistics, the energy expenditure of the human brain accounts generally for about 20% of the total energy expenditure of the human body.

discourse should be avoided, especially when calculating the above shares. For another example, an employee's current remuneration should be regarded as including remuneration for his knowledge and skills, and the employer should not be required to increase his or her salary because of a philosophical re-establishment of the substantive status of the knowledge and skills. Furthermore, the account of the forms of existence of thought should not be confused with the account of its contents. When we talk about the storage, reproduction, flow, growth, and interaction of thoughts in general, it is unnecessary to refer to their contents everywhere in text. On the other hand, since thoughts are, after all, familiar to us, some other times it shall be more appropriate to talk directly about the contents of thoughts. Such talk should no longer take physical activities as the only reality that is "on the stage", as has traditionally been done, and simultaneously take the mental activities as something merely "on the backstage" rather than "on the stage". Now, *all activities should be considered "on the stage" as the activities of different entities, belonging to these different entities.* The only exception to this is the activity of the researcher or presenter himself, which can continue to be considered the "backstage activity". However, because there is communication between the researcher and the actors concerned, this "backstage activity" will then affect the foreground, sooner or later, hence, researchers need to pay attention to this as needed in different contexts.

In this way, we further derive the concept of "Entity Completeness", that is, the entities that were previously identified as incomplete have caused difficulties and loopholes in analysis, and now, with the addition of thoughtful entities, the entities then become complete in terms of type, and they are all located in front of our eyes, or known to us, and *our analysis thus becomes only an analysis of the interactions between these objectified entities.* This is of great benefit and convenience for analysis. And, in this case, it is expected that certain conservation laws would return working well.

For example, in the conventional world, the first thing we can talk about here is the conservation of energy. If a person's physical strength and energy are invested in physical movements and external physical actions, due to the conservation of energy, it is impossible for him/her to devote more strength and energy to thinking activities, especially to those in-depth computational activities (which can be called "Deep Thinking"[5]), which leads to a prominent substitutive relationship between thinking activities and physical activities, so that thinking activities cannot be squandered as freely and unlimitedly as believed in tradition. Vice versa. From this conservation law, the equilibrium relationship between a total quantity and an individual quantity can also be deduced. The human capital case above is an example of it.

§45. The Generation of the Concept of Entity

The former two sections illustrate that a microscopic unit of thoughtful entities is small and finite, and thus can coexist with material entities, and can develop, grow, and expand in a spatio-temporal environment. Then, what are its specific properties, and how do these properties compare and interact with the properties of other entities?

The first question is, what is "entity"? In the ordinary usage of the word, it should refer to a basic unit of object. This basic unit must have been originally divided by visual effects. We

______

5. In "deep thinking", the brain intensively invokes data-processing instructions to work on large amounts of data from long-term memory; hence, its energy expenditure is significantly higher than that of usual simple computations. This can be analogized with the fact that a chip in a computer heats up when it is used intensively, as many auxiliary operations are concurrently ongoing. It is not a negation of the serial processing method.

observe that there are relatively independent objects in the physical world, each of which has a finite size and relatively clear boundaries with each other. This prompts us to divide and identify them separately as individual and different "entities", and to treat and study them separately as independent units. This is a kind of "obedience" or "tolerance" of the mind to the vision. Different objects often have different directions, modes, and trajectories of movement, making it even more necessary to treat them as different entities, because it is computationally economical to do so. On the other hand, if we look at the different entities all as one composite entity, we would have little way to speak, to describe them, or even to draw conclusions about them. Identifying such an "integrated entity" is only necessary when they share certain characteristics (e.g., being located in adjacent spaces) and hence can be described and analyzed together. In extreme cases, if they are moving in perfect synchronicity, it may be necessary to identify them as one entity. This example can be used to illustrate *the crucial role of the limitations of computing power in identifying entities; the natures of objects are combined with our limited and/or subjective observational, perceptional, and computational power to produce entities, through economic considerations.*

The above synchronicity and asynchronicity can also indicate that not all objects that are visually or sensorily independent must be defined as independent entities, and *when needed, entities can cross the boundaries of sensation to be identified.* This gives rise to *concepts such as "system", "structure", "molecule", "atom", etc.,* which either identify multiple visually independent objects as one big entity, or break down a visually holistic object into multiple smaller entities. It also leads to the distinction between entity and concepts of nature, relation, motion, and so on. For example, although "red" and "object" can be different concepts, observers have found that red can be attached to this object or that object, and it always exists and moves in synchrony with certain objects. This gives rise to the concept of "nature", "property", "character", "trait", "feature", and so on which is *subordinate* to the concept of "object", "entity", "substance", and so on. The same goes for "relation". Because the independence of entities is limited and relative, the relations between them lead to the fact that they are neither completely independent nor can they be merged into a single entity. This dilemma and imperfection re-affirm the emergence of the concept of "relation". *Both "nature" and "relation" can be seen as the complements to "entity"(or "substance", etc.) to make up for the shortcomings of entity.* The same is again true of the concepts of "movement", "development", "change", "evolution", etc.: because objects at different moments can be roughly the same in themselves except their differences in position and the gradual and continuous changes of position, then we identify these objects at different moments as one entity, saying that this entity is "in motion". *This is an economical way to process objects in a batch.* Otherwise, we would have to identify them as different entities, and the number of entities will increase dramatically, making analysis difficult. For similar reasons, we say that a certain entity is "developing", "changing", or "evolving", but not that there are different entities existent at different times. This again saves entities and replaces them with the secondary amendments to that single entity.

Concepts such as entity, nature, behavior, action, change, movement, development, evolution, and so on make up a "group of concepts" that complement and compete with each other to help us portray the world economically. Although the choices are diverse, their use in each specific context tends to be specific rather than indifferent, and one concept or one conceptual combination is usually preferred to another. This is also a stepwise, serial, and roundabout way that requires us not to use a single word to complete our statement in an instant, but to make it in a sentence or even an article, in a length of time. An undesirable consequence of this diachronic statement is that by the time we have finished observing and then burying our heads in our statements and analyses, the world of objects has changed to a certain extent, so that our statements may also become more or less outdated.

These processes and effects tell us how our human brain copes with the world in a rough, flawed, and even arbitrary way with specific structures and strategies. Furthermore, the lag effect on computations and statements can be further used as evidence that the existence of thought is real, and its specific traits also need to be portrayed.

§46. The Specific Traits of Thoughtful Entities

Although thoughts can be regarded as attachments to material organs, their natures and statuses are so special that they can bring us sufficient benefits and convenience to consider them as relatively independent entities.

Whether philosophically or scientifically, the natures and statuses of thoughts have long been vague and undetermined. However, computer science inspires us that a thought can be represented as a *state* of matter (electrical potential and/or electrical current) that can be replicated, transferred, propagated, altered, or reproduced for human beings to read and understand. While a computer offers only a "representation" of thought and its movement, it is an important clue that leads us to understand the actual, material, substantial, and/or physical natures of thought.

This "state of matter" theory could explain why thoughts (including Instructions, information, and knowledge) have no weight but take up space. Since a thought needs a specific state of a particular substance to be represented; when substance A represents thought A, it cannot be used again to represent thought B, and thought B will need substance B to represent. Since thoughts are quantitative, then the substances that represent them must also have a certain quantity, and if the quantity of substances that represent them is finite, then the ideas that these substances can "carry" are also limited. The "state of matter" theory can also explain why the sharing of a thought does not diminish itself: since the thought is shared by reproducing the state of matter with another substance, the sharer provides his/her own additional physical material for copying and storing that same state of matter. The deletion or oblivion of a thought is also a change in a specific state of a particular substance, and has nothing to do with other substances. Therefore, the fact that the mind is lost or abandoned here does not affect its continued existence elsewhere in other people.

In the above sense, there is at least a relationship between thought and matter, similar to that between goods and their carriers, and matter can be seen as the carrier of thought. Without a substance "supporting" a thought, the thought cannot hang itself in the air, and "exist" alone. It will fall to the ground like a glass bottle and "shatter", or it will scatter and lose like a puddle of water. The concept of "carrier" is used because we do not yet know exactly where thoughts come from, and whether there is a further close connection between a thought and its carrier. Although we can admit that the mind exists in the human body, that it moves with the movement of the physical body, that it is interrupted or deranged by the sickness of the physical body, and that it also disappears with the death of the physical body, the mere existence of the physical body does not entail the existence of thoughts, let alone the proliferation of thoughts. In order for thoughts to be generated and proliferated, people need to use their brains to *really* act. Without actions of the brain, there will be no thoughts, the carrier of the physical body will be empty, and there will be no corresponding physical actions. However, the fact that the mystery of the mind has not yet been revealed means that human beings are far from being able to establish a precise one-to-one correspondence between the state of matter and thought, and then to replace thought with matter. There is a wide area of grey or black in between that separates the two like a thick curtain. In this case, it is impossible to equate the mind with its carrier, nor do we need to refer to the body every time we mention thoughts, just as we do not have always to emphasize that a substance usually stands on another substance and doesn't hang in the air. This emphasis is often redundant.

Elon Musk's company of Neuralink has only done so far to extract information stored in the human brain,[6] and it has not yet been possible to re-"implant" the extracted information into another human brain. Even if all of these are done, they are only for memorization. Even more important than memory is the "human brain", the "device" that generates, reads, and manipulates memories, and the stored information is the "information" (or thoughts) only in relation to this "device". Of course, commenters can argue that computers or robots can be used to read and process this stored information, hence the human brain is not the most important. Another argument, however, is that in all these cases, the independence of thought has been justified or strengthened, and even the doctrine of immortal soul has been supported.[7]

The ancient doctrine that the soul can operate in the universe freely, or choose a material carrier to inhabit, may be the most supportive of a thought as an entity. However, I do not intend to go this far. Our core arguments are with the scientific

---

6. See https://neuralink.com/ for details.

7. Yew-Kwang Ng, "Could artificial intelligence have consciousness? Some perspectives from neurology and parapsychology", AI & Society (2023) 38:425–436. https://doi.org/10.1007/s00146-021-01305-x

methodology. William of Ockham said, "Entities must not be multiplied beyond necessity". It implies that new entities are set up only when they are necessary enough.

The essence of an entity is actually just the basic unit of object of analysis, which has specific characteristics and moves and changes according to certain rules or ways. As a result, it organizes the numerous relevant phenomena and elements in an orderly manner, making our analysis more convenient and efficient than it would have been without it. In this regard, physics provides a typical model, and one example of it is the concept of "energy". Energy is generally interpreted as a property of matter (e.g. temperature is interpreted as the kinetic energy of molecules or atoms), and in this respect it is somewhat similar to the view that thinking is a function of the human brain. However, the situation is far from simple. Energy can be transferred without a material carrier, and can travel through the void of the universe to extremely distant places, and can be inter-transformed with matter under certain conditions (as advocated by the special theory of relativity). This means that the concept of energy has actually been "materialized" as a kind of entity. When we talk about energy, we are actually imagining some kind of "tangible thing" flowing through space, or "passing" between objects. There is only one exception: some natures of this "thing" are not the same as those of a substance object, and it can be combined with the substance object in some *concrete* way. As long as we do not, by self-infliction, take the specific characteristics (e.g., the length, width, height, and weight) of substance objects as general criteria for entities, this recognition and this approach will be all right.

Today, the principle is similar: thoughts are generally placed in the field of view of theorists alongside other entities as separate entities, and when they interact with other entities, they operate according to their own specific natures. Then, don't ask: When the thoughts "hit" a cup, what will be the trajectory of movement of the cup? Thoughts cannot directly hit the cup. However, any thoughts are concrete, and their contents can be clarified. We can get to know whether we or others have the intention to make the cup move, and we can also influence or persuade others to generate this intention, and the other people can also choose, autonomously, to generate or not generate this intention. When this intention as a *decision* is made, the person involved will cause the mind to dominate the body to take concrete physical measures, to move the cup—"Physical" has traditionally been the core meaning of the word "real", but now the meaning of "real" is expanding. Any of the above situations requires that mental activities occur as real activities that consume energy and time, and that the associated decisions exist as results of these mental actions, and as a type of thought.

§47. The Novelty of Thought

Enormous mental entities coexist in space and time with enormous physical (discrete or continuous) entities. They generally exist in finite forms and have limited and real impacts on each other. We need to avoid both missing any entities and doubly counting them. We try to "attach" the otherwise independent objects we find to certain extant entities as much as possible. If this is not possible, then the types and names of entities should be coined so that they can be recognized as new entities. As mentioned earlier, one of the great benefits of this approach is that it simplifies our analyses. All phenomena are explained first by resorting to the natures of existing entities. This is especially true of social phenomena, which we can think of as being formed primarily on the natures of mental entities that we have recognized. The generality and specificity of social research methods can also be derived from this, without being fetched from far away.

Another implication of this perspective is that these mental entities in the "sea of entities" must be seen as novel, peculiar, eerie, grotesque, and outlandish compared to other entities. This is not to say that in the "sea of entities" only the thoughts are peculiar, and the others are mundane and indifferent. Rather, each type of entity here has its own characteristics and is different in principle from others. *It is only in this sense* that we say that the mind is also peculiar. This peculiarity or novelty coexists with its commonality and interconnectedness with other entities, and they do not negate each other utterly.

The information is novel or peculiar. Traditionally, a piece of information has been thought to be a "reflection" of the nature or state of an entity, but since the entity exists there, why should it be "reflected" again? Why should the entity "tell" itself to humans? Therefore, this view of information is a manifestation of anthropocentrism and a product of human narcissism. Human beings always feel that what their objects do or do not do is just "intended" to send some kinds of "signals" to human beings and to communicate and interact with human beings. This view also personifies the external objects, so that the external objects look similar to persons, and then are used as the subjects of sentences to unfold "their" statements. Such a sentence structure is relatively common in existing philosophical literature. This phenomenon is somewhat strange. If you read it a lot, one day you will have doubts: How so? I believe that the mystery of this is that information lacks its counterpart, especially its specific counterpart in the human brain, so that when philosophers want to say that "X is processing information", they can only say that "somebody is processing information", or "Mike is processing information", or "Mike's brain is processing information", and so on. The semantics here are not only ambiguous, but also lexically unequal.

The counterpart of information is just Instruction. Instructions and information are mutually defined; they should be co-produced as a "conceptual pair". Instructions define what information is, and what it isn't. This is like the relationship between eyes and color, ears and sound. The sensory organs, of course, are involved in defining information in the first place. "Objects" that cannot be sensed cannot give information, whereas sensed information is information because it is "sensed" and then concurrently processed by certain Instructions. Nonetheless, an object not sensed is an object and hence is deemed the source of information probably because it is guessed or imagined, and then is the result of Instructional operations. It is the Instructions that, combined with other data, make up the information. It is just in processing information that we discover the existence of Instructions. Although some Instructions do not process specific information according to computer principles, their functions are clear: they *directly* serve the processing of information by other Instructions, and coexist closely with other Instructions in the system.

This means that when we recognize the substantive status of information, we must logically acknowledge the substantive status of Instructions. There has been a lot of literature recognizing the substantive status of information. These documents not only favor the term "information entity", but some go very extremely, believing that information is the essence of the world, that matter is only the manifestation of information, and that the universe is a supercomputer.[8]

---

8. For examples, Paul Davies, Niels Henrik Gregersen (ed.), "Information and the Nature of Reality: From Physics to Metaphysics", Cambridge University Press, 2010; Luciano Floridi, "The Philosophy of Information", Oxford University Press, 2011.

Consider the context of the information technology revolution in the past decades, it shall be inevitable that this view will arise from traditional philosophical arguments. However, despite these authors' familiarity with computer principles, they ignored the importance of the concept of "Instruction". This ignorance determines that such "information philosophy" is just a copy of traditional monist philosophy and has nothing new. The word "information" has continued to grow in popularity over the years, being recited and chewed on to the point of inundation. Not only does it seem superficial, but it is also confusing and disappointing.

The rediscovery of Instruction could finally change that. Information is peculiar, and its peculiarity is not only caused by external objects and sensory organs, but also by Instructions. In the same way, Instructions must also be treated as peculiar or novel. The number of Instructions can simply be described as "scarce" compared to information. The number of Instructions is fixed, and their functions remain the same permanently, which exacerbates its peculiarity or novelty. Then, the results of these two strange or grotesque entities, i.e. thoughts or knowledge, are inevitably even more bizarre. It should be seen as a new species and a new kind of entity in this universe, and an "independent third party" between mind and matter. Its appearance has made this universe more crowded than before.

The disadvantage of the traditional "reflection theory" is not only that it cannot explain why external objects make us "reflect" them, or why we "reflect" them, but also why there are wrong ideas and thus wrong "reflections", and why such "reflections" develop and change again. Nor does it account for the existence of a large number of irregular, inconclusive "opinions" that lie between right and wrong. It is true that in order to process information, the collection of information is necessary and is a basic step that must be carried out before processing. However, the Kantian inspiration lies in pointing out that this "reflection" not only conveys the information of the external objects, but must also be regarded as adapting the information from the external objects to the specific structures and modes of work of the human brain, the preparations of the brain for its next job, and the arrangement or "customization" of the raw materials by the brain in a way that it can accept. The key point is not whether the reflection of external objects is accurate enough, but the concept of "reflection" and the "reflective" action itself, which is the requirement of human beings themselves, and has nothing to do with external objects. There is nothing out there that requires to be "reflected", and what are "reflected" are just for human's own use.

The sun shines on the earth, and there are mirrors on the earth that reflect sunlight. However, there are still living organisms on Earth that can grow and change in a variety of ways under the influences of sunlight. There are also air, water, and minerals, which have different consequences when exposed to sunlight. It can be said that these changes "reflect" the properties of the sun to some extent, but not in other senses (e.g., mirrors focus on "reflecting" the optical properties of the sun at the expense of reflecting other properties of the sun), but rather "reflect" the properties of the subject entities themselves. When there are more and more entities and factors involved in the above process, we can also say that it is the universe that is evolving, generating new things. In fact, the influence of the sun extends far beyond the confines of the Earth that occupies only a tiny part of the Solar System.

§48. The Novelty of Thought (continued)

In addition to the reflection theory, there is also a traditional theory that insists that the human mind and the world can be completely consistent, that is, human beings are completely capable of revealing the mysteries of the world and grasping its full truth. Such argument generally does not oppose the obvious processual characteristics of mental activity, nor the division of knowledge between different individuals, and can also accommodate the "temporary existence" of erroneous knowledge. It simply emphasizes that there is the ultimate truth far or near ahead, waiting to be discovered. While this argument emphasizes the continuous development of correct knowledge, it usually ignores the fact that the total amount of knowledge continues to grow. However, this fact needs to be confronted and explained. Second, while the existence of certain correct and successful knowledge is supportive to this argument, those arguers usually ignore the fact that some less perfect knowledge that is excluded from truth is also long-standing (such as some of the negative phenomena emphasized by non-cooperative games), and its existence is even as stubborn as the existence of the truth in their minds. *How can we explain the perpetuation of this mixture? They need to ask themselves whether this situation is in line with their ideals, and how it can be explained together with the growth of knowledge.*

Another serious problem with the above "ultimate consistency" is also manifested in the fact that it presupposes a point in time as the end of thinking processes. As a result, it has to assume a logical obligation to indicate exactly when that point in time is. Hegel confronted and answered this question with great courage. His answer was implicit. However, it is clear that his answer had to be implicit, because it would be too easy to verify if it were to clarify that this point in time was a certain day, month, or year. If such a specific prediction were made, it would inevitably cause a public outcry. If the world really believed him, it might cause chaos. This is tantamount to announcing a specific date for the "return of Jesus". One of the reasons for the outcry must be that at least a part of the readers would regard it as ridiculous from the point of view of common sense. Perhaps Hegel had this consequence in mind, then, while strongly alluding to this eschatological "Day of Judgment" in his book, he did not directly state it. However, this consequence cannot be avoided by him and his followers in any case, because it is an obvious logical obligation—despite the fact that they had been avoiding it. *Methodologically, this theory also makes a distinction between different historical points in time, preferring some ages to other ages.* In my opinion, this problem is also serious.

Moving on this line of thought, we will find another unjustifiable aspect of this theory, which is the fact that human beings can change the world. Even if the mind and the objects can be compatible, human beings are obviously not satisfied with this, and *human abilities and actions obviously exceed the requirements of the "consistent theory"*, and they have passed "Day of Judgment" and continued to move forward, so that the world has been changed. The world is no longer what it used to be. Should two things that are exactly consistent have such a relationship? Isn't it right that they should give each other neither more nor less? The fact that the world has been transformed by human beings clearly goes beyond the meaning of the reflection theory as well as the meaning of the "consistent theory". Moreover, there are times when the transformation of human beings fails, and there are times when human beings are dominated by external objects, and damaged by nature. These "reciprocal transformations" of humankind and nature do not happen only after "Day of Judgment", but have been happening since the beginning of history. Considering these macro and general facts, not just the partial facts favored by extreme rationalists, it is clear that the human capacity for thinking is likely to be something that is neither completely in contradiction nor in complete harmony with the external world. In this regard, the Algorithmic philosophy is inconclusive, because according to the Algorithmic logic, there is no need for us in the historical process to make such conclusions in advance. It is very likely that phenomena of human thinking are the results of the continuous operations and developments of some specific, and therefore "bizarre", "peculiar" tools, resources, or mechanisms. We are simply making this hypothesis cautiously and as neutral as possible.

The next step away from anthropocentrism is to realize further that, leaving aside the specific contents of thoughts, *thinking itself is a way in which humankind interacts with external objects*. Tables and chairs interact with each other through physical collisions, but, when they come to a person, the person can either choose to collide with them with his physical body or not do so but cope with them through thinking and research. Through a variety of computational activities, one can develop an infinite number of ways to cope with the tables or chairs. This is the characteristic of humans. This is not to say that these "human ways" are perfect (e.g., that the person might use this furniture for suicide), nor that human can adopt any other ways that other entities take. Rather, these ways are specific and distinctive. Using the word "specific" here does not mean that the human responses are merely mechanical. Human reactions can vary in different scenarios and evolve over time. The evolvement itself, or change, belongs to these "human ways", and is a characteristic of the "human ways".

As mentioned earlier, this argument, which is based on peculiarity and/or novelty, is on the contrary methodologically safe, generic, and all-encompassing. If the human mind is ultimately proven to be the "root" of all things in the world, or if there is an absolute boundary between it and external objects, none of these extreme conclusions will be missed in this approach. Instructions and information, two finite and specific kinds of things, must first interact in the framework of time and space, and *computational activities must first begin, and must be vigorously traveling on the road, and only then can metaphysical conclusions be considered again*. This argumentation will have a wider range of adaptability and persuasiveness than any existing philosophy.

Perhaps, some readers will immediately realize that this seems related to the established constructivism; then, how does it fit into the problem of truth? Let us answer this in the next section.

§49. "Truth" is Derivative and Partial

If knowledge is the "third party" that arises from the interactions of the brain's inherent Instructions with information from the outside world, it seems that knowledge has nothing to do with the problem of truth. This can be a question or a reproach to constructivism. However, such a constructivism as ATT does not exclude truth; on the contrary, it can answer the question of truth most accurately and comprehensively while placing it in an appropriate position in the philosophical system.

The gist is that *such computational activities must first (tentatively) produce a large number of different results, and the following comparison of these results inevitably leads to the question of "true or false" judgment, and then "truth" is selected for the results of relatively high quality.* Therefore, it is not that people have an innate grasp of the criteria of truth or the criteria of right and wrong, but that the computational activities themselves derive these criteria during the computing processes; and, in the whole body of knowledge, the truth and its criteria exist only partially and play a limited role; in general, they themselves are also changing.

What is innately present in the human brain is not knowledge in the first place, but tools for producing knowledge. Knowledge is the result of the work of these tools after the individual is born. Although we are not entirely opposed in principle to the idea that knowledge can be inherited, it is not our core thesis. Whether knowledge is inherited or not, or how much of it is inherited is not the most important thing. The major point is that we accept the existence of innate thinking tools, acknowledging that they play a role in the course of time, and then we will all at once come to the diversity or plurality of knowledge, and the differences between pieces of knowledge. Then, *we will come to this appropriate basis and premise for discussing the question of truth.*

Some writers argue that concepts such as truth and justice are innate[9], which is difficult for us to accept. Do people inherently know that a proposition is equivalent to its inverse-negative proposition? Do people inherently know that "all human beings are created equal"? Are people born to use empirical methods to test propositions? Although the assumption that a particular Instruction has a fixed and unchanging character and function seems to imply a certain innate (and a priori) nature of truth, we must, however, carefully analyze and discern what this truth is. A visible way to understand this truth is to understand the requirements for an Instruction in its format, which is designed to ensure that computations are performed in the way they can be performed and to exclude ways that cannot be performed. For example, if you ask "how much is 1 catty plus 2 feet", you just make a malformat of the data, and hence the computation cannot be carried out, and the result cannot be obtained. Conversely, if another computation has already yielded a certain result, it means that the computation must have met the format requirements. This formatting feature should be inherently

---

9. Rene Descartes is a pioneer well-known in this argument; see Rene Descartes, "Principles Of Philosophy", translated by Valentine R. Miller And Reese P. Miller, Kluwer Academic Publishers, 1982, pp. 1-50.

understood—even if it could not be clearly expressed for a while, it was studied in detail with the advent of computer science. Secondly, it is the logical correctness. This mainly refers to deductive reasoning. The essence of deductive reasoning is the rule of substitution of equivalents; that is, the reasoning, the substitution of one for its equivalent, is logically correct as long as we admit that it is equal to itself.

Since Nietzsche, the question of truth has rightly been transformed into a question of certainty. Therefore, the above two truths can be collectively referred to as the "Transcendent (or "a priori") Certainty". It is distinguished from the "Empirical Certainty" that pertains to the question of whether we agree with a certain conclusion about the external world. Such conclusions, even if they arise at an early stage of life (even in the fetal period), should be distinguished from the transcendent issues. For example, some philosophers argue that human beings are inherently equal. However, the concept of equality should arise in the process of knowing and dealing with others. If we agree that one only recognizes the existence of others after one's consciousness is formed, and then the question arises in one's consciousness as to whether people should be equal to each other, then we can only regard the answer to this question in one's brain as an empirical certainty. Given the identity of their Instruction systems and the similarity of their environments, babies must grow up with a large amount of identical, similar, or consistent knowledge, which can be explained Algorithmically. Anything that can be interpreted as acquired does not have to be interpreted as innate. This is the requirement of "Occam's razor".

"Transcendent certainty" should also be distinguished from instrumental disciplines such as logic and mathematics. It can be said that the goal of logic and mathematics is to explore this certainty, but it cannot be said that this certainty has been fully and unambiguously embodied in the existing logic and mathematics. It is one thing for an innate entity to work there according to its own nature, and quite another thing to unearth it and express it explicitly. At best, what has been explicitly expressed is only an approximation. To admit that this transcendent certainty has been fully expressed is to admit that logic and mathematics can no longer develop, whereas in fact they are still in the process of development. On the other hand, the development of logic and mathematics cannot be explained by the development of thinking tools themselves, but only by the shortage of prior understanding of such thinking tools, or the advancement of the working results of the thinking tools. This is the general view of the development of logic and mathematics. As for the development of logic and mathematics, it is rare for any author to claim that this is because the basic way of human thinking has changed, but generally that the previous logical or mathematical achievements were defective. Moreover, the slow development of logic and mathematics compared to the rapid development of other applied disciplines is all the more indicative of the fact that the objects of study in these disciplines, the basic tools of human thinking rather than empirical data, are likely to be constant and unchanging. This immutability often leads to certain deterministic conclusions in mathematics and logic.

Then, can something as "skewed and weird" as the Instructional system produce "correct" knowledge? If empirical evidence shows that it can, how can it be done?

In fact, knowledge such as "5" and "red" cannot be separated from the characteristics of humans themselves. Locke said that color as a kind of "knowledge" arose because people had eyes. In the same way, the number "5" also appears because people have the Instruction system that interacts with raw information from the outside world and can produce a large number of computational results. The efficacies of these results are usually pending. Judgments about the differences in their efficacies are also a gradually developed understanding. Usually, this understanding does not always lead to the examination and trade-off of the existing results. This is due to the economy of computations. The people concerned usually act only when a judgment becomes urgent and the last resort is compelled to do so. Since the skills of judging the results are also a kind of knowledge, when this kind of knowledge is insufficient, it is difficult for the actors to make the judgment, and they would be in a dilemma. This situation is common in the real world. People do not rashly define a certain knowledge as "truth", nor do they rashly abandon certain results. Those who are determined to claim a "truth", or those who are "disagreeable or hateful", are in the minority, and are often labelled as "extremists".

However, there are some techniques that will be developed to determine what is right and what is wrong. Much knowledge has a function of judging other knowledge, directly or indirectly, and is used in a particular context.

§50. "Truth" is Derivative and Partial (continued)

In principle, there are inexhaustible ways of measuring the value of knowledge or judging whether it is right or wrong. In particular, a very common method is to be discussed here, which is the logical analysis method. This means that the truth or error of a particular piece of knowledge often depends on how internally logically consistent it is, or how consistent it is with other existing knowledge.

This seems to be self-explanatory. How can a knowledge that is internally contradictory be accepted as "truth"? In the case of extreme rationalists, this alone is enough to reject this candidate. However, in an Algorithmic, and therefore real, environment (since we think that the real world is generated according to the Algorithmic logic, we have reason to equate the Algorithmic world with the real world), things are not so simple. Because here, conflict, plurality, and irrelevance are all normalcy, it is the normalcy for a person to hold two or more opposing views at the same time. Extreme rationalists tend to pay lip service to positions such as "a certain knowledge must be free from internal contradictions", whereas when it comes to specific pieces of knowledge, they are also often hesitant. This is because the appeals of some concrete pieces of knowledge are often so great that it is difficult to part with them simply because there are conflicts inside them. These conflicts are often local, even minor—from the "soft" Algorithmic perspective. In this context, conversely, *it is particularly meaningful to ask: why should we pursue consistency?*

This question is a unique problem under the Algorithmic framework. Also, it is prominent. However, once this question is asked, one Algorithmic answer will emerge. That is, consistency *represents a relatively high computational efficiency, thus it is often economical.* A piece of knowledge with internal consistency can be economically viewed and evaluated as a whole. When there are consistencies between different pieces of knowledge, it could be possible to combine them together for an overall treatment. Then, these mutually consistent pieces of knowledge may form a module or a model, up or down jointly. If one of them is correct and reliable, the other(s) can be inferred likely to be correct and reliable as well. Vice versa. In other words, *establishing consistency is a strategy for merging objects, reducing the number of entities, integrating knowledge systems, and improving computing efficiency.*

However, the problem that then arises is that when one type of efficiency increases, another may be to decrease. Since the pieces that make up the knowledge module are combined to rise or fall jointly, the overall risk of the knowledge module is increased. If the module would have contained some different, less consistent pieces, the risk would not be this high. This is similar to the fact that if an organization contains a certain percentage of opposition, the probability of the organization making extremely wrong decisions decreases. These similar effects cause *the criterion of logical consistency to be only relative*, not absolute, and even not necessarily preferential.

Another method, which we are familiar with, is empirical testing. *Since knowledge is used to explain and deal with the empirical world, empirical testing is "theoretically" logical. Therefore, empirical methods are not completely separated from theoretical or logical methods, and their difference lies mainly in the type of data used.* Empirical methods are characterized by direct correspondence between specific knowledge and specific facts, which is then judged by how well one fits in with the other. This "one-to-one" approach is much like a "Kanban system"[10] in that it aims to establish a correspondence (mapping) relationship that is quite mechanical in nature. In this approach, the process of conceiving choices for explaining phenomena or decision-making is often overlooked, focusing only on how to choose between these choices. A piece of knowledge that is strong in interpreting reality or has good practical results will be ranked higher, and otherwise, it will be ranked lower. It doesn't care why that's the case. It does not need and cannot step beyond its own boundaries to grasp the "truth" behind phenomena. Finally, at the end of the selective process, the knowledge piece that performs best is identified merely as the "truth". Yet, as Hume argued, the samples to be tested are always limited, whereas the conclusion to be drawn must be universal, which then has to be applied to unknown

---

10. A method of management of workflow, in which one worker acts as soon as he/she sees a very simple and regular signal from other workers, thereby smoothly connecting jobs of different workers in a factory. For a detailed introduction, see Taiichi Ohno, "Toyota Production System: Beyond Large-Scale Production", CRC Press, 1988, pp. 27-29.

objects. From this perspective, the advantages and disadvantages of this method are easy to identify.

The above characteristics show that the empirical method is often an inductive method. This method of induction can be extended to use interpersonally, i.e., the more people agree on a piece of knowledge, the more possible it is the truth; the longer it is used, the more credible it becomes. It can also be used to speculate on the future of the entire knowledge system. Some of the knowledge is of a remarkably high quality, which can arouse imaginations. In particular, some high-quality knowledge is simple in form, which aligns in line with people's inner desire for computational economy. Thus, Socrates called for the pursuit of knowledge, and Plato was agitated in his "cave". It had been so hard to imagine how such a wonderful discovery could be so flawed that it would be superseded in the future. They failed to recognize this as a form of "synchronic ignorance". The slow development of knowledge in ancient times helped to mask this ignorance. Thus, *the theory of knowledge was reversed, and the "truth" was given the priority and generality*. The ancients came to believe that the truth in their eyes would last forever, and that other thinking results would either be transformed and integrated into such truth or would be eliminated. Eventually, people would come to a perfect world containing the only truth.

This philosophical tone laid by Plato (and earlier, Parmenides) has remained unchanged to this day. The opposite philosophy only grew next to it, while the chasm between them was always there. Now, the reversed relationship can be reversed again. The Algorithmic solution is clear: we can admit that the development of knowledge for a particular object or a particular topic has a tendency to converge to a certain *relatively stable state*, but the general "combinatorial explosion" and the discovery of new information will broaden the field of knowledge, and thus the new various and heterogeneous knowledge will additionally and continuously emerge. From the mixed results of convergences and divergences, we do not see a *systematic* tendency that the proportion of "truth" in the whole knowledge system continuously grows. Knowledge is knowledge, and truth is only the results of limited selections after the generation of ordinary knowledge. We should not start by looking at all knowledge from the standpoint of truth, but rather the opposite: first look at the ordinary, numerous knowledge, and then, according to our needs, compare and evaluate them relatively.

Algorithmically, we can even speculate that *people deliberately maintain a certain proportional relationship between "good" (including correct) and "not-so-good" (including wrong) knowledge*. People don't assume that all knowledge is true or "good", otherwise, computing power will be idle to a certain extent. If there are not so many new issues that emerge fast enough, thinkers will have less to think. On the other hand, of course, people do not dismiss all knowledge as "not-so-good" knowledge, otherwise current computations will be unfounded and the quality of decisions will be seriously reduced. The knowledge *believed* to be correct must amount sufficiently to support current computations. As the Chinese saying goes, "once there is no tiger in the mountain, a monkey will become the king of animals instead." It can be speculated that if such correct knowledge is objectively insufficient, people would even exaggerate some knowledge of less quality in a "self-deceptive" way, imagining it as perfect knowledge, or claiming in a fatalistic tone that the world has been initially and always like this status quo, or that it has reached the boundary of possibility, and hence knowledge can only be like this status quo. Another possibility is that people will also retain some knowledge as the "negative types" and hence the objects to be further processed, thereby indicating that "the final whole truth will be reached sooner or later, but not now".[11]

Various distortions can also lead people to discriminatively treat different sorts of issues and different sorts of information, *favoring one over the other*, which in turn affects the judgment of truth. For example, if a piece of information is eye-catching, sonorous, or emphasized, people will react strongly, and if some information is low-key or tepid in their expressive forms, people will react weakly or even ignore them. It's like entering a gravitational world, where objects vary in density or elasticity, and therefore react differently to various impacts, and *rarely behave linear, proportional, uniformed, isokinetic, or monotonous.*

§51. Algorithmic Theory as a Minimized Whole

Since its birth, Algorithm Theory has encountered some doubts. This section examines Algorithmic Theory from a doubtful and critical perspective to see how acceptable it is.

The first is Instruction. Is it necessary to introduce the concept of Instruction? Is it indispensable to the theory of mind? Is there a need to change its name?

As explained earlier, the name of Instruction is used to analogize with computer science, which is always needed in the Algorithmic discourse. Moreover, this "strange" name is

---

11. Furthermore, once we recognize the effectiveness of this thoughtful development mechanism based on memory ability, it can even be said to the extreme that no matter how many Instructions there are and what the Instructions are, it is possible for this mechanism to produce phenomena similar to human civilization. A concrete thing, which has a context similar to the Algorithmic framework, interacts with external objects alternately and repeatedly, thereby producing various differentiated results; and then, by sifting these results, it will lead to continuous development. Although interaction of a physical object with other physical objects can also produce different results, there is no such a continuous development. Comparing these two different mechanisms allows us to further explore the mysteries of thinking.

conducive to indicating the uniqueness and novelty of the contents of Algorithmic Theory. Since Instructions are at the heart of the Algorithmic theory, what would the consequences be without them?

The first is that it would be impossible to explain the status of the aforementioned knowledge as an "independent third party" between human and the world, and knowledge will be unable to juxtapose with the two, and will be forced to "choose a side". Knowledge would be either the "reflection" of external objects or the "reflection" of the mind. The mind and external objects will be forced to engage in a "life-or-death contest". This was the main dilemma of the previous philosophy. False, imperfect pieces of knowledge will be used only as the props for this "show" whose end must be predestined, and these "props" will only appear superficially, then stand aside, and finally quietly fade out of the stage. The same will be true of diversity and plurality, let alone the "differences first". Not only must the end of the entire history of mankind be predestined, but the end of a specific thinking process must also be predestined: starting with a question or a message and ending with a "happy reunion" with the "ultimate truth". If you can't do this all the time (which is actually impossible), then pick the issues that can be done, highlight them, and neglect others. Or, as mentioned earlier, invent other "theories" to illustrate that this neglect is appropriate. For example, asserting that human cognition has absolute limits, or that the objective world itself has an inherent property called "uncertainty"[12], and so on. Then, all eyes look at the interactions of information with information, which eventually develop into "informational

---

12. Herbert A. Simon once mentioned the process of "uncertainty" turning from an epistemological phenomenon to the ontological entity (H. A. Simon, "From substantive to procedural rationality", in S. J. Latsis [ed.], "Method and Appraisal in Economics", Cambridge University Press, 1976). This process is similar to the generation of "universal in things" in Section §79.

determinism", or "Laplacian determinism".[13] Such determinism can lead to a radical loss of dynamics in theory of mind, and philosophy is then divided, persistently divided, failing to consider the possibility of synthesis or unification.

Then, is there an alternative to Instructions? Kant offered a solution. The "Kantian scheme" can be understood in the way that the Instructional system was seen as a whole, and then it was made to face the world. This move was significant, because it led to a "Copernican revolution" in philosophy, and the direction of philosophy was reversed all at once. Algorithmic Theory sees Kant as its forerunner. However, Kant's method also led to some major ills. One of the disadvantages is that because the Instruction system was not discrete and couldn't be divided into many Instructions, the thinking process lost its dynamic and developmentality. Kantian thinking process seemed to be a whole that couldn't be divided in space and couldn't be continued in time, and suddenly reached the end of history, and then the "thing-in-itself" that couldn't be reached by the human mind had to "appear" in the narratives, and the boundaries of various fields including morality, are inevitably absolutized.

From Kant's lesson, we can understand that *the discretization or pluralization of Instruction is a key factor* and an indispensable part of Algorithmic Theory. With discrete and plural Instructions, the smallest unit of mental activity is lowered by one level, and it is not the entire human brain or the entire intellectual system any longer that is directly confronted with external information, but the individual Instructions. In this way, there are tremendous permutations and combinations of Instructions with information, and hence the infinite

---

13. Pierre-Simon Laplace, "A Philosophical Essay on Probabilities", translated by Frederick W. Truscott and Frederick L. Emory, New York: Dover Publications, 1951.

development and expansion of knowledge happen, i.e., the combinatorial explosions. The thing-in-itself could exist, but thinkers can approach it infinitely through the course of history, without having to assume that the thinkers must stop somewhere on its periphery. Thought and knowledge themselves can also be discretized and pluralized. Individual concrete thoughts can also vividly indicate their specific contents, and the thoughts speculated by philosophers and theorists can be connected with the real thoughts of real actors. Objective and subjective thinking steps can be expressed and dissected respectively, and the "subjective turn" can be clearly demonstrated. Once a single computational activity is defined, the serialization and dynamization of computations can be described accurately henceforth, extending to the unknown future—only a dynamic theory like this can really make sense, not only for the mind and the human society, but also for the natural world. Literally, Kant did not completely fail to classify the specific forms of mental activity, in fact, the academic community continued along the line of Kant's tradition of microscopic analysis of mental activity, and finally discovered Instructions. However, it is true that this achievement did not happen in Kant's time, since we can't imagine that era would give birth to computers.

Other challenges relate to the assumption of interpersonal universality of Instructions and the finite number of Instructions. These two issues could be combined to explain. *If Instructions are not universal, the consequences are likely to be much worse than what the skeptics have envisioned, unfortunately.* They would include, for example, the problem of having different Instructional lists for different persons, the problem of how those lists would be compared to each other, and how people with different lists would communicate. If people can communicate, it means that their Instructional lists must be mutually agreeable and eventually consistent. If they can't communicate with each other, it will be contrary to our common sense. The point is, we can't give a case where an Instruction doesn't exist for somebody. There can be differences in the computational speed and memory between people, but a fundamental difference in the natures of their minds is unimaginable. Differences in the contents of thoughts are a common phenomenon, especially in the Algorithmic context. However, such differences in content can only arise from the fact that the thinkers have selected different Instructions in the same list of Instructions, or have selected different pieces of information, or adopted their different processing sequences, etc. This is a basic implication of Algorithmic Theory. Personally, I think that this is also a basic understanding that conforms to human common sense. This explanatory framework can already be sufficient to account for the interpersonal differences in thought. Thus, it is obvious that the assumption of individualized Instructions would be superfluous in the Occam's Razor sense, and that it will unnecessarily make the theory of mind more complex than we can handle.

The same rebuttal applies to the infinite number of Instructions. If the number of Instructions is unlimited, it does not correspond to the fact that human words in natural language are finite; and, it is not conducive to explaining the slow growth of human knowledge. In the case that the infinite development of knowledge can be explained by finite Instructions, there is no need to assume again that Instructions are infinite as well. If thinking processes can always be explained in terms of known Instructions, there is no need to assume unknown Instructions. Nor can it be assumed that Instructions will increase over time, as this would give rise to the burden of proof, which would require an indication of what Instructions were added in which dynasty and in which generation. Moreover, if Instructions can be increased (or decreased), it would be difficult for us to envisage that they will occur synchronously between individuals, thereby having to assume again the interpersonally different Instructions.

Summing up, the above interrogative discussions tend to show that Algorithmic Theory is a theory with a high degree of internal consistency; it is a whole, and a *minimized whole*. Its holistic and minimalist nature is reflected in the fact that its introduction can solve multiple theoretical puzzles simultaneously, and its cancellation will lead to the recurrence of these puzzles. I venture to think that it is difficult to conceive of another theory of mind with the same function that would be more concise in form than it is.

CHAPTER 5
THE PSYCHOLOGY

§52. Introduction

When Algorithmic Thinking Theory is proposed, we then have the answer to the "innate thinking tools" we talked a lot about in the first two chapters. The answer is just Instructions. Therefore, these many new principles and knowledge introduced in Chapter 2 can now be established. These principles include Algorithmic Logic, combinatorial explosion & infinite development, mental sedimentation & distortion & solidification, forced closure of thinking & different versions of knowledge, psychological objects as hard software, plurality & higher-order consistency, convergence & divergence & marginal adjustment, and so on. These new principles and new knowledge have been re-examined in detail from the second half of Chapter 3. The main task of the book is just to elucidate these new principles and knowledge. However, the order of the discourse needs to be adjusted, since the psychological contents that were generally discussed before now need to be advanced. We need to answer these pressing questions as soon as possible after the Algorithmic theory is proposed, so that readers know further how our "Algorithmic mind" is going to work, what resources it has from the beginning, what kind of structure it has to go under, and what goals it wants to pursue. These things take precedence over the development of general knowledge in time, and are possessed by an individual from the moment he/she is born. Previously, we were unable to effectively address these topics before the Algorithmic principles had been fully developed. However, now, since readers must have had a general understanding of these principles from the preparation of the former four chapters, these topics can return to their original position in the chronological order of personal development.

The goal of ATT is to put forward a theory about the spiritual life of mankind. This "spiritual life" should first and foremost refer to the mind, because the existence of the mind is generally believed to be the most reliable. However, the scope of spiritual life, as it is traditionally understood, seems to be much broader. "Spirit" sometimes refers to "consciousness", "heart", "soul", and so forth. According to common sense, activities of thinking are seemingly only one part of it, or even only the basis of it. However, the Algorithmic view is that *Algorithmic Theory is basically sufficient to be a comprehensive spiritual theory, and that the terms "consciousness", "mind", "soul", etc. are just synonyms for "meta-computations" or "computations".* The word "basically" is used here because we also need to introduce the assumption of "hard software". After all, hard software is not exactly the same as software. However, despite this, the word "hard" in the "hard software" still needs to be interpreted Algorithmically. In other words, the word "basically" can be basically neglected; and, under the Algorithmic framework, *psychology can be viewed mainly as a corollary or sub-theory of Algorithmic Theory.*

§53. Consciousness (1)

Start with consciousness. The word "consciousness" first and foremost refers to a dynamic activity, or a state in such an activity. However, in the traditional context, since the concept of roundabout method of production of thinking has not been clearly established, there is inevitably confusion and ambiguity in distinguishing flows from stocks. Therefore, consciousness sometimes seems to refer to the stock of instincts, emotions, and so on, in addition to thinking flows. The relevant topics of literature are scattered and lack a sense of direction, and it is unclear what their goals are and where they are going. This deficiency is even evident in literature based on computer science. The latter even exacerbates the confusions about the theory of consciousness, or simply grows new literature in addition to the existing literature. The object is still the same, but the literature on it has been pluralized before the problem of pluralistic consciousness is to be solved.

I believe that the failure of the existing literature is mainly due to the failure to grasp the key point of "Instruction", and thus the failure to establish a theory of *single computation* (or "meta-computation") clearly and concisely. Whenever this critical question is discussed, it is replaced by a discussion of either hardware, the cerebral tissues, or a multitude of seemingly related, but in fact futile materials. A firm foundation on consciousness should be found out first; otherwise, there will be no the subject of conscious activity, and hence no the theory of consciousness.

"Consciousness" is an active flow, which embodies the computational mechanism and computing power of the brain that is a "computing machine". Hume's distinction between self-knowledge and self (see §158, Vol. II) is actually meant by this. This computing power, "hanging there", is always ready to work. The existence of such "computing devices", computing mechanisms, and computing power is different from the existence of any stocks of information or knowledge (even about the self), or from the existence of any software or hard software. The latter is just applications, distinct from the "computing devices" themselves in computer principles.

In a nutshell, *consciousness refers to the computational behavior that is running or moving.* In the serial mode, since only one computational operation can be active at any moment, *consciousness refers to the "meta-computation" that is active, and the data processed by the meta-computation is what the concept of "attention" refers to.* This is the Algorithmical consciousness theory.

Such a theory of consciousness can explain the four basic characteristics of consciousness at the same time: intentionality, singularity (unity), selectivity, and transience.[1] The phenomenon of consciousness arises not first for anything other than for work, i.e., processing information, and the architecture of meta-computing clearly demonstrates this. This is just the "intentionality" of consciousness. Meta-computation is indivisible and is the smallest unit of mental activity. Only one meta-computation can be allowed to work at a time, which is the "singularity" (or unity) of consciousness. However, as in any computer, the contents of a meta-computation are arbitrarily conceived, and different meta-computations can be interrupted and interpolated, which is the selectivity of consciousness. A meta-computation is done all at once, without delay, stopping, or lasting; this means the transience of consciousness.

For the sake of figurativeness, we can further assume that the human brain has a "Central Processing Unit" (CPU) just

---

1. Robert Van Gulick, "Consciousness", The Stanford Encyclopedia of Philosophy (Spring 2025 Edition), Edward N. Zalta & Uri Nodelman (eds.), forthcoming URL = <https://plato.stanford.edu/archives/spr2025/entries/consciousness/>.

like in a computer, although the assumption of this "center" is not anatomically justified. The CPU is the "hotspot" in the human brain, where energy is consumed hotly and the "human stories" are performed. This scene was vividly called the "Cartesian Theater" by Daniel Dennett. Despite Dennett's ridicule on it, he still had to admit that it was a "persuasive imagery" about consciousness and that it "keeps coming back to haunt us".[2]

Many of the once perplexing phenomena of consciousness can now be answered Algorithmically. Before we do, though, let's explain and illustrate some of the details. Observation and probing of the brain have shown that during thinking processes, different brain regions are active in turns and then fall into silence. This phenomenon is consistent with serial computations. Of course, these perceptible or observable computing activities, even according to computer principles, generally do not refer to a single computing job, but always refer to a group or cluster of computing activities. As a result, the computational activities we talk about on a conventional scale often have a problem of intensity or scale. Highly-intensive or large-scaled computational activities refer to computational operations that are of big number or relatively dense in a spatiotemporal environment. Then, what are the operations "not dense"? Since any ordinary mental activities can be regarded as "computations", people can always be regarded as being computing when they are awake; thus, this question becomes an obvious problem.

The answer to this question is the same as that of a computer: when idle, in order to keep the machine running, the computer simply and cyclically executes Instructions that do not process data and only wait for the user to give tasks. In the same way, it can be assumed that the human brain also

---

2. Daniel C. Dennett, "Consciousness Explained", Back Bay Books, 1991, p. 107.

performs some of these simple Instructions when it is idle, which leads to a relaxed and comfortable state of mind, since it does not entail the concurrent cerebral operations on data. At this time, the rest of the brain is inactive and therefore consumes less energy. On the other hand, when the brain is thinking deeply, it needs to call up data in the memory, or write data into the memory, intensely and enormously, which leads to multiple organs and multiple brain regions being in different degrees of activity concurrently. Although Instructions run serially, they alternate so fast that a brain region that has been activated by the previous Instructions has not had time to fully regain its calm (variously depending on the running speed of the related biological tissues) before it is reactivated, repeatedly, by the subsequent Instructions. This is the same as the multiple components in a computer running concurrently to execute one instruction or more instructions. In the latter case, they appear to work simultaneously, but in fact, they serve different Instructional requirements, and are therefore in different stages of operation such as the preparation, execution, and the aftermath service of the Instruction. In other words, they are actually in a serial and overlapped relationship, not a parallel one. It's like a manager is in the middle of a shop floor commanding many different employees busily executing his/her serial but different instructions.

Another problem is that the contents of the "Cartesian Theater" may intuitively be richer than a meta-computation where it is stipulated that no more than two data are processed. According to the above discussion, the two-data rule can, depending on the context, be extended as long as the amount of data in processing is limited. The data can also be processed by certain advanced Commands. It is important to emphasize that the amount of data generated in a particular object is not directly related to the physical size of the object itself, but rather to the complexity revealed from other particular computations. The richness of the plot in the theater can also come from the difference between temporary and long-term memory. This is similar to the differences among CPU, internal memory, cache, and external memory (hard disk) in a computer. Data access is often not done individually, but in batches, and many data adjacent to the target data are often activated, so that the data trapped in the temporary memory (or internal memory) are enormous rather than a few. In addition, the access speed of each type of memory is different from one another, and the fast-accessing memories (e.g., internal memory) have the potential to form a phenomenon similar to "visual persistence", that is, when an image is formed by a computation, the image formed by the previous computation may have not completely disappeared from consciousness, thus overlapping into a continuous and motional "scene". Human vision and computer screens are all based on this principle to achieve the richness and continuity of the picture. In the same way, the "images" or "videos" in consciousness can also be thought of as being formed.

§54. Consciousness (2)

Narratives such as "information and knowledge flow in and out of the 'central processing unit'" may lead readers to think that the person concerned is completely passive in a computing process. However, this is not entirely the case. When the person receives the original information from outside intensively, his/her reactions may be passive, because the intensity of the informational input may not allow him/her to proactively respond in real time. However, once the intensity decreases, the opportunities for proactive responses and proactive computations must increase, and the person will regain dominance over his or her own thinking system.

This brings us to the question of "freedom". A key topic on

consciousness is freedom of will. We can Algorithmically interpret will and its freedom from multiple perspectives.

Instruction is the smallest unit of thinking tool, and the execution of an Instruction, i.e., the meta-computation, is the smallest unit of thinking activity. Each Instruction and each meta-computation is independent, can exist and run independently, and thus has its own computational significance. The consequence of this discreteness is that the actors must choose between many Instructions, information, and computations. Hence, *will and its freedom can be understood first and foremost as a "by-product" of this computing system.* "Free to choose" is, at this point, not only a right, but also an obligation, a task that *you have to do* (an existentialist perspective). Of course, this "task" also includes the fact that you can choose nothing. At the same time, *the selection is constrained, and the choices for the selection are limited to the above and nothing else.* On the other hand, as knowledge develops and individuals become more capable, the data in the brain grows, and the actual scope of choices *expands*, continuously. All of these meanings will concurrently arise from ATT.

Knowledge as patterns provides fixed values for variables, or directly guides how Instructions, data, and computations should be connected. Thus, *the immediate consequence of the use of knowledge is to shrink freedom*—or rather, to absolve people of the responsibility to choose. However, knowledge also increases the overall efficiency and benefits of the relevant computations, better serving human purposes that have been determined by people themselves. This is a combination of objectivity and subjectivity. By sacrificing a certain degree of freedom, people pursue the optimization of their overall interests. Nonetheless, since purposes need to be determined subjectively by people, it may create an additional burden that some people may be distressed about. They complain about the emptiness of life when they have no purpose, and complain about the lack of freedom when they have purposes. This is a contradiction in themselves. We can examine this contradiction in the Algorithmic context.

A person who has both a definite purpose in life and a wealth of knowledge to achieve the purpose may have the least freedom. However, as long as it is all decided by himself/herself voluntarily, in the sense of this voluntariness, he/she still has freedom. He/she could have given up a particular purpose, or he/she could have given up or dismantled a particular knowledge, but he/she didn't do so, which shows that it was worth giving up these freedoms, at least as far as his/her judgment was concerned. However, the situation is not so simple. This is because knowledge patterns are not necessarily developed entirely on his/her own, and even most knowledge patterns are introduced through learning activities from outside. Whether this knowledge aligns with the actors' own purposes is still questionable, and it is necessary to examine the circumstances in detail. Other knowledge, even if developed on his/her own, may be influenced by others to a greater or lesser extent, intentionally or unintentionally. From here, topics such as education, brainwashing, persuasion, convention, fraud, and interpersonal coercion can be brought out simultaneously. Since one person can use communication channels to directly influence another person's mental system, interpersonal coercion can be implicit and not show much in its physical appearance.

The concept of "will" is easy to understand in the Algorithmic framework, because the actors often need to subjectively assign values to variables: to assign or not to assign, and what to assign. Although the word "will" is generally used in conventional terms to refer to *decisions* about external actions, in fact, inside the brain, there are a large number of decision-making problems. The extension of the word "decision-making", like the scope of words "behavior" and "action", is now expanding to the realm of thoughts. Thus, even in scientific research, there is a question of will. The "will" or "consciousness", that is, the "hotspot" that exists at the *very bottom* of all spiritual things, is the "central processing unit", or "meta-computation". Whether or not the "central processing unit" is anatomically present or not, whether it is fixed or mobile in the brain, does not affect the above conclusions. Even if fixed, it is not contradictory to the subjective feeling that our consciousness can swim freely, autonomously, and proactively in the ocean of spirit. Because it's just a *relative motion, consciousness can be passive or proactive, fixed or mobile,* and its movement can be switched freely between various modes. These phenomena are all things that we can feel.

Consciousness can also decide whether or not it needs to monitor itself in the process of computations. This is one of the higher-order issues described above. The same is true for computers. A computer can be set up to record and proactively monitor its own activities. However, in the serial mode, this high-order activity will significantly crowd out resources for first-order and other computations, so its scope and frequency have to be limited. The same is also true for human computing.

First, because of the existence of temporary memory, we can assume that data about the computational activities are automatically stored in the temporary memory, and the actor must decide whether to "deliberately" save the data after the end of certain particular computations, or to ignore them and discard them. If you want to save them, you need to pause subsequent computations, transfer the data to the long-term storage (triggering certain storing computations), and then continue with subsequent computations, and so on. The accumulation of data stored in the long-term storage can be used to build a more comprehensive understanding of oneself, and the mechanism should be similar to that of other objects. Strictly speaking, although this understanding is aimed at the "*past self*" rather than the "*present self*", this "past self" is constantly refreshed with the addition of new monitoring data, then it can always continue to approach the "present self".

Some of the documents on self-consciousness have always puzzled why consciousness is capable of monitoring oneself while being object-oriented; this question can now be answered in the following way. In fact, Algorithmically, *consciousness cannot monitor itself at the beginning*, because the capacity of meta-computation is limited; if a computation can monitor itself at the same time of the computation, then two computations, the computation and the monitoring computation as another computation, are carried out concurrently, and the Algorithmic theory will not be strictly established. Moreover, when a computation is in progress, that is, when it is not completed, meaning that the object of monitoring has not yet been completed, then, what is it monitoring? Therefore, it is logically contradictory. That is to say, *the self-consciousness formed by the individual is always defective, because the current computation is always missing in it.* However, the content of this single current computation can be very small in comparison with the self-consciousness formed from enormous stocked data, hence this loss can be generally negligible. Even if it shall not be ignored, the next moment after this computation is completed, the data about this computation can be added to the stocked data to refresh the self.

The above reasoning shows that self-consciousness can never be complete, and has to be dynamic. This deficiency is not only due to the hindrance of the current computation, but more importantly, the records of the past can never be complete, and it is impossible to incorporate any details of any computation into the long-term memory, because this can cause a huge amount of computations, and even lead to a combinatorial explosion. If it is strictly required, self-monitoring activities as a kind of computation will also need to be monitored, which will exacerbate the issue of combinatorial explosions. Of course, in fact, only when activities such as self-monitoring, self-evaluation, and self-adjustment are carried out to a certain extent will there be a need to monitor, evaluate, and adjust these activities themselves. This will lead to the "second-order self-awareness". The second-order self-awareness may target less data than those of first-order. By analogy, the *process of self-consciousness will be believed to gradually shrink.* This is the "*attenuation effect*" mentioned earlier. In the social realm, the attenuation effect is a non-linear phenomenon, and the thinking economy is the reason behind it. This realization can help us get out of some confusions about our senses of the selves.

The above is the process of re-understanding oneself by computing activities. As for other aspects of the "self" (e.g., the physiological aspects), it can be assumed that consciousness will know them as if they were external objects, even if this process of knowing faces some special difficulties. However, consciousness also has other special difficulties in recognizing other external objects; hence, in principle, this is not different.

§55. Consciousness (3)

One of the confusing properties of the phenomenon of consciousness is that it is messy and "unruly", and hence difficult to grasp. It's not as orderly as a logical system or a scientific system. On the other hand, both the logical system and the scientific system seem to be only some of its components. However, these are all just traditional illusions. Algorithmically, it can be said that conscious activities have always operated "logically" and "orderly". From the traditional point of view to the Algorithmic point of view, it needs to go through two steps; one is to expand logic to the science of thinking, and the other is to expand traditional logic to the Algorithmic logic, thus making a comprehensive system.

The expansion of logic to the science of thinking is the inevitable result of the materialization of thoughts. As long as we understand that reasoning (as the core of logic) is the *real process* of generating new data from existing data, then we must ask, where do this "existing data" come from? Then, we enter into the scenario of the distributed data in space, where the necessities of data transmission and data search arise. Since data are transmitted or searched, it can be seen that "transmission" and "search" are the indispensable components of the logical system. Without these tools and their work, logical reasoning would be impossible. In this way, we will move out of the narrow and provincial logics to the broad, easy-going system of Instructions, or the "science of thinking". In it, traditional logical reasoning is viewed as real mental activities against data entities.

The operation of the Instructional system constitutes the phenomenon of consciousness, and forms free will. Then, will it run logically or "illogically"? To solve this problem, we have proposed the concept of "Algorithmic logic". It means that since ideas are entities, there are characteristics such as time, space, costs, and benefits relating to the entities, and the Instruction system then decides what operations to perform and how to arrange them according to the characteristics of each Instruction and information, as well as the expected costs and benefits of each planned computing operation. This logic is called "Algorithmic logic".

Hence, pros and cons analysis needs to be done for a specific computing project. The so-called "pros and cons" always refer to the pros and cons of certain computing activity. Therefore, the formation of this computing activity must take precedence over the pros and cons analysis. This activity can have already taken place. However, as far as the scheduling of the Instructional system is concerned, such an activity is primarily planned, proposed, virtual, conceived by the actors in their own minds. Therefore, as soon as such a pros and cons analysis is developed, it also means that the computational activities are self-objectified, and hence it must be in the orbit of time. Estimates of the pros and cons of a particular operating scenario are mostly prospective and most likely only approximate. Importantly, it is higher-order. Without the mechanism of self-objectification and higher-order, the pros and cons analysis cannot be carried out. Moreover, these related elements are all mutually necessary and indispensable. This is the reminder we want to give to economics.

We don't have to go into great details about how the pros and cons analysis initially unfolded, nor do we have to assert in a mystical tone that "organisms are born with pros and cons analysis". The pros and cons analysis is initially likely to be non-existent, or performed at a lower level with the support of hard software. The failure rate of thinking activities must also be high at this time. The concepts of pros and cons should be gradually developed in the experiences of successes and failures, from indirect to direct, from implicit to explicit, from subconscious to conscious, from qualitative to quantitative, and the methods of pros and cons analysis are gradually generated and cultivated, from rudimentary to advanced. This is where the Algorithmic approach is easy to carry out, and where it is "tolerant" and inclusive. Moreover, there is no such thing as a "standard" or "absolutely correct" analysis.

However, in any case, a wide variety of computations will be carried out in a certain order. The actors do not necessarily focus on the activities of a given sequence (like a computerized program), but rather assess the situations and move forward alternately and jump between different sequences, according to the results of the pros and cons analysis. He/she can postpone a sequence, advance a sequence, interrupt a sequence, and insert other activities into it. Computational operations can also be fragmented without a fixed sequence, or combined with serialized and fragmented operations. These actions can be work-based, or casual and enjoyable (e.g., concentrating on tasting food or watching movies). He/she can refuse to answer or set aside a question, or "respond" to a question with a bizarre answer or reaction (all as the results of the materialization of thoughts). He/she can also give many answers to a question, or hesitate. He/she can also be lazy, resting, mindless, and so on.

In my opinion, the above may be some important features of the seemingly "chaotic" and "confusing" activity of consciousness. In fact, looking at them with the Algorithmic logic, they are all fairly orderly, reasonable, or understandable phenomena. To put it in the language of economic theory, the actors seek to maximize the overall returns, and in most cases use the method of maximizing marginal returns to make decisions. The phenomenon of actors shuttling back and forth between different tasks is the result of this marginal analysis.

The above economic analysis is by no means perfect, and a further dissection and correction of it will be done later in the chapter. This is only an example of how these whimsical phenomena of consciousness can be subordinated to the principle of rationality. Nonetheless, because of the unavoidable analytic subjectivity (as we have also revealed), people may have different opinions on how to optimize their own decisions, and the observers and analysts may also have their own opinions, thus the application of the rational principle does not mean that people will unanimously agree on the relevant outcome. Free will and determinism go hand in hand here.[3] It could even be said that they have been combined

---

3. For an extant discussion, see Jaegwon Kim et al. (ed.), "A Companion to Metaphysics", 2nd edition, Willey-Blackwell, 2009, pp. 18-20.

here—or rather, reconciled.

These characteristics of conscious behaviors can also be further understood by observing the behaviors of robots. What are the characteristics of robots compared to ordinary machines? What is the difficulty of developing robots? Through observation, we can realize that, first of all, a robot lives in a discrete environment, and its relatively limited, specific, and small body has to travel back and forth between heterogeneous physical objects and perform different actions. This requires a task pattern that ordinary machines do not face. Even if the robot always responds the same way to a single specific problem or stimulus, the task becomes much more difficult when these many elements are mixed. Therefore, a machine that can handle a specific complex task within the right time is also considered to have a high degree of resemblance to a human. We will not discuss other deep questions about human intelligence for now, but we need primarily to highlight this basic mechanism.

Finally, I am reminded of Russell's "logical atomism". It should be said that the basic direction of Russell's thought is consistent with the Algorithmic theory. Russell also seemed to have tried to construct the smallest unit of mental activity in a discrete environment, and then based on that, to construct his philosophical system. He even put pluralism in an important position. Eventually, however, he focused his attention on external objects and tried to find the "atomic facts"[4], which made his pluralistic premise null and void. As a result, the philosophy of logical positivism has unfortunately developed into a narrow path of "scientism", leaving out a large number of subjective, vague, but important elements. As mentioned earlier, the modern logic, developed by Frege, Russell, Wittgenstein, and others, made important contributions to the

---

4. Bertrand Russell, "The Philosophy of Logical Atomism", Routledge, 2010.

creation of computers and the development of related disciplines. Now, we have to use Russell's contribution to correct his own biases.

§56. Consciousness (4)

The mysteries of consciousness are numerous and complex, but they are being revealed one by one by artificial intelligence engineering. Now, with the addition of Algorithmic Theory, we can explain more phenomena of consciousness. Everything in this chapter is related to consciousness. As a specific discussion, this and the following section deals with a number of conscious issues.

The first is perception. Much of the traditional scientific and philosophical literature has focused on discussions of the front-end of computing, such as sensation and perception. Sensation obtains the most primitive information, and perception further processes and organizes them to form cognition about an object as a whole. That is to say, the perceptual phase already involves information processing. A typical perceptual process is the synthesis of information, such as the synthesis of fragmented information from an outside object into a whole image in mind. This synthetic process is a process of summarization, that is, refining and simplifying, hence it can be said that the perceptual process is actually quite "Algorithmical". In addition, according to the requirements of computational economy, it is necessary to select, model, predict, and so on, the information. These Algorithmic effects are basically relatively anti-mainstream and alternative, but people often don't understand their "Algorithmicity", hence sometimes make a fuss about them.

An example of this is "pattern", such as the patterns in face recognition. There is a lot of information from the eyes; image technology, a branch of computer science, can tell us how huge information a picture contains (hence some traditional encryption techniques are based on graphics). If the brain's computing power can afford to receive and process all of this great information quickly enough, it would undoubtedly lead to the best effect for recognition of a human face. However, meta-computation and its speed do not allow for this, hence Algorithms come into play, and some trade-offs must occur. A better strategy (as an Algorithm) is to pick some prominent "feature values" and ignore other common information. These feature values can form a "pattern". It's like drawing a sketch, and in just a few strokes, a human figure can come to life. However, this is not where the brain is "smart", but it has to do it as a last resort. This simplification is really risky. For example, you remember someone wearing large, dark-framed glasses, but if that person takes them off one day, you probably won't recognize them. Hence, there's not so much to show off about the strategy of patterning. Since we want to simplify, of course, we must give priority to the selection of feature values, and it is impossible to first select the ordinary information that every face has! Nonetheless, in some past years I heard many praises that the human brain's pattern recognition ability was "amazing". This surprise reflected that we have had lived in a sea of distortive minds without knowing the distortions.

Another phenomenon is "binocular competition": when both eyes are confronted with different images at close range at the same time, the person's attention jumps between the two eyes.[5] This phenomenon can be a typical reflection of the serial way the human brain works. If the theory of meta-computation had been established earlier, this would not have been an explanatory problem. Another example is mispronunciation: shuffling the order of words in a common sentence and

---

5. Blake, Randolph; Logothetis, Nikos K. (1 January 2002). "Visual competition". Nature Reviews Neuroscience. 3 (1): 13–21.

presenting it to readers, who will quickly "read out" its correct order. Obviously, it is not that the readers discover the wrong order of the words and then corrects them and reads them "correctly", but that readers usually invoke their own memories (the invoking is obviously faster than they read at this point), aid the reading with the correct words they remember, and simply "pick up" some of the feature values of the image presented in front of them, and then synthesize them into the one answer. Such experiments reveal a big secret, that is, whether we listen to lectures or read, we must frequently use this synthetic mode to improve the speed of information reception and comprehension. Why? The reason for this is obviously the economics of computations: the need for speed outweighs the need for accuracy. The benefits can be illustrated by the fact that native speakers of a particular language generally speak, read, and write much faster than non-native speakers, who tend to have significantly fewer text samples stored in their brains. If the former do not adopt this aggressive strategy, they will probably understand and use language at the same speed as the latter.

Such *predictive mechanisms* can explain numerous puzzles about consciousness. In fact, the brain should be doing what it is doing while preparing for the stimulus it predicts. A well-known example is Pavlov's experiment, in which a dog drooled before he could hear the meal-opening bell and not even see the food. The same is true for people. The human brain is clearly happy to prepare for this in advance, even if it turns out to be a waste. This makes economic sense. For example, in the "rubber hand illusion" experiment, the subject hides one of his real hands and places a similar prosthetic hand in the usual position of the real hand, and then the researcher alternately hits the prosthetic hand and the subject's other real hand, with the result that the subject appears to feel the "pain" of the prosthetic hand.[6] In particular, the experiment requires a bit of Algorithmic explanation: the similarity of the prosthetic hand to the real hand, the position of the prosthetic hand, and the alternating hits to the two symmetrical targets all generate and reinforce the subject's cerebral associative or analogous computations, making the subject mistakenly believe that the real hand is being struck; or, the subject subconsciously believes that the real hand he is hiding is in danger of being hit, and then he/she mobilizes his/her physical and mental strength to prepare for the hit, and the painful memory of past hits is then awakened.

Another mechanism related to prediction, which I call the *"authorization mechanism"*, can be used to explain the phenomenon of so-called "time delay". For example, the subjects were asked to do a certain action, which the subjects did, but a probe of the subjects' brain systems revealed that the "decisions" to act had been made before the subjects were aware of them.[7] In this regard, I believe that this is the authorization mechanism at work: after some routine operations are carried out repeatedly, the subjects will feel secure and relaxed, and then the decision-making mechanisms will be simplified, and the "programs" in the subjects' brains will become shorter and shorter. Then, as soon as a condition appears to trigger such a short program, it starts to run immediately. This is not to say that the process is fully automated and the consciousness is completely uninvolved, but rather that the amount of computations that require consciousness to do has been reduced to such a level that it might not be easily detected by researchers. When the subjects

---

6. Botvinick, M.; Cohen, J. "Rubber Hands 'Feel' Touch That Eyes See". Nature 391, 756 (1998). https://doi.org/10.1038/35784
7. Soon, C.; Brass, M.; Heinze, HJ. et al. "Unconscious Determinants of Free Decisions in the Human Brain". Nature Neuroscience 11, 543–545 (2008). https://doi.org/10.1038/nn.2112

enter the experimental site, they must have made a judgment that the environment was safe and thus they could respond to the instructions of the researchers without examination or hesitation. In other words, they have temporarily added the "researcher's instructions" as a trigger condition of the above-mentioned mini programs in their minds, so that they could be executed quickly. However, an authorization may need to be reviewed. When the authorization is set, the actors would have decided whether, when, and how to review it. Thereafter, a general arrangement of the actors shall be that certain instructions can be executed first, and then reviewed and re-affirmed. As a result, the conscious reviewing and re-affirming processes detected by researchers lagged behind the executions, despite the possibility that it might be too late to intervene in the executive actions. If the reviews were not passed, the actions that had been performed or were being performed would be revoked or stopped. Presumably many people must have this kind of experience.

§57. Consciousness (5)

There is also a mechanism, which I will call the "*Alarm Mechanism*", which means that the consciousness will usually set up an alarm system when awake to monitor the surrounding situation. In the event of a major emergency, the alarm system will interrupt the ongoing work of the person concerned pursuant to the prior authorization, insert a task process and report it. This mechanism can be used to explain the classic problem of consciousness: in a noisy party, A and B talk face to face, seemingly undisturbed by others, but when someone else mentions A's name elsewhere, A interrupts the conversation with B and responds quickly. My explanation for this is that although A seems quite attentive when chatting with B, he/she is also running his/her own alarm system at the same time. The triggering of the alarm system is conditional, and those conditions have been gradually accumulated and built up by one's past life experience, and additional adjustments may also have been made on the spot of the party. An alert is to be raised once one of the conditions is met, such as being called by A's name. Some people may ask: since the consciousness activity is singular and serially carried out, how can A be able to monitor the surrounding situation while chatting? The answer is that meta-computing frequently switches between the two tasks of "chatting" and "monitoring" (and even others). In serial jobs on computers, this kind of interrupt and insertion operations happen actually very frequently. However, because computers are running so fast, it is often not easy for observers or users to notice that the current operations have been interrupted and plugged in. My own observations and experiences can tell us that we are generally not very attentive in our chats in public, and our consciousness has been continuously aware of the surrounding situation. On the other hand, our minds can be much more attentive in private places. This shows that the operating intensity of the alarm system is actually generally flexible and contingent. The amount of insertion work can sometimes be very small and short, depending on our overall judgment about the situation of the environment. But, in any case, it's hard to imagine that it would be completely absent.

Each of the above cases is not complicated, and even falls into those that "once it is proposed, it is commonly agreed." Then, how did they become "puzzles" of psychologists? In my opinion, this is the undesirable consequence of physicalism and behaviorism, which has caused psychologists, from the very beginning, to habitually regard any object as existing and moving like a physical object. Even if the object of study is a mental activity familiar to each of us, it is treated preferentially as a physical object. An inevitable influence of this is that consciousness is firstly regarded as a "dumbheaded" thing, and its processing of information is also mechanically straightforward, completely losing the quick-witted, flexible, reflexive, jumpy, and mixed properties of consciousness. Then, the researchers let out a startled cry, and all of a sudden, the problems arise. In front of consciousness, consciousness has turned into a strange object!

Now, we have to adopt a different methodological principle: we do not resort to other methods for phenomena that can be Algorithmically explained.

While the mysteries of consciousness are being unraveled one by one, we can ask the following question: After various explanations, is there anything left in the phenomena of consciousness that needs a further explanation? In this regard, it has been suggested that consciousness has a special *experiential* quality, which is exclusive and cannot be copied by external objects. Just as it is impossible for us humans to understand how a bat in the dark feels about sound waves[8], it is impossible for a person who has never seen red to know what red really looks like. Such a defense seems plausible. However, we need first to consider the philosophical and social science implications of this view. This view is nothing more than an emphasis on the flaws of our knowledge and the limitations of "scientific explanations". In a group that pursues perfect knowledge and thinks they already have "fairly perfect" knowledge, the point alleging the existence of such an absolute boundary seems earth-shattering. And, as mentioned earlier, this view of absolute boundaries also seems to be to the taste of this group—they therefore do not have to be disturbed by the reality of intellectual imperfections. However, in our bounded rational, and thus Algorithmical approach, we are in a sea of

---

8. Thomas Nagel, "What Is It Like to Be a Bat?", The Philosophical Review, Vol. 83, No. 4 (Oct., 1974), pp. 435-450.

"imperfections", and this "exception" is not at all surprising—here, neither various "absolute perfections" nor "absolute unknowables", as a few extreme cases, are groundbreaking.

Secondly, the experiential process is also a computational process, or in other words, preparation for data processing. When we mobilize our physical and mental resources to "experience" an object, we are discovering a wealth of information that can be used for subsequent computations. After these experiences have occurred, they are further reflected in the process of computations as our evaluations and reactions to the external object (e.g., a commodity) that caused the experiences, perhaps leading to a change in our physical or mental behaviors. We can also "confide" in, compare, or "affirm" each other's experiences through verbal and other communicational channels between us. That is, the experiences can at least be partially externalized and socialized. Out of respect for these experiences, and for other reasons, philosophers such as Kant shouted the slogan "Man is the end".

Next, not only are the spiritual experiences unique, but also the thinking of humans, as well as the objects, are all unique to each other. As mentioned earlier, it cannot be assumed that the fact that a computer can *simulate* human thinking activity means that the computer does have a mind. Since the knotted rope simulated human counting, so did the rope have a mind? "Thinking" is the unique way of the human brain itself (and animals), and of course cannot be "understood" by inanimate objects. There is no question of "understanding" in those inanimate objects. Now, isn't it a little funny to say that our experience is unique? If these inanimate objects could speak, perhaps they would ask: Aren't we unique? Do you humans really already know us? How can you guarantee that any so-called "knowledge" you have about us will continue to work in the next second?

Finally, under the Algorithmic framework, the uniqueness of personal experience is especially accompanied by the uniqueness of personal knowledge. Given the universality of Instructions and how they operate, although the production of specific knowledge does not vary from person to person, due to the role of big data, the knowledge gathered in the human brain is different from person to person, and the computations and results performed by specific individuals are not necessarily duplicated with others. The uniqueness of individual knowledge will now coexist with the uniqueness of individual experience and reinforce the ethical principle of "respect for an individual". On the other hand, the above discussion acknowledges the exclusivity of the human experience relative to other species, but this exclusivity can hardly be considered absolute. For example, if one day in the future, the human nervous system can connect with bats, and humans and bats may be able to communicate with each other about their experiences. How can this possibility be entirely ruled out? I argue this not only for the sake of arguing, but to stress that although the Algorithmic method is boundedly rational, it can also include developments. If readers think that the above possibility is somewhat reasonable, then it will also be found that this "Algorithmic position" can be much more flexible and inclusive than the traditional mainstream position, and its methodological advantages are obvious.

§58. Consciousness (6)

As the main target of our Algorithmical argumentation, the philosophy we call "extreme rationalism" has many manifestations. It can even be said that, in almost every context, we can discern what is extreme rationalism and, therefore, what is the "Algorithmical". For example, "perfect rationality" is a variation of extreme rationalism. And in the context of psychology and consciousness, one of its variants is the idealization of consciousness as something complete or unified, even mystical. In the professional literature, this topic focuses on the concept of "unity of consciousness". In a broader field, it is sometimes expanded to concepts of "the unity of the individual", "the unity of the self", consistency, systematization, and so on.

It is quite plausible when the unity of consciousness refers to the "singularity" of consciousness, which suggests the smallest unit of mental activity. This singularity makes consciousness indivisible, or makes its meaning change dramatically after it is divided and hence ceases to be consciousness. For example, we don't discuss the meaning of "half Instruction" or "quarter meta-computation". Although we clearly know what components are needed to perform a meta-computation and what kind of micro step(s) is required for a meta-computation, its significance as "a computation" is not established until it is completed as a temporal process. Conversely, after a meta-computation is completed, it obtains an independent meaning, just as an Instruction and a piece of data (information) have their respective independent meanings. Their singularity and independence happen simultaneously and inseparably. Therefore, I believe that ATT based on computer science has perfectly portrayed the unity of consciousness, no more and no less.

However, the confusions that have occurred on this issue seem to be linked in the first place to the issue of "singleness of information". For example, researchers have found that people sometimes treat multiple pieces of sensory information (e.g., sound and pain) from different channels as one piece of information rather than as multiple pieces.[9] This question

---

9. Andrew Brook and Paul Raymont, "The Unity of Consciousness", The Stanford Encyclopedia of Philosophy (Summer 2021 Edition), Edward N. Zalta

sharply raises the question of the unity of consciousness. It is true that a format of Instruction has made it clear that there is a limit to the number of pieces of information that can be contained in a single Instruction. Meanwhile, this concept shows that "computation" itself requires that its processing object(s), i.e. data or information, have a certain "customization"; that is, it requires that "information" have a fixed unit, just as a machine has requirements for the volume of its raw materials, which can neither be too small nor too large. Also, it measures the size of the information in a discrete, integer manner, such as 1 piece, 2 pieces, 3 pieces, and so on, rather than 1.1 pieces, 2.39 pieces, 3.05 pieces. However, it is important to distinguish and emphasize here that this format requirement does not mechanically correspond to the *division of information in its physical natures*. The physical signals that produce information sometimes have their natural physical boundaries, but the human brain can collect information from them in its own formats—and then process it. For example, noise and pain are usually processed separately as two different pieces of information, but when they come from the same object, the human brain often deems it necessary to merge them. Since a metacomputation can generally process two pieces of information, we can assume that noise and pain can be "synthesized" by a metacomputation into *a new piece* of information (or symbol), and then this new information (or symbol) participates in any subsequent operations representing the object as a single message. If there are any other pieces of information generated from this object, they can also be concocted in a similar way. We can understand this process as an integral part of the process of producing a perception or a concept. Obviously, such merging does not have to be limited to

---

(ed.), URL = <https://plato.stanford.edu/archives/sum2021/entries/consciousness-unity/>.

the information of the same nature exactly. This is different from arithmetic operations. Considering that not all different pieces of information are processed in this way, it can be speculated that when the above-mentioned commenters are surprised in their experiments, such a process of synthesis and conceptualization must have taken place repeatedly in the subjects' mind beforehand, and hence they must have already been familiar with it, so that such "unity" could be exhibited in the experiments.

Theorists have been usually familiar with the process of "analysis". No matter how small an object is subdivided and how rich the data it generates, theorists will not feel surprised, weird, or deviant about it. On the contrary, the "synthesis" process is more or less "alternative" to everyone. This is because in the process of "synthesis", it is inevitable that some operations of approximation and omission will occur, which seems contrary to the spirit of science. However, computations must be seen as *interacting* with external raw information in the established structures and ways of our human brains, and we both conform to information and distort information; we magnify the small and shrink the large, complicate what seems simple and simplify what seems complex, and so on. Information produces information (knowledge) in the human brain, and the information produced then generates new information, and so on. The infinite depth of processing will make the forms and contents of information more and more distant from its origin's (and perhaps closer and closer to the "truth"). It's all commonplace. The physical properties behind information must have an influence on the division of information in the human brain, because the observance of physical properties leads to computational convenience and economy, but *the view that information has naturally an absolute, standard way of division is consistent with the "atomic fact" argument that we have refuted in §55. The mistakes of this argument can be ascribed to the metaphysics of extreme rationalism.* It can be inferred that if information can only be processed in a given form, and cannot be decomposed, altered, or synthesized, the consequences must be very serious. In particular, when it cannot be synthesized, we human beings will never be able to make a concise and general statement. This consequence would be grossly contrary to our life experience.

Further, the Algorithmic principles necessarily require the argument that *in principle, the information contained in any object or entity must be regarded as infinite.* While the form and content of a particular piece of information are limited, its use expands with the depth of processing, and must therefore be seen as infinite.

The next issue is the coherence and systematicity of consciousness. When the perspective of analysis enters the human brain, in the face of many stocks of knowledge, arguers tend to assume that the active "rational homunculus" can take care of everything. Another manifestation of this perception is that an organization is considered to have the potential to practice some sound management, provided that its head is rational enough. As a result, such a sage-like, one-man center is often expected by society. Through this path, the unity of consciousness becomes a theoretical basis for centralized governance as opposed to democracy.

The first thing I want to say about this point of view is that the question of "unity of consciousness" is not, first of all, a question of the degree of coherence *within* consciousness. Because meta-computation is consciousness, and meta-computation is the smallest unit of mental activity, strictly speaking, this question is meaningless. It's not that the coherence or consistency in consciousness can be judged by the outside world, but that the consistency comes exactly from the consciousness, which dictates what "consistency" is, and then works hard to bring the consistency to information, and then to the outside world. All of us judge the coherence or systematicity of other objects according to how consciousness and thus meta-computation "tells" us, and not conversely judge consciousness itself according to the "criteria" from elsewhere. Since metacomputation cannot be meaningfully divided, this problem cannot be determined from outside. It is the source of theoretical analysis.

In other words, such judgments can only occur *between* information and information, or *between* meta-computation and meta-computation. We can even say (not exactly) that there is only as much consistency in the world as how many metacomputations have been done. Because the number of computations of any history is limited, we can only ask "how much consistency is there in this world at present", but not "whether there is a contradiction" (if no, then the consistency in it would become "complete"). As far as the human brain, thinking system, or Instruction system is concerned, we cannot think that the knowledge we have, or the knowledge in anyone's head, is completely consistent, and *we also cannot think that these many Instructions are completely consistent with each other* (although there is a certain degree of compatibility and collaborativeness between them), *or that computations are completely consistent with knowledge, or that any parts of the thinking system or any thinking operations are completely consistent with each other.* This is the basic way in which we reconcile pluralism with consistency.

Well, now we're finally at pluralism. In this pluralistic world, consistency or systematicity (or order) is always local. Then, within any delimited spatial range, there is the question of more and less consistency, namely, the degree of consistency (as the "softness"). And it is in this sense that because the internal communication of the human brain is far more convenient than that of people, and the processing of information in close proximity is more convenient than that of information processing in distance, the internal consistency of a person's thoughts is often higher than that of a group, and the internal consistency in small areas (e.g., a cluster of temporary computations) is often higher than that in large areas (e.g., the long-term memory in the human brain). Obviously, because phenomena such as these are unfortunately misunderstood, they are wrongly reduced to the question of the unity of consciousness and then idealized.

A related problem is that in philosophy and social sciences, the functions of a single organism are often regarded as an "organic" unity or continuum, ideal and absolute. In this regard, my view is similar; that is, this unity can only be viewed in a limited way within this framework of relativity.

§59. Desire

Let's start by considering the Instruction system as a toolbox for individuals. Then, what is the purpose of this "toolbox"? The question sounds plausible at least to common sense, because the word "tool" is actually symbiotic with "purpose", pairwise. However, the Algorithmic approach requires us to interpret any object as much as possible with the instrumental, namely, traditionally the "rational" and "scientific" logic, so as to give full play to the role of the Algorithmic principles. This is also a common requirement of the "grand synthesis".

However, it should be recognized firstly that just as the concept group of "entity-behavior-change" was created, the *concept group of "end-means (tool)" is also a product of the serial computing method in the case of limited computing power.* It's not that we naturally have these concepts in our minds, but that our computational objects can't be "contained" by meta-computing all at once, therefore, we have to divide them into two parts, end and means, and study them separately, and then study the *relationship* between them. As an example, this consequence reflects that knowledge is the product of the collision and run-in of our subjective structure with external information, rather than favoring any one party and relegating or neglecting the other. It can be inferred that such "arbitrariness" will inevitably lead to the following undesirable consequences at the same time: end and means cannot be completely distinguished in some places; one or both are missing; and even if they are identified, it is impossible to effectively compare or calculate the relevant cost-benefit items, and so on. As long as we realize that this division is partly of our own making, we will not make a fuss about these undesirable things, blame the objective world, or insist on looking for any "final truth" in the objective world.

The above approach of "pluralism + higher-order consistency" is our higher-order way of synthesizing end and means. Of course, this is not enough, and we need to go back to the first-order analysis.

At the first order, desire is a spiritual thing that the individual can perceive, and thus it is a presence in the individual's consciousness, or a mental "variable". It reflects the "requirements" of the human body's physiological system for the psychological system, or the hardware system for the software system; that is, the former "tells" the latter what to do. In computer language, this is a "hardware-software interface". At this point, the software work comes to its beginning. In other words, desire can be an "exogenous variable" for philosophical, psychological, or social science analysis. This is where the analysis starts, and we don't have to go any further.

However, here, the Algorithmic analysis can allow us to take a step forward and cross the boundary between hardware and software to understand the generation of desires. This does not mean we have abolished our own principle of "mind-body separation". This is only a temporary, exceptional trespass that is still intended to demonstrate and illustrate the Algorithmic approach.

There are many conditions that need to be met for an organism to survive. Providing and configuring the "equipment" of the spiritual system is one of the ways in which the organism satisfies these conditions—this understanding can be useful in this context, although it assumes a purpose on the organism that transcends the thinking system and stands on the "perspective" of its "designer" or "creator". The "designer's perspective" has been a common approach. We have not intended to build a flawless analysis. Obviously, the "designer" has a variety of means or schemes to provide and configure the equipment, e.g., the establishment of an automated system outside of the thinking system that works on its own without intervention of the thinking system. Suffice it to say, most of the systems are automated. Hair and nails grow on their own. Although they grow on our bodies, we can neither feel their growth, nor know how they grow, nor can we directly control them to grow faster or slower. The heart beats on its own, and we only feel it occasionally and cannot directly control its beating. Food is digested automatically, but chewing needs to be learned on its own, and this is something that the mind system can be involved in a little. More interesting is breathing: the consciousness can both feel it and control it moderately in order to avoid choking in the water, so that amphibiousness can be achieved for a short time.

Why are there such different "arrangements"? Obviously, many functions need to run continuously and stably; *if they are left to the command of the thinking system, it will do more harm than good.* The thinking system is limited in its capabilities and ever-changing, and its instability will bring danger to the operation of many systems. For example, if the heartbeats are controlled directly by the brain, we may sometimes forget the "beating". If the liver's work requires direct intervention from the thinking system, the process of food digestion and absorption may be disrupted. On the other hand, there are tasks that cannot be done by automation. For example, the acquisition of food is not something that can be "decided" by one's own body, but must be intervened by the thinking system. The thinking system directs the body to produce physical movements, acting on the outside world, in order to obtain food. Compare the way food is obtained with that for the acquisition of air, and we will see the ingenuity of nature's arrangement: air is supplied everywhere and at all times, hence breathing is basically automatic, and if air requires our subjective and conscious efforts to obtain *intermittently*, it may be supplied in the same way as food.

That is to say, there are multiple relationships between the thinking system and other systems, such as competition, division of labor, collaboration, etc. The result of this "overall weighing" is that *the "designer" has given it only the "work" that is appropriate for the thinking system to undertake.* These "jobs" are specific, limited, and varied in type and nature. They are mainly manifested in various physiological desires of people. For the sake of operational reliability, these desires are based on biological genetic mechanisms and thus given in a "hard software" manner and remain largely unchanged throughout one's lifetime.

We don't need to enumerate and analyze each of these desires in detail. The next question is: what is the relationship between these desires and Algorithmic Theory?

§60. Desire (continued)

The above hypothetical analysis from the perspective of the "designer" leads us to recognize the various Algorithmical natures of desire. In particular, desire is like the subjective ideas and patterns that arise from mental distortions; it is crude and sketchy, but it is stable and reliable, and thus has a computing economy.

The human body lives in the natural environment, not only to adapt to the variability of the spatial environment, but also to endure the long-term nature of time, and the resulting concrete demands must be complex and changeable. Fortunately, the human body has a thinking system. Neither ordinary inanimate objects nor plants have such a system of thinking, hence their operations can only be mechanical (or comparatively mechanical). Although ordinary animals have a thinking system, they are not as advanced as humans. Since the human thinking system is highly precise, flexible, and developmental, it is assumed that it can meet the various needs of human survival in a relatively comprehensive way. Imagine if there were precise communicational mechanisms between the various biological tissues of the human body and the thinking system, as if customers could precisely tailor products and services to restaurants, wouldn't it be more ideal?

However, these biological tissues of the human body no longer have their own "thinking system" that should have been responsible for communicating with the thinking system of the human brain. As a kind of "hardware", a biological tissue can only use its own way and its own "language" to "speak" to the thinking system. *Desire is just such a "language".* The sensory system is the channel to convey such a "language". A message in the language crosses this mysterious wall between hardware and software, from the biological tissues to the mind, like the Chinese "Laoshan Taoist Priest" who can break through a wall[10]. The mental activity is also interesting in this way: it cannot directly feed back to biological tissues, as is often the

---

10. A Chinese fable tells of a Taoist priest on Mount Laoshan (崂山) whose body could pass through walls without being harmed. See Songling Pu, "Strange Stories from a Chinese Studio", translated by John Minford, Penguin Books, 2006, pp. 50-54.

case with waiters in restaurants, but it has to compute the messages, turn them into decisions that cross this mysterious wall again, turning the decisions into physical actions, and then generating certain feelings to satisfy, procrastinate, or "reject" (suppress) desires. They just communicate with each other in this "silent" way.

On the one hand, biological tissues need to be "wary" of the thinking system and not to give it a job that is unsuitable for it, and on the other hand, they must use it sparingly, due to its limited capabilities. This explains why the types of desires are very limited, from a few to a dozen (even including the so-called "spiritual pursuits"). This amount must be significantly less than the amount of the wide variety of "demands" of an organism. *There is also clearly a mechanism of "generalization", in which a multitude of related needs is expressed in a generalized way as a single desire.* For example, the needs for nutrients in many organs, and for tastes in the digestive organs, are uniformly expressed as "appetite". As long as the appetite is satisfied, the requirements of a large number of related organs and tissues are basically satisfied—I say "basic" because the guidance of desire is obviously not precise enough. For example, a person who pursues health only by satisfying his appetite may end up with obesity and disease.

At the same time, we realize that the most direct messenger of desire is the senses. The sensory system is not only a messenger of the outside world, but also a messenger between the human body and the thinking system. Feelings can be divided into at least three categories: positive, negative, and neutral. Positive feelings are pleasant, while negative feelings are uncomfortable. This is like the reward and punishment mechanisms that induce or force the thinking system to make some tendentious decisions. A desire can be expressed as multiple feelings, manifesting differently in dimensions such as intensity, time, space, etc. However, they are often associated with the acquisition of a single object, and are therefore rationally and abstractly generalized as a certain desire. For example, sexual desire can be expressed in many ways, but sexual activity calms all these feelings *simultaneously*, thus we rationally say that people have the "sexual desire".

Various Algorithmical characteristics of physiological desires can only be seen more clearly in comparison with psychological, ideological, or abstract "wishes", "intentions", "goals", "values", "preferences", and so on. Physiological desires, whether permanent or cyclical, are very stable in time, and not as fickle as the latter. Comparatively, they have a high degree of interpersonal consistency (although they are also interpersonally different to some degree), while the latter ones are rife with interpersonal differences. Things like "wishes" are like unreliable friends who can dump you at any time. On the other hand, the reliability of physiological desires is worth paying for or saving for at any time. Even if you make extra efforts, they will come as promised and will not fail you in the end. The *one-way* and stable character of physiological desires can create conditions for *continuous* development. Therefore, physiological desires have become the most basic and main driving forces for economic and social development. Even if the wealth accumulated by the rich people far exceeds their own needs, it can be used for the future, bequeathed to descendants, or donated to others to satisfy their desires without being wasted. In contrast, mental whimsy can sometimes develop into wild ideas that are divorced from reality, causing serious damage to oneself and others (e.g., suicide). Ideological aspirations can be contradictory, which is also detrimental to the construction of developmental mechanisms. These contrasts can highlight the positive social significance of physiological desires.

The flip side of the above characteristic of thoughts is that they grow and develop rapidly. Physiological tissues, as well as their "requirements", are largely set in stone, and their evolutions, if at all, are extremely slow. And the growth of thoughts is one of the outstanding characteristics of the mind. In particular, the growth of the mind is most pronounced when it serves a stable goal, such as a physiological desire. The mind can take the initiative to look back at and study the organism it "inhabits", to recognize it, to maintain it, and to develop it. In this way, *there are two layers of structure in the human body to maintain itself*: one is the "desire-feeling" system, which is mainly based on the innate hard software mechanism and characterized by simplicity and stability, and the other is the thinking system, although complex and changeable, but having good development. For example, agricultural engineering, nutritional engineering, biological engineering, medical engineering, and so on, which have been developed through the system of thinking, might have already achieved more than the expectations of the "designer" in maintaining physiological and mental health. This also highlights the limitations of the "designer" perspective.

§61. Purposefulness and Purposelessness

Although desire attracts or pushes the thinking system in certain directions, the thinking system could not succumb to it. The thinking system can, relatively independently in acquired activities, develop its own goals, objectives, wills, intentions, preferences, values, etc. and form complex and multifaceted relationships with desires. In general, all of these can be seen roughly as Algorithmical. However, we also need to understand the mechanisms in more detail.

A basic way of understanding them is that *a purpose is a derivative of the limited capacity of metacomputation and its serial mode of operation*. A finite and tiny thing exists in a much larger space, with abundant places to go around it, so that it can move, and hence comes the problem of direction in its motion. The purpose arises from this reasoning. It is a concept prepared for the processing, evolution, and change of metacomputing. Moreover, human attention is limited because of the limited capacity of metacomputing, then *the "purpose" must also be a relatively small thing*, not many things or everything, so as to match the size of computations. By establishing purposes, actors need no longer to go too many ways futilely in too many directions simultaneously; computations are hence simplified and can proceed quickly and efficiently. Otherwise, the person concerned would be in disorder. For this technical reason, and because of the heterogeneity of the world, the actors classify the things around them according to their values and meanings, some of which belong to the "ends" that can be pursued, the more the better, and some of which belong to the costs that need to be avoided, the less the better. *Thus, the concepts of ends and means are differentiated.* As a result, *people often need a purpose, regardless of the content of the purpose.* Even if one does not come into the world with a purpose, and even if one can actively examine one's desires, one needs a purpose and often actively seeks one's purposes—otherwise there are no behaviors or actions.

As far as the content of the purpose is concerned, desires must, of course, be given priority, because desires have been existent there, persistently and inveterately. A newborn individual lacks knowledge of the world and society, so it is impossible to establish other, more abstract purposes before birth. Moreover, even if the spiritual purposes arise later, they should first be regarded as *derivatives of desire*, the instrumental purposes established by the thinking system in the process of satisfying a desire. This is the effect of a serial, boundedly rational thinking system in the pursuit of any goal. Because *metacomputation cannot accommodate all the thinking operations needed to achieve the original goal at once*, the operations are divided into many, even lengthy, steps. And, the operations are not nuanced in many aspects, but only outputting some rough ideas of what is good and what is bad, what should be pursued and what should be avoided. This is the effect of mental distortions. It gives these things that should be pursued a status that is relatively independent of the original purpose, as the new "purposes". In order to achieve the original purpose, the actors must now pursue these derivative purposes. Therefore, this derivative phenomenon is a typical "Algorithmical phenomenon", which can be called the "*Derivative Effect*". According to actors' original intents, the derived purposes should be abolished after the original purpose has ceased. However, some of the original purposes are long-lived or cyclical, hence the derivative purposes may also be long-lasting. Or, when an original purpose has died out, the person concerned forgets to cancel the purpose derived, or finds out other purposes that can be served by this derived purpose, which will result in the derived purpose not only perpetuating, but also becoming part of those elements that are most closely related to the person's daily life.

Another way to understand spiritual purposes is to think of certain spiritual pleasures as the nervous system's own "desires". As mentioned earlier, although we have developed the principle of mind-body separation, we still believe, in principle, that the thinking system is a function of the human body, not of other entities outside the human body. Specifically, the thinking system is a function of the human nervous system including the human brain. Although the nerve serves other organs and tissues, it is also a biological tissue itself. Since other organs or tissues can signal pain and happiness to the conscious system for their own needs, why cannot the nervous system itself? This logic could be consistent with the former. For example, too heavy a computational task may be detrimental to the nervous system, then it is reasonable to assume that the nervous system will signal "pain" at this point. Conversely, a moderate computational cadence can be pleasant. The nervous system itself has a feedback mechanism that evaluates various computing tasks and objects from time to time. From this, we can distinguish between physical pain or pleasure and spiritual pain or pleasure. They are distinctly different in experience.

However, it is not enough to explain spiritual purposes on the basis of *biology alone*. Since the mind is regarded as an entity that exists independently of matter, and matter can produce desires, why can't spirit again? It doesn't make sense! Moreover, in fact, the purposes of living organisms are precisely through the way of thinking. The cliché that says that the primary goal of living organisms is to survive comes actually entirely from *the way of thinking and its syntax*. The accuracy of this cliché can be questionable. Living organisms never "tell" us this "truth". It's just a metaphor, a method that we reluctantly and improvisationally take when there is no other way to the explanations. On the contrary, the thinking system knows best what the concept of "purpose" or "goal" means, and it is its own understanding and definition of this concept that is the most "authentic". The freedom of the mind system to set its own goals is a fact that we directly experience every hour of every day. This fact is more reliable than any other fact we have come to realize. Even if all the facts that are perceived can be challenged, this fact should only be questioned less than other facts. Not only can we refuse, suppress, and procrastinate any request from a physiological desire, but our spirit can, on its own, autonomously, deliberately, and independently set any goals, objectives, wants, motives, intentions, preferences, values, and so on. These things can have any imaginable characteristics and may or may not have any relationship with other things or purposes. A person can be mediocre regardless of his or her family's livelihood, can pursue any absurd and bizarre goals, can modify or revise them at any time, and set new goals after all the goals have been achieved, and this list of one's doings can be endless. An extreme, but not uncommon, example of spiritual freedom is that many individuals choose suicide as a way to reject any "request" from their bodies.

§62. Purposefulness and Purposelessness (continued)

This freedom is also manifested in the fact that one does not set any goals. The freedom to set goals means in itself that the goals set can be zero. As the existentialists emphasized, a human does not come into the world on purpose, but is "thrown" into the world by others. After that, one has to think about one's goal. This reflection often occurs after alleviating urgent physiological needs, and thus reflects a structural dissonance caused by the asymmetrical developments. It's like holding a bow and arrow in your hand, but now you don't know where to shoot it. *It's not that the target needs a bow and arrow, but that the bow and arrow need a target.* This is also an irregularity. In a context where regularity has been the criterion, any articulation of irregularity would have been innovative. Now we would like to point out that regularity is not the way the world is; it is first and foremost the expectation of us humans. In order to be lazy in computations, researchers deliberately chose a preference for regularity, leaving irregularities behind.

Some people may say, "You are making a contradictory statement. What is the point of economy when there is no purpose?" This is a witty question, but also a sophistical one. We're talking about the *current* lack of purpose for a person, but his/her purpose may not necessarily be lost before or after; both the lack and possession of a purpose are generally all temporary. Secondly, the lack of purpose of actors does not mean that scholars themselves and the whole world are lacking purposes. At this time, the actors and the researcher should be separated and treated differently, discriminatively; their difference should not be ignored. One of the underlying rules of mainstream approaches is that the actors and the researcher must be consistent or even identical, or that the researcher is completely absent from the discourse and hence is not considered. That is, ontological and methodological discourse are completely separated. The Algorithmic method is characterized that the researcher and the actors concerned are intermittently separated or connected, depending on the specific contexts. To borrow a physics term, this can be called the "entanglement" of ontology and methodology.

Another sophistry in the above question is that the goal the mental activities are seeking is not the goal of the mental activities themselves, but the goal of the person to whom the mental activities belong. Second, the absence of an actor's goal usually does not mean that the actor does not intend to pursue any goal at all, but that the actor's *specific* goal is absent. What does this mean? This means that the person lacks a *viable, actionable* goal that can be applied to the real dynamic world and matched with the serial way of behaviors. Saying "I want to pursue happiness" is undoubtedly too abstract; since the ability to act is limited, it is necessary to set goals that are in line with the limited *scale* of behaviors. Many of the goals that people have chosen in the empirical world can be considered to fit this scale, because they have been tested by people through their own practical actions. This is how the meaning of "experience" emerges to us.

The statement that "the person was thrown into the world" means that the cost has occurred first and is continuously occurring, and this cost needs to be offset with benefits. Cost, benefits, economy represent a general and vague value that is relatively independent of other concrete goals. This is a plurality, vagueness, and asynchrony in the area of values or purposes. And, this is also the true mindset of many people who are struggling to find their purposes in life. Their intention was to admit that there should be a goal. This admittance is a recognition of an abstract general value or interest. This abstract value is a concept created in the human consciousness, and it can be used to act as an intermediary between various concrete values. Money, for example, is such an abstract value, although it cannot be strictly considered the most general value due to its limited use.

In this way, the purpose and meaning of life are neither determined at the time of birth, nor at a particular age or point in time. The phrase "purpose and meaning of life" itself ignores the pluralistic contents of the concept of "life", i.e., it is a collection of relatively independent actions over a long period of time, and the practice of prescribing them as a whole is itself an arbitrary distortion. In fact, purposes unfold (or not to unfold) in the spatio-temporal environment dispersively (which can be called the "*Dispersion Effect*"), which requires hard and explorative work to discover. Thus, it is often a pleasure for a person to obtain and establish a purpose. Moreover, ends are often hidden in the means, to be discovered as happiness only when people work and give (it can be called the "*Affiliation Effect*"), hence many people love their work and are willing to give. On the other hand, if a person lives alone for a long time, the result is often negative and misanthropic, in a loss of motivation. Another situation that arises from this is that the generation of goals cannot be predicted in advance, but is endless; new goals are generated as old goals are achieved, so goals are like the carrots dangling in front of our eyes, which we seem never to catch up. Of course, this is an illusion, because the series of goals achieved in this process are all different. Second, this reflects the perpetuality of computing and development, which causes people to live in a state of satisfaction for a period of time, then discover new goals that will bring about dissatisfaction and then initiate new efforts. If human purposefulness does not have this characteristic, there will be no continuous development of humankind.— Otherwise, if one's goals are too ambitious, too distant, or difficult to achieve, he/she will suffer too much pain in his/her life. And, if everyone's goal is only once for all, and no more goals are generated afterwards, the world will definitely be different from what we see now. Generally, people will continue to adjust their goals to certain status and rhythms to match the characteristics of computing and physical behaviors.

The above is mainly about the many irregularities of purpose. Another type of irregularity is the absence of means, i.e. an end is there, but it is not yet known how to achieve it. The latter are more common than the former, but both are normal in the dynamic, serial behavioral streams and networks. Revenue items and cost items exist and interact with each other in a real space-time environment as relatively independent and real entities. Freedom of purpose and intention cannot rule out the objective laws and their inevitable influences, although the person can subjectively choose to respond to the objective laws actively, or to ignore them. It is in this sense that physiological pains and pleasures gain the upper hand in the long-term games. Once a spiritual pursuit is recognized by the person concerned as costly and painful, he/she may retreat, and return to his/her basic needs. Spiritual pursuit is a kind of "arbitrary power" of the human being, but after experiencing the world, and comparing and weighing, one can give up this "power", or prudently implement it to be more constructive. As people often say: if you want to develop hobbies, why not develop hobbies that can benefit you? Thus, although theoretically people can pursue anything, in practice their pursuits often have a certain regularity and commonality.

Finally, it should be emphasized that "purpose", as a variable in consciousness, must be what the person concerned is aware of, not unconsciously. For example, if a person subjectively does not pursue a certain purpose, a bystander cannot assume that he/she has that purpose. Even if there is some methodological interest in doing so, this distinction needs to be noted, and addressed. Another situation is that the words and actions of the person concerned are considered to be "potentially" pursuing a certain purpose, even if he/she does not explicitly state it, or is not directly aware of it. What distinguishes this potential from the unconscious is that in the researcher-actor dialogue, an honest actor would, after a reflection of oneself, acknowledge the potentiality. If these distinctions are not emphasized, there is a danger that they will go out of the orbit of our consciousness approach.

§63. Emotions (1)

The distinction between ends and means is a structural differentiation of the mind that occurs in the early stages of its development. The desire part of this differentiation can be seen as being done in the form of hard software before one's birth, and other spiritual purposes are developed in the form of pure software during acquired practice. Another differentiation is the generation of the emotional system. Based on general observation and understanding, it can be assumed that the emotional system is innately developed in the form of hard software.

Based on our own experience and the available literature, we can conclude that the emotional system has the following characteristics: First, human emotion has a difference between the latent period and the active period, and its onset is always related to the person's recognition that a certain event is beneficial or detrimental to the realization of the person's goals (including desires). That is to say, the onset of emotion is caused by the person's recognition of whether an event is a "good thing" or a "bad thing". In other words, the affective process contains the *evaluative* process. "Evaluation" is to judge the "value" of an objectified event, and the so-called "value" refers to how the event contributes to achieving the goal: beneficial, harmful, or "neutral"? And, to what extent is it beneficial or harmful? A large number of objects, and the rich knowledge of these objects, generally do not have obvious value implications. Most of our daily life is about following various routines and doing common things. There are few prominent "good things" or "bad things". Even if these things ultimately lead to a virtuous end, most of them are not independent but are part of many links to the end goal. It is clear that emotional responses are not for ordinary events with weak value meanings, but *those rare events with prominent value meanings*. It's like a teacher supervising the performance of students, most of the time he/she doesn't take a stand on them, but only occasionally praise or criticize someone or something.

Second, although an emotion can be strong or weak, there are only several *types* of emotions, each of which points to a quite different type of action. Several kinds of emotions, similar to several kinds of desires, reflect their *discreteness, simpleness, and economy*. Emotional outbursts bring about intense psychological experiences that are often sufficient to interrupt the current mindful or physical activity. Meanwhile, an outburst of emotion can be accompanied by several physiological occurrences (e.g., rapid heartbeat, breathing, reddening or whitening of the face, etc.) that physiologists can detect and measure in certain ways. At this point, the person concerned feels some urge to engage in certain inclined behaviors. For example, the emotion of "joy" asks for celebration, the emotion of "anger" asks for an attack on its source, the emotion of "fear" asks for an escape, and so on. This urging is immediate, requiring the actor to perform the act quickly. Even if it is not very specific, the actor can use it as an important parameter to form a specific decision and action.

Based on the above two characteristics, we can say that an emotion is a *decision-making program.* It is not an end, but an instrumentality, which serves the realization of an end. Moreover, it does not output cognition, but directly the decisions, or the tendency to make a decision. As with the alarm mechanism mentioned above (§57), we can think of the emotional system to frequently search the thinking system to see what of its outcomes can be *significantly* related to one's purposes; if any, it is triggered, and then is tried to interrupt the current operations and promptly turn to the relevant action. For example, parents take their child to a party, the parents are busy socializing while the child's focus is on what is good to eat or to have fun. If any, take the opportunity to enjoy right away!

Why, then, is the child so *eager* to enjoy, or why is there a need for such a *roaring* emotional system? What is the rationale for the "Creator" to make it this way?

This involves Algorithmic concepts such as "forced closure", "factor completeness", and "mental distortion" under time pressure. A newborn person, who has been born out of his mother's body and born into this world, has achieved physical and physiological independence, then he/she needs to make decisions, whether a decision is for an active behavior or for a passive question such as "whether to accept the feeding of a stranger than mom". The decision must be made in a limited time, or instantaneously, and the computations must be forcibly shut down, not allowed to proceed any longer. Regardless of how much knowledge is introduced or established, certain variables must have values (e.g. whether this is a good or bad thing, whether he/she should welcome or avoid it, etc.). This is the requirement of the "factor completeness". The quality of decision-making can be somehow inferior, but its structure must be "complete" in a certain sense. At this time, he/she may not care about whether his/her mentality is distortive, but feel lucky that it can be "bent" to make an answer (e.g. to smile or to cry).

That is to say, the *emotional system can be understood as the most rudimentary and primitive decision-making system*, regardless of how much knowledge is available to support the decision-making. Especially, it is a simple mechanism managing temporal processes, forcing computations to conclude themselves intermittently. It prevents those instrumental operations from running too far from purposes. This is like the difference between a nerd and a worker. A recent university graduate may have a wealth of professional knowledge in some specific areas, but lack practical experience, or even never conduct a whole practical project, thus it is difficult for him to work independently, but can only cooperate with others, or, complementarily, learn practical knowledge under the guidance of a practical master. On the other hand, a person with a low educational background who has worked for many years may not be able to perform complex, advanced work, but can complete some ordinary tasks independently. The clinical case on the lack of decision-making capacity in people who lack affection[11] can be used to support this view.

For a newborn baby, such a decision-making system cannot be established or introduced by oneself, hence one can only be equipped with it congenitally; that is, it must be arranged by hard software, otherwise the baby will likely be difficult to survive. Moreover, according to this logic, any animals must be congenitally equipped with a similar system so that they have basic decision-making and behavioral abilities. Since an individual organism needs to be renewed from generation to

---

11. Mario Fahed, David C. Steffens, "Apathy: Neurobiology, Assessment and Treatment". Clinical Psychopharmacology and Neuroscience. 2021 May 31; 19(2):181-189. doi: 10.9758/cpn.2021.19.2.181.

generation, or, since the individual organism will die and give birth, then such an arrangement is indispensable.

Further, the above theory also provides a rationality for the innate inheritance of other knowledge. "Instinct" can be such a kind of knowledge. It is also possible that this knowledge is individualized, so that different individuals can be born with different personalities from each other[12]. We can study this innate knowledge in categories. Since they are hard software that cannot be changed once formed, they can affect a person's entire life persistently.

§64. Emotions (2)

After an individual leaves the mother's body, the emotional system cannot be changed. This "arrangement" has both advantages and disadvantages. The upside is that, just like desires, the emotional system can be used to balance the thinking system and prevent it from becoming obsessed with computations and forgetting time and decision-making. Even if an unstable mental system is really lost in computations, the emotional system can, in place of it, play a role in ensuring that individuals stay awake and don't forget what they are busy for —that is, what their "true interests" are. The disadvantage of this "arrangement" is that individuals must develop purely software-based decision-making systems in addition to the emotional system, and these two systems are relatively independent and complete, and conflicts will inevitably arise between them. Here, the word "complete" means that they meet the requirements of factor completeness, i.e., they both

---

12. Empirical research on the causes of personality differences among people has reached a relatively consistent conclusion, that is, innate and acquired factors roughly account for half each. See Alan E. Kazdin, "Encyclopedia of Psychology", Vol. VI, American Psychological Association & Oxford University Press, 2000, pp. 142-143.

may answer the same questions that must be answered at the time of decision-making. Since they are different versions of decision-making systems, formed in different historical periods, the answers to the same question are likely to be different. As a result, there shall be *direct* conflicts. Then, *our thinking system often perceives the emotional system strongly opposing us* and feeling that it is a stumbling block, thus we label it "irrational"!

This effect is quite different from the relationship between two different versions of a software-only decision-making system. Imagine what happens when two software-only decision-making systems collide? Obviously, there is a high probability that one will negate the other, or rewrite the other, and end up with another newer version of the decision-making system that will be left for use, while the leftover materials will either be scrapped or diverted for other purposes. This is because rewriting ideas or software is easy and can be done directly. In a small probability, both versions will be retained, as the actors may not have time to take care of them, or it may be difficult for them to select between them. But that being the case, the actors will not simply judge one of them as "irrational". There is also a situation where the person concerned has already decided on the merits and the inferior, but is still willing to keep the rejected version as a model of inferior knowledge in order to serve other purposes of the research. In this case, the actors retain a particular knowledge, but do not "adopt" it, so there is no conflict of logical thinking. Knowing and retaining a certain kind of knowledge without believing in it is a "higher-order" attitude that our human thinking system can have towards a particular piece of knowledge. Of course, in the usual context, unless otherwise specified, the application of a particular knowledge is generally understood by default as having accepted that knowledge.

Consequently, the conflicts between the emotional system

and some parts of the thinking system would be *acute* and *significant*—even though the conflicts within the thinking system are also sometimes acute. Considering that the thinking system is constantly improving itself, and the emotional system remains unchanged as hard software, then it is recognized that there is a danger that these conflicts would continue to increase.

This theoretical understanding can be used to explain an interesting psychological phenomenon called "sham rage": in some experiments with mammals such as cats and monkeys, the cerebral cortex, which is mainly responsible for mental activity, is deliberately removed by researchers, so that the hypothalamus, which is thought to carry the emotional system, is exposed and works independently. At this time, the animals tested were very emotional, surprisingly sensitive to external stimuli, and very easily angry.[13] These experiments can be used to show that there are indeed conflicts between the emotional system and the thinking system, and that the latter usually suppresses the former, causing it to not function to the fullest.

In fact, human beings have both vigilant and suppressive attitudes toward the emotional system, as well as an attitude of worship. Humans' understanding of their own spiritual world is also constantly evolving. Under certain understandings, some people may think that there is a "true meaning" of life in the emotional system, so they attach great importance to emotional experience, and even deliberately and actively stimulate their own emotions. There are quite a few nationalities or ethnic groups with such a traditional tendency. This is also the case, for example, with traditional Chinese Confucianism. This tradition still deeply influences

---

13. For an introduction of sham rage of both animals and humans, see Wortis, Herman; Maurer, William S. "'Sham Rage' in Man", American Journal of Psychiatry, 98(5): 638-644, March,1942.

contemporary Chinese. Of course, since one is free to determine any object as one's own goal, there is nothing ethically wrong with doing so. However, in any case, understanding of the emotional system still needs to be refined.

The worship of emotions is like the worship of the past. Thus, usually it is common as a characteristic of conservative cultures. Empirical observation shows that countries with these conservative cultures tend to be economically backward or make slow progress. Values are freely chosen, but such knowledge still needs to be understood and mastered. On this basis, the actors remain free to choose and adjust their values. Hume's lever knife doesn't work well until it's a useful strategy.

In the case of having to accept the existence of hard software, *thinking systems can positively adapt to, or manage hard software.* In the context of mainstream rationalism, rational and irrational systems are separated and cannot merge into a whole, thus there is no such a perspective or such a problem. However, since the thinking system is highly flexible, how can it simply allow the gap between hard software, including the emotional system, and itself to widen? How can it never recognize the real characteristics of hard software? If the reader acknowledges some truth in Algorithmic Theory, then Algorithm Theory itself can be used as an example to illustrate the progress of our understanding of ourselves. In fact, opinions and propositions on managing one's own emotions have long been known[14], and now, on the basis of ATT, such a "psychological construction project" can be carried out more groundedly and confidently.

Thinking systems can manage hard software systems, and this principle does not need to be elucidated under the Algorithmic framework. This is because, after all, hard software

---

14. For example, see Anna Freud, "The Ego and the Mechanisms of Defense", International Universities Press, 1936.

is only a kind of applied software, which is subject to the scheduling and use of consciousness and the Instructional system. Although hard software cannot be consciously rewritten, and even the triggering of hard software is automatic in many cases, the *thinking system can control, process, and rewrite some input and output of hard software*, thus a "decision" as output of hard software can only be regarded as a parameter of the thinking system. Moreover, even if a particular thoughtful outcome directly triggers a particular piece of hard software (e.g., an idea that angers oneself), the mind system can control the final product of the entire processes; that is to say, it controls the hard software just as the upstream of the data flow. These mechanisms can be used as the theoretical basis for the "psychological construction projects".

The above arguments can also be used as an illustration of the entanglements of ontology-methodology, science-engineering, and actor-researcher. There is no way out of these entanglements; because academic work of our researchers is also serial, we cut the research task into pieces or fragments so that they conform to the computational scales of our brain, and then we advance our discourse sentence by sentence, aspect by aspect.

§65. Emotions (3)

A concept that is close to but slightly different from emotion is called "sentiment", such as disgust, surprise, envy, jealousy, embarrassment, guilt, shyness, pride, and so on. What are the differences between sentiments and emotions? That is, the degree of an emotion is generally stronger while the sentiment is relatively mild, although they both imply some tendencies. In addition, emotions often require the person concerned to take some actions immediately, while the expression of sentiments is relatively restrained, and bystanders can only, by paying close attention, find out that the person is *in a certain state* of "sentiment". A sentiment can only be "triggered", meaning that it does not usually interfere with others except that when stimulated by a particular event, it may explode or be reflected in subsequent behaviors. Others learned one's sentiment only by analyzing one's words, actions, expressions, and postures.

Based on the above characteristics, we can propose a small "sentiment theory": in the multiple phases of computing, the output of the emotional system is biased towards the downstream close to decisions, while the output of the sentimental system is in the middle and is mainly used as a parameter for other computations.

Does this distinction matter? Of course not, fundamentally. But this distinction shows us again the diversity and irregularity in minds. This is the inevitable effect of lifting the veil of extreme rationalism. The emotional "gear" shall not be rich enough, and then be added with sentiments. Where the emotions are too intense, they are diluted by sentiments. Emotions may be extroverted too much, and thus they are restrained by sentiments. In particular, this distinction shows the characteristics of a dynamic theory and its causal relationship with diversity. Propensity and decisiveness occur not only at the end of the computations, but in the whole process, at any links.

The sentimental introversion leads to the effect that the person concerned will be silently and unnoticeably in a certain "mood" or "mindset". What does it mean when we often say that someone has a certain "state of mind", "mood", "mentality", or "mindset"? By introducing the dynamic theory formed with time and computing processes, we shall define and explain such a topic with relative satisfaction: this means that the person's state of mind at the moment is not in the so-called "standby state" (i.e., just keeping the computer on and not running any specific application), but in the "internal working state", that is, "internal memory" is occupied, and certain programs and data related to that state of mind (e.g., a certain sentiment) are called in and are *running*. While it has not yet exported decisions and launched explicit behaviors, it is busy on its own, and is not as "casual" as it is on standby. Because the program is running, it is possible for the person to respond quickly to a specific stimulus (e.g., when he/she is feeling disgusted with somebody, the latter happens to act disgustingly) rather than at the same slow pace as others normally respond. This, in turn, explains the above "triggering" nature of sentiments.

In the end, it is very simple: under the dynamic theory, all the details of the spiritual processes are *real* beings or *real* events, and they must be *truly* unfolded in time and space, so that if you, horizontally, look at the social state at a specific point in time, you may get insight of *any parts or links* of a particular dynamic process, and these different links can be presented to the observer *concurrently*. When we feel confused or unfamiliar with these phenomena, it is because the deep thoughts in our minds tend to be static, and we have been taught by mainstream philosophy to value certain states and despise others. The mainstream philosophy has not adopted the *situational equality* (i.e., equal treatment of the world states at each time or place, which can be further divided into "*temporal equality*", "*geographical equality*", etc.), but *situational bias* or *situational discrimination* (i.e., differential and unequal treatment of the world states at different times or places).

The next question is: are these sentiments hard software or software only?

The reason for asking this question is that certain sentiments, such as shyness, seem to be based on social knowledge that obviously cannot be innate. For example, how can one feel shy about being naked if one does not know that one must put on clothes before engaging in social activities? And, how can one feel embarrassed in a particular situation without understanding social concepts such as "reputation", "public image", and "decency"?

Some behaviorist studies are arguing eloquently that many psychological tendencies are innate. I do not intend to take a specific position on this issue. Again, let's return to what has already been made: the robustness of the Algorithmic approach is that it inspires us not to have to take a particular position on issues such as this. It doesn't matter whether sentiments are innate or acquired, at the end of the day, because hard software operates similarly to pure software, where their differences are minor and technical. Even if certain sentiments are not innate, they may arise rapidly in postnatal practice (just as human interaction can quickly create ethical and moral problems). The key is to understand that the mind itself produces things like this in a "bent" way all the time. A little friend who sleeps next to a baby gets food, but the baby doesn't get it oneself, which is awful for the baby. He/she can rightly protest to the feeder, or wrongly hate his/her companion (if the companion has refused to feed, he/she would not feel unfair and would not be miserable) to the point of being considered "jealous". These situations are normal in a world of bounded rationality. Young people are considered to have a strong sense of "curiosity" because they live in a prominently contrasting environment. By comparing oneself with adults, a kid can discover his/her own ignorance, but "curiosity" is not the self-evaluation of kids, but the evaluation of adults for kids. Since the Instructional systems are identical for everyone, such mental knowledge may be produced in each person so quickly after birth that experimental researchers have misunderstood that they are all innate. Much of the so-called "inherent humanity" may have arisen this way.

§66. Subconscious

Many of the above arguments have been formed on the basis of inspirations from our predecessors. Sigmund Freud, for example, was one such inspirer. He believed that the human mind is not completely transparent, and that there are many things in it (such as sexual desire) that are in the dark and quietly affect us.[15] He called this the "subconscious". However, Freud only opened a loophole. Somewhat similar to behaviorists, he also used the method of enumeration, trying to reveal the subconscious elements one by one, and misunderstanding that as long as these demerits are repaired, the mind would still be transparent, and quite "perfect".

Our approach is the opposite. We think that *everything else is dark except those the attention of consciousness illuminates* (perhaps there are some gray areas at the junction of the two). Therefore, the bright place is a constant and fixed "dot", while the dark places are enormous and infinite. This completely *reverses* the relationship between the finite and the infinite, the normal and the exceptional.

As mentioned earlier, we can think of this arrangement as a result of the biological mechanism that numerous parts of the human body are outside the direct supervision of consciousness, and hence the "unconscious". No matter how hard the consciousness tries, it is not possible to reach these places directly. This refers to the lack of a direct neural connection between them. However, with the help of scientific instruments, a person can also learn about the internal structure of their own body and brain. In this sense, the scope of objects of conscious activity is infinite and developing. But this indirect way of understanding is different from the

---

15. Sigmund Freud, "Introductory Lectures on Psycho-Analysis", translated by Joan Riviere, London: George-Allen & Unwin Ltd., 1970.

mechanism of neural connection. In addition to the unconscious caused in this case, we shall think that everything that belongs to the *thinking system* can in principle be directly perceived and understood by consciousness, while the limited capacity of meta-computing entails that such perception and understanding can only be in a serial and time-consuming way. Metacomputing is like a flashlight, shining not only in the world, but also in one's own heart. Wherever it shines, it is bright, and where it does not, it is naturally dark. As mentioned in §55, the contents of any external object are in principle infinite, and the data in memory is massive and nearly infinite, hence metacomputation can always illuminate only a part of it. Not only does this result in a limited knowledge of an object, but also that our attention, mention, description, and control over it generally involves only a part of it—Although with the help of tools and knowledge, the scale and scope of what we can operate on the object currently can continue to expand. This is because we need to compute and control concisely, economically. To do this, ambiguity needs to be adopted frequently. An example of this is the authorization mechanism discussed in §56. For other examples, an old man who meets several of his grandchildren, of course, knows their names, but has a hard time recalling, so he calls each of them "child" or "young man" in general terms. And, when a doorman of a stadium checks tickets, in order to save time, he may skim the tickets quickly only for a critical mark or feature rather than checking their details accurately. This literally provides an opportunity for someone to sneak into the stadium (as in the case of "slips of the tongue"[16]). A group of strange guests came to the office of a company, but the manager Zhang deliberately avoided them, maybe because he was too busy, or he knew that this group of guests had nothing to do with his interest, or

---

16. Ibid, pp. 13-48.

maybe he already knew that these guests would bring trouble to himself. Nevertheless, he did know that the guests had arrived, and he did have the power and ability to go directly into the guest room and get to know them personally.

That's the truth of the subconscious. Before Freud, humans did not know that their actions were greatly affected by their sexual desires. After Freud's reminding, readers begin to self-reflect and self-monitor their own inner world. In other words, the flashlight is starting to try to illuminate certain areas that have almost never been touched before. Although the mechanism of formation of libido is hidden and cannot be directly detected by consciousness, libido itself is a variable, an existence, and an interface that is "invested" into the scope of consciousness by that mechanism. That is, it is the content of the mind. Then the consciousness grabs it, feels it, starts to examine its activities, and to analyze its relationship with other existences or other activities. At this time, the person concerned feels the great force of sexual desire, and hence he/she begins to agree with Freud's psychoanalytic theory.

A similar principle applies to dreams. Dreams can be seen like a self-learning class without a teacher. With no one to manage and maintain order in the classroom, the students began to mess around on their own. At this point, it's likely that you would have done anything you usually wouldn't have done (given the combinatorial explosion effect, there's always no limit to what you can do). Therefore, dreams can bring unexpected computations that allow the person to gain something that is not possible in the waking state. However, there is no need to be obsessed with a dream because even the "automatic computation" in dreams is still subject to the limitations of its ability, speed, knowledge, and resources, and in principle it is still an ordinary computation. Although the ordinary computations in a waking state can also produce surprises, people rarely become obsessed with them. In the same way, if we were to do the statistics, we would definitely find that the frequency of surprises in dreams is not necessarily much higher than when we are awake. This can now be inferred.

By the way, intuition also needs to be mentioned. Intuition can be understood as a kind of automatic computation, that is, the automatic processing of information by the human brain. Is there such a mechanism in the human brain? We can't completely rule it out. However, as mentioned earlier, even for fully conscious computations, the human brain will establish similar mechanisms by "authorizing" and so on, so that it may seem that the computations there appear to be "automatic" and "unconscious". From this point of view, the mysterious "intuition" is no longer mysterious. In other words, Algorithmic Theory understands intuition and automatic computation first and foremost as a computational phenomenon and a mental economy. There are at least two ways to prove this. The first is that when we recall and actively monitor a so-called "intuition" process, we will often discover some details of the process, such as what information or means are used to arrive at a particular "intuitive view", and so on. The second is that intuitive processes can obviously be consciously intervened in. For example, if you don't like a person, you will "automatically" associate him/her with negative things. However, one day, if it is discovered that this is a misunderstanding, and then when you see him/her again, or think of him/her, the things you automatically associate with may become nice and positive. Therefore, intuition is likely to be as peculiar as ordinary mental activities. For those who worship intuition, we need only ask them one question: If automatic computing is more efficient than conscious computing, does it mean that a student will do better if he or she does not study hard, but only relies on intuition?

The popularity of psychoanalytic theory not only proves

the truth in Freud's theory, but also proves that the common basic understanding of ordinary thinking activities is flawed. Not only is a large amount of hard software in the mind suitable for such a "subconscious" mechanism, but any mental activities and stocks of knowledge are also governed by this mechanism. Now we will realize that under the Algorithmic framework, this doctrine, which was once shrouded in a mysterious aura, is really ordinary and commonplace. Nonetheless, psychoanalytic doctrines basically adhere to our rational analysis, and its method of pros and cons analysis will continue to be carried forward by ATT.

The below paragraph provides a conclusion to the previous sections of this chapter.

I used to think that the contents of psychology were just a general application of Algorithmic Theory, then I generally arranged these contents in the later chapters of any previous Algorithmic writings, until one day, I suddenly realized that intergenerational inheritance can not only inherit the Instruction system, but *must also* inherit certain hard software. We must look at the roundabout production of mental activity from the perspective of the whole of "humankind reproduction". This perspective requires that *some minimum stocks of knowledge must be established directly in the infant before birth for after-birth use*. A large part of these knowledge stocks can of course be used for the whole lifetime of the person. Because there is no other means of biological inheritance for this minimal stocked knowledge to be transferred to the future, as if a teacher educates a student, then, only the hard software mechanism is adopted. In this way, when the baby is born into the world, he/she not only carries the "Instructional system" as a tool for developing knowledge, but also carries some ready-made knowledge. He/she uses this *dual structure* to face the lifetime in front of him/her. Henceforth, "psychology", or hard software, is not a "quasi-member" of the Algorithmic principles, but should be a full and essential part. Only such an Algorithmic theory is reasonable.

§67. Personal Growth, Education, and Evolution

In this section, the human mind, which has the above structural characteristics, will move in the world and in the orbit of time. We can theoretically speculate and see what will happen to individuals.

Whether the activity of consciousness begins in the embryonic period or after childbirth, it is likely to be first and foremost information-driven, i.e., passively processing the information imported. This passivity can also manifest itself in the passive responses to physiological desires. After the passive processing produces some results, there may come some predictions and expectations, hence the actors will turn to proactive searching for specific targets. Not only will the innate "hard software" come into play, but it will most likely play a key role in guiding the completion of basic activities. For example, children communicate well with animals, and this phenomenon can be interpreted as the effect of hard software, because at least a part of human hard software can be inferred to be the results of animal evolution. Objects of computation in infancy and early childhood should be mainly physical and concrete, since abstract objects are only derivatives of a large number of concrete objects.

Furthermore, the above logic shows that the growth of an individual's mind and personality is phased and structural. This means that *each of the knowledge and capabilities of adults has not grown at the same rate as one another*, but every phase of growth has its own focus, and the focuses alternate over time. This seemingly simple truth actually needs to be theoretically supported by an Algorithmical and boundedly rational framework. "Human nature" is obviously a concept connected with hard software. The conditions of hard software and its interpersonal differences determine fundamentally the characteristics of one's nature. Then, the newborn children of the same age kick off their growth from the same starting line, thus there must be a lot of similarities in their journeys, showing obvious synchronicity, which may be misunderstood as "human nature" or an innateness. However, given the differences in hardware, software, hard software, environment, and specific behavior trajectories, the heterogeneity and asynchronicity in them must also be obvious. Both the similarities and differences exist hybridly, or in parallel. Mental growth and physical growth are intertwined. Some skills are the products of integrating hardware with software, and can therefore only be effectively produced when physical and mental activities are combined. As the children grow, their physical and mental activities increase dramatically, hence the gap between the highest and lowest values of any dimension in the child population is likely to widen. This conclusion will be logical. These speculative conclusions can further point to the empirical research on children's behaviors and developments, and then form a positive interaction with theoretical research.

However, in any case, education is crucial. Relying on children's own spontaneous computations, there is not much knowledge that can be deduced in a limited number of years. *Knowledge must be efficiently "indoctrinated" into children and adolescents as an abrupt, blunt uninvited "guest", arranged by adults.* This is a manifestation of humankind's "collective rationality". The role of stocked knowledge in current computing can be used to illustrate how education can "shape" future generations into what predecessors want them to be. It's really a compulsion. But with the serial computational method, this is also a last resort, because knowledge can only be questioned and revised after it is acquired and understood by the child. Therefore, even if it is more humane and clever heuristic education, it must first be premised on the indoctrination and memorization of ready-made data. Students combine the knowledge they receive with their own experiences and ideas to form their own personalized knowledge system.

The knowledge accumulated during human history is so great that education must be carried out over a number of years. Even if students' majors have been divided into many different disciplines, the years of education have been extended over history. Education is first and foremost a copy of knowledge. The importance of education reflects the importance of copies of knowledge in society. From this perspective, we can especially appreciate the characteristics and significance of knowledge as real entities. However, once you have learned knowledge, you must use it. Since an individual's lifespan is finite, the more years of education, the fewer years of using knowledge. Therefore, society must maintain a certain balance between the two. To this end, society must also appropriately streamline the knowledge that needs to be passed on. In the era when the physical means of recording and transmitting knowledge were not yet developed, people streamlined knowledge to save costs; now that recording and transmitting knowledge has become increasingly convenient, it is also necessary for people to streamline knowledge in order to improve the efficiency of use of knowledge.

After an individual has attained a certain level of education, he or she gradually approaches or even catches up with the paces of adults. This phenomenon is understandable, because the speed at which knowledge is learned is, after all, faster than the speed at which knowledge is developed. This apparent difference in speed can be used to distinguish the minor ages and the adult ages, and finally, one day, an individual will be evaluated as *"mature"*, and his/her personality and performances enter a period of relative stability. Another meaning of "maturity" is related to factor completeness, which means that the knowledge and qualities by which an adult makes decisions and behaviors finally come to an end after being socially cultivated. And, due to the huge amount of computations that an individual has experienced and the huge amount of data one has had, as well as the individualized hard software, there must be a high degree of complexity in one's personalities. Even if different personalities can be empirically roughly divided into a number of types, their specificity must widely vary. A large number of their differences coexist with a large number of their similarities, and a large number of their congruencies coexist with a large number of their conflicts. The unchangeable hard software will also interact with software or knowledge in a complicated way (to be continued in §129).

The use of knowledge is intended to yield certain benefits. The good thing about knowledge is that its application does not lead to its diminishing or disappearing, but rather to its improvement, generally. Knowledge grows automatically in computations. Innovation doesn't have to be deliberate; it can happen naturally by following some existing experience and skills. Since stocked knowledge was formed in the past, even in very early times, it may become obsolete. This is an embarrassment that the education system must face. This outdated knowledge then needs to be patched up during its use. Individuals also need to learn the latest knowledge from time to time. An adult's personality will not remain completely the same, but will evolve relatively slowly.

The "bother" caused by learning and innovation can motivate the person concerned to use the existing knowledge as much as possible, or even reject the new knowledge. It's like old things are often used as much as possible in tinkering. This is where conservatism originated. It is especially prevalent among middle-aged and elderly people.

Young people are open, radical, and curious, while older people are closed, conservative, and nostalgic. These characteristics are present in comparison with each other. On the other hand, the development of the mind is sustainable compared to the degeneration of the body of old people. The mechanism of intellectual progress is so simple, straightforward, and ubiquitous that it is difficult to stop. This can be used to explain why in many fields, middle-aged and elderly people are mostly in charge, and young people seldom surpass them.

Another topic is group psychology, regarding issues such as self-determination, self-esteem, and human dignity. Algorithmic Principles tend to affirm these concepts. People do not always communicate and argue on specific issues, but often divide the decision-making power and assert their own rights to self-determination. Within a certain range, they prioritize their own ideas and put the opinions of others only in a secondary or advisory position. This is an inevitable phenomenon in the world of dynamic computing. As "human objects" are different from physical things, people deal with other people in ways that are different from those for physical things, forcing others sooner or later to recognize their own and mutual "personal dignity", a concept that may seem illusory but actually has important practical value. Of course, these social systems are not innate, but develop gradually. This is also the method people use to deal with subjectivity: in an environment full of subjectivities, the role of rational communication is limited, then they have to divide their decision-making scope from place to place, or establish some other public mechanisms. For example, "respect the old and love the young" is a public mechanism. In situations where young people and old people can only have limited communications, young people are sometimes required to blindly obey the elderly while the elderly are required to tolerate and love the young people, and not to criticize them as harshly as they treat other adults.

Finally, one more example. People's knowledge, abilities, preferences, and behaviors are often logically asymmetrical, therefore, what a person appreciates or criticizes may not be what he/she is able to do or avoid. A person himself is a certain character, and what he likes is another. A person may believe he knows people well, but conversely, he may know very little about how he is perceived in the minds of others, and so on. Why is there such an asymmetry? The answer is bounded rationality. It causes a lot of irregularities, and the asymmetry is just a category of irregularities. Hence, *the key is to provide a theory of appropriate bounded rationality (or "concrete rationality", or "real rationality"). Inside and outside the body, everything is mostly just its manifestation.*

The above many exemplary deductions are intended to show that the application of ATT in psychology is extremely broad. A large number of psychological phenomena can now be explained in a coherent and synthetic manner by using this theory, and *psychology can thus become a holistic and quite theoretical discipline, and will also logically become an essential and indispensable part of the humanities and social sciences.* This chapter is only the beginning of this work and is only used to assist us in obtaining a basic philosophical perspective and method of psychological problems. As long as this goal is achieved, the discourse here can be put on hold temporarily.

CHAPTER 6

THE FUNDAMENTALS OF PHILOSOPHY

§68. Definition of Philosophy

It is said that philosophy is difficult to define. However, in my opinion, this difficulty does not come from elsewhere but from philosophy itself. Mainstream philosophy has adopted a posture that, obviously unintentionally, and unfortunately, renders the classification of knowledge meaningless. The situation is similar to that of economics, which takes an attitude of rejecting the materiality (or substantiality, or physicality; similarly hereinafter) of ideas, thereby making money lose its theoretical status and thus making economic activity indistinguishable from other social activities. Now, the way to the redefinition of economics is to introduce money by introducing the materiality of ideas, and then define economics as the study of activities that use money.

Plato's theory of Idea absolutizes, idealizes, and confines knowledge as the truth. An absolute, ideal thing shall not be fragmented, nor shall it be changing and developing. That is, it must be a complete "thing", "being" or "substance". If philosophical knowledge can also be counted as a part of it, how can it be distinguished from other knowledge? In particular, the objects of philosophical research are also studied by other disciplines, and philosophy does not have its own relatively independent object of study like other specific disciplines. For example, botany and zoology have a very clear boundary between their respective research objects, so there is no need for a further clarification. Philosophy is the study of the "philosophical aspect" of everything. Then, what are these "aspects"?

Let's go back to the common sense of philosophy.

These "philosophical aspects" refer first and foremost to the "fundamental aspects". What does this mean? This indicates a place that can be called the "root" where the research in a particular discipline will stop. In other words, under the pattern of division of research, specific research only starts from here, develops upward or forward, and then becomes a specific discipline. If we retrace again from here, where we are going does not belong to the scope of the specific discipline, but to philosophy. This may seem like a common statement, but it actually acknowledges the following three premises.

First, the scope and depth of human knowledge is finite at any given point in time, not complete. Perfect knowledge does not need a starting point, because the starting point, if any, it must be arbitrary. Perfect knowledge should be infinitely retraceable, so as to eliminate the starting point and connect it from beginning to end, thus becoming self-evident. In contrast, our human knowledge system can see the heads forward and the tails backward. Although it is evolving, there is really only so much knowledge as of now. Knowledge is limited in general, as is its foundation, which is the philosophical aspect. It's like a tree standing in front of me, I can see where its root is, how much it's growing upwards, and where its edges are. I'm in a lot of space, and it's only a part of it at the moment. Only in such a context do words such as "basic", "fundamental", and so on make sense.

Second, human knowledge is *structural* and *functional* to a certain extent. That is to say, knowledge does not correspond in isolation to a single object. There would have been knowledge A for object A and knowledge B for object B, and A and B would have been arranged in parallel and independent of each other. Really, this is not the case with knowledge systems. As we already know, knowledge developers conduct research on a large number of objects in batches, and, for division of labor and specialized research, extract specific *aspects* of a large number of individual objects to form the structural and functional knowledge. Such knowledge shall be not sufficient to support a comprehensive study of any specific object, but it may involve a very large number of studies of all objects. This is the case with logic, for example. It's like a functional department in an enterprise, which can't produce any product independently, but is related to the production of each product. Why is this so? This involves the question of efficiency and optimization of the research activities, namely, the thinking economics. Economics requires that research activities be divided into certain specialized modules. Even if each module can only study an individual aspect of an object, it deserves.

Third, human knowledge is *hierarchical* to a certain extent. This means that the above functionalization is not enough, and the knowledge system is stratified. At the bottom end is philosophy, which proposes the most basic assumptions and methods, on which other sub-categories of applied research are based. Since it is a hypothesis, it must be highly subjective, and it is an estimate and conception made by philosophers based on a lot of thinking. At the same time, it is also vague and is only used to indicate directions roughly. To a certain extent, vagueness is related to universality, and precisely because of the vagueness, it has a wide range of applications. Vagueness is also related to the human brain's ability to synthesize and generalize. According to the discussion of synthesis above, *there is some distinctions between synthesis, generalization, and universality*, and the directions provided, although generally not empty, are not precise enough and generally contain *distorted* and *approximate* meanings. There will also be controversy over how it applies to specific issues. However, in any case, specific researchers and ordinary people cannot do without them. Considering the "Algorithmic person's problem", we will see how helpless specific researchers and ordinary people are in general. Their thinking is to answer questions and gain knowledge, but they need knowledge first to answer questions. It's like doing business to make money: in order to make money, you have to have capital. That's when philosophy came to the fore. It uses vague but concise language to point people in certain directions. This "concise universality or comprehensiveness" is in fact a masterful skill, and the resulting cost-effectiveness is very attractive to helpless people, who now can, based on the philosophical knowledge, have a glimpse of the whole world in a small amount of time, so that they can primarily determine the directions of their future computations or actions. "Hierarchical" refers to the logical order. In a specific chronological order, the thinker can start with philosophy and move into specific fields, or they can start from specific fields and work back to the philosophical fields. Bad guidance only adds to troubles, keeping people spinning around and obtaining little, whereas good guidance can have a cumulative effect, like building an edifice, extending it continuously upward.

These hierarchical and functional structures are intertwined together to "wrap" the human knowledge system. It's like the bract of a corn, wrapping around the growing corn. *Within* this package, concrete knowledge is like the grains of the corn, and the discreteness is then manifested, and the specific knowledge corresponds to each specific object. The above-mentioned finitude, structurality, functionality, hierarchicality, and discreteness are combined to portray the human knowledge system. People treat the objective world like cutting a watermelon, which can be cut vertically or horizontally, hence different knowledge modules will be formed according to the different and intersectant dimensions. Without this Algorithmic perspective of bounded rationality, we cannot gain this understanding.

Since the advent of logical positivism, the vagueness and subjectivity of philosophy have been rejected, and the work of many philosophers who have led the trends of their times, although beneficial somehow to the development of philosophy, is fundamentally inclined to deny philosophy itself. This shall be the short-sightedness that once occurred in the twentieth century. Now, with the new perspectives, we can "Algorithmically" justify vagueness and subjectivity, and then synthesize the existing philosophical achievements of various schools to form a unified system. In this system, philosophy will give itself a rightful place. According to this unified logic, even if we do not immediately come up with a new literal and rigorous definition of philosophy, readers will be able to do it themselves.

§69. Classification of Philosophy

To examine a discipline, one needs to examine its history. Why is it? This is because no discipline has developed all at once only with current raw materials and a kind of unified logic. This ideal situation is not allowed by limited computing power. As a result, the discipline can only develop historically, and improve marginally, from time to time. Also, there will be different factions and styles within the discipline. Also due to the finitude of computing power, each of these factions can only rationally optimize to a certain extent, and then (at least temporarily) they will be in a pluralistic and quasi-static state.

This compels scholars to adhere to the tradition of literature, more or less. In other words, in the absence of the possibility of completely preserving all the literature and treating all of them in full equality and justice, it is necessary to continue and develop the discipline on the basis of the existing literature, and even, to a considerable extent, taking the existing literature as the standard of dialogues among researchers. This is what Thomas Kuhn meant when he used the word "paradigm". The domination of the community of professional scholars will inevitably cause a certain degree of suppression of new ideas, but "Algorithmically", this suppression cannot be *completely* avoided. The rise of the fringe doctrine to the mainstream is a risky operation that must be supported by investment. When a revolution is finally complete, the scholars who made the revolution will have the dominance like the previous "mainstream", and in this same way they will recoup their investment or make up their earlier losses.

In the early days of human society, the work of scholars was often synthetic. Because its contents were not so rich. This synthesis is in line with the Algorithmic economy. The division of labor in academia originated from an expansion of the professional workloads. Although these principles are very simple, it is necessary to restate Algorithmically here. This restatement is intended to illustrate: 1. The earliest scholarly work in the West was collected under the name of "philosophy". 2. Later, science was able to separate itself from philosophy. 3. Today, philosophy is divided into four branches: metaphysics, epistemology, logic, and ethics.

There are historical reasons for the formation of these four branches. Logic and ethics, for example, remain within philosophy, apparently because they have nowhere to go for the time being. In other words, they have not yet been fully scientized. We can envisage some kinds of sciences to contain them. For example, as some scholars have referred to as the "science of thinking", it may be possible sooner or later to "merge" the highly technical discipline of logic—although the foundations of logic (and the science of thinking) can still legitimately remain within the purview of philosophy. As mentioned earlier, behind ethics are social sciences and social engineering, and once the latter two have been satisfactorily established, the time has come to reform and reclassify ethics.

However, from an Algorithmic point of view, the meanings and logical structures of these four branches are very clear at the moment, and *it is particularly suitable for an Algorithmic elaboration.* The study of logic can be broadly understood as the basic study of the human mind. This research has been softwareized since ancient times. As a theory of thinking, ATT also adheres to this software-based style. Human minds act on information from the outside world and form thinking activities, which has become the objects of epistemological research. Philosophy of science can be used as a branch of epistemology, which specializes in epistemological issues about science, a type of knowledge. Then, as Algorithmic Theory emphasizes, although the processes of knowing are endless, it is necessary for people of every age to draw some conclusions about their own research on the world (even if they know that these conclusions are just temporary makeshifts). While some scholars admit that they only draw conclusions in the course of history, they are still highly convinced that some conclusions are permanent and final. Thus, this forms metaphysics. And, the metaphysics formed in ancient times shall be understandable for its lack of recognition of the temporariness of its own conclusions.

However, according to the view of thoughtful entities expounded in Chapter 4, *epistemology can no longer be elaborated completely separately from metaphysics.* Why? This is because the processes of knowing, or the processes of thinking more generally, are now the real, substantial activities in themselves;

they are the substantial or material entities, and they form new entities all the time. If metaphysics excludes them, it is obviously incomplete in its content. Moreover, although the thinking processes are developing, as mentioned above, we have come to a large number of relatively definite conclusions and understandings. Some parts of these conclusions and understandings are of a higher order, but this higher order does not prevent it from becoming a definite knowledge at present. The "higher-orderness" itself should also be one content of the "metaphysics of thinking" (or "ontology of thinking"). This is where Algorithmic philosophy is particularly different from traditional philosophy. In line with this understanding, the "Algorithmic metaphysics" (or the "Algorithmic ontology") began in the previous chapters and continues in this chapter. Now, *ordinary epistemology, along with Algorithmic Theory itself, should be included in ontology or metaphysics. Outside ontology, we should only discuss the "scholastic epistemology", namely, the philosophy and methodology of science.* Given that the principles of interpersonal differences and division of labour can now be elucidated Algorithmically, this ensures that this distinction in epistemology is meaningful.

In the sense that ethics is a prelude to social science and social engineering, ethics is particularly suitable to be the content of Algorithmic philosophy. This is because one of the major purposes of Algorithm Theory is to provide a basis for a unified social science, so that the category of "social science" can be *formally* established in a *strict* sense. A primary means of achieving this goal is to provide an ontology of the human mind. With this ontology, people, society, social sciences, and humanities all emerge spontaneously, and we only need to discuss them step by step. Algorithmic Theory comes from the problems and inspirations of the social sciences, and it is also used in the social sciences. We will recount in Chapters 8-11 of

Volume II the work that ATT has done for the social sciences, as well as some recent new developments.

This re-organized system is not only comprehensive, but also new and revolutionary; it is a reversal of the traditional philosophical system and a fundamental change in the direction of philosophy. The clear logic provided by this change will allow us to see the new flourishing that will take place in philosophy and relevant disciplines in the future. At the same time, with this relatively satisfactory solution to the problems of traditional philosophy, we can also foresee the inevitable decline of traditional philosophy. The theory of mind will develop in the direction of "the science of thinking", which may eventually lead to the separation of its main part from philosophy. The formal establishment of the general social science, as I have thought, would inevitably lead to the decline of the role of ethics in the hall of philosophy. However, according to the Algorithmic logic, philosophy will never die, it will look for new topics. The development of specific disciplines will also continually raise new questions for philosophy. These changes will happen slowly. Although it is still too early to tell the details, such a prospect is already visible, and we must mention it here—otherwise our main points will be incomplete.

§70. Epistemology and Ontology

After epistemology gained philosophical importance, there happened a great crisis in ontology or metaphysics. In fact, this crisis can be explained in one word: if knowledge is developing, how can we form a definitive conclusion about the world? Furthermore, should we draw conclusions about the world? If there is no need to make the final conclusion, is it necessary for metaphysics to exist? and so on.

Nonetheless, the retreat of metaphysics was done only

slowly. Descartes' methodology of science, and Kant's conception of the scientific metaphysics[1], can be seen as actions to deviously save metaphysics. The logical positivist assault on metaphysics was well-known and once considered fatal, though it was not so pertinent actually, and metaphysics has been on a slow revival shortly thereafter. This was because the concrete practice of research forced scholars to recognize the indispensable role of philosophy in their research. However, the above dilemma remains. In the absence of appropriate solutions, simply asking questions and acknowledging the crisis will not save philosophy itself.

There is also a strange optimism that philosophy has satisfactorily solved its problems and that its mission can come to an end. Both Wittgenstein and Heidegger[2], for example, held this view in different ways. Since then, twentieth-century philosophy has gradually fallen into a situation of triviality and disorganization, which could be related to this understanding. The picture is similar to that of economics today. The growth of literature coexists with the suspension of fundamental questions of the discipline. This situation is unfair to readers of the public who have to endure the obscurity of professional literature and terminology while the practical philosophical and economic problems they encounter in real life have not been solved. There is a lack of concise and effective doctrines to provide a basic, exercisable theoretical framework. In fact, theorists are sometimes there to create problems and cause trouble—As the saying goes: If you don't say it, I still somehow understand, but the more you say it, the more confused I become.

---

1. Immanuel Kant, "Metaphysical Foundations of Natural Science", translated and edited by Michael Friedman, Cambridge University Press, 2004.
2. Martin Heidegger, "The End of Philosophy and the Task of Thinking", in Martin Heidegger, "On Time and Being", translated by Joan Stambaugh, Harper Torchbooks, 1972, pp. 55-73.

Throughout the ages, philosophers have been tormented by a phenomenon that has not been alleviated to this day: the emergence of correct knowledge. This kind of knowledge is either the knowledge that was *believed* to be correct by the person concerned in a specific spatio-temporal environment, or it is the "correct knowledge" that was objectively proved as a consensus over time. Philosophers needed to explain this— and, above all, in an environment containing much false knowledge. Of course, computer principles and the derived Algorithmic Thinking Theory did not exist at that time. One easy way to do this was to claim that there is a "truth" or its analogue somewhere, and then, as if I have turned to the back of a hill and found a rock, that "truth" is assumed waiting to be discovered. If you find it, you find it; if you don't, then you need to keep trying. Obviously, such a doctrine actually facilitated the peddling of specialized knowledge by intellectuals in society.

Since truth (or "substance", "essence", etc.) exists *somewhere*, its relations to what exists *in front of our eyes* need to be clarified, as does its relationship to the less correct knowledge (or "opinion") in people's minds. Philosophers have gone to great lengths to explain how truth is reached, what truth looks like, and how truth in turn determines phenomena. These are the main contents of philosophy. The more head-scratching questions, which are relatively in the dark zone, are why is essence different from phenomena, and why do we human beings suffer so much from the toil of this process? Hegel answers these questions by using the concept of "the cunning of reason". This is an anthropomorphic explanation that became well-known for a while and was finally rejected by the world. A greater crisis comes from the "development" of "correct knowledge", that is, inside knowledge that was once accepted as correct by people, a considerable part of it was later denied again. These denials were not easy to detect in everyday life, but after a macroscopic and historical examination by scholars, a deep crisis was felt. The long-term stability of a small amount of knowledge coexists with the variability of the majority of knowledge.

These are the fundamental crises and difficulties of philosophy. These difficulties had actually existed since the early days of philosophy. Although later philosophers have developed philosophy in many different directions, these basic difficulties have not changed to this day. Personally, I believe that the mystical and obscure style of philosophy are more or less connected with these basic difficulties. Since the "big truths" have not been found out, some "small truths" will prevail or even spread. The world needs philosophy, but philosophers fail to provide exactly what they need.

Despite its terminology that may sound puzzling at first glance, Algorithmic philosophy is committed to building a philosophy that is plain, basic, close to ordinary life, and dedicated to making sense of those "big truths". My philosophical attainments are not profound. I have tried to read various philosophical texts over many years, but, to be honest, I was disappointed with the results. I don't think it's entirely my fault. Philosophical texts have not captured the heart of an enthusiastic and sincere reader like me, but instead aroused my will to criticize and reconstruct philosophy. In my opinion, the state of philosophy, and the states of humanities and social sciences closely related to philosophy, do not match the current epochal trends and spirits, and hence need to be updated and even reformed. For this reason, my idea is that, first of all, I should *completely* and *intensively* speak out what I want to say. Henceforth, I would rather behave less "professionally", and will not hesitate to do it. Even if existing philosophies are really profound in some aspects, they are by no means comprehensive. What I want to express shall be as indispensable to philosophy as if everybody needs air. In the past, they were in the dark, but now they need to be explicit.

§71. Epistemology and Ontology (continued)

The reformative scheme of Algorithm Theory is as follows: First, a discrete and pluralistic environment is constructed, in which the mutual "reactions" of Instructions and information intermittently causes local and many equilibria, which represent not only "correct knowledge" but all other cognitive stagnations; More importantly, we understand that this whole, which contains all the positive and negative phenomena, is infinitely expanding, and that the infinite development of knowledge is a core content that philosophy needs to introduce, and on this premise, we can then study how (and why) the development of knowledge stops to rest for a while; The factor completeness and the forced computing closure provide the answer to this question, which forms a particular version of knowledge, which is then to be updated intermittently; discreteness and heterogeneity, as a result of the Algorithmic bounded rationality, lead to different rates of change in different parts of the knowledge system, and the local equilibria are sometimes broken and reconstructed; however, the stability of Instructional performance provides permanence and absoluteness, avoiding the fall of philosophy into relativism. As mentioned earlier, while reforming logic, this scheme also endogenizes social, spiritual, and humanistic activities.

Then, how can the ontology or metaphysics under this scheme be reformed?

First, the localization and minimization. Where logical positivism criticizes metaphysics is that it has a lot of unnecessary redundancy. Since philosophers want to make certain conclusions about the basic, overall, or future things, and these conclusions need to be relatively reliable and easy to accept, what should we do? One of the strategies is to draw conclusions *only* about something that is necessary and compelled to be concluded, or about what is *relatively* certain or reliable while avoiding other unnecessary or unreliable conclusions. This is not a new strategy, but a reaffirmation of the extant economy of thought (e.g. the "Occam's Razor"). Now, Algorithmic Theory provides it additionally with a new foundation.

Second, high-order and versioning. This means firstly that in the case of the materialization of thoughts, the philosophy of mind itself has become an ontology. Second, the rest of the ontology shall be incorporated with the Algorithmical *self-consciousness*, that is, to recognize that this ontology is limited and, in general, temporary, to be replaced by a later version. A first-order doctrine about a particular phenomenon may be indeterminate in itself, but there may be some certainty (the "high-order certainty") in a second- or higher-order doctrine about it. For example, philosophers and economists may not know exactly about the pricing of specific commodities, but economists can point to certain patterns or important factors in pricing, as well as the laws of price movement, while philosophers (or economic philosophers) can point out the incompleteness of price information in reflecting other economic conditions, the difference in prices, the inevitability of price changes, and so on. With such a self-awareness, the ontology can claim or hint in the text anywhere the limitations of its conclusions, indicate where it is not possible to reach a conclusion, provide a number of possible options for a conclusion, or illustrate some of the computational processes, and so on. Note that there is a strong need for concise propositions for both scholars and ordinary people, and that the readers' expectations for our academia are by no means as detailed and rigorous as logical positivists have assumed.

Contemplative philosophers, as long as their words are meaningful and recapitulatory, will always be welcome. This is guaranteed by the law of the economy of thought.

Third, as mentioned in §40, it is envisaged that there is an objective *"human knowledge thesaurus"* which consists of all the results of all Instructions processing all information. It is used as a new "Being" or "Substance" to replace Parmenides' "Being", Plato's "Idea", or the medieval "God" in philosophy. Since Instructions are given and information is quite objective (although the subjective human factors also participate in the formation of information), it is possible to think of all knowledge as predestined as traditional philosophers assumed, but we observers have limited computing power and cannot exactly know all the "predestined" things at any point in time. This super-database also contains imperfect and false knowledge. However, false or imperfect knowledge can be just as false or imperfect even if it is computed in the same way by another person. In this sense, all knowledge of right or wrong is *objective* and predestined, but due to the limited computing power, each person can only possess a part of it. It can be argued that debates between people are always about the comparison between one part of the knowledge base and another. This database cannot depend on the existence of any particular individual person, but it depends on the existence of humanity as a whole. If humans don't exist at all, there wouldn't be this database. The process of knowledge development can be seen as a process of wandering within this database, or a process of clarifying the contents of this database. Therefore, it can be set both between people and at the very front of the evolvement of humankind. Of course, this database cannot simply and exactly replace Parmenides' "Being". This replacement will inevitably lead to a series of substantial changes in philosophy, and eventually to a philosophical subversion.

Algorithmic people who think according to ATT, equipped with all kinds of innate tools and resources, are now about to enter the earthly world. In other words, the Algorithmic ontology is now to unfold with a new rhythm and attitude.

We will begin our discussion with a review of logic, and then look at the various computations and actions of Algorithmic people in the world, and what their consequences are. It's a new attempt to see what we can say.

§72. Logical Reasoning is Productive Activities

The delineation, narrative, and analysis of human thinking processes involve a wide range of disciplines. In addition to logic, psychology generally describes and analyzes thinking as behaviors and thoughts as entities, but psychology, as a quite new discipline in history, has been separated from social sciences for a long time in the absence of a thinking theory, and it is not until the late period that it approaches the core of social sciences. It can be argued that different social science disciplines describe and analyze the process of thinking and its consequences from different aspects, but they are mainly problem-oriented and do not directly explore thinking itself. Meanwhile, literary writings are often rich in mental activity, but are imprecise and overly subjective or "irrational".

As mentioned earlier, logic describes and analyzes certain segments of the thinking process in a narrow sense. Higher-order logic has still been generally narrow in scope.

Now, we need to integrate the achievements and methods in the above fields with the Algorithmic principles and methods, to try to construct *a comprehensive and unified basic framework of logic or thinking science.*

Whether classical logic or modern logic, the basic form they take is literally discrete and consistent with ATT. Even though some parts of the objective world are continuous, the human brain first uses its discrete ways to describe and analyze them. That's not to say that humans won't use a continuous approach. Mathematical functions and analog radio signals are mainly examples of products of the continuity approach. However, taking continuity as an object and a problem or using it as a method is different from recognizing discreteness as the basic way of human thinking. Second, continuity and discreteness as two different approaches need to be used in combination in order to complement each other's strengths. Where the continuous approach is overused, the value and necessity of the discrete approach rises. At present, the establishment and use of Algorithmic Theory is just to correct the excessive proliferation and use of continuity methods.

In fact, the discrete approach demonstrated by logic has been precise and vivid. The process of inventing a term or creating a concept is really the process of preparing a single piece of information, a "datum", exactly, which then becomes the object of computing. The process of making a single proposition or judgment is like the meta-computation, which connects different pieces of information or data. A reasoning process is to connect the two meta-computations and further process them to produce a new result. Therefore, reasoning is the prototype of a computerized program. It's like there have been islands in a lake, and then come the bridges. Or, in geometry, there are dots first, then come the lines and figures.

When Aristotle and other philosophers tried to describe activities of the human mind, this was the first method that came to mind. Later, when scientists tried to use machines to simulate human thinking, they came up with this discrete approach as well.

Computer scientists were inspired by logic before building computer science. However, after computer science, our understanding deepened, and then, in turn, we could use computer principles to reform existing logic. This is the return and feedback of computers to logic.

The first step in the Algorithmic reformation of logic is to re-understand and re-interpret the concept of "logic". When we say the word "logic", what does it mean at the core? It refers to the connection between data, or how to generate new data from old data, right? It's like drawing a line between data and connecting them, or "drawing a line" from existing data to the future, *extending* it diachronically. Since there is the concept of space and the concept of time, the reason why data are "crossed" between each other is because they are in different places (or in different places in the brain) and this discreteness creates the need to connect with each other, while data extends into the future firstly because there is a dimension of time, and secondly because data can move and interact with each other —or they can interact with Instructions. This involves the element of change and behavior. Therefore, logic since ancient times has implied or explicitly stated that the theory of thinking should be a theory about the *existence* and *movement* of thoughtful entities in the *environment of time and space.*

In particular, the theory of thinking is not only about the existence and movement of thoughtful entities, but especially about the *generation* of thoughts. The growing popularity of the word "generative" reflects the fact that people are breaking through the confines of determinism or statics and embracing innovative ideas as everyday worldviews. However, "generative" can first and foremost refer to the replication of old data, and this replicative process also makes a lot of sense. People don't just copy things, or copy information. Where replication activity takes place or data are transferred, there must be its own reasons that cannot be ignored. Moreover, strictly speaking, the result of copying or moving can also be regarded as "new data", because the resulting data are likely to be something that one did not have before, so these data are "new" to him/her. Even if one had them at this place, but missed them at that place, then they would still have been new at that place. What doesn't constitute new data for another person can still be meaningful to this person as long as it's new to this person. Of course, data that constitutes new data for all of us are of the greatest significance, because they shall be an innovation for humanity as a whole. This is how we usually understand innovation in the narrowest sense.

Nonetheless, compared with the copying and moving data, what is more important is the generation of data, that is, the generation of new knowledge from existing knowledge. That's exactly what reasoning does. Deductive reasoning is undoubtedly the most important type of reasoning. However, the mainstream view in academia is that deductive reasoning does not produce new knowledge. This is because they believe that what deductive reasoning "produces" is "implicit" in its premises, and this deduction has only made it explicit. This argument actually negates the significance of much of the work done by theorists throughout history, the significance of the main work of mathematicians, and the significance of the most reliable parts of everyday mental activities. This type of thinking activity, because it is the most reliable and often in the highest priority, is considered "meaningless" while activities such as induction, imagination, etc. are considered unreliable and non-mainstream on the one hand, and the most "creative" on the other. This is a paradox! Moreover, this view is often held by no one else, but by those who are best at deductive reasoning. What a complete, selfless self-denial!

Since we believe that even the reproduction of data is important, we certainly cannot agree with this view. Deductive reasoning is about the production of spiritual products; and, all reasoning activities are about the production of spiritual products. Based on what a person already has, reasoning activities produce something new that the person does not already know and hence is novel from what the person already knows. As a result of such productive activities, the total amount of knowledge in the mind of the person, and thus in the world, has increased, from less to more.

We need to re-examine the nature of deductive reasoning. I don't agree with Aristotle's emphasis that deductive reasoning is a kind of deduction "from big to small"—hence he interpreted deductive reasoning as "reducing" ("deduce" is near "reduce") something. This interpretation is too complicated to be correct. Deductive reasoning is obviously similar to what mathematics calls "*the substitution property of equality*". Because two things are equal, one can be used to replace the other. In this sense, deductive reasoning does not seem to "produce" anything. However, if this is the case, why is this kind of "substitution" carried out? Isn't this useless work? Of course not! *The two things in the substitution are only equal in their contents, but in their positions and functions in the computational operations and thus in the thinking economy, they are different, of course.* It is exactly this characteristic of "both equal and different" that leads to the occurrence of such substitution and reasoning. This principle is actually similar to the meanings of data copying and moving, that is, they are all related to spatial locations and temporal processes. The discovery of another proposition that can deductively match one proposition is creative in itself. Second, with the help of these two equal variables, a new relationship is established between the other two variables in those two different premises, which has not existed before, and has not been perceived by the person; isn't this a kind of productiveness? Isn't it through this process of production that the knowledge of the person concerned is increased? It's like a long distance that cannot be reached by one step, and thus requires two steps. The stance of extreme rationalism is that, as an afterthought, there is "no difference" between taking two steps and taking one step; however, it was clear that one step was not enough to go through the distance at that time! Wasn't this success, and even this afterthought, achieved really by taking two steps? Isn't this a kind of "ingratitude"?

§73. Extension of Deductive Reasoning

Thoughtful entities move and interact with each other in the spatio-temporal environment, resulting in the formation of new ideas. To do this again, the above deductive approach needs to be extended in two ways, one to functional and service operations, and the other to a wide range of less reliable inferences, even beyond the scope of the word "reasoning".

The expansion into functional and service operations, as revealed by computer science, includes data searching, transferring, replication, storage, deletion, and other controlling operations. We can argue outside computer principles, but only the generalized statements made in computer principles are more comprehensive and reliable. For logic, the most important thing is to answer the question "where does the data come from?" In other words, it is a problem of memory management. Human memory is like an ocean, and its contents are extremely large and complex, so how to search in it is a big problem. The fact that a valuable material has not been available for computing does not necessarily mean that it does not exist in the memory. There are problems with the formats of data stored, as well as problems with the paths to certain data, which is similar to computers. For example, the same information can be saved both in text format and in image format. When we recall it, we don't necessarily find any of them at once. Sometimes, it is possible to catch it by first recalling a specific event associated with it. Thus, the search strategy is important. Some other times, we don't know exactly what we need to search for; this is when "association" comes in. A person who is good at association is someone who is good at finding useful information in memory. In doing so, another prerequisite for an excellent association is the discovery of certain unnoticed features of the object in front of us, which in turn requires the ability to observe and analyze the object. In short, along such clues, numerous thoughtful steps, operations, functions, and thus "Instructions" will enter our field of vision, and hence be included in the scope of logic.

Sound reasoning is wonderful, but it's not easy to obtain. Sometimes, a process of reasoning that we engage in with confidence is found to be flawed, because we often tend to work on a large scale and do not pay enough attention to details. One way to clarify the details is to record and analyze the computational process stepwise with the help of computerized simulations and programmed methods. This is our passive way of getting into "uncertain reasoning".

The main way shall be the positive way. Reliable reasoning is mainly achieved by means of "equal substitution", and its conditions are strict and not easy to satisfy. Even if it can be satisfied, the direction of reasoning may be wrong, not towards solving the problem. Or, it's cumbersome and costly. The word "high cost" may sound insignificant, however, it can be so severely costly that the person concerned cannot afford it, and the time can be so long that it is impossible to wait. However, the timeline of decision-making may force the actor to make some changes to the computational steps. Then, the actor may actively design and apply those unreliable reasoning methods. Another motivation for this is that the actor might *first* draw certain unreliable conclusions and *then* assess their qualities and reliabilities. This is an experimental operation, as well as a serial and stepwise operation. Rational choice theory only emphasizes the identification of options, but does not deal with the generation of the options. However, there is no doubt that only when there are options can we discern them. There is no "subject" other than human beings themselves who provide us with the service of "making options". A large number of "opinions" in real life need to be produced first before they can be taken as the basis for discussion. Being good at analyzing and answering questions is a kind of ability, and raising questions is also a kind of ability, and providing preliminary ideas, options, and solutions as the basis for analysis and discussion is an important kind of intellectual activity as well. These clichés are actually unconsciously telling the Algorithmic truth.

Algorithmically, in detail, there are often only minor technical differences between the many different ways of reasoning, and they are also closely related and can be transformed into each other under certain conditions. For example, a complete inductive reasoning is equal to a deductive reasoning, and only when the inductive samples are incomplete, it is conventionally called the "induction". Induction is unreliable, but it doesn't matter—let's pull out the conclusion first! This raises the question of "true or false" of a proposition. This is an application of the serial method: make a hypothesis before making a judgment on it. Since incomplete samples can tentatively come to a general conclusion where these samples can be extrapolated to others, it is also possible to consider doing the same for similar samples—Anyway, nothing is reliable here! This is analogical reasoning. Since it is possible to deduce from the premises to the conclusion, it is also possible to try to deduce from the conclusion to a premise. This is known as "abduction". Sometimes, reasoning cannot be done continuously; some parts are difficult whereas others are easy. This is a key reason to use a hypothetical approach. The core of the hypothetical method is not whether the hypothetical premises are reliable, but the *strategy* that *firstly,* to draw the *relatively* easy and reliable conclusions downstream and *then,* to speculate on the upstream situations *based on the existing conclusions.* This strategy can be called *"computing selectively"* or *"certainty in priority".* This indicates the importance of the computing order: "dealing with uncertainty first, then with certainty" and "dealing with certainty first, then uncertainty" often have very different effects. As long as we realize the serial, dynamic nature of mental activity, it is easy to understand the causes, characteristics, and uses of this method and its comparability with other methods.

Since computing costs can lead people to seek unreliable conclusions, the reliable and precise conclusions are not in themselves indispensable. Sometimes this accuracy is unnecessarily wasteful, and sometimes it leads to high costs for subsequent processing. Therefore, simplification, approximation, fuzzification, and so on have important uses, because their concise conclusions are often easy for actors to remember and apply. Philosophical propositions are often vague but concise, then they are loved by the world.

The difficulty of computation and its costs can be so great that the actors sometimes would rather do tentative operations or experiments than do computations anymore. From this substitutive perspective, we can say that *an object runs on its own, which is somewhat equivalent to us doing computations. An analogy can be drawn between the two* (see "thought experiment" in §170, Vol. II)—albeit with their different natures. We can approximate that the operations of the object are carried out according to certain mechanisms or ways that we have conceived or understood, and therefore, the operational results of the object themselves can also be understood as the results of running in these mechanisms or ways. In this sense, the object acts as a "computer", which can form a cross-reference, competitive, and complementary relationship with our theoretical analysis. Objectively, the tentative or experimental results can be interpreted in multiple even infinite ways;

therefore, without a proper specific theory, the implications of these results would be quite arguable, and they are of little use. Theory can help make an experiment more efficient and productive. On this basis, one can selectively do computations (including conceiving theories) through one's own brain or turn to experiments as the "physical computations". This is an extended understanding of the experimental method, as well as the combination of theory and practice.

Since we know that the conclusions are unreliable, there is still the probability that some are correct, and then various Algorithms related to probability will be generated. For this topic, we will turn to §90.

By setting the object in the above discussion as a human rather than a physical object, we will get all sorts of "social Algorithms" such as Persuasion, Negotiation, Fraud, and Threat to deal with social problems.

§74. The Algorithmic Logic

After the extension of logic to the theory of mind, it is necessary now to propose the "Algorithmic Logic", why? This is because many logical operations, Instructions, or Algorithms that are produced by the above extension need to be permuted and combined again. The logic required to make this permutation & combination is what we call the "Algorithmic Logic". It is a type of higher-order logic (or meta-logic), namely, logic that performs operations on operations of lower-order or first-order. The relationship between it and ATT is a two-sided relationship. In other words, Algorithmic logic is the counterpart of ATT in logic. After having Algorithmic logic, the unified logic and the unified thinking theory can have their rudiments.

Under the framework of "thinking = computing = (Instruction + information) × speed × time", what kind of logic is used to organize, construct, and arrange Instructional sequences (and logical operations)? *What "Algorithmic logic" indicates first is this question.* It is raised in the context of Algorithmic Thinking Theory, so it is an Algorithmical problem (and also an "Algorithmic person's problem"). This question is based on the independence of a metacomputation (including a logical operation), as well as on the presence of time and space, because computations now need to be extended within time and space.

The answer to this question begins with the recognition that the substantial and Algorithmical natures of thoughts allow for a multitude of non-traditional options for answering a logical question. For example, the logically incorrect or flawed answers are possible and allowable. Computations made to answer a particular question, as *actions*, can be wrong, and an error (or imperfection) is logically unacceptable in itself, but not entirely unacceptable as an acting result. The person answering the question, although he or she may answer incorrectly, is literally providing an answer to this question, subjectively or objectively. This is one of the ways in which we introduce errors into our theoretical system that is supported by logical reasoning. It embraces mistakes without defying logic. Another option is to set the question aside, divert oneself from the question, or procrastinate the question. On top of that, the options of computing jobs that can be substitutively used are almost limitless. The suspending, diverting, delaying, or avoiding are all the deliberate *responses* made by an actor to the specific question, so each of them can be regarded as an "answer" to the question in common sense. It has a meaning, which may only be understood after a reflection. In other words, this is still a causal relationship between the specific question that precedes it and the specific reaction that follows. As a manifestation of this causal relationship, the reaction sometimes does not have a direct relationship with the question in traditional logic, but may only have a specific, indirect, distant, or weak connection. However, *in the eyes of the actor*, according to the Algorithmic logic, the reaction he/she made that was not deemed related on the surface was Algorithmically *the most direct* reaction. After a series of Algorithmical reactions, the person may turn back to the "traditionally direct" answer to this question. This chain of phenomena may even be strictly logical. A critical aspect of determining this logic is the economic pros and cons of the various and many steps in this entire computing process. He/she has to assess the whole situation and try to marginally optimize the choice of which operation to do next. The computing process is arranged just with this in mind.

The core of Algorithmic logic is to put forward such a requirement for computing on the premise of recognizing Algorithmic Theory and computational economy: strive to ensure that each step of computation is economically optimal at the moment and the place where it is performed. After such optimization, the seemingly unrelated computational steps can have this economic connection, which is just a logical connection between them. As this logical connection has not been found out before, we give it a new name: Algorithmic Logic. Furthermore, we can give a new understanding or definition of "logic", that is, *"logic" is the method of extending computations in the flow of time*. Computations are extended not only by a variety of existing logics, but also by Algorithmic logic. Algorithmic logic, in particular, links computations from one logic to another. It builds an additional "logical bridge" between different logical operations and logical systems.

As a result, a computing job typically has a two-tier architecture: it uses Algorithmic logic to decide what logical operations (as computations) to perform, and performs these computations. The two types of logical operations are alternated diachronically. This two-tier system shall be familiar to people who use computers a lot: either run certain applications, or go back to the desktop, wait and choose which application to go to next.

With the help of the bridge built by Algorithmic logic, we can now form a comprehensive vision, that is, to gather various existing logic systems into a list, and then compare and analyze their respective conditions, requirements, functions, and operational and economical characteristics, so as to seek advantages and avoid disadvantages in computing, learn from each other's strengths, and thus realize the optimization of the overall benefit of thinking activities. In the past, various logics existed independently, and the perspective of comparison, connection, and trade-off was lacking. However, this integrative perspective is actually necessary for computations. Due to the limited time and resources, the actors must make such comparisons, combinations, and trade-offs. If scholars don't do this, the actors will do it themselves, consciously or unconsciously. Or, in the absence of anyone doing so, the human minds are in a state of fragmentation and unconscious "ignorance" about the economic problems of thinking.

With the concept of a comprehensive or unified system of logic, the meaning of the term "Algorithmic logic" is automatically expanded and rises to the name of this unified system. This is because, since Algorithmic logic is the logic of comparison and selection between all other logics, the mention of the word "Algorithmic logic" naturally means that the "presence" of all other logics is simultaneously recognized, then the concept of "Unified Logic System" also arises. *In this unified system, any other logic can, in principle, exist as a special case of Algorithmic logic.* When we ignore the factor of computational economics for any reason, the unified system collapses and decomposes into the various specific logical systems.

However, this argument is incomplete, and the

computational economy has penetrated deeply into traditional logic. Not only does a syllogism take a discrete form, but it is also a way of "agglomerating" data, namely, the way data approach each other. Since scattered storages of data over long distances are not convenient for inference, syllogisms show how propositions can be gathered and re-organized in a way that makes the reasoning quick, clear, easy, and accurate. This "agglomerating data" feature works with all existing logical systems. After the agglomeration, when they see the data before them are so close and so simple, the actors might ignore or "forget" the economic factors in them, and even mistakenly think that all logical operations, no matter how many they are, can be carried out costlessly or "frictionlessly". This applies in particular to the formalization of a logic. The formal factor in classical logic was weak, then "formal logic" strengthens the formal factors in logic. What does "formalization" mean? That is, you transform a logical operation into a series of symbols that have no practical meaning but only the *finite meanings* given by yourself, and then, *when an operation is performed*, you *only need* to consider the categories and positions of the symbols, and the finite meanings given, *without any other factor.* This greatly speeds up the computing process, and the operations then become a purely proficient exercise. This is also how the principle of computers came about. It is only after the operations are completed that people need to restore the symbols to their original meanings. It can be said that the development of logic in modern times has actually been driven to a large extent by this economic idea.

The application of the inductive method is also deeply based on the economics of computation. With limited computing speed, a complete induction is often unachievable and unnecessary. This is because, in time and space, our usual problem is to infer the unknown from what we already know, or from the past and the present, to infer the future. If it can be fully inducted, the induction itself may lose its meanings. Therefore, *expansively interpreting the finite samples is the soul, value, and significance of induction*, and how it pursues the computational economy.

Without the Algorithmic perspective, any higher-order logic is in principle questionable, and the rationale is similar to what we discussed in the previous chapter on self-objectification: higher-order logic is for first-order logic (or lower-order logic), and it presupposes that the first-order operations must exist as a *fait accompli* (an established fact). However, if we ignore the economic aspects of computations, we admit that computations must have been done profligately and modified freely, then the objectified first-order logical operations cannot exist as the fait accompli, and *they must foresee the occurrence of the current higher-order operation that is objectifying them at this moment and then proactively adapt to it in advance.* This exactly shows that they are not a fait accompli, but "to be determined". This is like, say, I ask you how old you are this year, but you reply to me, "How old do you think me to be, or how old do you want me to be, then I will be." In the face of this difficulty, the theory of rational expectations in economics takes such an approach that it assumes a *particular* situation in which the actor's current optimal decision does not change according to how the actor foresees the future, and that the predictions of others, or the reflections in the future, have no effect on the current decision. Relevant economists exaggerate this particular situation as "standard" and "ordinary", to make a sophistry.

§75. None of the Four Laws of Classical Logic Hold True

With Algorithmic logic, I find that the four laws of the famous classical logic are now in question; strictly speaking, none of them can be established any longer. Their positive, truthful components, while still present, require the Algorithmical interpretation, restatement, or reconstruction.

The four laws are the law of identity, the law of contradiction (or the law of no contradiction), the law of excluded middle, and the law of sufficient reason. Now let's explain each respectively.

The law of identity means that a thing is equal to itself. This seemingly undoubted "law" is very problematic if it is placed in the environment of time and space. The first is that the boundaries and scope of the things we are referring to are commonly approximate, not very precise, and the things often change, but we ignore their changes to a greater or lesser extent. The reason for ignoring these "details" is that we want to keep the names of the objectified things the same in order to save on computational costs. For example, we generally do not distinguish between the different Mikes of different days, but refer to Mike in different days indiscriminately as "Mike". This risky approach is successful most of the time, but less often, mistakes occur. At this point, we may be accused of "disguised replacement of concept", i.e., the objects we are talking about in different contexts are actually different, and the differences have reached the point where they affect the conclusion; and we ourselves either don't know, or pretend not to know. This kind of mistake can happen even for abstract symbols. This is because the meaning of an abstract symbol is given by ourselves, and with the passage of time, the context changes, but we forget its original definition, or are too lazy to strictly adhere to its definition, and eventually mistakes occur. Even if we don't see it as a mistake, we need to know that the meanings of concepts we use in our everyday thinking and discourse are always in a state of slight flux. *This state of imprecision must now be seen as a normalcy.* Meanwhile, we need to re-understand the nuanced meanings of classical logical discourses, that is, they may have assumed some ideal conditions, or implicit preconditions, for certain referential or propositional activities, or they may have assumed a consensus or common-sense knowledge base with listeners, and so on.

Now the turn to the law of contradiction (or the law of no contradiction). This "law" cannot be secured at all in the case of Algorithmic discrete computations. There are usually a lot of data and computations, and their basis is not exactly the same, and the actor is not usually fully aware of it. In such a case, there is no guarantee that the actor will reach two completely non-conflicting conclusions on the same issue or the same aspect of different objects. Until the conflicts between the two conclusions are resolved, they may coexist in the mind of one actor, and the actor may be in a dilemma. Moreover, *since contradictions can exist temporarily, they can also exist for a long time.* There is no insurmountable gulf between the two situations. A person can make contradictory statements or behaviors. Since thoughts, words, and actions occur in a serial manner, they occur in different moments and therefore *do not directly "collide" or contradict each other.* The only thing we insist on is that metacomputing can't contradict itself. This is the constancy of the function of meta-computation, i.e., the same Instruction processes the same information, and the result is always the same—except in the case of "lottery" where the results may be different. However, this constancy does not guarantee that there will be no conflicts between different computations. Even the Instructional system itself cannot be considered to be completely self-consistent and complete. We have not put forward such a hypothesis. This hypothesis is unnecessary.

From an Algorithmic point of view, the value of the law of contradiction does not lie in a strict requirement that there be no contradiction in thinking activities, but in the context of widespread and unavoidable contradictions, *it respects and pursues consistency in this context.* As mentioned earlier, consistency stands for relatively high quality or efficiency, which leads to savings. The *disadvantage* of a conflicting, pluralistic, or erroneous system (note that it is merely a "disadvantage") is that it needs to retain more computational results concurrently, and it can only give conflicting or ambiguous answers to problems, or provide the potential for future answers, or it may not give answers. This is not the case with a consistent system, which is generally concise, clear (these effects are economical), and relatively speaking, often effective. Therefore, throughout history, people have favored consistency and prioritized the pursuit of consistency. Something wrong, even if it is intentional (e.g. using the method of reverse verification), is often only useful when it helps to find the right answer, and hence is a devious way. This is an illustration that can be used to show why the direction of traditional philosophy has been reversed, and how it can now be reversed again.

The problem of the law of excluded middle is even more obvious, because it is based on the premise of a "known wholeness", and the conclusion is inferred by a deduction of the whole. Under the condition of bounded rationality, firstly, we often do not know the overall situation. Second, we can't know for sure whether we are categorizing things or problems correctly, so how can we apply "either/or" thinking to it? If the categorization is not right, any proposition related to it may be wrong. The positive aspect of this exclusion law is that it can be used as a method of exploration, allowing us to speculate on the unknown from the known and then try to verify it. This extends the chain of thinking. Because, in some cases, we do have a sense of the big picture ahead of knowing its parts. Second, since most alternative methods are not reliable enough, why do we have to exclude this method alone?

The problem of the "law of sufficient cause" is even more serious. Under the condition of discrete and big data, the knowledge system is an irregular and huge network, in which the connections and disconnections are so mixed and varied that we can never strictly know what kind of reasons are "sufficient" for what kind of phenomena. In principle, the reasons behind any phenomenon shall be infinite and cannot be fully enumerated. The "law of sufficient reason" assumes that the causes can be enumerated, implying that "people can know the world completely", or "truth is simple", etc., or it assumes that forms of knowledge can be standardized and that any contradictions and plurality can be eliminated. It misunderstands that when people pursue consensus, standard answers, or standard statements in everyday discourse, there are many implicit common premises and contexts in that scenario, and therefore, such forms of knowledge must never be regarded as the *universal* standard forms of knowledge. The "law of sufficient reason" reflects a form of German-style (even Kantian) extreme rationalism, which attempts to establish some ultimate standard knowledge by means of human's innate way of thinking—even if it also acknowledges that this "ultimate standard truth" is different from the true truth of the external world.

The deconstruction of classical logic opens the door to all kinds of non-classical logics. However, this does not mean that Algorithmic logic is useless in a non-classical logic. However, a preliminary investigation of non-classical logic shows that there have been more and more Algorithmic elements, and the development of logic from classical to modern is generally in the Algorithmic direction, and even becoming more and more "Algorithmical". In order to maintain the balance of the overall structure of the book and avoid getting bogged down in costly details, the work of using Algorithmic methods to re-interpret existing logic is to be stopped here. This is just a starting point and an illustration; readers can build on it if they are interested.

§76. The Algorithmic Pros-Cons Analysis

The Algorithmic logic constantly asks questions and requests a pros-and-cons analysis of the computing steps, and the filtering and sorting of them, but it cannot do this analysis on its own. This analysis needs to be supported by other specific knowledge. The pros-and-cons analysis, or the "cost-benefit analysis" as it is called in economics, can only be carried out using those specific pieces of knowledge.

Objects of the analysis are the plans for computational jobs. An actor first formulates a plan and then analyzes the plan as a whole. The plan can be for a single meta-computation. More commonly, it is a set of metacomputations in chronological order, i.e., a program. The actor needs to assess the overall feasibility of the program.

One might ask: since the assessment has not yet been carried out, how can the program be constructed in the first place? How can the structure of the program itself meet the economic requirement? And in particular, how can it be ensured that it meets the specific economic conditions of the situation?

These are good questions. For the time being, questions like these are more important than the answers to them. In fact, under dynamic conditions, *there is no completely ideal, well-established way to solve such a problem.* The actor can only construct the program utilizing his/her past experience, common practice, the rationales of the matter itself, a rough estimate of the specific circumstance, etc., and then evaluate it. Theoretical methods and empirical methods must be used alternately. The results of the evaluation may lead to modification or refactoring of the program. After the modification or refactoring, then evaluate it again; and so on.

However, there are limits to these feedback and interactive processes. Constructing a program requires one type of knowledge, and evaluating its economic viability requires another type of knowledge (the transparency, simpleness, and purity of Instructions are particularly useful for showing that computations always require various types of knowledge). These types of knowledge are all limited. As a result, actors are unable to establish a *fully* clear, precise, one-to-one correspondence between each step of computation and its economic consequences (including costs and benefits) so that such an assessment can be as simple as the work on an accounting book. Another factor is that the evaluation and modification of the program itself are costly, and if the costs are too high, it is not worth a careful investigation. Such costs would inevitably limit the accuracy and frequency of the assessment, and the actor would prefer to do it hastily to a certain extent. Thus, it can be assumed that assessments *are usually carried out intermittently, in batches and approximately.* The assessment will not be detailed unless the scale of the computations to be carried out is large and/or long-term. These costs also limit the modification and refactoring of the program. Even if it were to be amended, the person concerned would have to amend only a small number of its links, and such an amendment would only be made if it is obviously or certainly necessary. The actors can also reconstruct the program, because the costs of refactoring are sometimes less than the costs of making step-by-step changes to the program (an "Algorithmic effect"). In the case that these operations are more cumbersome, actors may also choose to carry out the program directly and let the consequences naturally occur, because they may prefer to live with the consequences rather than do the pros-cons analysis.

In short, nothing can unfold perfectly and precisely. This dilemma is by no means a special case, but a common problem in dynamic conditions. Without a plan, there is no object to be evaluated; however, once there is a plan, the plan cannot be adjusted perfectly. This is like a company hiring an employee has to negotiate the salary and make the decision based on an assessment of his conditions and the prediction of his/her overall performance over a period of time in the future, but once the salary is determined and he/she is hired, his/her performance may not meet the expectations, and the salary cannot be changed flexibly enough. Such a contradiction cannot be completely resolved. Theorists are often obsessed with constructing ideal models, whereas they tend to overlook the realities of such obstacles and their significance.

Another insight is that when the knowledge used to construct programs was initially constructed as modules or patterns, the economic factors have been considered and embodied somehow in the knowledge, which inevitably reduces the need to re-consider them on the spot of current computations in real time. This is as if before a technology is put on the market, its inventor must have considered the costs and benefits incurred for the users of the technology, and have in principle believed that the users would make profits to use it. That's true. Since the analysis of pros and cons can be carried out at all times in principle, how can it be assumed that a knowledge producer will only produce knowledge without any economic considerations? Nonetheless, these ex-ante considerations generally cannot be precisely fit in the real-time and on-site applications. Obviously, the so-called "habit" can be such a kind of knowledge produced according to such logical steps.

Another confusing but grossly erroneous view comes from mainstream neoclassical economics, which assumptively holds that there are perfect market prices for all products and all factors of production, so that all cost-benefit analyses can be quantified, monetized, and thus precise. It misleads readers to believe that any deviation of reality from the analyses shall be approximate and secondary, and therefore, any discussion of the deviation is insignificant. This view is a manifestation of extreme rationalism in economics.

Algorithmical, and therefore practical, is that market prices are not readily available and that they are volatile and imperfect, so that quantitative analysis is either difficult to carry out or can only be carried out partially or intermittently; or, its conclusions are not accurate. That's where the concept of "data type" comes in. The difference between qualitative and quantitative analysis is just in the types of data used. If we consider the distinction between qualitative and quantitative analysis to be important, then we must assume that the differences in data types are important. In fact, people often use non-quantitative data to analyze the pros and cons, and the resultant judgment is not "whether the net profit is 2.3 or 2.4", but "high" or "low", "big" or "small", "good" or "bad", "yes" or "no", and so on. Although they may not be precise, it does not mean that such conclusions are necessarily inferior to a quantitative conclusion. Such computations can be called "*Structural Computations*". *Qualitative analysis is or entails structural computations.* As for the terminology, we can optionally limit "cost-benefit analysis" strictly to quantitative analysis (which is more in line with everyday usage), or broadly define it as any structured or "unstructured" analysis. It depends on the need of the context. At the same time, since any knowledge may tell us what we shall think or do, it can be assumed that they all indicate, more or less, consciously or unconsciously, some meanings of costs, benefits, etc.

Another issue arising from this is the distinction between the meanings of "implicit" and "explicit". This distinction is similar to that between intentional and unintentional, or conscious and or unconscious. That is to say, when a certain knowledge is produced, if the producer does not think about the economic problems in it deliberately, but only subconsciously, or if he/she does not explicitly consider the economic problems at all, then will this knowledge produced be the same as if the economic issues are explicitly considered? This question is somewhat absurd in common sense, but the implication from neoclassical economics is that the two cases should be regarded as equivalent. This view abolishes the importance of conscious activities, and in fact implies that all knowledge can be perfectly produced for use at the moment when it is needed. How can a meaning (e.g., the economic implication) understood from an opinion that an actor inadvertently contributes be exactly tantamount to a clear opinion that the actor contributes deliberately after a careful consideration? How can there be no difference in quality? These differences may be degreed, technical, or "soft", but they are not necessarily unimportant, because an important function of intelligence or knowledge is just to transform the unconscious into conscious, the implicit into explicit, and so on. If we deny this importance, we are denying the importance of ourselves as scholars.

Extreme rationalism is on the one side and Algorithmic Theory is on the other, and the two will be "fighting" everywhere in this book. Without understanding the infinite variants of extreme rationalism, we cannot understand the importance of Algorithmic Theory, and we will not know what this book is talking about, and hence we will not understand the necessity, approach, and method of philosophical synthesis.

§77. Traditional Entities

In §48 we refer to the problem of "correct knowledge". "Correct knowledge" is here only a convenient term for the knowledge that is commonly respected. Philosophers and ordinary people may call it by different names in different contexts.

Correct knowledge was first used as the banner of philosophy, and it was the basis for the emergence of philosophers and their existence in society. But it gradually became the burden of philosophers, the monkey on their backs, which still cannot be shaken off. I believe that the introduction of Algorithmic methods will solve this problem in all aspects, making it a key step in our reformation of traditional philosophy.

The knowledge that people have acquired at any time and in any situation varies from person to person. This is a basic Algorithmic principle. Completely leveling people's knowledge would entail unimaginable costs. There are many Algorithmical reasons (e.g. people who hold "wrong knowledge" disagree with this "correct knowledge" and therefore refuse to accept it) that make this "leveling" idea very unrealistic. That is to say, people do not level their knowledge first and then develop it together, but that from the very beginning their knowledge has both similarities or coherences and differences or gaps, and develops in the same or different ways or rates, mixedly.

There is firstly no such a thing as a judgment about right and wrong. Even if, according to some transcendental claims, such a judgment existed at the earliest, it is unlikely that the actors would have known about it. The person concerned just uses their transcendental thinking tools to process certain information and then come up with some results. Judgments about what is right and what is wrong are then produced in the comparison of these results. "Right vs. wrong" is just a simplified mode. In fact, one is bound to draw a large number of irregular conclusions in comparisons, rather than just making clear judgments about what is right and what is wrong. A more rigorous way to say this is to distinguish between high-quality and low-quality knowledge.

People don't even know it's merely "knowledge". Although people do not think that all opinions, ideas, or thoughts in their heads are correct, when they are convinced that some knowledge is true, they think that they have had the "truth" of an object. In particular, when this kind of knowledge is concerned with some "mechanism" of the movement or change of the object rather than with its mere superficial characteristics, because this mechanism is invisible, people will think that it is hidden in the "inside" of the object, and regard its changes and movements as the results of "operations" of this mechanism.

This process refines and compresses the data. That is, less knowledge explains more information. This is an efficient way to deal with chronological changes. It is relatively satisfying, because computations aren't always like this. Sometimes, it takes a lot of efforts and a lot of information to explain a single phenomenon. Horizontally, if many objects in the same space share the same or similar property, then the cost of discussing this property can be prorated among the many objects, and thus the discussion will become more economical. This economy is similar to the previous one.

From the very beginning, human thinking must have been deeply involved in the pursuit and fascination of this computational economy. Just like what we see today, a person who says only what he/she sees is a mere honest person, not a wise one. "Wisdom" lies in discovering the *laws* behind many phenomena. Only those who are able to do this are generally counted as smart people. Moreover, only this kind of knowledge, with high efficiency, is most worthy of dissemination. The more it spreads, the greater the benefits it brings to people and society, and the more respected the inventors and disseminators of this knowledge become. This is a productive approach, both on personal and social levels.

Moreover, different pieces of "correct knowledge" found can be interconnected, so there is a need to continue to explore the further "truth" behind them. We should not underestimate the ancients and mistakenly think that they were able only to make small parts for our current grand theories and grand narratives, or that those grand theories and grand narratives were not generated until later generations. According to the view of forced closure of computing and factor completeness, since the world needs to be summarized in every era, the grand theories and narratives of humankind must be generated every moment. Hence, something like the "general equilibrium theory" in economics today must have been enthusiastically constructed by philosophers in ancient times.

What governs the change and motion of an object is a thing "inside" or "behind" it. What, then, governs the movements of so many objects and the whole world? The answer is obviously the common "thing" behind these different "things". It can either be directly all-encompassing, or it can be transformed into the infinite everything—for example, into the "essence" of a concrete object, and then into the object itself. Thus, the words "Being", "Idea", "substance", "essence", "universal", "truth", "Absoluteness" and so on appeared, and "God" thus enjoys a place in philosophy as a variant of "Being", the last of all things.

A key, difficult, and easily overlooked question is where this Being or these things above are staying; that is to say, it needs to interrogate their *spatial* properties. As mentioned earlier, the original Being is naturally thought to exist *within* or *behind* the object(s) (or at least in its vicinity). However, this difficulty becomes exacerbated when the objects become numerous and hierarchical, and thus move towards a final "Being" (or "substance"). We can imagine the existence of a virtual "world of truth" that governs the real world in front of us. Then, where is this "world of truth"? To portray it as something akin to the "kingdom of heaven" would be too much like a religion. This is unsatisfactory. In fact, philosophers have been either vague or controversial on this issue.

However, in any case, looking at the world from this system

of truth has been established as a mainstream approach. From Plato to Kant, from Husserl to Karl Popper, they have tried to give a special place to this "correct knowledge"—for example, in Popper's division of three worlds, "objective knowledge" enjoys one of them alone. Such "correct knowledge" is above everything, not an ordinary member of knowledge. It attracts, dominates, and pushes everything like a magnet, rather than being done the other way around. Other intellectual or spiritual life has only "temporarily existed" as a supplementing and supporting role—although a great deal of philosophical achievements since the twentieth century have otherwise tended to emphasize the importance of the latter. This is a root cause of philosophical failure and splitting, and a central problem that we need to break through in order to build a comprehensive philosophy.

§78. Dissolution of Traditional Entities

Being misled by the correct or high-quality knowledge, being controlled by it, worshiping it, and making excessive imaginations in the wrong direction, are grave mistakes made by traditional philosophy. The task of this section is to provide a solution to correcting this.

First of all, it shall not be that the system that is worshipped goes to expand and engulf the whole system of thoughts or knowledge, but quite the contrary, it now shall be pulled back and placed in the comprehensive system of thoughts or knowledge, so that it becomes a part of it, and grows with the whole system. Priority, therefore, should be given to elaborating this all-encompassing overarching system. The construction of this general system should be the primary mission of philosophy at present. This shall also be the main and key principled knowledge that philosophy can provide for other disciplines—and this is, in fact, something that other disciplines, especially the humanities and social sciences, urgently need.

This "correct knowledge" exists relative to other knowledge and is selected in comparison with other knowledge. However, there is no essential difference between the method of making it and other knowledge. A classic example of "correct knowledge" is science. Science is the result of using specific research strategies to pursue goals such as certainty, universality, persistence, and systematization. However, while these goals are partially achieved, scientific research often loses the timeliness of its conclusions, thus playing a "slow" role in the overall body of knowledge. It also loses the breadth of the questions it answers. While it may involve a large number of individual objects, it tends only to address specific aspects of these objects and ignore the other aspects. Different types of knowledge are, in principle, different styles of knowledge. This is an important conclusion that can be drawn from Algorithmic deductions. In particular, they are the results of pros and cons analysis and optimization of computational activities under Algorithmic economic conditions—although some of the results are satisfactory to the actors, some of them are resulted from the actors forced to do so, some of them are the final products, some are simply on hold, and so on. *Different types of knowledge compete with each other and complement each other.* People with different types of knowledge are also in relationships of competition, collaboration, and exchange. Scientific knowledge cannot survive alone, and it is the income generated by those who cater to the timeliness of decision-making at the sacrifice of certainty that feeds the scientific community, allowing scientists to concentrate on their work that would typically be difficult to achieve in the short term.

We don't need to dwell on how scientific research can benefit from common sense. Some of the methods used in scientific research are also used in other fields, but they differ in the scale and intensity of their uses in different fields. The other fields also pursue goals such as certainty, universality, persistence, and systematicness, but they are less demanding in these regards, and their natures are different from those of science. For example, the importance of ethics and morality is universally recognized, but because ethics is clearly something "man-made" and dependent on human wills, the attitudes of philosophers and common people towards it are complex—even though Kant and Chinese Confucians have placed it in parallel with something like scientific truth (this interesting attitude exposes that what is seen as the sacrosanct and permanent "existence" is actually a mixture, a "hodgepodge"). In order to act effectively, the average person must find or establish a lot of certainty, that is, a lot of variables that can be convincingly assigned fixed values. Only in this way can computations and actions be happily addressed at the margins. In fact, there is a great deal of certainty in everyday life, which, objectively speaking, is not necessarily less certain than scientific knowledge. For example, many aspects of people's patterns of behaviour may have changed little since ancient times, but scholars have seldom focused on and systematically summarized them. Historically, by contrast, scientific knowledge has crumbled and revolutionized from time to time. This is especially important. Because scientific revolutions tend to span a long period of time, it can be mistaken for the idea that scientific knowledge is static, and some parts of it are even "ultimate".

We don't need to stress for a moment that some knowledge outside of science is important because it answers different questions than science. The key Algorithmic principle is that human computations are like a person crawling forward, he must have one hand and one foot sticking to the ground, and thus the other hand and the other foot can move the whole body forward. Therefore, one has to fixate a lot of conclusions.

If they can't be fixated permanently, they must be at least temporary. If this relatively fixed knowledge cannot be discovered, it must be produced artificially (including by making agreements with each other on ethics and morality), as long as they can, by this "production", deal with the problems in front of oneself—It needs to be perceived that for this purpose, people would even deceive themselves and each other (even in good faith). Philosophers have always posed that "you cannot live without the pursuit of truth", but if the above logic is recognized, the necessity of pursuing the ultimate or perfectly reliable "truth" itself is problematic: why must it be pursued? Even if such a "truth" is occasionally available, its benefits are obviously limited. The historical fact is that most of the "reliable knowledge", including scientific knowledge, morality, and so on, is actually versioned and updated historically.

There are many reasons why people are surrounded by what they think is "correct knowledge" and indulge in it while ignoring, marginalizing, or forgetting other types of knowledge. First, other "less correct" knowledge is deliberately eliminated and discarded because it is "not quite correct". Because of the limitation of knowledge storage capacity, people give priority to the preservation and inheritance of relatively high-quality knowledge, especially those pieces of knowledge that are deemed universal, persistent, and systematic, which are compiled into teaching materials and taught in schools. Fragmented, practical, or low-quality knowledge often does not enjoy such a treatment, and can only exist silently in the shadows. This, in turn, reinforces the impression that the latter are only minor, temporary, complementary, transitory, contrastive, pathological, or procedural. Meanwhile, "correct knowledge" is like a treasure box, constantly collecting treasures and expanding its territory, making people feel that it is about to swallow up the entire knowledge system one day and reach the "other shore of truth".

The dominance of "correct knowledge" also stems from the logical effect of a "paradox": "correct knowledge" is stored because the person concerned believes that it is "correct", otherwise people would not have retained it. Why should people doubt or deny a piece of knowledge if they have kept it, and why should people value, preserve, or even believe in what is "wrong"?

It can be seen that in order to start from "correct knowledge" and reach the entire knowledge system, it is necessary to concurrently establish the "knowledge" about the finitude and developmentality of common knowledge, namely, the knowledge about knowledge itself. This is a kind of high-order knowledge. People can't get to this state in the first-order dimension. We must observe and compare different types of knowledge and their historical evolution on a broad and long-span perspective. In the past, the pace of knowledge evolution was slower, so that static perspectives prevailed. Nowadays, the speed of knowledge evolution is relatively fast, and it is easier for people to recognize, more strongly, the changes in knowledge itself. The scope of people's activities, travels, and exchanges has expanded, and it has become easier to compare different types and styles of knowledge horizontally. This is the social condition that produces higher-order views. Under this view, while people accept and adopt a certain kind of knowledge, they might simultaneously anticipate this knowledge to be denied and renewed.

This brings us to Algorithmic Theory. In it, "correct knowledge", along with other knowledge that has been relatively static, is considered to be some local, temporary existences that were achieved through specific convergent computational processes. Divergent, dynamic, negative, improving, and creative processes are also widespread, preventing the overall convergence of the knowledge system and instead taking on the form of the "Big Bang". "Big Bang" can explain the question of why the scale of correct knowledge has increased while the body of knowledge as a whole has not converged, and it can be compatible with the results of both earlier and recent observations of the knowledge system. The above-mentioned heterogeneity of the knowledge system is also within the scope of Algorithm Theory, because bounded rationality and finite computing power will inevitably lead to the unevenness of the knowledge system. In it, the existence of certain permanent or ultimate knowledge, if any, is also non-detrimental to the overall situation, because it must be partial, individual, and scattered. The slow updating of correct knowledge itself can now bring less embarrassment to us, because when some equilibria are broken, new "correct knowledge" would settle down and coagulate again into the new equilibria.

§79. Dissolution of Traditional Entities (continued)

A seemingly superficial but very important question about knowledge is: where does knowledge really exist? We have asked this question, but the answer to it is not yet over.

The traditional concept of knowledge is narrow, i.e., confined to the "correct knowledge". This creates a condition in which different types of knowledge can be distinguished. Correct knowledge (or "Being") is thought to exist in a *distant, hidden* place outside of the human body, and only other "less correct" knowledge is allowed to exist *within the human brain*. Of course, correct knowledge is sometimes also allowed to exist within the human brain, but this knowledge is only seen as a copy of the "objective knowledge" (i.e., correct knowledge) that is assumed to exist originally outside of the human body, which can only be obtained or reached by living beings. There is another understanding that a "being" exists within an object, and that there is a one-to-one correspondence between a piece of correct knowledge and the being within the object, as an equivalent or identical relationship.

How do we discern the merits of the various points of view and synthesize them into a whole doctrine? The previous section discussed that correct knowledge must be merged with less correct knowledge and then find a home for them all. Of course, this place of settlement cannot be anywhere else, but only in the human brain. This is where the traditional *"conceptual theory"* is correct. Any knowledge, or anything that we humans talk about or think, is firstly a thought in itself, and can only exist in the human brain. Even if it is recorded outside of the human body by physical means such as books and disks, it is something that is intended for the human brain to use. That is, knowledge or thought, in its *form*, is *directly* manifested as a product of the human brain and nothing else. As for its right and wrong, true and false, valid and invalid, it is only a matter of its *relationship* with *external objects*. In other words, it is a matter of the *content* of it. Distinguishing and discussing the forms and contents of thought separately is a special attitude and method that we can have towards thought, which corresponds to the distinction between hardware and software in §9. When describing a purely physical object, such as a box, we also use terms such as "form" and "content". This can be used as a metaphor to allow us to understand the relationship between software and hardware. Nevertheless, I think that the use of the terms "form" and "content" in relation to the object of thought is still different from its use in relation to a purely physical object.

The mind is within the human brain (or human body). It is only when books, computers, and other physical objects are used as auxiliary computing tools for the human brain that thoughts temporarily and "technically" exist outside the human body. With this strict exception, there can be no thought or knowledge existing anywhere else, much less in other hidden places outside of human society. One of the key reasons why we must hold this view is that our minds are constantly renewed. Especially for the same, unchanging object of knowledge, the knowledge itself can be divergent and changing. These different and contradictory pieces of knowledge may all have been regarded as "truth" in different eras. There may be not only the changing knowledge of a stationary external object, but also the stationary knowledge of a changing foreign object (e.g., different tables in different eras may all be regarded as the prototypes of the "Idea of table", thereby contradicting each other). The changes or movements of thought and its object are often asynchronous and sometimes interlaced, with inherent conflicts, irregularities, and a large number of defects. Therefore, an ideal relationship that ontology requires is difficult to *concretely* establish.

It is necessary to return to the position that "thought is human's own business". The primary question is not whether a thought is right or wrong, but that thought itself is a way of dealing with external objects, a way of one's own, and has nothing to do with external objects. The distinction between right and wrong is a concrete manifestation of this way, and it is only one of its many manifestations. This way also manifests itself in a multitude of other thinking phenomena. Knowledge is a product of this way of working. Correct knowledge is, of course, also a product of it. It is not the right knowledge that actively controls humans or the world, but humans who generate, store, use, modify, develop, or destroy knowledge, right or wrong. It is the human body and the human brain that are alive and working, not the knowledge itself.

However, it is not enough for us to recognize the higher-order truth that "thought is thought, not an external object". Algorithmic Theory not only emphasizes the importance of higher-order knowledge, but it can also be used to demonstrate the importance of lower-order knowledge from a non-traditional perspective. The most useful thing for an ordinary person who is busy thinking and acting is not to recognize that "I think, therefore I am", but to establish some concise, powerful, or convenient argument for a particular object to work on. This argument should be economical in terms of computational operation. For example, if an apple falls to the ground, I can imagine that the earth has some kind of "gravitational force" that is able to pull the apple to the ground. This gravitational force is invisible, and I can't *fully* confirm it, but I still imagine that it exists between the earth and the apple (or inside each of them), *not just in my brain as an idea.* It is only when this idea would have turned out to be my own pure fabrication that I could consider it "only within my brain". Otherwise, it would be verbose and therefore computationally harmful to think that gravity is only a hypothesis that exists in my brain. In turn, I assume that there is such a thing as "gravity", which *attaches* to a mass object, moves with it, and exists within it as an inseparable "whole", which is *computationally concise and efficient.* The economy attained here is, firstly, the fact that the "gravity" is an imagined entity is temporarily "forgotten", or suspended, and is replaced by the belief that it is an objective fact like the apple, juxtaposed with the apple as two similar entities. An advantage of this is that, since gravity has now become an objective fact and entity, it no longer needs to change with the changes in the thoughts of the person who is thinking about it. Before this, gravity, as an idea proposed by the person concerned, must in principle be adjusted at any time with his/her other ideas; this adjustment process can now be avoided. In mathematical terms, this "self-correlation" problem can now be temporarily avoided. Secondly, the gravity is further treated as a property of the apple, thereby merging into the one entity. To a large extent, this principle of Algorithmic economics influences or determines how we divide, define, eliminate, and save entities, e.g., how we define some other entities as "characteristics" of an object rather than other "objects". These characteristics are attached to the object and move with it. Thus, the number of independent objects is reduced, and the economy is obtained.

This is the logic that concepts such as *"universal in things"* arise from. Such a hypothetical entity existed as a hypothesis at first, and it is also possible to be confirmed later (e.g., the philosopher's concept of "atom" was later visually confirmed). Once confirmed, it is *further* identified as a "being", "substance", etc.—although even what is visually "confirmed" can still be questionable. On the other hand, once it is denied, it is removed from the collection of beings or substances and *recouped* into the set of "pure fabricated thoughts". This is *the transformational relationship between thoughts and objects.*

Now, knowledge already exists in two places: in the human brain and in the objects (as a hypothesis). Then, is there any positive significance to the above-mentioned "Being" that was thought to exist in a hidden place but has now been dissolved? And, should we re-explore the rational factors in it within the Algorithmic framework?

My attitude on this issue is similar to that on other issues: to critically synthesize it; that is, to "sublate" it.

It is not enough to imagine that knowledge is scattered in everyone's brain. There are drawbacks to this kind of imagination. One of the drawbacks is that it can lead to verbosity in statements. Especially with regard to what is accepted as "correct knowledge", why is it still necessary to emphasize that it is someone's idea? At this point, it would be a little ridiculous to add the word "I think" to every statement of everybody. Therefore, since ancient times, people have held the idea that this "correct knowledge" does not belong to any specific person, but *"among people"* and is shared by everyone.

This knowledge does not change because of the death or birth of an individual, nor does it even change because of the existence or absence of an object. Thus, it becomes the *"universal before things"*. For example, before the first "table" appeared in the world, the Idea of the "table" should have existed, as Plato assumed. Even if it is a bit exaggerated, it is not impossible. The first table was by no means created out of thin air without any subjective design on the part of the inventor. The design might start out rudimentary and vary from one to another, and then gradually improve and develop. The marginal law would cause it to historically converge into a certain form(s), then it was called a "universal" while the economy of thinking caused the instances and particulars that produced it to be gradually ignored or forgotten, and the universal was elevated and absolutized into something like "correct knowledge". On the observers' side, under time-bound and serial conditions, people generally give priority to understanding the current "new" objects based on existing knowledge. According to the comparability between one and many, it is inevitable that a universal is used somehow to suppress its particulars, and its essence as "the common characteristic of the past particulars" has been further ignored. Now we are back in §77. From this perspective, some of the origins and rationality of traditional metaphysics can be found. Although it is difficult to clarify the exact location of the "correct knowledge", this drawback seems harmless to our study.

Nevertheless, we still need to make a change in this traditional thinking, that is: Is it true that the "wrong" knowledge is only private, and cannot be "merged" among people in the way above? Can't a mistake made by one person be made again by others? This is clearly not the case. Algorithmically, this is even more so: if one person makes a mistake in his computations, another person will inevitably make the same mistake if he/she were to compute in the same way. The only difference is that the person who pointed out the mistake would not compute it again this way, but would do it in a different way. Therefore, *all "mistakes" are actually objective and therefore can be combined.*

Thus, we come to the perspective of the "human knowledge thesaurus", that is, the above "correct knowledge thesaurus" should be expanded into the "human knowledge thesaurus". *All knowledge is actually objective*, because they are the results of Instructional processing of information, and hence they are "predetermined" and can exist before specific individuals can *concretely* produce (or "realize") them, while "subjectivity" arises because of the barrier of limited computing power and big data, so that different persons can only occupy *different areas* in this all-encompassing super database. Another conceivable reason is that, since much knowledge is in direct conflict with each other or negates each other, there is often a lack of interest in appropriating the whole of the knowledge that is comprehensively made up. Consistency as an economy prevents them from doing so.

Of course, because this general database is the result of the consolidation of human knowledge, if human beings as a whole do not exist, they cannot be considered to exist.

CHAPTER 7
THE ONTOLOGY

§80. Generation Algorithmic Entities: substances

Apart from the Being, Western philosophy also has a long tradition of materialization and discretization. This means that it always tries to correspond concepts to concrete, tangible objects, and overall it appears as a combination or accumulation of the fragments. This feature is relative to Chinese philosophy. Chinese philosophy does not pay so much attention to materialized objects, it does not even distinguish between material and immaterial objects, but combines various objects and imagines them as something that is integrated. This is how concepts such as "Tao"[1] (like logos) and "Li"[2] (like reason or rationality) come about. "Tao" or "Li", as a universal, unified law, then produces concrete things.

From the above distinctions, it can be seen that Chinese

---

1. Chan, Alan, "Laozi", The Stanford Encyclopedia of Philosophy (Winter 2018 Edition), Edward N. Zalta (ed.), URL = <https://plato.stanford.edu/archives/win2018/entries/laozi/>.
2. Thompson, Kirill, "Zhu Xi", The Stanford Encyclopedia of Philosophy (Spring 2025 Edition), Edward N. Zalta & Uri Nodelman (eds.), forthcoming URL = <https://plato.stanford.edu/archives/spr2025/entries/zhu-xi/>.

philosophy has a more dangerous tendency than Western rationalism. Of course, there are also other heretical elements in the respective knowledge systems of China and the West, which are used to supplement and correct their extreme rationalism, so that many aspects of their cultures are converging on different paths. However, these convergent paths have not yet completely reached the same end of unity, but still stayed in their respective midway of mixednesses. In other words, many major and fundamental philosophical problems have not yet been resolved. This is an amazing synchronous phenomenon!

Now, the Algorithmic narrative is first and foremost based on the Western tradition. Plato pushed objects and their Ideas (or "Forms") to the forefront, and we intend to do similarly.

A single object in the visual world is often taken as a single object of study by the person concerned. The natural boundaries of objects are also the boundaries between them in the world of thought. Even if the activities of the mind later adjust to them, these natural boundaries are still the main, basic, and priority. Why? The answer is just convenience or economy (or, as §50 mentions, the "eye-catching" feature of visual information). This is the "Algorithmic" answer. To understand the economy and convenience, we can get a deeper understanding by comparing it with the following situations: not according to the natural boundaries of the objects to define a single object, but to divide them arbitrarily, or use a ruler to divide them mechanically or geometrically, then it can be imagined how much trouble this method will bring to the subsequent activities of description, interpretation, analysis, decision-making, action, etc.

Identifying a single object as a single object of study implies the *merging* of the elements that make up the object, as well as the *exclusion* of other elements outside the object. The elements that make up this object are numerous. In a specific analysis, when the object is identified as a single entity, it indicates that its components are not identified individually as entities. As we have already said, the Algorithmic principle is that *everything (including thoughts, weightless things, intangible things, etc.) can be generally and Algorithmically seen as an "entity", or a "real entity", or that every entity is real.* In terms of usage, the "entity" in this proposition is equal to the phrase "object of study". However, this does not mean that the entity status of an entity cannot be canceled, or that the status of a research object as an independent object cannot be canceled; nor does it mean that it is meaningless to use words such as "virtual" and "false" to state an entity. On the contrary, since entities can be determined at our wills, any determination is in principle "legal", which also means that they can be changed or revoked at our wills. This is like when eating at a buffet, I have the right to taste every dish on site, but this does not mean that I am obligated to do so, nor does it mean that I will actually do so. Secondly, the words "virtual" and "false" are used in a specific rather than a general sense. For example, when thought is used to cognize an external object, errors and falsehoods might occur. This is in terms of the consistency between the specific cognition and the object, that is, it is talking about the relationship between the two different entities or objects rather than canceling the status of these entities or objects as entities and objects.

The fact that everything qualifies as an entity (or "real entity", similarly hereinafter) does not mean that there must be an objective and immutable criterion for the identification of "one entity". The way in which objects are divided is due to both the nature and characteristics of the objects themselves, as well as the subjective reasons of the dividers. One of the most important subjective reasons is the limitation of meta-computing capability. There are limitations to the ability of sensory organs to collect information, as is the ability of the human brain to process information. This is especially clear in the format of an Instruction and at the level of a meta-computation, where discrete information or data are used as the processing objects. It can be said that *this kind of computing mechanism directly requires the division of the objective world and the creation of a single or "unit" object.* Although the data operated by a single Instruction does not necessarily correspond strictly to a single entity or a single object in all cases, the simplicity of data and the finite number of these data decisively limit the complexity of the object(s) to which a particular computing task is directed. On the other hand, the economy of computation requires that objects should not be too simple to avoid cumbersomeness. These multifaceted and conflicting factors together influence the definition or division of the basic unit of objects in each specific thinking process.

This process of definition and division is also a process of interaction and reproduction between entities. Now, the definition and division of entities are no longer carried out by an unspecified subject. *This divider, or definer, is just among the entities as one of them.* He/she divides or defines objects through his/her own mental activities. This division or definition is not entirely based on natures of the objects, but also from one's own subjective desires or needs, and the combination of the subjective and objective aspects. That is, it is a process that utilizes raw materials for production. What is produced is some concepts as new entities, stored in one's own brain, and spoken or written.

Another reason I say above that it is "among the entities" is that I can frequently objectify myself. I'm imagining some other people constructing objects, and I'm imagining myself doing it as well, and I'm one of them—though everyone might do it differently. Although the "I" who is thinking or writing does not have time to objectify itself at the same moment, this fleeting "I" is negligible as a very small part of "I" (This was explained in §54). Therefore, we can say that nothing is now outside of our scope of study, and the entities are complete.

A single object acts as a unit of analysis, carrying the many elements that make it up, and together they exist and move in space. When we say "it exists" or "it moves", we are generally referring to the movements of these many elements together, synchronously, and in bonding with each other. Meanwhile, this presence or movement does not involve other entities in the near or distant places. The existence of empty space encompasses the existence of this entity, as well as its movement. A benefit of "space" is that it can prevent this entity from overlapping with other entities in the same place, or from colliding with each other in motion. Otherwise, the computation of this entity will become more complicated. When the complexity rises to a certain level, the meanings of defining or dividing entities will be lost, or it would be necessary to redefine or divide entities.

That is to say, the definition and division of entities not only meet the needs of meta-computation, but also meet the needs of serial computation. With this definition or division, we can *then* speak of other parts of the world outside of this entity, or we can *then* talk about the movement and change of this entity. This is part of a holistic approach and an initial, preparatory step of it.

§81. Generation of Algorithmic Entities: split, merger, relation and change

The reason why an ordinary object is regarded as a typical entity is not only because of its visual convenience, but also because it can be used as a basis and "carrier" (i.e. Aristotle's "substratum") to merge many other entities (or objects), thus bringing significant computational economy.

Compositionally, an object includes the various physical

materials that make it up. Therefore, the change or motion of the object means that the compositional materials change together. The computations of the object include the computations of its materials. Thus, in principle, the materials do not have to be repeated to compute, hence they are temporarily removed from the list of entities and stayed backstage. As a result, the number of entities has decreased. It saves.

Secondly, certain phenomena perceived by the sensory organs in relation to the object, which could have been regarded as separate entities, can now, after identifying the object entity, be re-characterized as the *natures, properties* or *manifestations of the object*, and thus attached to the object. In this way, the effect is the same: the number of entities is reduced, and the computational efficiency is increased.

Entities at different moments can also be considered different, especially if they are more or less different in themselves or located in different spatial positions. However, since most of these entities are identical, or whose main contents are identical, it is resolved to merge them into a single entity and to refer to their differences at different moments with terms such as movement, change, etc. which are also viewed as a nature, property, or manifestation of the entity. From this, it can be recognized that *the so-called "movement", "change" are actually a way for people to merge entities and pursue an Algorithmic economy.*

However, this division and definition of entities is imperfect, and some things are left behind. Thus, the term *"relation"* was coined to refer to those objects that could not be included *inside* the concept of a single entity. "Relation" is like a rope that connects different entities. However, it is intangible, thought to be due to some (often implicit) natures or characteristics of the entities in question, and it often manifests itself as certain phenomena in the movement of time and space. Thus, when the concept of relation arises, the phenomena to which it refers lose their statuses as independent entities and become subordinate to the other related entities. The gravitational force mentioned above can be deemed a relation. We have also referred to the inclusive relationship between an object and its components, as well as the ancillary relationship between an object and its properties, characteristics, or manifestations.

This was the beginning of philosophy and physics. People prioritize constructing concepts, creating entities, establishing relationships, and then analyzing and calculating around those most common objects in life. *Concepts such as entity, nature, characteristic, relation, change, etc. complement each other and combine into a team to share the mission of computing.* As mentioned above, under the pressure of economics, computations become efficient, but they are also inevitably distorted. Therefore, this combinatorial approach is necessarily imprecise, and can only work roughly. The concept of entity will continue to undergo great expansion and change, but objects with weight and volume are not only the original basis of the concept of entities, but also a basic way for modern people to understand the world.

Along the direction of "entity merger", with the expansion of the scope of human activities and the improvement of thinking ability, some macroscopic and large entities are created, such as planets, galaxies, universes, countries, gods, and so on. On the other hand, microscopic research is also progressing. The latter requires not to merge the entity in the first place, but to decompose it. This is how phlogiston, molecules, atoms, etc. were produced. Instead of simplifying the computations, they complicate them. This is not a disregard for the requirements of the computational economy, but is caused by the weakness and simplicity of the power of meta-computing. This finite computing power requires objects to be broken down and decomposed again until they become fairly simple, so that the analytical units can be stabilized and the computational activities can be relatively competent and pleasant. Therefore, this should be understood as another manifestation of computational economy.

The above refers to the material components that make up the objects. In terms of the properties or characteristics of the objects, people generally first divide them according to their types, such as weight, color, smell, texture, sound, dynamics, and so on. When an object is red, people study its red as a whole, not "half red". By classifying the characteristics of objects according to their purity, it lays the groundwork for the next steps of abstracting them, building models, identifying generalities, finding patterns, and so on. People will pursue the economy of computing on a larger scale.

§82. Generation of Algorithmic Entities: information

In philosophy and the history of philosophy, the following comical question has been debated from time to time: Does the human brain operate on certain "materials" or parts from external objects, or the external objects themselves?

First of all, I would like to reject the absurd idea that the human brain has been *directly manipulating an external object* (or its any part; similarly, hereinafter), because direct manipulation of the external object is the function of motor organs; if the human brain can directly manipulate it, then what do the motor organs do again? The human brain collects information about the external object through sensory organs, processes it, and then forms a decision, which is handed over to the motor organs for implementation, with or without the help of other physical tools, which is a basic and common-sense process. The Algorithmic philosophy prioritizes the collation and refinement of common-sense knowledge, doubting and marginalizing absurdity. I generally believe that obscure and absurd theories often arise from a lack of basic knowledge, leading to the inability of common sense to be correctly explained, so that philosophers fall into struggling. This is especially true when it comes to the relationship between body and mind. It is precisely because philosophy has failed to establish a basic, minimal theory of thinking that it has led to many absurd theories.

What the external object inputs into the human body is firstly the sensory materials. Locke convincingly pointed out that these sensory materials are not a direct reflection of the external object, but synthesized with the functions of sensory organs. In other words, the sensory organs are involved in the formation of these materials (the so-called "secondary qualities"). This well-known argument can not only be used to refute the idea that the human brain directly processes foreign objects, but it also leads to the question of what exactly this "sensory material" is.—the meaning of the phrase "sensory material" is quite ambiguous.

This question was not answered until the concept of "information" came along: the material of sensation is information. Previously, philosophers had struggled and debated a lot on this issue. The concept of information is enough to quell the debates. That is to say, foreign objects do not directly enter the human brain, but what enters the human brain is information, *information is constructed by combination of physical media and sensory organs, and meanwhile, it conforms to the format of thought*; or in other words, it is a kind of primary thought—it is said to be "primary" because it is only transported and stored by functional and service Instructions, and has not yet been processed, or intensively processed, by data-processing Instructions.

In this way, *there has happened a major leap or qualitative change in the concept*. Physical media (light, sound waves, etc.)

are converted into information through the sensory organs, which crosses the line between mind and matter. *Sensory organs are like devices connected to computers called a "transcoder" or "modem" (modulator-demodulator) that does this conversion.* When we advocate the "mind-body separation", we do not directly explain this transformation, but rather discuss them separately, or in parallel and correspondingly with each other.

"Parallel" means to exclude the consideration of the reciprocity whereas "explain" is about establishing a relationship of reciprocity. To explain A as B is to equate A with B. This is not possible for the topic with current scientific knowledge. By acknowledging that we are not yet capable of explaining mental activity accurately as physical activity, we cannot admit that the physical phenomena, the so-called "physical media", is equated simply with information. In this sense, biological equipment such as eyes, ears, and nerves are magical, connecting the outside world at one end and the human brain at the other, and acting as a bridge between them.

We have said many times that thoughts are the business of human beings. The mind counts external objects, which has nothing to do with external objects. This is because the mind cannot act directly on external objects, it can only use information to understand external objects and to conceive solutions to actions on external objects. The solutions cannot be carried out by the mind itself, and can only be transferred to the locomotor organs to implement. If the locomotor organs cannot implement them, the solutions would be in vain. Information now has an important role to play in explaining this point. Foreign objects cannot directly enter the human brain. Inside the human brain, foreign objects are only *represented* by information. The word "represent" is now in vogue, and its significance is to establish a one-to-one correspondence between mind and matter, namely, between mental entities and physical entities. This relationship is mathematically called "mapping". Under the mapping relationship, the human brain's manipulation of information *corresponds to* the manipulation of specific physical objects by material organs and tools. This correspondence is not strictly and mechanically one-to-one, but is based on a specific definition in the context. Some thinking activities do not correspond to external entities. This is often clear to the thinking system itself. In the correspondence, the specific situations also vary, and different correspondences are different in their meanings. The Instructional system is also different from the locomotor system in nature and type of their contents, and it is also impossible to carry out a simple one-to-one correspondence between them.

§83. Generation of Algorithmic Entities: models

The first step of the human brain in recognizing external objects is to reconstruct an image of an external object in the mind. The "materials" used in this reconstruction are "information", "data", or "ideas". These three must be considered to be the same kind in terms of "material" and distinct from physical materials. For example, we use wood to build a model of an iron tower, or draw an animal on paper with a pen. The materials used in these models differ from those in their original objects. By saying this, I mean that I apply the language and analytic method for physical objects to thoughtful objects, that is, I distinguish between material and form, so this expression is necessarily imprecise. However, these analogies can help us understand that what we have in our minds are indeed models of external objects, not the external objects themselves.

Moreover, such models are generally concerned only with *some parts* of the properties and characteristics of foreign objects. Limited functions of the sensory organs, coupled with the limited speed of computation, determine that the information we collect from external objects can only be partial and limited, either focusing on appearance and ignoring content, or focusing on certain aspects of traits and ignoring others, and so on. This refers to the kinds of information. The amount of information is necessarily limited as well. It's like the difference in pixels of photos, or the difference between an oil painting and a sketch. A detailed model necessarily requires careful observation of an object and memorization of data over long periods of time. The human brain is actually as difficult as a computer to do this kind of work.

A synonym for the above argument is that the information that can be gleaned from any physical object is in principle infinite and inexhaustible. In the Algorithmic framework, this is a conclusion that we must reach. This is not to say that any conceivable piece of information can be gleaned from any object; rather, it is difficult for us even to fully obtain certain information in a certain object. This is like when we use a meta-computation as an infinitesimal denominator to divide the physical object, the result will be close to infinity, regardless of how "big" or "complex" the physical object is. Physical objects generally seem infinitely subdividable, and our ability to disassemble them is limited at any historical moment. And, physical objects can be combined or interacted with an infinite number of other objects, and the phenomena in the process may be beyond our expectations, and these phenomena may eventually lead to some new understandings of the properties and characteristics of specific objects, and so on. These are among the ways in which we can understand the above proposition.

The models built will not only be biased and omit something, but also probably contain errors. If we agree with the view that bias and omission are some errors in themselves, then it is easy to understand that other errors would arise. This leads to the fact that a model built is the model only in a certain sense, and in some other sense is not a "model" but something outside models.

We need to further understand how this "out-of-model thing" comes about. Capturing information is like using the physical object as a template and duplicating the parts on this template. After these "parts" enter the human brain as information, the human brain can rebuild them as they are, thereby making a model of the object. Since this can be done, then the human brain can also not do it. The human brain can make a mistake in the model, take out a part of model A and transplant it to model B, or collect different parts from multiple models and assemble them into a new "model". This model may not have a real-world counterpart, making it a mere intellectual creation. It can also be absurd, even morally evil, and so on. Further, *when this new model is compared with the facts in the real world, it is found that it does not exist in the real world, which gives rise to concepts or statements such as "nothing", "zero", "something does not exist", and so on.*

Ancient philosophers were so confused by the concept of "nothing" that they questioned whether there could be something out of nothing. In my opinion, the fundamental reason was that they did not understand the real natures of thought: its independence, specificity, objectivity, creativity, etc., so that they simply looked at the physical world while forgetting thoughts. After forgetting thoughts, of course, they would be confused by the creation of "nothing", because "nothing", as a concept in the human brain, was obtained precisely after *comparing* an imaginary model with reality. *Without this comparison, how can we know what is "not" or "does not exist"?*—and how can we know what "does not exist" and ask why it does not exist since it does not exist? Literally, people do not go out to look for the prototype or counterpart of any thought in the external world, but, in the case of the above, people have been deliberately creating models of real things. This creation is first and foremost a kind of "fabrication", even a fiction. This saying is because a model cannot be essentially identical to its original thing, but is only similar or analogous in specific aspects or meanings. We humankind can only do so. The so-called "virtual" or "real", "true" or "false" are defined usually merely in a comparative, technical, and degreed context, rather than denying the materiality or substantiality of thoughtful entities. Since thinking activities can start with the input of external information, in the endless interactions between the internal and external worlds, of course, they can also take the initiative to start with thoughts. After completing fabrication of the model, we can go to the objective world to find a counterpart and confirm or falsify our thoughtful model. For example, I see a white horse, and then by displacing its color, I think of a green horse and a black horse. I would have found black horses in the real world, thus confirming my fabrication. It is also possible that I will not be able to spot a green horse and thus not be able to confirm my fabrication. In other words, "nothing" is a *concept* that arises as a result of the *computational operations* of "comparing" with the "existence", the fabricated entity, in my mind. In addition, I may also try to create green horses through physical actions. If it succeeds, "nothing" will become the "reality".

This brings us to the "entity completeness" of §44: after thoughts are materialized Algorithmically, the *types* of entities (or "real entities") have become complete (except for entities that have not yet been discovered in the physical world, of course), and any activity in the world is only the activity of an existing entity, or the interaction between them, and any entity can only find its causes in other entities and their interactions, and there is no longer anything that comes out of thin air rather than existing entities. In this sense, *nothing can no longer be created out of nothing*.

It may also be questioned that since the understood "foreign object" is, in fact, only a model, constructed by the joint work of the sense organs and the Instructional system, is it true that all entities actually have the same nature, namely, the nature of thought? Is the distinction between different types of entities therefore unnecessary? My answers to this question are: First, although all knowledge of entities is concepts, the mind itself has to distinguish between different concepts and different entities, and this is where the inclusiveness of the mind lies. This inclusiveness is based on the higher-order function of the mind. Second, the original information from external objects is of only the "format" or "form" of thought, but its contents are foreign and given from outside, and the mind itself generally acknowledges this. The mind itself is able to distinguish its own subjective creations from external objectivity. A concrete external objectivity, whether felt or inferred, is not necessarily less reliable than a concrete mental model. This self-consciousness is also based on the higher-order function of the mind. Thirdly, the same logic can be applied to human-made objects: since human-made objects are formed by the joint actions of human's physical organs and their physical objects, can it be said that the human-made world is only physical or material and not ideological? If an interrogator denies this, then he/she can deny his/her own above claim. Clearly, this assertion simply reflects the habit of traditional monism—the habit of over-simplifying and distorting oneself.

Finally, it should be added that objects with weight and volume, as classical entities, are no longer typically used as a criterion for identifying entities. Because weight and volume are not analytically important in many cases, there is no need to establish such a "standard" generally. The concept of "entity", or "real entity", can now be applied to any physical or mental object, whether or not it has weight or volume. Under this premise, the combination, decomposition, and re-division of entities only need to be based on Algorithmic economic considerations, namely, the methodological considerations. Such considerations are now only technical and not substantive.

§84. Generation of Algorithmic Entities: universals

The brain builds a model of a foreign object that can be used to recall and "see" and, more importantly, to *manipulate* it in the brain. We imagine how, under various hypothetical conditions, it can connect, interact, and evolve with other objects, resulting in a wide variety of phenomena.

The question shall arise: why are these processes carried out over and over again in the mind when the external object itself is in motion and people can manipulate it with their limbs and tools? The answer obviously lies in economics. The thinking processes are usually easy to carry out while the manipulation of the physical object is not so easy. The thinking processes run usually fast while the practical processes run slower. The thinking processes can assume that numerous or bizarre scenarios are "experimented" in the mind, but the same numerous or bizarre experiments are often difficult to carry out one-by-one in practice. In particular, many experimental practical activities can cause disruption, whereas computational activities in the brain have no significant disruption, and a "disruption", if any, usually simply means that a thought is denied.

The following example can be used to illustrate this economy. Today's dinner plan includes allocating one apple per person. Well, our human rational solution is usually this: count the number of people who attend the dinner and then prepare the same number of apples. Math is involved here, and while it's simple, it's a way that is unique to humans. The numbers themselves are models of the foreign objects. Although these models are simple, they extract the specific properties of foreign objects in terms of quantity. The addition of the numbers is an operation that runs the models to produce a certain result, which is then equated to the number of apples. After the actors have prepared apples according to this number, their pre-set goal of "one apple per person" will definitely be achieved at dinner. On the surface, there are very few physical actions involved in this process, and the physical actions can be said to be somewhat discontinuous. This is because a part of the actions is replaced by the internal activities of the human brain. If other species could understand this goal, perhaps "he/she" would be surprised or confused that this goal was precisely achieved.

The above analysis also shows the relationship both of *competition* and of *substitution* between computational processes and physical processes. Obviously, computational processes are carried out only when the economic comparative advantage is obtained, otherwise actors are likely to abandon the computations and, as mentioned above, turn to use the method of tentative practice or experimentation—of course, the latter cannot completely depart from the former, and thus in fact can partially replace the former.

However, this is only the beginning of computing activities to unfold their economics.

A typical economy comes from the discovery of the so-called "universal". This means that a person discovers that a large number of objects contain the same elements. This discovery originates first from the large and diverse data collected from objects. The finitude of metacomputation entails that these data must be distinguished from each other and then processed separately. A universal is a result of comparing the data from different objects with each other. The properties of objects are only "dead" in the objects, but when they become data and enter the human brain, they come to life, and the connections between them can be established.

The discovery of universals brings great economic benefits, because the computations of the universal characteristics of objects concern not only an individual object, but a large number of objects. Thus, the results of the computations can be applied to a large number of objects than only one object. In this way, the actors avoid getting bogged down in the dilemma of building an entirely separate knowledge system for each object. Universals are usually found in a limited number of samples and then provisionally *extrapolated* to all objects of the same kind, i.e., a universality. For economic reasons, it is often impossible, or unnecessary, to test all the kindred objects that exist in the world, let alone the object that will appear in the future but do not exist today. After the emergence of a new object, people usually try to apply the knowledge of universality to it, so as to test or even modify the universality. On the other hand, some people put forth a universal proposition and other people test it, and then, after the proposition has been popularized, the masses of people continue to test it, confirm it, question it, or revise it in a long and large-scale practice.

The word "universal" is used to encompass all the objects. A subordinate concept is "commonality", which refers to the relationship between a finite number of objects. The opposite of commonality is difference, while the opposite of universality is particularity. Since universality means the refinement of the local features of an object, the remaining features are particularities. The same is true of commonalities and differences. However, in the relationship between commonality and difference, commonality and difference are more equal, while in the relationship between universality and particularity, universality is often used to suppress particularity and put it in a secondary position. People model objects based on universality, leaving blanks as the places for particularities, like the spaces in a table to be filled. For example, people build a model of horse and leave blank spaces in the "Color" column to fill with the different colors of each specific horse.

Associated with "universality" is the word "summarization" (or "encapsulation"). In many cases, the result of the work of the "summarization" is the extraction of universals. With a slight difference, summarizing activities tend to *ignore* particularity or specificity. That is, in its statement, no "spaces" are left for particularities to fill in. It has a clear goal of simplification, focusing on the universal and ignoring the particular, whereas in the context of "universality", the status of particularity is almost explicitly respected.

Algorithmically, the above processes are relatively clear and understandable, but in ancient times, due to the fact that the Algorithmic theory was not established (including that the concept of "information" was not produced), people made many mistakes in understanding these processes. One of them, as mentioned earlier, was that the discovery of universality was mistakenly believed to herald something more mysterious, thereby enlarging the imagination to the point that all knowledge can be reduced infinitely until it reaches a single minimalist form. Why do we think this is an over-imagination? This is because this view has not been proven in the subsequent scientific research, and it is believed that there was no mysterious way for ancient people to discover this "final truth" in advance of the subsequent scientific research. As soon as we recognize that this is a wishful assumption made by human beings out of the need for computational economy, then all relevant confusions will clear up.

Another mistake was to mistakenly believe that the ideological model established is an entity with the same properties as the prototype object, rather than an ideological entity that is different from it, thus increasing the number of object entities. The concept of an abstract horse is not a real horse in the physical world. If there are ten horses in the physical world, then a person abstracts the concept of "horse", the number of horses would not be eleven now. In the same way, when we say "white horse", we may imagine the image of a white horse in our minds, but we don't actually have a real white horse in our minds, and the white color of the virtual horse in our minds is supposed in principle to be different from the white color of the real horse, but only information, data, thoughts, or knowledge *about the real white color*. With the help of sensory organs, a relationship of one-to-one correspondence is established between this information and external objects. It is unnecessary to be alleged as an equality relationship. The brain remembers the sensations given to it as information by external objects through the sensory organs, and reversely, retells or restores these sensations in other circumstances— such as making other white objects with the help of the memory of the white horse.

An extreme manifestation of this correspondence mechanism is the distinction between colors by color blind patients. Although this distinction is different from ordinary people's, it is still valid for the patient's own purpose of understanding and grasping colors—even if this validity cannot be completely equivalent to that of ordinary people. *In this sense, the nature of the sensory information is very apt to highlight our Algorithmic proposition,* that is, the thoughts (including information) act as an "independent third party" between people and objects, and the mind perceives and handles the world in a way similar to how people with color blindness perceive and handle color. It can even be said that the more confused you are about the nature of this kind of information, the closer you get to the Algorithmic theory.

§85. Generation of Algorithmic Entities: types, essence

Universality and commonality are only properties that are distilled from objects and exist as concepts. Based on these concepts, people go on to classify objects. A certain type or class of objects refers to a number of objects that share certain common characteristics. Thus, the computation of an object of a certain type can be a computation of any object of that type. This is a way to deal with problems in *a batch*, bringing significant computational economic benefits.

This economic interest largely dominates the activity of classification. Different pros and cons lead to different ways of classification. Change in the relationship between the pros and cons will inevitably lead to a new way of classification. Therefore, it is inappropriate to think that the division of objects is absolute and immutable, as some traditional philosophers do.

The division of objects is a route that pursues computational economy through "merging entities". As previously noted, this approach is flawed and hence can only be optional. Another route to computational economics is not to merge entities, but to merge relationships, and then apply the merged single relationship to different entities. When these two methods are combined, the resulting computational economy is even greater.

This approach is known as the "theoretical approach". Theories are often directed at a certain kind of objects rather than a single object. Some of the relationships or laws described in theories can be applied to a large number of objects rather than to a single object. This brings with it a huge Algorithmic economy. Different kinds of objects can also be further merged with their commonalities to form a larger classification and, further, a hierarchical classification system.

Different theories characterize relationships in different classes of objects.

A variable is a type. A mathematical formula illustrates a typical pattern of relations for certain types or sorts of objects: a relationship between them is often fixed, and this relationship can be applied to many individual objects of the same type. Variables have different values, which means that the formula is being applied to different objects. The results of the operations are in principle different from each other, meaning that an object entity corresponds to another object entity in another kind. This is how people combine fixity with change, commonality with difference. In other words, the regularity in the objective world is found to be discontinuous, fragmented, rather than ubiquitous, which requires us to do selectively and mixedly, to deal with the heterogeneity or irregularity.

Numerous entities can also be linked to a single entity through certain relationships. The latter may be real or virtual, extant or newly created for this particular operation. The latter is often referred to as essence (or substance), while the former is called "phenomenon". This approach to economy is slightly different from the former. However, it is the same regarding "merging entities", "batch processing", and so on.

In the long run, the "merging and batch-processing" method will certainly bring about computational economy, but is it impossible not to merge or merge less? Of course not. It will be slower and require more memory or storage, but it may be more accurate. For example, language exists mainly in a discrete way, and words and phrases are compiled into dictionaries for us to learn and master one by one. Although there are regularities and commonalities, these are relatively weak. The biological world is extremely rich in diversity, and therefore, the priority of biological research is to exhaustively collect and organize information about plants and animals. The same is true for historical research. Historians are first and foremost people who have specific and rich historical information.

For a long time, people in the world have placed theory above experience, and have looked up to theories and down on experiences. Now it seems that the reason for this is nothing more than that theory has brought about a huge computational economy, so it has the effect of "one as ten" in the face of experience. Therefore, this emphasis on theory is reasonable and understandable. However, *theory (and the laws it describes) should never be so important as to be entirely separated from experience, or fundamentally different from experience. Their advantages and disadvantages can be compared, and their differences are only in degree, quantity, or detail, not essential.* It can be argued that the main reason for that misconception is that in the pre-IT age human knowledge developed slowly, so that the issue of computational efficiency was obscured. Now, as the ability of human beings to store data, transmit data, and compute has increased dramatically due to the advent of information technology, the importance of whether to merge entities, i.e., whether to deal with problems in batches, has been protruded significantly, in a highly sensible way.

For example, in this current situation that large amounts of data can be stored and processed rather than discarded as before, the topic of "big data" has emerged, which examines how to quickly manipulate vast amounts of data, rather than confining the object data within a small range, intentionally or unconsciously, as was the case in the past. Many practical computer models now have millions or hundreds of millions of variables, making computations more granular than ever before. Individuality, specificity, and differences are no longer discriminated against as they used to be. Without high-speed computation, the "large language models" like ChatGPT[3]

------

3. For an introduction to large language models, see Melanie Mitchell,

would not have been able to produce valuable results. Now, they have already been done. These new products became popular all over the world overnight and were hailed as a milestone of great innovation.

In the IT age, due to the principle of "a rising tide lifts all boats", the dominance of the Algorithmic economy is still prominent, which must have been deeply understood by the algorithm economy experts who help design computerized programs. Data can be conveniently and almost permanently stored and disseminated, which means less repetitive human labor. *Computer programs can be used repeatedly and at a low cost without being learned personally, which is another alternative to the traditional pursuit of economy.* Traditional mathematical formulas can only be written very short, whereas a computer program acts as if extending the length of a formula and running it automatically. Most of the parameters are also filled in or valued automatically. In addition, automatic programming can result in an economy that is not ordinarily large. ChatGPT can replace traditional writing jobs to a certain extent, indicating that white-collar jobs will also fall within the scope of labor that can be saved in the future. At the same time, the explosive growth of computing volume, in turn, requires a continuous increase in the speed of computers, hence the upgrading of chips continues to be the focus of the industry. Although the efficiency of energy use has improved, the total energy consumption has increased significantly, and it can already account for a considerable proportion of the total energy consumption.[4] When you realize that the heat emitted by the data center can already heat an entire mountain range,

---

"Artificial Intelligence: A Guide for Thinking Humans", Farrar, Straus and Giroux ebook, 2019.

4. International Energy Agency (2024). "Electricity 2024: Analysis and forecast to 2026", P. 8, https://iea.blob.core.windows.net/assets/6b2fd954-2017-408e-bf08-952fdd62118a/Electricity2024-Analysisandforecastto2026.pdf

you would realize that the era of the Algorithmic economy is not going away, but just emerging.

§86. Generation of Algorithmic Entities: spirit and its freedom

The operations on the sensory materials will gradually detach from the sensory materials.

This "detachment" is first reflected in data types. The processing of information such as images and sounds will gradually transition to the processing of numbers and characters. The numbers were mentioned above. If you stand in the shoes of a physical object, you will find the characters quite incomprehensible. Although characters, whether hieroglyphic or alphabetic, are also a kind of graphics, they are not used as common graphics, but as representations of "meanings". What is a "meaning"? If I were a physical object, I would "think" it was strange. But because I am human, I do not find it strange; I know for myself what it is, and I know it is made by me and my kind, or for me to read and understand. In the past, I had to establish a one-to-one correspondence between external objects and meanings, but now, while I can still do this, I don't necessarily have to. I only do this in certain situations (e.g. when I get to "know" a foreign object) according to my clear definitions, and the rest of the time, I am fairly free to manipulate and compute on the stocked data. In the past, I established a hierarchical relationship between meanings and external objects, and I had to let one dominate the other. Now, I'm not so stubborn on it anymore. Instead, I juxtapose them as different concurrent entities, and study the relationships between them.

Of course, they can also have no relationship with each other, or they may have fewer, looser, or less important relationships. On the one hand, it is difficult to conceive of a mind that has no empirical background at all. Most of the thoughtful objects that people compute today are the results of the computations of their predecessors, the ones of hundreds of millions of processing times in history. Who knows how much information from the outside world has been synthesized into them? Therefore, even what we think of as the most abstract ideas must inevitably have had rich empirical elements. From an Algorithmic point of view, this should be assured. On the other hand, information is processed by Instructions, and they are always paired; and, the same is true of Instructions. When a specific original information is processed repeatedly and deeply, we can think that the proportion of Instructions contained in the computational results, namely, the subjective weight, will be higher; on the contrary, when computations are mainly aimed at the original information and does not pursue the depth of processing, we can consider that the factor of information, and hence foreign objects, is heavier in the results.

In this way, we establish a perspective that as the depth of computation increases, the human mind gradually moves away from the outside world. Of course, from the perspective that the understanding of external objects may also be deepened, the deepening of understanding also means another "proximity" to the external objects. However, let's continue with the former.

Since the processing of data by Instructions is guided by imperfect knowledge stock, the incompleteness of knowledge allows for a large number of attempted computations, and the results of these attempted computations might be strange and not completely evaluative. The target data to compute shifts from raw information to data stored deep in the brain. No matter what kind of computations are conducted, they are all computations, all equal substantive activities. This determines the *great richness of human thoughts and mental activities.* Whether results of the computations are instrumental or purposeful, they are tremendously abundant. Moreover, there will inevitably be a large number of results whose meanings are difficult to determine instrumental or purposeful. Thus, this opens the source of the "spiritual life" of humankind.

It is impossible for external objects to "know" the meanings of spiritual life, or to "understand" the meanings of artistic and literary works. It is also impossible for them to "understand" interpersonal relationships, or to "understand" the love and hatred in the social world. The spiritual elements and the social elements thus gain *relative independence*.

What was discussed earlier was either an external or a mental entity, and now, "human" has finally appeared as an entity and an object. A human is a combination of mind and body, equipped with a system of Instructions, hard software, and common software, and is therefore a relatively independent "computor" and doer, and belongs to the same species as the observers with intellectual equivalence. The human brain stores a lot of data. Not only are these data in close proximity to each other, but they also have direct neural connections to each other, and there is a separate Instruction system that processes these data at any time, which leads to the fact that the "human" entity carries a large number of other mental entities, so *that the human being is a unique way of merging the mental entities*—and the way in which they are recombined with the physical entities. As a relatively independent entity, a single individual is a very distinctive entity. *Frequent processing in close proximity inevitably results in each person having rather unique individual characteristics.* The uniqueness of a human also lies in the fact that he/she is *alive, autonomous, active, proactive,* and *developmental.* When we speak of any other entities, they themselves (even specific thoughts or knowledge) are either rigid or generally less prominent than humans in these characteristics. For example, it can also be said that animals are like this in a certain sense, but they are not as strong as humans in these aspects.

Since an individual person can be seen as an entity, namely, a relatively independent object, the combination of individuals can also be viewed in the same way. This brings us to families, groups, organizations, and societies. Since a person can see the other in this way, the other person can also see him/her in this way. These objectifying activities can be one-way, bidirectional, or networked. Moreover, since an individual can be seen as a way of merging thoughtful entities, the individual can be "disassembled" into many thoughtful entities again, and the dismantled thoughtful entities can in turn compete with the "individual"; Then, according to the economic pros and cons, the analyst can choose whether to identify a thoughtful entity or the individual as a unit for analysis; Thus, sometimes we have people in our eyes, and sometimes there are no people, but only the thoughtful objects.

§87. Generation of Algorithmic Entities: spirit and its freedom (continued)

When an individual is *free to imagine* in the spiritual world, a determinist may think that he/she has been implicitly constrained by certain "laws", that his/her freedom exists "mistakenly" only in his/her own subjective feelings, and that objectively or "actually", the freedom does not exist. Humanists, on the contrary, believe that "noble" spiritual freedom is not only real, but also the main mark that distinguishes one as a human being from other external objects. Then, how do we reconcile the two?

First of all, people can only think about what they can think, so the scope, ability, and performance of thinking are all limited. Specifically, it can only be thought in the way of "Instruction + information" (we will not repeat other relevant limitations such as speed). In other words, mental activity is limited both by the availability of information and by the type of Instruction. One cannot think using other "Instructions" (or some other "thinking tools" or the like) that are not Instructions. This restriction may not be felt by the actors, but we can logically conjecture it. What the person directly feels is that whatever he/she wants to think, he/she is able to think. One has complete and absolute control over one's own conscious activities. Given that this control has been refuted by the subconscious theory, we can now adjust it to be more precise, that is, "We have complete and absolute control over our metacomputation (or current computation)." This control shall not extend to the stock of knowledge. On the contrary, a meaning of knowledge stock is to affect current computations, telling them to do some predetermined things, while a current or meta computation does not necessarily accept the attempt of knowledge stock, it can break free from knowledge stock, putting it only in the position of tools or resources.

Another meaning of "spiritual unfreedom" is that no matter what one thinks and decides, one must undergo the consequences. Now that ideas have been substantiated, this view has gained a foundation and will certainly be strengthened in theoretical analysis. Since the function of an Instruction is specific and constant, the result can be predestined when it is executed. Furthermore, when the results of computations are put into practice as decisions, if we believe in the determinism of the objective physical world, then the consequences of human actions are also predestined. However, while the execution of Instructions generally has certain consequences (except the "Lottery" Instruction), this is not the case with the choice of Instructions and information, especially with behavioral or economic considerations, which lead to a great deal of uncertainty in the selection of Algorithms. The specificity and constancy of Instructions do not tell us the final truth of the world, and do not lead to the final establishment of a completely definite knowledge system, but rather to an explosion of knowledge systems, so that the knowledge available at any point in time is limited and flawed. This clear logic shows that the two are not contradictory to each other, but coexist with each other. Thus, even if the person believes that the consequences of a particular act are "predestined", he/she may not fully know what those consequences are. Even if an observer knows more than the person concerned, the observer's advantage is still limited, and it is impossible for the observer to be fully aware of the consequences. Between subjectivity and objectivity, freedom and necessity, *big data constitutes the ultimate barrier that prevents people from knowing the "final truth"* (if any). Determinists often use the technique of sophistry on this issue, to imply that the consequences are limited and easily known by pointing out some "certain" consequences of a certain act. In the past, this sophistry was not easily debunked due to the lack of a basic framework such as Algorithmic Theory; now, under ATT, this sophistry would not be so lucky.

As for the Algorithmic subjectivities, we will continue to argue again and again in the following text. Many of these subjective characteristics tend to protect the freedom of thinking and spirit, and even tend to justify the willfulness and self-appreciation of the mind. One aspect of ideological willfulness is the establishment of the legitimacy of words such as purpose, value, preference, intention, spirit, etc. From an idealistic, extreme rationalist perspective, there should really be no substantial distinction between ends and means. However, because this underlying perspective does not conform to political correctness, it eventually becomes an absolute separation between the fields of purpose and instruments, and there is no essential consistency between them. The Algorithmic approach not only allows the two to communicate with each other, but also makes them relatively separate and independent. As a result, the person concerned can now talk about "I like so-and-so" and "I want to be how I want". Curiosity is now one of the valid reasons to initiate computations. Alternatively, the person concerned may allow his/her thinking to flow freely, unchecked, and regardless of the cost. It's as if society allows the humanities and arts to govern themselves to a large extent, and allows professors to enjoy the highest control over a university.

There are moments when willful thoughts are creative, and there are also times when they have to restrain themselves because they are taking regret pills. Objectivity's intervention or coercion on it manifests itself only intermittently, and is only perceived intermittently. As far as the physical world is concerned, it doesn't know what these "tricks" in the human world are all about, and they have nothing to do with it. And if these "tricks" are separated from the Algorithmic language, they are difficult to explain clearly, and more difficult to explain clearly in one sentence. It is only when we get to the Algorithmic realm that we can only use a formula, or a sentence, to clarify this large number of philosophical questions.

§88. Relationships between Entities: plurality, conflict, consistency, scheme

So many entities have arisen, and we seldom talk about their relationships. Discourses about relationships are always scattered and discontinuous. As discussed above, relations can also be regarded as a kind of "entity", and the concept group of "entity-nature (characteristic)-relation-change" as a whole scheme aims to merge entities, or connect entities, thereby reducing the number of independent entities and pursuing computational economy. In this *specific* context, the entity status of a relationship is thus revoked, and it is instead attached to specific entities. However, on the other hand, it is also a way of establishing a "relationship between entities", i.e., when the relationship is attached to particular entities, it can also be considered that the subsidiary relationships are established between those entities and that relationship (as a kind of entity). There is an equivalence between these two ways of understanding. The same applies to concepts such as nature, characteristics, change, etc.

The number of entities is large. According to the principle of permutation and combination, the relationships between entities are even quantitatively richer. What happens when entities meet or interact with each other? It's like what happens when atoms interact or combine with each other, and what the properties of the newly created matter are. They are often unknown, and you need to do experiments to know. The same is true for the traits of entities, which are specific, and so are the relationships between entities—even though they may be infinite in observers' eyes. Infinity and specificity are not contradictory here. Because they are specific, we need to study them specifically, document them one by one, and deal with them one by one. It's like there are many small islands in a lake, and to connect them, you need to study the ships, bridges, tunnels, etc., and their specific routes.

Numerous relationships between entities have been discovered, and a variety of words have been used to describe them. However, there is little mention of this relationship between entities that these entities coexist in the same circumstance and keep a distance from each other, and because of this distance, they often "live in peace". This is called "plurality". Plurality, though much talked about in common literature these days, has not really gained a place in philosophy. Especially in the field of metaphysics, where philosophers study the truth behind phenomena, how can plurality be tolerated when plurality is generally considered a temporary, epistemic, and procedural relationship?

Now, since all the elements of thinking and human knowledge are included in the ranks of entities, it is logical that plurality should be included in philosophy and metaphysics. The word "plurality" *at least* describes a temporary state of peace between entities—between physical entities, between physical entities and mental entities, and between mental entities, and so on. The existence of space prevents them from "intimate contacts" and entails their interactions in specific ways (e.g., gravity, light, waves, etc., involving other entities) and in timely processes. This is known as "events". In the absence of such an event, the relationships between them are *potential* rather than real. Potential relationships can only be transformed into real relationships under certain conditions in the future, and thus can be observed or perceived.

One might argue that there are relationships that do not need to arouse events to be recognized as "relationships", such as similarities or opposites between two entities. Similarities or opposites, however, are not revealed by themselves for no reason, but are recognized by human (as another entity), and *the recognition of them by human (and thus Instructions) is just an event*, through which the "relationships" between them are "revealed" in the human mind and are only to be understood and used by the human. As far as these two entities themselves are concerned, if they were not intervened by the entity of the human, there must not be such relationships between them! This answer can be used as a concrete application of the entity view in the Algorithmic framework, especially the view of "entity completeness".

The pluralistic existence of entities must be an essential element of metaphysics. The introduction of this element brings in the human element, the element of thinking, the element of time and space, the element of event, the element of phenomenon, as well as potential, essence, and so on, in short, everything. In other words, philosophy cannot make sense without it and the new elements that come with it, and philosophy can only have a basic and acceptable completeness by introducing all of these in conjunction with each other.

The existence of plurality is a kind of "base". Only on this base we can explore other things. All other things are only some parts here. The scope of plurality is indeed much broader than we usually think. For example, as long as we admit that there are differences, gaps, and so on between things, we are admitting plurality, admitting that it is not enough to just know a single object (or holds a single thought), and therefore, we must also go to other objects to absorb what is in them and what the former object does not have. Extreme rationalism and idealism demand that all entities eventually be reduced to one entity and generalized by a simple, singular idea. Any rejection of this principle means, to a greater or lesser extent, a move towards pluralism.

The next issue that comes to mind in a pluralistic world is conflict or contradiction. As mentioned earlier, the word "conflict" has a broader meaning than contradiction, so we mainly use "conflict" in the text. Logically and historically, the first thing that appeared in front of the actors must only be some scattered entities of different forms. Differences do not directly constitute conflicts. The occurrence of a conflict means that knowledge has taken a further step. The confusion of an actor about a phenomenon is one conflict, and a gap between a resource and a need constitutes another. Conflicts can take many forms, as we usually define or refer to. Philosophers can point out new types of conflicts and propose ways to resolve certain conflicts, but in principle cannot negate the recognition of conflict by real actors.

The same applies to the concept of consistency. What exactly "consistency" means has not been defined, as it is generally known to the average actors, although its specific meanings in specific circumstances might be different.

However, in the Algorithmic framework, we can make an analogy to understand conflict and consistency more conveniently.

This is with the help of the concept of "entity". An entity cannot simply be equated with a physical object, but, in some cases, it is possible to draw the analogy to a physical object. As long as we are careful to use metaphors, not only will we not make mistakes, but we will also get certain benefits. Plurality resembles the dispersion of physical objects in space, while a relationship between entities is like a phenomenon that occurs when the physical objects come together (or a phenomenon of knowledge about their information "gathering" in the human brain). The physical objects are all "hard", that is, they have their own relatively definite shapes. Then, when they come together, the question arises about whether their shapes fit each other or not. It's like patching a lot of pieces together. It is conceivable that if this kind of gathering, patching, or even collision is carried out at random, then in most cases, they cannot be perfectly fit into each other, so the inference brought about by our Algorithmical "chemical method" will first of all be the occurrence of conflict; and, various conflicts and contradictions will appear as a normalcy in the Algorithmic world, rather than the consistency taken as the normalcy in the mainstream paradigm where conflicts are regarded only as a few abnormal phenomena.

Of course, even in fewer cases, consistency will come naturally. Conflicts are found in local places, just as consistencies are found in other local places. Moreover, they produce each other in contrast to each other. Due to the limited computing power, the conflicts and consistencies that people find or focus on are small in number and relatively prominent in degree, and the other less obvious ones are pushed to the background and left to their knees. This means that "problems" occur. A "problem" is a conflict that an actor is determined to resolve—to find some explanations, or some decisions.

These solvent schemes can be other entities that "populate" between the conflicting entities, individually or jointly, to complete the patching of the picture. Although the original conflictive two entities cannot be directly compatible, they might now be compatible by such intermediaries, and eventually they would form into a holistic and harmonious consistency with the intermediaries. Nevertheless, as we already know, such intermediary entities are often not entirely readily available; some need to be searched in existing entities, and some need to be produced on-site.

§89. Relationships between Entities: cause and effect, and categories

Results of the interactions of Instructions and information, that is, the forms of knowledge, must be diverse. Even if some of these outcomes can be connected into a whole, the parts of the whole are diverse. This is like a car, although the engine has always been regarded as the core of the vehicle, but how can other parts be missing? The lack of any parts may cause, at least, some discomfort or inconvenience to the user. This principle, although it may seem simple, is often forgotten philosophically. For example, in recent discussions about ChatGPT, some philosophers have expressed their serious doubts about the large language model.[5] These commenters apparently mystify the process of understanding. As everyone knows, any computation we make about an object is, in principle, related to "understanding". Even just giving an object

---

5. Gary Marcus and Ernest Davis, "Rebooting AI: Building Artificial Intelligence We Can Trust", Vintage Books, 2019.

a name reflects the namer's understanding of it. The so-called "real understanding" is actually indicating that the philosophers have taken their own specific understanding as an authority and the standard; however, the "understandings" of the computer with ChatGPT, which they despise, may have been inferior to the philosopher's today, but may surpass it tomorrow.

The complex computing results need to be sorted out and classified in order to meet the economic requirements. Philosophically, this classification eventually leads to its foundational part, the categories. Category is the "highest" classification in philosophy. The so-called "highest" does not come from a definition of some authority, nor does it reveal any secrets in the universe, but the philosophers' own terms, which are relative to other contents of philosophy. Because the contents of philosophy, like the contents of other knowledge systems, are limited in quantity, this creates a relativity, and it is possible to distinguish between "high" and "low". Of course, the word "highest" is a bit misleading, and the other way to say it is "basic" or "foundational". In this way, the concept of category is not the highest, but the lowest. It's a pure matter of terminology.

Categories give philosophers the basic concepts they use when they speak, or when they are confronted with a particular object, or rather, *they list some of the basic characteristics of an object.* In mathematical language, categories provide the most basic *variables* for describing and analyzing an object. Think of them as concepts that were built up from scratch during operations of the Instruction system of the human brain (just like how a computer system accepts functions). Other variables are generated on top of these basic variables. Whether it is a philosopher or an ordinary person, he/she always has to think, and always has to speak. It is not conceivable that anyone can speak perfect words at the outset, or speak a primitive language with no insight at all. He/she can make use of the knowledge that already exists in the world in which he/she lives. At this point, philosophers can hand over the basic tools they have invented. These tools are the empirical products of the limited history of human computations and the pursuit of computational economy. From these points of view, we also come to the corollary that *there can be no perfect system of categories* in which the generalization of objects, or of knowledge, is everlasting, neither repetitive nor omissive, as if the God's secret file system of the truth of the world has been stolen, taken out, and solemnly announced to us. If we do not believe that such "stealing" exists, then our Algorithmic, economic understanding and interpretation shall be a preferable view. This view shall be more acceptable nowadays. However, it took a long and difficult struggle for philosophy to reach the views alike. For example, even with Kant, the traditional perfectionist view prevailed then, thus Kant attempted to make a list that was supposed to exhaust all categories. The transition to this view would not have been possible without the help of ATT.

After the above preparations, we are to discuss another type of relationship between entities, that is, causality.

The relationships in the Algorithmic world are diverse, some loose, some tight. Causality exists only partially in it and is a relatively close relationship. It can be said that the mainstream philosophy of the classics is mainly focused on this relationship. This closeness is so close that it obliterates the independence of each relevant entity, resulting in the entities eventually merging into one. Now, our Algorithmic job is to relocate causality into the Algorithmic framework, then localize and relativize it, thereby restoring it to its original status.

Causality first refers to the relationship between different individuals and local objects, which requires analysts either to look for causes *elsewhere* for a specific phenomenon, or to clarify the mutual influence between certain objects, etc. Thus, when using the term "causation", an analyst is not trying to say something about the whole world. Even if he/she attempts to do so, for example, by searching for the cause of the entire world, this "cause" has been preconceived as existing *outside* this "world" to be explained. In this way, he/she gets back to local analysis. Moreover, looking for cause and effect implicitly assumes that the relationship between a specific cause and a specific effect can be relatively independent of the rest of the world, and can be clarified *first before* the other relationships in the rest of the world are to be clarified. Therefore, it must be more or less arbitrary. Without this presumed arbitrariness, the forced closure and bending, it is impossible to identify and determine any causal relationship. The person involved neither completely knows all parts of the world at the same time, nor does he/she first determine those macroscopic relationships in the world or the relationships between other parts of the world and then come to understand this specific causal relationship, but start here, determine the causal relationship here (even if it is temporary), and then use this causality as a basis to expand the scope of his/her understanding. Obviously, this causality has already been supposed to be easier to identify than others.

However, even if the causality identified is ideal, we can't find it everywhere and all the time. Recorded human history is only a fragment of the history of the universe. If this is true, how can we clarify everything just with our limited computing power? We can't know exactly where the universe came from and where it will go. Even if someone happens to reveal the "truth" of the universe by chance, he/she cannot fully verify it, and thus neither he/she nor anyone else can fully confirm his/her success. The more realistic and ordinary situation is that we may usually grasp part or fragments of causality. These fragments are also often scattered, and their further relationships to each other are unknown or irregular.

As for the method of grasping a causal relationship, it may rely partly on computations embedded with existing theories and partly on empirical observations. Regarding theoretical analysis, how can we determine a specific causal relationship in the vast network of things interacting with each other? In my opinion, this problem is actually very serious. The usual attribution of specific phenomena to specific or a small number of causes can be clearly questionable. Any phenomenon or event occurs only in a specific context or environment, and in the final analysis, the whole world is just the background. How can we determine that other elements have no influence on a particular phenomenon or event, and how can we determine whether the influence of each element is positive, negative, and to what extent? By considering these questions, we can agree that the "marginal method" (i.e., the method of linking the most recent cause in time to the most recent effect) is crucial.

The intrinsic connection of the objective world is largely a black box, and it is unlikely that we will directly probe the truth into it. The "truth" we discovered is actually mostly questionable and relatively valuable, and sometimes it's just a little bit better than nothing (and even it isn't some other times). This is how theory itself was developed, because it is impossible for us to employ nothing in a particular empirical observation. For example, in the use of marginal methods, theories can help us identify in advance what types of elements are causes and what are effects, and then use empirical observation to concretely relate them. It is impossible to accomplish empirical induction without a theoretical framework in any real space-time condition.

In this way, we can further conclude that the so-called "causality" can be reinterpreted as a discourse with a specific meaning. What it means is that, in order to have real use value in real computational activities, the "causality" as a conclusion must be fairly simple (although it can be admitted that it originally had a complex, even infinite context), can be reduced to a single or fewer elements, and can be expressed in relatively brief language. The aim was to serve other activities that are currently underway: either discussions on other related topics, or the proposed actions, and so on. Thus, the variables to which it boils down are often controllable, and thus the relevant actors can control or influence them by action (within an acceptable spatial or temporal range).

With this in mind, the Algorithmic framework is even more indispensable as a background. A contextual framework can both protect and limit the meanings of causal discourse. For example, the existence of time, and thus dynamics, is indispensable, without which marginal analysis cannot be carried out. The existence of space is also essential, otherwise it is impossible to distinguish between internal and external causes, since internal causes are nothing more than the "causes of proximity (to the point of entering the interior of the object)", which can affect the object conveniently, quickly, and continuously, while external causes are the "causes of longer distance". Because of the long distance, the speed at which the causal force arrives is relatively slow, the interferences encountered on the way may be much, the attenuation may be more significant, the frequency of action may have to be lower, and so forth.

§90. Relationships between Entities: certainty, possibility

In a framework where statics is mixed with dynamics, and convergence is mixed with divergence, the statics and equilibrium have a variety of cases. For example, when a particular problem is set aside because it cannot be solved, it results in a statics. Another different situation is the conviction that a certain state is an established fact, or that a certain thought is the truth, and so on. This is called "certainty", a much modern term. At first, it was believed, undoubtedly, that people had unfettered access to the truth in the objective world. Later, theories of subjectivity emerged, arguing that any perceived fact contains subjective components, or even some subjective constructs. However, such a theory needs to be prevented from going to an extreme. For example, facts (such as colors or sounds) constructed with the help of sensory organs have literally subjective components, but the functions of sensory organs can be objective and beyond the control of consciousness although they coexist with consciousness in the human body. This objectivity is not much different from the objectivity of physical phenomena.

What is distinct from the objective physical phenomena is the human mind. For example, people can hold a consistent evaluation of an object, but *will not consider this evaluation objective because it is interpersonally consistent.* The evaluation as an opinion is still considered subjective. At this time, people usually do not attribute this phenomenon of unanimity to external objects, but to people themselves. However, "certainty" refers in particular to a situation in which people agree on an inference about the state of a foreign object (often based on some causal relationship, of course), such as the state of an unknown object, or the future state of an object, and so on. If the results of their inferences are the same, i.e., interpersonally consistent, people do not say that their "opinions are unanimous", but that the object *itself* has a "certainty".

This subtle language has sparked controversy. I understand you so easily that I have come to certain conclusions, but I do not boast of my own cognitive abilities, but saying that you have a nature that is "easily known to me", why do I speak in such a devious way?

In my opinion, the first issue regarding certainty is to avoid a misunderstanding, that is, to mistakenly believe that certainty is a "naked fact" that has nothing to do with cognitive activities, and meanwhile, it is also necessary to realize that the spread of this term from scratch and from experts to the public reflects a certain rationality of this term in common sense. This rationality, like the reasonableness in the word "possibility", is yet to be revealed.

Now let's do an Algorithmic deduction. The combination of Instructions and information can never lead to the development of knowledge everywhere and at all times; the development of knowledge for each object cannot be completely synchronous or at the same speed. As a heterogeneity, the knowledge of specific objects is almost immutable, or, at least, changes more slowly than the cognition of other things around it, so that it looks like an island in the ocean, not only singular, but can be relied on by other computations—for example, a computational strategy is to prioritize a deterministic question and determine its answer first, and then use it as a constant parameter for other computations. That is to say, the computations about a specific deterministic question always converge to a definite answer(s). This is not only due to the Instructions used, but obviously due to the unique natures of the object concerning, or the way it relates to other objects. Other objects in the vicinity may be changing, but those changes are not affecting it, or the effects of those changes, after offsetting each other, are not enough to affect it. In short, it is not surprising that this phenomenon occurs in a heterogeneous, discrete, and mixed world; it is neither ubiquitous nor completely unavailable. Even, it is endogenous, and as long as one perceives a *relative stillness*, it can be identified and named "certainty"—even if, in fact, it changes slowly or accidentally, and is not completely "certain".

In particular, this cognitive phenomenon is "object-dependent". The computational activities of the person concerned do not have this effect on other objects, but only when they come to this particular object will it occur—and always occurs. The person concerned must have recognized the "object dependence" of this cognitive phenomenon, so he/she simply binds this cognitive phenomenon to the object, and for the sake of convenience, he/she insists that the object has the nature of "enabling human to produce a certain knowledge", which is referred briefly to as the "certainty", as if there is this nature inherent in the object, and if the object exists, it exists, and when the object disappears, it disappears. This principle is similar to the "universal in things" mentioned earlier (§79): although we know that it is a cognitive concept, we insist on reducing it to the object for the sake of computational (and expressional) convenience.

The same applies to issues such as uncertainty, probability, randomness, and so on. Since certainty is local, there is also uncertainty. If certainty means "100% knowing", then there are many levels between 0 and 100% that can be used to characterize the degree of certainty (or uncertainty). Following this logic, it shall be a common phenomenon that various ideas and viewpoints have varying degrees of certainty; and, according to our speculation and empirical observation, the existence of ideas with different degrees of certainty should be a normalcy, and a "100% certainty" itself should be in the minority cases.

Among the many uncertainties, it can continue to be speculated that most of them should be difficult to quantify, or that even if quantitative assessments are insisted on, the results are not easy to reach an interpersonal agreement. Further, this conclusion can be extended as the following: although in most cases there is interpersonal inconsistency, in a few or individual places there can be agreement. Why? Because the situation of "the evaluation results can never reach an agreement" is too regular and neat, which is unusual in the Algorithmic world.

Only by allowing a few consensuses to exist can it be normal. This can be regarded as a fuzzy reasoning method under the Algorithmic framework. I believe in its effectiveness. When we make this reasoning or speculation, it's actually the common sense in our heads that has already stepped up and started to guide us. This reasoning or speculation may not work well on any issues, but can direct us to places that conform to common sense. Moreover, at this time, the readers and I will carry out this reasoning together and reach the same idea. This is because we all have similar experiences and common sense.

This brings us to the concept of "probability", i.e., on some issues, where people's judgments of possibility are not only quantified, but surprisingly mutually consistent and always objectively the same—the estimate of the degree of uncertainty is always "certain". I believe that probability is a comprehensive, typical, or extreme reflection of many *Algorithmic elements* such as subjectivity and objectivity, convergence and equilibrium, qualitative and quantitative, discrete and heterogeneous, etc. *The subjectivity and apriority of thoughts are concurrently exposed here*, because even if the estimated probability is definite and interpersonally consistent, we cannot help admitting that it is merely a thought and not a "naked fact". We can't reach the completely naked fact (the "thing in itself"). But it is not because the mind is so subjective that it is not *objective*, nor is it unable to achieve interpersonal consistency because the knowledge it has reached is less certain. The interpersonal agreement in probability estimation is like any other "certainty" in that it only signals the objectivity of knowledge to us in an extreme way. This approach eventually leads us to the Instructional system, and the binary structure of "Instruction + information". Here, since "one palm cannot clap", subjective Instructions and objective information together create thoughts, which also lead to the probability estimation. *Here the two are "stuck" into a "deadlock", unable to move forward, resulting in a constant conclusion, but not fully knowing the object.*

On the other hand, we cannot be obsessed with probability and certainty, because the holistic Algorithmic framework can simultaneously explain probability, certainty, and numerous other qualitative or quantitative uncertainties. We shall not exaggeratively interpret, imagine, or play on the minor phenomena of probability and certainty. We shall not, based on these extreme cases, question why other things are not like these, or demand or predict that sooner or later they will converge to these. These neat, extreme cases are loved by us simply because they are easy to handle. Computing stops here, freezes, or recycles, but it doesn't necessarily follow that all computations will end up on this path. If this is the case, then the opponents can also ask for an opposite position. In fact, there are other ordinary, irregular cases much more than these. Such questions or speculations are bound to be not much tenable on both sides. Convergence, divergence, and development of knowledge need to be argued from other more defensible angles—and the "combinatorial explosion" seeks to provide such an angle.

§91. Conclusion: the metaphysics in the unified philosophical system

Algorithmically, philosophy can be a whole, and meanwhile, it can be divided into several closely related parts: the theory of the mind, the epistemology (including methodology) about the actions of the mind on objects, and the metaphysics as a result of the actions of the mind. Since the mind, thinking activities, and the results are now all considered real entities, these parts are both different parts of the knowledge system and different parts of the world, or those pertaining to different parts of the world.

In order for philosophy to have its place in the body of knowledge, philosophy must articulate the importance of the idea that human knowledge is not a self-consistent closed loop, but rather a combination of processes or fragments that have a beginning and an end. I now recognize that this point is becoming more important and therefore needs to be emphasized. Under the Algorithmic framework, this view can be quite clear: in the history of the objective world, human beings, as thinkers, only capture information in some spatiotemporal stages, and then process it with a finite number of times and a limited depth; therefore, the thinking processes as a whole has a beginning and an end, and correspondingly, the ideological system thus formed has its body and boundaries. Philosophy is at the beginning, end, or edge of the body of knowledge. In other words, a logical retrospection of knowledge systems often ends up in "philosophy", which supplies the most basic and often subjective things for knowledge systems. The reason why philosophy is quite subjective is because, after arriving here, a philosopher must use vagueness to economically deal with big data, and it is impossible for him/her to make a precise argument. What philosophy proposes depends mostly on whether the reader agrees with it or not, and cannot be directly proved. A philosophical proposition can be proved ex post facto indirectly by its applicative effects, or by looking for indirect and weaker arguments in facts, common sense, or other knowledge. At the same time, philosophers love to argue, and they have established an image in public as "eloquent" and even "bellicose".

However, in any case, any thinking processes will come to some conclusions to a greater or lesser extent. A philosopher thinks about the world, and then he/she comes to some conclusions in due course. He/she cannot just talk about the structure and process of thinking itself without saying something *directly* about the world at which his/her computations aim. The fact that thinking processes cannot be completely terminated shall not prevent anybody from reaching certain conclusions about the world. At this point, the general equilibrium theory in economics contains an element of truth. The latter argues that we must, and can always and everywhere, draw perfect and consistent conclusions about the world. While this view is overly optimistic, we do have to draw certain conclusions about the world. This is because we have to act, and thus have to draw conclusions. Even if the conclusions are not perfect, some of them cannot be left undone. We can only draw certain conclusions with the limited stock of knowledge we have, plus the current computations with limited capacity—and then revise them from time to time in the future. This gives rise to different historical versions of metaphysics.

Metaphysics can conceive itself on the basis of a self-awareness of the inevitability of its own versioning. This is a new strategy that it can implement under the Algorithmic framework. In addition, the strategies that can be implemented are: acknowledging one's own limitations and answering only questions that have to be concluded or hypothesized and avoiding answering all questions; acknowledging the temporal process of thinking and answering only questions that have already been matured and keeping other questions open; appealing to epistemology and higher-order nature to try to provide higher-order answers when first-order answers are unavailable; acknowledging and arguing heterogeneity and plurality to justify the strategy of topic selection; choosing topics with relative significance to avoid wasting research resources (unfortunately, some philosophers used to be good at this and proud of this, which hurt their social images); clearly proposing the slogan of "Minimized Metaphysics"; studying the influence of human on the physical world under the premise of infinite development of human knowledge, and so on.

I am not an expert in the philosophy of the physical world, so I have to stop here temporarily in this book on general metaphysical issues. Next, we will turn to the specific discussions of social issues. In my view, the philosophy in this area is in a state of serious weakness and flawedness, and the Algorithmic method can be used to make significant and comprehensive improvements to it.

ABOUT THE AUTHOR

Bin Li, a visiting scholar of Center for Urban & Regional Studies, University of North Carolina at Chapel Hill, used to be an independent scholar and a columnist in Shanghai, China. Email: libinw2025@hotmail.com

Personal Webpages:

    https://pcc.web.unc.edu/faculty/bin-li/

    https://unc.academia.edu/BinLi

    https://www.researchgate.net/profile/Bin_Li197

    https://scholar.google.com/citations?hl=en&user=qkCLlowAAAAJ

    https://algorithmicalbinli.wordpress.com

    Chinese site: http://blog.sina.com.cn/libinw

    Chinese Weibo: https://weibo.com/u/1400692850

    Chinese Podcast:

    https://www.ximalaya.com/zhubo/185996474

Books:

Li, Bin (2005). "Reformation of State-Owned Enterprises: A New Scheme" (in Chinese, original title: "The Constitution of State Capital: A Mechanism-Design for Management of China's State Capital"). Beijing: Economic Daily Press, 2005.

Li, Bin (2009). "Algorithm Framework Theory: A Basis for Unification of Social Sciences" (in Chinese). Beijing: China Renmin University Press.

Li, Bin (2012). "A Preliminary Inquiry into Principles of General Social Science: The Algorithmic Approach" (in Chinese). Beijing: China Renmin University Press.

Li, Bin (2019). "Foundations of Algorithmic Economics: The Cognitive Revolution and the Grand Synthesis of Economics" (in Chinese). Beijing: Economic Daily Press.

Articles:

Li, Bin (2006). "The Algorithmic Economics: A General Theory on Bounded Rationality" (in Chinese). Economic Research Information, No.6. 3–14.

Li, Bin (2011). "The Synthesis of Various Economics: An All-in-One Solution". Annual Conference of Association for Heterodox Economics (AHE), Nottingham, UK. https://www.hetecon.net/wp-content/uploads/2019/12/Li_AHE2011061R.pdf

Li, Bin (2014). "The Grand Synthesis of Economics" (in Chinese). The Chinese Symposium On Interdisciplinary Theoretical Innovation, Unirule Institute.

Li, Bin (2015). "The Endogeneity of Institutions & Organizations: The Algorithmic Approach" (in Chinese). The annual conference of China's Institutional Economics.

Li, Bin (2019). "How could the Cognitive Revolution Happen to Economics? An Introduction to the Algorithm Framework Theory". World Economics Association (WEA) online conference: Going Digital. https://goingdigital2019.weaconferences.net/papers/how-could-the-cognitive-revolution-happen-to-economics-an-introduction-to-the-algorithm-framework-theory/

Li, Bin (2019). "Ten Lectures on Algorithmic Economics" (in Chinese). free e-book online, downloadable at the personal English webpages.

Li, Bin (2020). "The Birth of a Unified Economics". MPRA (The Munich Personal RePEc Archive) paper, downloadable at https://mpra.ub.uni-muenchen.de/110155/

Li, Bin (2020). "Why is Algorithmic Theory a Necessary Basis of Economics?" MPRA (The Munich Personal RePEc Archive) paper, downloadable at https://mpra.ub.uni-muenchen.de/110581/

Li, Bin (2022). "How Various 'Irrationalities' Proven to be Rational". Academia Letters, Article 4579. https://doi.org/10.20935/AL4579 [peer reviewed]

Li, Bin (2022). "Algorithmic Economics as an Economics of Thought". The International Journal of Pluralism and Economics Education, Vol. 13, No. 2, pp. 176-191. [peer reviewed]

Li, Bin (2022). "The 'Algorithmic Logic' as a Synthetic or General Logic". Academia Letters, Article 4936. https://doi.org/10.20935/AL4936 [peer reviewed]

Li, Bin (2022). "How can a Human be Modeled 'Alive'? The Scientific Endogeny and Manifestation of Subjectivities", in "Human Rights, Religious Freedom and Spirituality", edited by Yashwant Pathak, A. Adityanjee. Pune: Bshima Prakashan, downloadable at the personal English webpages.

Li, Bin (2022). "Algorithmic Economics". MPRA (The Munich Personal RePEc Archive) paper, downloadable at https://mpra.ub.uni-muenchen.de/113563/

Li, Bin (2023). "A Unified Psychology as Part of a General Social Science". Qeios. doi:10.32388/GGSOLK.3. [peer reviewed]

Li, Bin (2023). "From General Equilibrium to Algorithmic Equilibrium". Qeios. doi:10.32388/3WoJ51.2. [peer reviewed]

Li, Bin (2023). "The Unrevealed Causes of Prosperity". Qeios. doi:10.32388/KLR222.4. [peer reviewed]

Li, Bin (2023). "Como Várias 'Irracionalidades' Dão Provas De Serem Racionais". Revista Paranaense de Filosofia, v. 3, n. 1, p. 220 – 232, Jan./Jun., 2023.

Li, Bin (2024). "The Algorithmic Philosophy: A Synthetic and Social Philosophy". Qeios. doi:10.32388/SoAQEE.2. [peer reviewed]

Li, Bin (2024). "The Thinking Theory Unifying Grandly". Under review.

Over one hundred column articles (in Chinese) in Securities Times Newspaper, mostly on China's public economic policies.